THE FIFTH DIMENSION

Also by A.E. Dyson

THE CRAZY FABRIC: Essays in Irony
THE INIMITABLE DICKENS
BETWEEN TWO WORLDS: Aspects of Literary Form
YEATS, ELIOT AND R.S. THOMAS: Riding the Echo
DICKENS'S *BLEAK HOUSE* (*editor*)
EDUCATION AND DEMOCRACY (*editor with Julian Lovelock*)
MILTON'S *PARADISE LOST* (*editor with Julian Lovelock*)
MODERN JUDGEMENTS ON DICKENS (*editor*)
MODERN POETRY (*author with C.B. Cox*)
POETRY CRITICISM AND PRACTICE (*editor*)
THE PRACTICAL CRITICISM OF POETRY (*author with C.B. Cox*)
THE TWENTIETH-CENTURY MIND (*editor with C.B. Cox*)
THREE CONTEMPORARY POETS: Thom Gunn, Ted Hughes and R.S. Thomas (*editor*)

The Fifth Dimension

A.E. Dyson
Honorary Fellow of the University of East Anglia, Norwich

First published 1996 by
MACMILLAN PRESS LTD
Houndmills, Basingstoke, Hampshire RG21 6XS
and London
Companies and representatives
throughout the world

ISBN 0–333–65173–1

A catalogue record for this book is available
from the British Library.

10 9 8 7 6 5 4 3 2 1
05 04 03 02 01 00 99 98 97 96

Printed in Great Britain by
The Ipswich Book Company Ltd
Ipswich, Suffolk

For

CLIFF TUCKER
1912–93

A good man and a great friend

'Where your treasure is, there will your heart be also.'
(Jesus of Nazareth, *Matthew* 6: 21)

Contents

Acknowledgements

The author and publishers are grateful to the following for permission to reproduce copyright material: J.M. Dent Publishers for poems from *Collected Poems 1945–90* by R.S. Thomas; and to Faber & Faber Ltd and the Eliot Estate for extracts from 'Burnt Norton', 'Little Gidding', East Coker and 'The Dry Salvages' in *Collected Poems 1909–1962* by T.S. Eliot, Ch. 4 for 'Everyone Sang' by Siegfried Sassoon; and for 'Everyone Suddenly Burst Out Singing' in *Collected Poems 1908–1956*, published 1961. 'Anyone lived in a pretty how town' is reprinted from *Complete Poems 1904–1962*, by e.e. cummings, edited by George J. Firmage, by permission of W.W. Norton & Company Ltd, Copyright © 1940, 1968, 1991 by the Trustees for the e.e. cummings Trust.

Every effort has been made to contact all the copyright-holders, but if any have been inadvertently omitted the publishers will be pleased to make the necessary arrangement at the earliest opportunity.

Part I

Where Am I? Man's Place in the Universe

1

Where Am I? Space/Time

The thrush is a killing machine, Ted Hughes tells us. My elderly, much cherished cat is bad news for the thrush. But they look beautiful, and lost in thought, to my human perceptions. The garden is serene, and I ponder. 'Where Am I?'

In this chapter, the question is pragmatic, with no tinge of mysticism. I am concerned with locating myself, if possible, in space. But it is vital to what follows, since not only are the three dimensions of space relevant, but so too is the problematic fourth dimension, time – considered here in its specific relation to space.

Time is not confined to space, but it is deeply entwined with it; in one aspect, it is the duration which is space's fourth side. From here onwards, I shall refer to this aspect of duration as 'clock-time', for convenience; and to distinguish it from time's Janus-faced role in a fifth dimension, where its nature is dual.

So, I begin in the garden with thrush, cat and serenity, and allow my mind to wander from here. The layer of soil is thin, not rich or fertile. It allows a basic garden to flower, but no great trees, or exotic plants. Beneath, there is rubble, then clay and chalk, and the things London is built on. Then, a little below, a mazelike network of man-made pipes and tunnels: water, sewers, gas, electricity, phones; how many more? The London Transport tube tunnels run very deep here. You detect no rumble, as trains pass two or three hundred feet below.

And then? Well: not in London, but elsewhere, there are explorations underground. Dangerous risks in caves, taken by potholers. Miners, bringing resources up from deep in the earth. The potholers do it for fun, the miners for commerce; a skilled and dangerous livelihood, stretching far back in history. The miners serve us all and are felt to be special. They are touched with heroism, in myth and in fact.

The Earth, much below its surface, is a mystery. The human race has not tried to dig much deeper than the deepest mine workings (or so I believe; diastrophic geology makes new advances all the time). There is no generally known plan to dig down to the Earth's centre, or even through the centre to the 'other side'. What conditions would prevail much below a few miles we must largely conjecture; brooding on deep natural chasms, and on the stuff that volcanoes and earthquakes throw up. At the Earth's 'centre', if there is one, would direction reverse, and the tug of gravity gradually, or suddenly change?

Downwards then, we have surface knowledge, and not much that goes deeper. Look upwards, and we have the Sun by day, the stars and all other objects visible by night. It is upwards that astronomers search for their knowledge, using radio-telescopes that probe far through space, and intriguingly far backwards in time. The distances now are vast, and yield innumerable data; but the layer of breathable air is alarmingly small. Our aircraft cruise well above breathable air, through alien coldness, with only death outside for humans if something goes wrong. Meanwhile, we destroy the ozone layer, that protects us from toxic solar radiations. We destroy the rainforests, increasing carbon emissions with effects that are bound to be for long-term ill. We have invented and recklessly use the internal combustion engine, as 'an extension of liberty'; failing to acknowledge it for the savage destroyer of our planet that it is. We play appalling new games with nuclear fire, like half-witted children. Our shallow layer of breathable air is daily defiled and depleted – and these things are 'not on the agenda', in serious political terms. Earth Summits, yes – for politicians to talk at, and make 'long-term resolutions' – mostly for 'the next fifteen years', or 'the middle of the next century'; by which time they be will safe in their peerages, or their graves. Some few limited decisions are taken (and for these, much gratitude); but trees fall, species perish; irreversible poisons steam up through our thin licence to breathe.

But at least in the garden I breathe 'fresh air', or its London equivalent; and at least I am stable, or seem so, as I sit and think. The thrush and the cat are at ease; they are not the Earth's enemies. And there are no earthquakes or hurricanes; no vertiginous terrors of some Disneyland ride.

This stability works well enough, for reasons codified by Newton. The force of gravity steadies us, and keeps us from harm. But the whole thing smacks of illusion? We sense this instinctively, without recourse to Einstein; without grappling with the 'uncertainty principle' of quantum physics. The fact is, the garden I sit in is so far from stable that I should be flung off into space if gravity faltered at all. The garden is travelling at various speeds, all of them large and at least one unimaginable, in three or more differing directions, with no perceptible steering or brakes. The most hair-raising Disneyland whirligigs dwindle, in comparison. If it were not for the mercy of gravity (as one anthropomorphically judges it), we should speed to vertiginous extinction in one, fearful collapse.

First, the Earth revolves on its axis, one complete turn daily. It spins in space, its great shadow following. Every day of our lives we are carried with it, moving in and out of the shadow. At twenty-four hour intervals it returns, to a similar position; though the movement on its axis, relative to the Sun, ensures that it can seldom (never?) return to the same place twice. The speed would be a thousand miles an hour, very nearly? It is above the sound barrier and slightly faster than jumbo jets. We are fortunate not to hear any sonic bang.

And then, there is our movement round the Sun, in counterpoint – the whole, spinning ball speeding in three hundred and sixty-five days (very nearly) round its central star. Distances from the Sun vary (between ninety-three and ninety-seven million miles, or thereabouts), and the elliptical orbit is subject to various other slight tugs, some constant, some variable. This time, the speed is much greater than that of the sound barrier (indeed, very much greater? 'Someone would know: I don't', as Larkin said of the major landmarks in his churchgoing jaunts). We know that our natural satellite, the Moon, has its own phases, but that it is dragged, with its parent planet, on this dance round the Sun. Beyond the Moon, there are asteroids (mostly between Mars and Jupiter, but some of them wandering); likewise, meteors, meteorites, comets and the like. This side of the Moon, there is an amazing orbiting collection of purely man-made junk: all brand-new as astronomers calculate, but now riding there too.

So. Here we have two forms of movement, both in differing directions, and best not thought of, if one has the least tincture of honest doubt about Newton's main 'law'. But there is a third movement too, cutting through the others, which is spectacularly more mysterious and sounds far, far worse. The Sun itself moves, with near and far stars attending it, in our own tentacled spiral of the Milky Way. Dragged with it, Earth, and its other planets and their assorted satellites, follow along, at new speeds and angles much harder to chart. The Sun moves, relatively to the unnumbered other stars in its galaxy, at speeds really huge now: and does anyone yet, with certainty, plot these tracks?

But the entire galaxy is moving, at speeds to boggle our thinking. It is flying out, from Big Bang to Black Hole (says Hawking), through astronomical time. Other scientists vary and embroider this scenario, with quasars and pulsars observed, or sometimes deduced, in the abyss.

Perhaps Black Hole (or Black Holes, in the plural) will not be the 'real end' of it all? Perhaps Big Bang – producing everything out of nothing in a manner to remind us of *Genesis* and, if we fall into heresy, even of Aquinas – wasn't 'really' the beginning: or didn't 'really' bring about the whole cosmos, without *fiat* or help? Perhaps at some future moment, the process will stop, and actually reverse itself? The whole universe will recall Big Bang and start contracting backwards towards it? And then, perhaps, it will vanish backwards still further, leaving the nothing that was as if nothing had been? Or perhaps, the unimaginably huge cosmos will go in and out, like giant lungs, or a Heath Robinson bellows – winding up and down, in perpetual or near-perpetual motion, with its galaxies surviving, after a fashion, this yo-yo fate?

Be this as it may, the present game is expansion. We on Earth depend on the thing going ahead smoothly (if 'smoothly', as a word, stretches this far). It has gone smoothly enough during 'our' eye-blink history – man's few thousand year-reign, as lord of the earth. (Though what on earth did happen to the dinosaurs, after their multi-million year tenancy before we came?).

A collision of heavenly bodies, even a comparatively tiny one, could do the human race no good at all. Make it a larger collision, and the moon might come down on us; the Earth might smash to powder; the Sun might blink, or explode, or roll grossly off course. For the present, I ponder this third direction (or set of directions) in which I am moving – at odds with the first two, and further unsteadying the nerves.

At this stage, I refer to the purely physical universe; or rather, to the scientific models and theories served up, currently, to the popular mind. Scientists warn us against 'dogma', very properly. Their own 'hypotheses' vary; but for the most part, the theories and models are presented as 'true'.

And indeed, though scientists will not ask 'metaphysical questions' and do their best to deter them, the dramatic 'laws' they discover do have reasonable proof, of a pragmatic kind. The day and night cycle of Earth on its axis; the seasonal solar cycle – these are universal experience as far as they go. Eclipses and conjunctions and the general position of visible planets and stars in the heavens accord with the routines that scientists have mapped.

Further, we have used the 'laws' of gravity for remarkable exploits. Man-made contraptions have been sent to the moon, and have arrived promptly on schedule. Two satellites were sent on long voyages, many years in length, to the outer planets. From their original send-off, by rocket, they utilised the gravitational force of various planets in orbit to speed and direct them on, in predicted paths. These two arrived on time, in outer parts of our system, returning splendid pictures to us at the speed of light. We now see Jupiter, Saturn, Uranus and Neptune in some detail, along with a number of their extraordinary and very various moons. The whole process is extremely impressive, and beautiful; and very alien to us, even though achieved, as a spectacle, by mankind.

So 'laws' postulated or discovered by scientists really do work, to our reckoning. To this degree, we can 'trust' them; at least to the verge of deep space. Speculations about galaxies – our own, and others – may be partly included in this realm of the 'trustworthy'. But other data are tentative, and still subject to 'proof'. Even the 'red shift' effect, so basic to interpreting distant objects, has at the moment to be 'assumed' (on very strong grounds).

We have reason to know now to a high degree of certitude that the entire solar system is inhospitable to man, except for this planet, with its numerous resources and conditions that sustain our lives. There is no other planet, or planetary satellite, to which we could transfer, or hope to survive if we did. Whether other stars have planets, in this or more distant galaxies, is still blocked to our knowledge, and likely to remain so, given the vast distances now known to exist. The very nearest star is a mystery, four-and-a-half light years away (or thereabouts): which is to say, four-and-a-half years away from us, supposing we could invent a machine to travel at the speed of light.

But the speed of light is mind-blowing. It turns us to pygmies. We are left with science-fiction dodges of 'time-warps', or machines beyond all imagining, if we are to try to find any use for deep space travel at all. Maybe, the speed of light is an absolute, as Einstein speculated; or maybe, further discoveries will bring this in doubt. What is certain is not only that the speed of light is beyond us; it is beyond any scientific progress we can realistically hope to achieve. We have to assume that the known universe has produced humanity on this planet, and that man is unable to find, anywhere, an appropriate alternative home. In the fullness of time, man appeared, replacing the dinosaurs. And, at the rate we are currently achieving our planet's destruction, our tenure is likely to be scarcely more notable than a single insect's prematurely snuffed-out day.

Very likely, other suns have planets; very likely, life exists there. This Earth has produced life in abundance, with the human race currently lording it at 'the top'. We tend to assume that a carbon base is needed for life, and perhaps it is; or perhaps, this is a generalisation from Earth-life, with no basis in fact. Who is to know what types of life and evolution may go on, elsewhere? Perhaps vastly intelligent beings exist, and have cracked the light-barrier; and have achieved wisdom enough to cherish and sustain their own home. Or perhaps it is a law of intellect, that when intellect discovers the means to self-destruct, in its upward evolution, it will use this knowledge – by some power-urge also endemic in this space/time cosmos – and end with a bang, as we seem destined to do ourselves.

Perhaps some life-forms are not driven by power, with its attendant struggle, and madness; and develop vast, beneficent faculties, with no built in violence. Perhaps some life-forms can move more freely in the cosmos than we currently can. Perhaps some life-forms have evolved to move freely in space, without our need for contraptions. Perhaps the mere size of the physical universe is a ringfence against travel in space.

The basic facts are 'known' now. Others are thought of, but doomed to the sphere of fiction rather than fact. The space/time continuum is awesome, but requires no 'faith' of us. We need no religion to 'believe' it, and most scientists (not all) keep religion at bay. Perhaps we should say, these facts are our human baggage in this scrap of history, as other world-pictures, now gone, have been in the past. There are certainly some of us who suspect (or more than suspect) a Creator: a mind behind and beyond the space/time continuum, huge though it is. Perhaps a majority of scientists still set their face against this Creator, along with Hawking; but they live by faith, not science, if they do.[1]

It will be seen that though my own concern will be chiefly with the 'metaphysical questions' (the basic questions proper to all seven ages of man), I am starting from the facts of 'Where Am I?', as they are generally agreed by science today. In this sense, 'Where Am I?', touching space and its four dimensions, is an awesome question; and one takes as firm a grip as possible on cat, thrush, garden, 'self', to keep oneself safe. I am on planet Earth, and held in place by the force of gravity. But planet Earth is on the move, in at least three, and most likely more, complex directions, at wholly dizzying speeds. These journeyings will continue for each of us individually, until we cut loose at the process of death.

In saying this, I approach at last, my 'fifth dimension'; but I want to leave that pending, until I get my general context in place. But 'the fifth dimension' (a hint) points to what may seem missing, to those who reflect that our corpses, or ashes, remain with this earth and its wanderings after death.

The 'fifth dimension' (another hint) is where I enjoy the garden; and where my consciousness wanders, in somewhat differing ways, again, from Earth's wanderings in space.

'Where Am I?' includes certain other assessments, made by scientists, as well as the general precariousness so far perceived. Chemists look at me, I gather, as a handful of chemicals; many ingredients, but mainly water (and some, in transit through). The total cost of the *ensemble* is not impressive. My memory dredges up £1/4/6 (£1.23 now?) as a figure once given; but perhaps this was satiric understatement? I forget. Allowing for inflation, there might still be enough change from a £20 note for two pints at the local; and these would rapidly lose their value in becoming 'me'.

No cheer from the chemists; and what of the medics? They offer a dismaying mix, held together by skin. Heart, lungs, stomach, liver, kidneys, bowels, bladder, lights assorted; blood, veins, arteries, nerves, teeth, and all the head to foot bits and pieces and appendages; tonsils and appendix if present; oh yes, and the brain. And of course, a bone structure – highly complex, and full of symbolism; but not really worth very much, in 'market' terms.

Dismaying enough, all this, and a great source of trouble. Every item is important to our peace of mind, if functioning; painful or fatal, in varying degrees, if not. The medics tend to have their own names for our components, boding ill when one hears them in a consultant's mouth. For the past twenty-one years my mandible (the right one) has had a lurid history, which I refrain from expounding, since this is not that kind of book. Then, there are the bacteria lurking by the million all around us. Fleming did something to tame most of them; but the major ailments left over are best ignored. And the viruses: surely millions of these, also? The viruses have yet to meet their master, in their game with us. From the common cold up to HIV, they resist treatment; mutating when necessary; 'viral infections', all searching out our weak spots or tired moments (or both). Our immune system does its best for us, working overtime (unsleeping?). It wears out, in clock-time, or maybe meets its match earlier; but it has done wonders, just keeping us going till now.

In my lifetime, medical men and women have made advances and also suffered setbacks in their war against microbes; in their important business of vaccinating us against plagues, patching us up by surgery; getting us going again when some germ gets through. Some have gone in for *hubris* on a scale scarcely dreamed of by Aristotle. A few have plunged into horrors, with genetic engineering – akin to genocide? – well to the fore. The hope of defeating death, thereby making earthly life eternal (interminable?) has lured a few: perhaps it still does? (I suppose they are mad.) For those getting older, the 'life-support-system' looms as a threat worse than death – a last, horrible fling of life's worst nightmares. Molecular biology, in contrast, seems to offer a prospect akin to hell upon earth.

Altogether then, our bodies are not worth much, though they can be torture. They are not worth much *in themselves* – not when abstracted from whatever worth the whole man or woman may have to those who admire them; or better, whatever unique worth they have, to those who love. Perhaps, if the outside *ensemble* is attractive, we have some cash value? But this is a matter of social valuation, not of substance itself. There is value in good looks in the world of theatre, film, entertainment; there is some value from painters seeking models, from predators seeking sex for payment. Still: only a privileged few, and the young, count for much here. The distinguished elderly are more likely to pay than be paid. Just possibly, a medical researcher might pay, for this or that organ. But it is more public-spirited to 'give' organs, when one is dead. Bodysnatchers and resurrection men worked, a bit earlier, on similar principles. And, bodily organ by organ, we are worth very little, whether alive or dead.

Yet we cling to life: so doctors and surgeons prosper: plastic 'beauticians' make fortunes disguising, repairing, or touching us up. The clergy come out of it well. They baptise, marry, bury – all for small fees; but all with our happiness here and hereafter chiefly in view.

No doubt, undertakers do best out of 'the remains', when life has departed. A 'good burial' is widely coveted, for reasons social and psychic. A lavish memorial may be required by the rich.

So 'Where Am I?', touching the body – once again, the answer is, 'precarious': the 'thousand natural shocks that flesh is heir to' take care of this.

What, finally, of the physicists? Their cosmic theories overlap with astronomy, and have already been touched on; when they turn to microscope and microcosm, what do they find? Not much for our comfort: for them, I am cells and atoms (and the structure of atoms? – 'an electro-chemical machine', says one; meaning 'me'). When I was young, atoms were simple, or seemed so. 'The smallest possible unit of matter' was my first belief. But then, it appeared that the atom is itself broken up, into a mini-solar-system. Moreover, it behaves at times like a particle, at times like a wave. The huge power latent in atoms was talked over in my young days in the realm of science fiction, though the major breakthrough had in fact been made, just before my birth. Then in 1945 (I was 16), an altogether new measure of this formidable miniature appeared. Two Japanese cities were devastated, to end the Second World War nightmare. The 'objective correlative' to everyman's desire to destroy the world, was fiction no more. The tiniest particle was, now, the mightiest solution: *homo sui juris* (*animal disputans*), was in the second phase of his history; about to be put to the test.

Though not a scientist, I read of continuing wonders. Maybe, each atom is a complex universe, in itself? Then Hawking tells me (can I hear aright?) of new hypotheses in the making. Perhaps atoms (and everything) amount to vast tangles of string?

It was almost a comfort to come upon the *Guardian* piece I quoted earlier (see n. 1): to discover that my brain has (had?) 100 million million synapses; and that these can be connected in ways outnumbering every atom in the universe. Good for the synapses (how can I have gone so long, without saluting them? How can I picture them as small things on sticks, interspersing the cocktails, as this new word struggles, even now, for some image to clutch?).

One could go on, with these external perspectives, pondering data for the poser 'Where am I?' in merely physical terms. One could even touch them up, with some good PR. But there they are: not religious theory, not somebody's dogma, not philosphy; just the facts of the self in the universe, as science conceives them to be. No doubt, the Big Bang, and the Black Holes, and the tangles of string are conjectural; but a formidable consensus presses around them, these days. In our solar system, we have tested the hypotheses with space-craft, and found them accurate: or rather, the moon and most planets, and several satellites and Halley's comet have been visited to schedule, just as calculated, by our rules in clock-time applied in man-made machines.

For the very literal-minded and the blinkered, there are still loopholes? 'Far-fetched' is a lovely, all-purpose word to reach for; and there is that blessed, old standby, 'common sense'.

Surely, everything in this opening chapter is 'far-fetched', not to say un-commonsensical? Don't I know that I am 'really' here, enjoying the garden; along with the unsuspecting cat and thrush? No, I am not whirling through space, in conflicting directions, and at speeds varying from the simply supersonic to mindboggling accelerations in the Einstein scale. And yes, I am who I think I am (for the doubters): I am not a mere sack of chemicals, atoms, DNA, electric waves bound in a gruesome package of organs, with no market value to speak of, in our money-mad world.

Well. Far-fetched it might be, but there is science to speak for it: and so, may some far-fetched religious ideas be stirred in, as well?

Many pagans thought that we come to Earth when conceived in a womb, through Lethean waters of forgetfulness, to live out a period of testing, or punishment, or education, before returning back home. The waters of Lethe, or some benign forgetfulness like that dispensed by Prospero to his daughter, wash over us, taking away all previous memories of who or what we were, and may soon be again. In childhood perhaps, some lingering wonder remains, but it is soon lost in 'experience'. The waters of Lethe wash away previous memories, leaving 'hints and guesses/hints followed by guesses'; leaving sudden far-back remembrances, numinous moments, that come as they will and are hard to speak of, even to ourselves.

To this theme I shall return, since I myself believe it; Eliot's *Four Quartets*, quoted in the previous paragraph, is one seed of this book. For the moment, the basic idea needs fuller statement. We are born in a body which, though highly cramped, and devoid of many ultimate faculties, is truly connected with 'us'; is part of our eternal and inviolable and, in the fullest sense, 'real' life. The purpose of our visit to earth is clearly open to question; but its necessity, in the eternal economy, cannot be in doubt. Perhaps we need a period on earth, where we know love only as it is linked to mortality, to sharpen and purify our joy in love itself? Perhaps we need a period when the people we love best are not only unique, but transient; in order to cherish better the uniqueness of each godgiven thing? Perhaps we have sinned in some way – grown bored with eternity, even – and need a short, sharp shock to bring us back fully to life? Perhaps the Earth is indeed education; a very hard one – with glimpses of heaven few and far between (or *are* they?) in a purgatorial ambiance of exile and pain.

Plato's image of the Cave is righly celebrated; St Paul, from his different perspective, said much the same. 'Here we see as in a glass, darkly; but then, face to face'. The fifteenth chapter of *1 Corinthians* is a pure well of wisdom, deep beyond plumbing. So also is much in the *Epistle To the Hebrews* (not by Paul, but by another remarkable mystic): 'Here, we have no abiding city; but we seek one that is to come'. In a sense, these words should be inscribed on every tombstone; and be taken as read for people whose bodies have vanished from Earth, with no visible remains to dispose of, and no shrine to affirm that they ever existed at all.

The wisest of all men, Jesus of Nazareth, spoke of 'the kingdom of Heaven': and this takes us beyond the space/time *continuum*, if my thesis is followed, into God's wholly other reality in counterpoint, everywhere, with all that Jesus meant by 'the world'. 'Lay not up for yourselves treasures upon earth . . . but . . . treasures in Heaven', Jesus told us; adding, 'For where your treasure is, there will your heart be also' (*Matthew* 6). St Paul, in 2 *Corinthians*, offered a powerful rider, no less part of the equation: 'But we have this treasure in earthen vessels, that the excellency of the power may be of God, and not of us.'

In this area of the 'far-fetched' there is art, with its haunting resonances, deeply sensed as icon: poems by Vaughan, Wordsworth and Eliot; a prophet like Blake; a phoenix-wonder like Shakespeare; all the painters and sculptors and designers of shrines and great palaces; the Mozart G Minor Quintet and the Schubert Quintet in C and the Mahler Ninth Symphony, all three sounding 'farewell, and return'.

There is 'nature' itself – the Earth, beautiful beyond measure; a place fitted to man, and speaking of wonders far off.

And there are the Greek Tragic Dramatists, and Plato and Plotinus; and the huge wisdom infused, from the Greeks, through so much that uplifts and delights our daily lives.

And – to return to it – there is Christ's great teaching of The

Kingdom, which is truly the summit; a peak from which all the glories of Earth can be viewed. Christ was taken up high, by the Devil, to be tempted to destruction. Through his victory, he was able later to take Peter, John and James to the Mountain of Transfiguration – a lifting of the veil, before his descent again, to face betrayal and death.

Will we be taken up that mountain ourselves? If we are, will we notice?

Who is Christ, in our 1990s world of wars, and money, and pollution, and plague? He might be anyone. We need discernment; a gift of the Spirit, as St Paul always stressed. The question 'Who is my neighbour?' was asked, of Jesus; his tale of the Good Samaritan came in reply. But Jesus himself; who is he, and how do we know him? 'Anyone who has done it to the least of these my brethren has done it to me' (*Matthew* 25: 31–46).

Human art is 'far-fetched', in my view of it; so is Nature; so, without doubt, is all Christ's teaching on the Kingdom of God.

And so too, I am suggesting, are we: and I quote Wordsworth, using a famous stanza from his best-known ode. For many critics, these words are metaphor, not literal doctrine. Elsewhere, Wordsworth did profess an open mind on the doctrine of 'pre-existence' (in *The Prelude* itself). It has always struck me, however, that he wrote of pre-existence from conviction. And my own conviction – not dogmatic, but clear – is very close to these words, understood as the closest we are likely to get to a guess at the truth:

> Our birth is but a sleep and a forgetting;
> The soul that rises with us, our life's star,
> Hath had elsewhere its setting
> And cometh from afar.
> Not in entire forgetfulness,
> And not in utter nakedness,
> But trailing clouds of glory do we come
> From God, who is our home.

But before proceeding, there is another port of call on the quest for 'Where Am I?', and this I now turn to; an experience basic to my analysis of Eliot's *Four Quartets* elsewhere.[2]

It is worth recording that this key insight of my life came to me on the night when Coventry was badly hit by German bombs, in November 1940. It was a few days before my twelfth birthday and, laying awake in the night, hearing the raid on a brief stay in Bletchley, sensing the danger (though for once, I was away from London), the realisation that I lived 'now', and 'now' only, swept over me, with amazing power. Perhaps it was the realisation that I might not be alive in (say) five more minutes; perhaps the thought, coming with it, that I had no way back to 'five minutes ago'. Later, I found the idea in St Augustine, later still in T.S. Eliot – so, like all major 'discoveries', it is clearly, in no sense, 'mine'.

But I note that few people speak of it; as a theme, it is *tabu*, almost? I suspect that many people find it familiar, but – well, far-fetched; hard to speak of with ease.

So: Time, the great mystery. In one aspect, Time is the fourth dimension of the space/time continuum, and it is in this role that it has featured here.

But in another aspect, Time is the impingement of a mystery far beyond the space/time continuum: a stream flowing backwards, not forwards, over the unchanging 'now' where our all-important fifth dimension rightly belongs.

In fact, our fifth dimension is indeed Janus-like – in clock-time dwindling towards mortality and apparent extinction; in this other timescale, opening out 'from glory to glory' – or maybe, from darkness to deeper darkness: for here is the rub; here the purpose, of our rough ride in exile; and the theme of this book.

Such things are 'far-fetched' in the metaphorical sense, if one shuts the doors of perception; they are far-fetched literally – from a place not in space/time at all. Christ called this 'The Kingdom of God', and it is infinitely more distant than Black Holes. It is also immediately and always present, in the 'now' where we are.

2

Where Am I? Time, the Mysterious Dimension

In Chapter 1, I began with reminders of the very slender hold we have on space. My concern was mainly with the three dimensions of length, breadth and depth, and with 'time' in its role as duration, the fourth dimension of space. This I call 'clock-time', as a reminder that we measure our lives by it daily, from cradle to grave. In direction it moves forward, from Big Bang to Black Hole in the cosmos (one of Hawking's 'arrows'). We know it in early life chiefly as growth and development; then, as change and decay. My focus was on scientific accounts of time as on current offer. The religious paradox lurking was merely implied.

In this chapter, the religious dimension will be to the fore, though only because the inherent mysteriousness of Time dictates its own terms. My consideration of some pervasive objections to religious or metaphysical 'questions' is reserved for Chapters 4 to 6. Meanwhile, the nature of time has inbuilt ambivalence, with its profoundly mystical aspect not far off, but near.

So my reminder now is of the extremely slender hold we have on time.

As I write this, or as you read it, most of what 'we are' is in abeyance. We can see in one another something of what we have 'become', through a lifetime of actions. But we are not being, or possessing at this moment, remotely all of 'ourselves'. You have only to recall your best, or worst, experiences, to realise this vividly. How do they match, or even touch, what you experience 'now'?

Or it can be dramatised by recalling all the books you have read, all the music you have heard, with pleasure. What hold do they have on you, or you on them, in this moment of time? Where is 'your' past, 'your' life, with its varied intensities? Where is the child's day at the sea; the dance; each catch of the breath?

'Who Am I?' is a familiar question; in modern experience, almost always confined to social, and psychological frames. But 'Where Am I?', witticisms apart, can also tease us (though it is not a subject to embark on in the pub). Is your 'total' self stored only in memory, distorted and fading, and is it otherwise 'lost in the past', wherever or whatever that is?

That we came into existence at conception is a truism, though the day we celebrate our 'beginning' skips the womb, and homes in on birth. We celebrate it yearly as 'our' birthday – which is to say, the point when we entered that finite scrap of history where our story is set. That we depend on God for creating us and keeping us in being, is a belief held by most Christians, and by most others with belief in 'One God'. In one form or another, it has a meaning for numerous other religions; and, certainly, for all men and women with a mystical strain. But, unless all we 'have been' is also in 'God's keeping', we seem to be already more than half-bereaved of ourselves; more than half ghosts?

This riddle of lost potential can come home, sharply and painfully, whenever a very young child, or a very old person, dies. The young child has missed the experience of adulthood, and it is a bleak observer who says merely, 'Thank God, he was spared the pain'. The old person may have fallen apart in body, in mind, to all appearances in identity, surviving as a seeming parody of all he or she once was. Are we to assume that infancy, youth, maturity, all 'seven ages of man' have been extinguished in mortality? Can it really be that 'what has been' is *de facto* dead, before death intervenes?

Or is the power that called all creatures into being still guarding them; still perfecting rather, through 'becoming', a work once begun? On one showing, we come from oblivion and return to oblivion. This may sound soothing, even attractive to some (some are scared stiff by it). Can one listen, unmoved, to Swinburne's hymn to oblivion?

From too much love of living,
From hope and fear set free,
We thank with brief thanksgiving
Whatever gods may be
That no life lives for ever;
That dead men rise up never;
That even the weariest river
Winds somewhere safe to sea.

(Swinburne: from
'The Garden of Proserpine')

But such lotos-music tells us, 'all achievement is transient; all human struggles ultimately wasted – even if they did briefly influence one or two fellow humans, for good or ill'. In particular, it tells us that the growth of goodness which we admire in loved people through a lifetime of kindness and courage, has no true fulfilment, of the kind Jesus promised, and named 'the Kingdom of God'. Even transfigured men and women (a rare few) lose their beauty in death, as if the progress 'from glory to glory' had been only a trick.

But if some God does exist, superhuman in power and loving in nature, would it truly be odd if our struggles, defeats and victories are the best and nearest measure we have of truth? It is easy to see why this view is regarded, by some, as 'wishful thinking'. But are not such wishes (if that is the word) central; to creation, dignity, striving, in the battle of life?

II

I turn next to our attempts to find images for eternity; which set a further conundrum, for scrupulous minds. Moving towards death and knowing change daily, how can we imagine the absence of death and change? How can we start to imagine 'the timeless' except by abstracting; except by draining out, from 'normal' experience, all colour and grace? We think perhaps of an end without ending, a future with no future, a deprivation; a deeper darkness, or a glare of white light. The imagination grapples with and tries to grasp emptiness; a grey and nebulous residue, left after time.

This is bad in itself; but how, yet more urgently, can we truly desire or long for such a state? How are we to warm to the traditional pictures that force themselves into the vacuum – to angels, golden streets, harps, and endless praise? At best, such images are fated to seem insipid (even to those who delight in music, and find heartsease in the kindness of men). Could this be because negation obtrudes into the concept 'eternal', so that we imagine all full-blooded joy as we know it, away? No friendship, no sex, no Venice, no warm human bondings; only, a school-prizegiving, with real life *tabu*? Or is it that beauty seems irrevocably married to sorrow, so that we say, with Shelley, 'The sweetest songs are those that tell of saddest thought'?

Yet Plotinus insisted that the works of time are beautiful, though tinged with illusion; indeed, are the revelation of *Nous*, second person of his Trinity, as he looks upwards to God the transcendent, and downwards to Earth. Blake wrote, 'Eternity is in love with the productions of time'. And, as religious people, the particular beauty we celebrate on earth in things, and more especially in people, will surely impress us as seed of very great splendour to come? 'I am convinced', said St Paul, 'that the sufferings of the present time are not worthy to be compared with the joy that shall be revealed in us; for the earnest expectation of the creature waits for the manifestation of the sons of God'. If we reread Paul's exhilarating letters with this in mind solely, we can be overwhelmed by their continual grip on the *weight* of glory waiting release. Our religious instincts assure us that all life creates and strives to perfect our potential. We are told, also by Paul, that the resurrected body will surpass every highest earthly splendour, as a great oak tree surpasses the acorn from which it began. It must then be true – if such intuitions hold – that however young and unformed, or however old and decayed, a mortal body may be, at its moment of dying, its inner glory remains the true seed of what will be reaped, when the harvest is home. The treasure has been in 'earthen vessels', in the time of our pilgrimage. This mortal puts on immortal, when our earthly moment for 'It is finished' comes round.

We must therefore believe that our past does remain, with God, as the seed of this future; when we are translated from mortal to eternal soil, as clock-time runs out.

But the Christian understanding is that eternity is here, as well as hereafter; that changes towards wholeness cut across, and counterpoint, all decay. Platonism places our being in time 'at one stage removed' from reality, and finds aspiration to return to the real at the heart of our quest. Tibetans speak of a reality to which we return, between human incarnations – an ongoing pilgrimage, on this showing, related to our deeds in each life. Hinduism agrees that ascent to 'higher reality' is the goal of existence; though the total duality of 'body' and 'soul', favouring the latter, poses a problem that in theory, at least, Christianity tries to avoid.

And before I pursue these themes, one natural analogy might be helpful. Are we not less ready to doubt the glory a seed can hide in itself, if we recall that the male sperm includes its *whole* genetic potential, when it enters the womb?

III

One problem of imagining eternity (to return to this) clearly links with the paradoxical nature of time. The problem of locating oneself in the here and now accurately, is akin to the problem of locating oneself in 'eternal life'. The former problem (in the aspects my last chapter looked at) is largely scientific, the latter, religious: but both tend to tease and alarm the imagination. Both are wrestlings, in territory strictly ill-adapted to human minds and imaginations. We can only be helped therefore if we can find as firm ground as possible for our 'intimations of immortality'; and for some disciplined confidence in God.

Tiny atoms in space and time, almost unlocated in either, we are still richly conscious of ourselves and of others, as agents of love. But do we measure our conscious 'reality' by the ticking of clocks? We know five minutes, ten minutes, next year, as general notions. We know yesterday, last year, never again as pangs of the heart.

And do we know where to seek these, or any other experiences in their *essence*, as we wonder, how they came into being; and what they portend? Are past and future 'real' only in the present? And if so, do they exist, in the present, in a radically altered form? Yet, if they exist only in the present, where are they? The present passes almost before we can give it a name.

Where – to take one instance – is music? Where, in past, present or future, is the texture and structure of Beethoven's 'Ninth'? There are printed scores of the symphony, with their written notations; but these are not the music itself. There are performances of the symphony in concert hall and on recordings; but where does the performance, the sound, really exist? Each second, a resonance shapes, holds, and passes. The echoes may prolong it briefly, as it leaves. We guess at the sound to come from the still unfolding patterns, and are delighted equally by the expected completion, or by some unexpected departure which is, gloriously, right. If we are familiar with the music from past performances, we are helped by memory: which, anticipating things still to come, very variously and subtly enriches the 'now'. We form the strongest sense of some kind of space, where the whole work is gathered. But the fleeting sounds, as they move, are all that we actually have.

In fact, are we not teased by the near-tangible illusion of architecture? – of a shape, or a palace, somewhere only just out of reach? The work seems to exist in some space-not-quite-space where our minds have access; a location easier to intuit than to define. We say 'Mahler's Second Symphony', or 'Schubert's String Quintet', and some vision, as exotic as Venice, is conjured up. When I first heard these works I knew that they had always existed, and that I have always known them: Plato's doctrine of 'remembrance' was no longer theory, but fact. I knew too, of course, that the works were constructed with considerable creative anguish and revision by Schubert and Mahler, at particular moments in clock-time, as they refined and developed their art. This is indeed the Janus-faced quality I shall be returning to, on and off, as central. People, and things, live in clock-time, to the laws of growth and mortality. Yet they face outwards also from an unchanging now, to a wholly other reality, with its own, different 'time'.

Works of music possess this 'architectural' quality, which we further experience when reflecting on them from some distance away. Perhaps it is a little like revisiting a great cathedral in memory? – except that it isn't, except by analogy, remotely the same. We 'remember' a great cathedral in its general aspect and its atmosphere; but we cannot count the columns, or exactly visualise the mosaics. None the less, the columns and mosaics have spatial existence and solidity, and we can return, if we want, to check our memory against the facts. But a symphony can be revisited only in a further performance, where the elusiveness of all, except the sounds as they gather and pass, must always remain. For the rest, we don't have even the real sounds present, in our memory. We have only the memory's reconstruction of what sounds are like. There is a sense, perhaps, of what sounds *sound* like – and for most of us, this is essentially imprecise. But, since the work can never be extended in space, or held in time, for our full inspection, how do we get nearer to that triumphant structure which, still, we somehow possess?

IV

These reflections include a reminder – in no sense original, yet overlooked sometimes – of the precarious temporal existence of 'art', as well as of 'life'. A work of art may outlast its creator, for so long in 'clock-time', that it can become a quasi-symbol (in Keats' 'Ode to a Grecian Urn', in Yeats' 'Sailing to Byzantium' and so forth), for 'eternity' itself. (Or for a step on eternity's 'way'?) But this is indeed an illusion, as such poets well know and perfectly calculate: 'Foster-child of silence and slow time' is Keats' further image, for the Urn. With this in mind, we can admit that Music, in which many of us find our nearest apprehension through art of eternity, is none the less among the most elusive of all experiences in time.

Yet is this elusiveness not still more true of our love for people? Not of the dead only (though of them especially), and not only of the living but absent; but, by a slight extension, of the living and normally accessible themselves? 'Man is in love, and loves what vanishes, What more is there to say?', wrote Yeats. Of course, he did say more – a great deal more, as we all do, though without Yeats' genius. But the tormenting dilemma remains. We come back to it through every real experience of love or of suffering, even if there is an attempt to retreat into 'everyday commonsense', 'normal life' (stability without God, and without glory?) in the spaces between.

Now there are, of course, famous explorations in this territory, and I should have no wish to compete with them, even if I could. And while St Augustine's *Confessions* (Book XI) and T.S. Eliot's *Four Quartets* stand out, even among the very greatest classics, much other memorable literature, memorable art, can also be invoked.

My present attempt is to throw into this complex area one simple suggestion – which is, that eternity may not be *more* of a mystery than is clock-time. In fact, in one aspect, Time has one foot in clock-time, one foot in eternity; and its foot in eternity *could be the more familiar to us, of the two*. We know clock-time by the feel of transience, with all its riddles. *Do we know eternity by the feel of existence itself?*

I approach this idea not for its novelty (though some people claim to find it novel), but rather, to establish a clear path and a firm foothold among manageable, indeed normal, ideas.

For Christians, a 'relationship' with Christ homes in on certain landmarks: manger, parables, 'signs', transfiguration, cross, empty tomb. These things are not conceived of as belonging chiefly to the past, and as permanently receding; they are not simply held in records, or even in the memories and images of succeeding generations of men. They belong, for believers, with daily consciousness; with the signs of dereliction, and joy, and the map of these polarities, stamped through our lives like the 'Brighton' in Brighton rock. The church stresses this aspect of permanence in its central action; in the perpetual re-enactment of the breaking of bread. The priest says 'Therefore with angels and with archangels and with the whole company of Heaven' . . . and it is as if the sanctuary, and the congregation, tilt out of time. The mighty dead and the hosts of Heaven are summoned, and a change which is 'theirs', not 'ours', starts to take place. As sacrifice and glory happen, linked in cross and resurrection, there is a different, more glorious, offer of change. Not change, in clock-time, from past, through present to future; but change, by grace, to eternal life, which is Christ's offered gift. 'For the love of Christ constrains us, because we are thus judged, that if one died for all, then were all dead . . . Therefore if any man be in Christ he is a new creature. Old things are passed away; all things become new.'

From meaninglessness to meaning, from torment to serenity, from desolation to glory; is this not the direction of all willed change, towards wisdom and love? The change which comes upon Christians as Christ moves into them was called, by Christ himself, 'eternal life'. 'Eternal life' is not merely 'life after death', and still less is it merely 'survival'. It is bringing the human consciousness back to God (back to its true being, if one sees life this way). This change cuts across all the changes of transience, as did Christ's Transfiguration (though like that, it does not suspend mortality, or cancel it out). We remain subject to the laws of the space/time continuum, which is the place of our exile. Yet a change which transcends death *because it has nothing to do with death*, starts to take place.

The Christian religion is amazingly rich; its Liturgy, in the Russian Orthodox form especially, can become a window, like the icons it cherishes, directly out of 'this' world. But the quest for God through prayer, icons, worship and service, is near the heart of most religions aspiring upwards, from earth.

And 'timeless moments', properly associated as they are with religion, have humbler, occasional roles, in our mundane affairs. Though the phrase 'in and out of time' is in essence elusive, there are fairly common analogies to point the way. The first day of the holiday; Monday morning; the dentist's waiting room; staying-in for the plumber; waiting for the specialist's report. The difficult interview, which cannot be avoided; the red-letter day, for seeing a friend. These circle round in their season, with a special feel to them; perhaps filling all the horizon when they come. And in the background, there are the great hopes and fears that attend us; the lurking tension between our limited present, and our intuited fullness of joy.

V

Let me now suggest a simple experiment, both to close in on the mystery, and to clear verbal barriers away. Say 'It is now': Yes, say it out loud, as you read this. Now, what do (did?) the words mean; and how are they true?

The words 'It is now', as you said them, are already receding – five, six, seven seconds ago. Are they disappearing (have they disappeared) into nowhere; set on an endless (or ended) one-way voyage to the past? Do they remain now only in memory? And if so, are they the memory (eighteen, nineteen, twenty seconds ago) of a lie? In what sense were they true, when you uttered them? In what sense are they true, 'now'?

If you say, 'It is now' again, do the words have the same meaning – as this repetition also moves, second by second, into the past? Do they have some different meaning, because circumstances differ in clock-time; or do they have the same meaning, to the degree that the statement is true?

No: I do not propose to institute a game – reflections in mirrors – but to suggest that the words were, and are, in one important sense 'true'. The apparent problems hinted at are merely verbal, since the word 'now' shifts and changes, in normal use.

'Now' can be used to describe limited vision, the bondage of the present, blinkered preoccupation – 'confined to the present; no way out', one might say. It is the politician's temptation, short-term expediency rather than the sweep of the future: 'without vision the people perish'. Where now, are the prophets and seers?

But 'now' can be used also as a word implying stillness, clarity. It can be calm, delicate observation – exact cloud formation, the precise texture, the fine shade of light. It can be a claim, or call, to exactitude as at the start of a race: 'One, two, three, steady: NOW'. It can be that other call to exactitude when skills have to test themselves: the student in the exam room, the pilot coming in to land on one engine; the surgeon about to operate for the hundredth, or the thousandth time, but this time on you.

'Now'. But 'now' is also a word for eternity. Eternity, we say, is an unending 'now'. But *is* eternity the only 'now' without an ending? Or rather, is there ever an end to our normal 'now'?

An unending 'now' *is* our consciousness, as we daily experience it. It is our fate to exist 'here' and 'now', and nowhere else. Whenever we say 'it is now', it *is* now. 'Now' is the entire space we are given to exist.

'We' don't move from the unknown future, through an infinitesimal present, into a past that is always receding (or always nowhere?): 'we' are the still point through which everything moves. We cannot get one second ahead of, or one second behind, ourselves. Whether we are anywhere or nowhere, we are held in 'now'.

Try saying 'It is five minutes ago'. Well, that is clearly untrue. And how could you now hope to get there, even if 'five minutes ago' really exists? Try saying, 'It is five minutes in the future'. How does that sound? You can no more get to it than fly. It is coming towards you, at the measured tread of clock-time. But as it nears (four minutes ahead? three minutes and fifty-six seconds?) it is as inaccessible as the remotest past years, or the farthest reaches of the remotest galaxy. It will of course come very soon, unless you fall dead now. It will be here quicker if you dread than desire it, or seem so, maybe. But, when it comes, it will instantly pass, before you can touch it. It will be one second, two seconds ago (where the dinosaurs are?).

You exist 'now', and now is the still point of consciousness, through which future moves into past inexorably, and faster than thought. We wake into 'now' and 'now' stays with us. It is 'now' while we read, and 'now' after we read. Things flow through us, continually – changing us, attracting or repelling. What we choose, as this process goes on, is our personal destiny, our dance of 'becoming', in clock-time, what we now really are. All is touched by heaven or hell, and *they* do not pass by; heaven and hell battle in us, for the grey ground: and living and choosing 'now', our colour is formed. Within consciousness, we live richly in now, one way or the other. Our free-will (where does *that* originate?) touches us nearly, moving us always towards darkness, or light.

So: from the moment we come into consciousness at (or very slightly after?) conception, to the moment we die, we are always – except when asleep, or rendered unconscious – living in 'now'. 'Now' we hope, and fear, and imagine what might be. 'Now' we are, and we always are, the dance going on.

VI

What then is this fixed 'now', the centre? By definition, it is oddly related to time. Clearly, the passage of clock-time affects and colours our consciousness; and our choices in clock-time (from past, through present, into future) determine what we become, and so what we currently are. Clearly, clock-time prescribes the immeasurably mysterious way in which we 'know' things; which is no doubt, why the passing of time seems so real, to reflecting minds. By 'know', I refer in this instance not only to the experiences which come through our nerves and senses and, by whatever process, arrive in the mind as images and ideas – but also to the feelings and associations fused with these things, forged in the dance of becoming that proceeds, to laws of its own. While systems of belief, or creeds, may be one fruit of our impulse to structure experience, most of us remain aware of unresolvable complexities in flux, in unending play.

Our experiences themselves are modified by many factors, ranging from lethargy or inoperancy of one or more faculties to inattention, faulty structuring, poor memory, malfunctioning nervewaves, or the extravagances of hallucinations, delusions and dreams. Yet in the middle of experiences – and of 'experience' – we are conscious of existing. We exist: and our consciousness of 'self' does not recede with time. It seems, then, that if the mystery of 'time' that passes over us, from future to past, is at first hard to imagine, yet it is as familiar as consciousness itself, where the passage takes place.

The complexity in both notions of time – one moving forward, the other backward – is added chiefly by the factor of mortality: which seems to belong with the former; but affects the 'becoming' of the latter, as well. Touching clock-time, we measure mortality by ageing, by loss, by the death awaiting all that we love; by the death awaiting ourselves, at the last. Touching a present that goes on – well, very simply, we live in it. Yet we live with mortality, too.

Mortality is so important, in both equations, that it can virtually be used as a synonym for 'time'. Familiar lines from H.F. Lyte's great hymn remind us of this (often at funerals) – drawing a distinction between the real God (behind all our notions of God) who made and sustains us; and ourselves as creatures doomed to clock-time – our element for choosing and becoming, here on earth:

Change and decay in all around I see;
O Thou, who changest not, abide with me.

Yet, though mortality is brutal, and our ride in exile a rough one, mortality does not 'mix' us with the time that leads to death. Mortality may steal our memories, our faculties, our vitality – indeed, very large parts of us; yet when all is said, it in no way steals our *selves*. The very word 'us' testifies to an obstinate sense we have (I speak for myself; but is this not general?) that there *is* a self, which is anything but an eternal flux. Though Hume, and certain other sceptics and solipsists have denied this, the reality of a continuing 'self', a 'me', is most widely experienced and assumed. From our earliest moment of consciousness to our very last living conscious moment, we assert and build up the 'self' in the 'now' where it truly seems to be at home. I think it important that this is as true of saints as it is of the most selfish egoists; it is as true of Eastern mystics, who may seem to deny it, as it is of Western religious and romantic traditions which grant to 'self' a very high place. Nearly everyone takes the 'self' for granted, and seeks to find or build an identity.

In Chapter 5, I shall argue that questioning the existence of the 'self' is a philosophic game, or tease; obsessive in some: for most, not a serious concern.

Christ taught that peace, love, joy are fruit of 'The Kingdom', where our life grows, in total counterpoint with decay. Christ called his gift not simply 'enrichment', but 'Life Eternal'. This is our true life, experienced here, though in exile, in 'the world'. Eternal life is distinct from and finally immune to mortality, despite the death, perhaps on a cross, that we know to be our immediate doom. Eternal life is discovered in ourselves by 'remembrance', as Plato told us. It is nurtured by the Spirit, 'from glory to glory', in Paul's larger view.

Our 'now' of being is redeemed, and returned to its native wholeness, in balance with the inescapable bondage of change and death. 'Eternal Life' does not fade with memory, energy, and the physical decline of mind and body. It is safe in our perceived and accepted sonship of God.

VII

My concern has been with some analogy between life 'in time', and our 'now' that continues. Naturally, no further exploration of 'eternal' can be made, touching the nature of God. 'Eternity', in God's being, is a mode of consciousness we cannot guess at, and will surely never be able to share. We are, after all, creatures; and the Consciousness to which past, present and future are always available is far indeed from our own. We risk confounding ourselves, and our language, by trying to probe it (even though thought about prayer leads irresistibly in this direction, at times). Undeniably, in our life on earth we are denied access to many questions we are strongly prompted to ask. There must be further questions which will elude us permanently; and with no harm done – since it is not in our nature ever to know what they are. Only God can know God fully, and we are not God. Our human ideas of God set often intractable posers; as Jung (for instance) explores, in his *Answer to Job*.

For Christians, the practical aspects of 'eternity' are twofold and, if I am right, less wholly lost in mystery than is sometimes supposed. First, 'eternal life' is the promise of consciousness that will not cease at physical death and sink into oblivion. Rather, it will continue in its true dimension, refined and healed by this life. Christ said that he 'went to prepare a place' for his disciples. If this had not been so, he would have told them; to make the terms of life clear beyond doubt. He spoke of 'many mansions' waiting in the life beyond death, attuned to human diversity. He said there would be 'no marriage or giving in marriage' (no procreation; no one-to-one relationships, excluding to some degree others); but that we should meet those we love, and all close friends; and possibly, all whom we grow to see with the eyes of God. His 'kingdom', 'not of this world' is, therefore, our final goal; as well as our spiritual way.

The committal of the dead into God's keeping is a solemn occasion. For the beareaved, there is grief at loss – many men's sharpest experience of suffering; yet also, love's most striking tribute to the person now lost. Celebration of a life, final blessing, the proclamation of promise, join with grief – in recognition that all life is unique, and irreplaceable, and dependent on God. The great proclamation from John's Gospel (11: 25–6) fittingly sums up 'the hope that is in us', ringing true to Christ's teaching from the exotic and unearthly vision in which it is set: 'I am the resurrection and the life. He that believeth in me, though he were dead, yet shall be live. And he that liveth and believeth in me shall never die'.

What the resurrected body will 'be' is a mystery. But St Paul is convinced that it is the vital link between our identity here, and our truest self. The resurrected body is a guarantee of our identity: body, mind, spirit truly fulfilled, not 'absorbed in oneness', or half-cancelled-out. We shall know and love one another as individuals for ever; we shall know all creation. Not a bird worth less than a farthing falls to the earth, unnoticed by God, Christ also said. The Christian good news is unquestionably 'romantic', if the 'romantic' affirms unique individuals as the prime work of God. Christ's promise is more, but it is not less, than this.

In this insight, we converge on the second implication of 'eternal life'. It is a quality of life discovered here and now, beyond the reach of mortality; and 'in Christ', through the Spirit, assured of its direction and way. We shall love for ever, not possessively or destructively, but in a freedom that on Earth we glimpse only far off, at times of great joy. Eternal life is not 'just' survival, or 'just' continuity. It is life delivered from evil, and made perfect in love. The life of prayer initiates us into the eternal, and is the means of our growth there. This activity, which to humans reduced in their vision may seem useless or even meaningless, is the activity most natural to humans, and the activity most important in linking daily routine to the direct life of God.

If left until crisis or death make us 'need' it, prayer is almost negated by most human tests. Perhaps God *will* honour such prayer and even refine us, belatedly – but can we sensibly delay to the hour of 'our' need? Prayer is really the service of God, through words and deeds equally, and the activity in words and deeds that make a life. Prayer is the building up of the eternal, deep within us, through every season of joy, pain and indifference that life brings.

The change towards holiness is sure, though painfully gradual. Most of us so fail to grow in glory, that we seem devoid of any tincture of glory at all.

'By their fruits you shall know them' is a true, helpful saying; but the grace that transfigures is as rare as any numinous gleam. We can be glad that the writer of *Hebrews* invokes the saints as a 'great cloud of witnesses'; the body we aspire to, but most usually sense – in their presence – from very far off:

Moments of great calm.
Kneeling before an altar
Of wood in a stone church
In summer, waiting for the God
To speak; the air a staircase
For silence: the sun's light
Ringing me, as though I acted
A great role. And the audiences

Still: all that close throng
Of spirits waiting, as I,
For the message.

Prompt me, God:
But not yet. When I speak,
Though it be you who speak
Through me, something is lost.
The meaning is in the waiting.

(R.S. Thomas, 'Kneeling')

VIII

For believers in eternal life, whether Christian or not, these Christian beliefs are a summit on the horizons of faith. This is why many (like myself) would like a Christian burial, even if the church on Earth, as it now is, may seem to preclude this, on grounds of its own.

The hope is that when our 'now' resumes, after physical death and beyond the space/time continuum, it will be the absence of *mortal* change that will strike us most. The fact of mortality is the chief sting of time, as we know it. The city we seek is elsewhere, however lovely this Earth can often be.

And, though eternity after death will be free from further loss and bereavement, I see no reason why it should lack diversity and change. Indeed, since 'glory to glory' is the ultimate promise of holiness, change itself, in eternity, is splendidly transformed. There is no reason to think that Heaven will lack procession or colour, or the marvellous diversity found in nature and art.

Nature and art are complex in clock-time, where suffering makes more than half of their beauty and power. We must believe that the complexities stored up for us will transcend, without cancelling out, the glories we already experience on earth.

Heaven is defined as our 'real' home, our true fulfilment. It promises more, not less, of whatever fulfils us here. If certain physical things cease to exist as we have known them, this will be because a beauty they concealed as well as revealed can at last fully break through. I see no reason why things and people should not still be individual and particular, differing only in clarity; since nothing that gives rise to love will be lost.

The Christian vision is of the whole creation coming home in triumph, of every seed that has been planted, and prospered, reaching full fruit. It seems that what we cease to experience when we move on after death to the phase of real existence, will be not change and diversity, but change and diversity irrevocably wedded to death. When love has been finally purged of whatever let death into it (egocentric possessiveness?), love will finally be purged of the *need* for death. That this final triumph will be no mean or partial end-game is apparent when we see the works of 'the kingdom' on Earth. The 'meanest flower that blows' – acts of daily kindness, nameless and unremembered – it was in these things, as much as in skating at evening as a child, or crossing the Alps as a man, that Wordsworth discovered 'thoughts that do often lie too deep for tears'.

Will the fuller life have its own matter and density, its own time even? This also seems likely; though we cannot be sure. In these first two chapters, I have concentrated on the mystery of our known world, and our precarious hold on it. I have used as focus not religious facts (though these have come into it – especially with the 'now' where time becomes ambivalent); but observations common to science, and to normal human reflection on the state of this Earth. We find that our minds cannot imagine, with any precision or concreteness, even the ascertainable, scientific facts of our here and now. Physicists baffle themselves, and us, with tentative images, and it is a confident man who thinks that a spade is a bloody shovel, and nothing more. A world created at Big Bang with unimaginable fury and drama; expanding at vast speeds 'outwards'; our own Earth a wildly-spinning speck round a smallish star in a galactic arm. The end, a Black Hole, or Black Holes, with or without interim spasms. Encounters with comets and meteors and meteorites for sure and, maybe, with mysterious pulsars and quasars some billions of years off in space. All this: and the atoms that compose us; mysterious microcosms, mirroring in miniature the larger confusions, and in no way easier to grasp. Meanwhile, our bodies – precious to us, though perpetually threatened – reduced to no market value to speak of, when the chemists have done.

And time: one aspect of the space/time continuum, for all practical purposes; but more mysterious, more elusive, than the *continuum* can contain.

The mysteries of 'Where Am I?' surround us, in this space-age; almost everyone engages with them, in the physical world. But by choice – or is it, as a hangover from the recent, scientific ascendancy? – we often ignore or deride the spiritual questions which, in close parallel, lurk.

But, though we cannot imagine 'eternity' and may be mocked if we try to, we do have data: we have a point of contact, in the continuous 'now' of the consciousness which is ours. My point has been to suggest that while eternity is mysterious, it is not more so than clock-time. Indeed, it may be even less so, since it is – not in theory but truth – the mode of our experience itself.

In the next, deliberately brief, chapter, I shall state this books's thesis, in its concise form. I shall then tackle three obstacles to clarity, in our search for wisdom, that are man-made; then point to three paths, for pilgrims, that have proved important to me. But perhaps I can end this chapter with a quotation which, when I first encountered it, came as revelation: for reasons that the speculation, up to now, will have made clear.

> It is in my own mind, then, that I measure time. I must not allow my mind to insist that time is something objective. I must not let it thwart me because of all the different notions and impressions that have lodged in it. I say that I measure time in my mind. For everything which happens leaves an impression on it, and this impression remains after the thing itself has ceased to be. It is the impression that I measure, since it is still present, not the thing itself, which makes the impression as it passes and then moves into the past . . .
>
> When we measure silences and say that a given period of silence has lasted as long as a given period of sound, we measure the sound mentally, as though we could actually hear it, and this enables us to measure the duration of periods of silence. Even without opening our mouths or speaking at all, we can go over poems and verses and speech of any sort in our minds, and we can do the same with measurable movement of any kind. We can estimate that one poem takes proportionately more, or less, time than another, just as if we were reciting both aloud. If a man wishes to utter a prolonged sound and decides beforehand how long he wants it to be, he allows this space of time to elapse in silence, commits it to memory, and then begins to utter the sound. It sounds until it reaches the limit set for it, or rather, I should not use the present tense and say it sounds, but the past and the future, saying that it both has sounded and will sound. For as much of it as has been completed at any given moment has

sounded, and the rest will sound. In this way the process continues to the end. All the while the man's attentive mind, which is present, is relegating the future to the past. The past increases in proportion as the future diminishes, until the future is absorbed and becomes wholly past.

But how can the future be diminished or absorbed when it does not exist? And how can the past increase when it no longer exists? It can only be that the mind, which regulates this process, performs three functions, those of expectation, attention and memory. The future, which it expects, passes through the present, to which it attends, into the past, which it remembers. No one would deny that the future does not yet exist or that the past no longer exists. Yet in the mind there is both expectation of the future and remembrance of the past. Again, no one would deny that the present has no duration, since it exists only for the instant of its passage. Yet the mind's attention persists, and through it that which is to be passes towards the state in which it is to be no more. So it is not future time that is long, but a long future is a long expectation of the future: and past time is not long, because it does not exist, but a long past is a long remembrance of the past . . .

You, my Father, are eternal. But I am divided between time gone by and time to come, and its course is a mystery to me. My thoughts, the intimate life of my soul, are torn this way and that in the havoc of change. And so it will be until I am purified and melted by the life of your love, and fused into one, with you. (St Augustine, *Confessions*, Book XI)

3

The Fifth Dimension

'To be conscious is not to be in time.'

(T.S. Eliot, 'Burnt Norton')

The quotation from Eliot is a key to this brief chapter, and to the book.

I am referring to 'consciousness' as the 'Fifth Dimension', for two reasons that together form my theme.

The first, is to place 'consciousness' in relation to the opening two chapters, and the 'Where Am I?' questions that have to be asked.

The second, is to relate the quest for Wisdom – and the particular paths towards Wisdom that will be touched on here – to 'eternal life'.

II

Strictly speaking, 'consciousness' is the Fifth Dimension of 'clock-time', since it is the dimension without which the space/time continuum could scarcely be said to exist. As far as we know, without 'consciousness' there is no reality. Even Hume, the solipsist, tactily allows this. Though he pares consciousness down to a mere flux of impressions, with no unifying centre, at least impressions occur, related to whatever reality the perceiving flux has.

Berkeley had avoided solipsism by postulating God as perceiving Consciousness. He asserted that things and people go on existing in the divine consciousness; which encompasses everything, and never sleeps. Even if no human consciousness is attending, space/time remains safe in God's eye.

My concern here is chiefly with human consciousness, since for us, this is the place where everything always and only is.

Our whole human awareness and discourse is within this area. Epistemology represents various attempts to define, and perhaps enlarge, its scope. Locke's empiricism confines us within data received by the five senses, which are then conveyed to the brain, where they are received as ideas and images, and made the subject of 'reasoning' in its form of discursive logic. Hume's solipsism, working inside Locke's system, reduces rational empiricism to near vanishing point.

My own instinct as a Christian Platonist is, naturally, to include further spiritual faculties within Epistemology, notably those receiving Beauty and Goodness (and perhaps, 'spiritual truth'). The resultant complexities of attempting to sort out which of these spiritual data are received 'directly' into the soul, and which of them relate partly or chiefly, through aesthetics, to the human perception of Lockean data, is luckily not my business (though Kant and Coleridge – and a little before, the Third Earl of Shaftesbury – are names to which I turn).

I also attach great importance to numinous moments; to perceptions of holiness; and to vision. I take 'prophecy' seriously, as a creative and religious activity, while holding no definite views of it's 'kind' of truth. I am personally extremely interested in the field of the paranormal, though I have no direct gifts or experiences in this realm. Brian Inglis's *Natural And Supernatural: A History Of The Paranormal* (Hodder & Stoughton, 1977) is an interesting account of explorations from 'early times' to 1914. It is good to know, also, that serious scientific attention is at last being paid in the 1990s to 'near death' experiences, telepathy, numinous moments, and other possible inroads upon consciousness of supernormal truths.

God's consciousness is different in kind from ours, as I have already acknowledged. The lesser cannot contain the greater, and we are not God.

The consciousness of animals appears to lack language, with its consequent possibility of structuring and reasoning from concepts; and animals do not appear to produce art 'for its own sake'. But animals have their own instincts and intuitions; as well as a strong instinct for survival, which they share with us. Their data perceptibly goes beyond ours in some areas (how far, is a mystery). Their lack of 'reasoning' has saved them from many ghastly man-made messes, as well as separating them from our distinctive creative achievements.

There might also, of course, be angels, spirits, extra-terrestial creatures and other entities, with a consciousness of the universe pertaining to themselves. A lot will depend on God's use for this cosmos, apart from providing a fleeting home for human life on Earth. Our faculties do not run to knowing these, and it seems to be no part of God's plan to reveal them.

III

I return now to human consciousness, and its complex relationship with Time, the fourth dimension. The two are perfectly distinct, of course, with wholly different functions. Yet they are oddly alike, in the ambiguous role they share.

In the space/time world, 'consciousness' is the Fifth Dimension, moving with time in its forward movement, from beginning, through middle, to end. Here we are born, grow mature, suffer, grow old, die finally; moving to the tug of mortality from the first moment that our consciousness is aware of itself. 'Time', as the scene of our 'becoming', is the process where, dented and shaken as we are in this place of exile, our 'identity' forms and shapes to a unique, perceived 'self'.

But there is that other time also, explored by Augustine and Eliot (among others), which flows over us backwards, from the future, through the present, into the past. For Augustine, the future and past are non-existent, and the present is too fleeting to measure at all. No wonder, experiencing such precariousness, he turns to his Father, as the Lord of Time and Identity, Who alone makes sense of such a flux. For T.S. Eliot, this backward flow of time poses the threat of determinism. If the future moves towards us, like a film unwinding on its spool, what scope is there for human prayer, and free-will? What scope is there for changing God's Mind, if you like; for altering the 'plot'? *Four Quartets* confronts the dilemmas of determinism in explicit questions at the heart of its wrestling. The insight 'If all time is eternally present/All time is unredeemable' is seed, at the opening of 'Burnt Norton', of much still to come.

In this timescale, man is the 'still point' whom time washes over: the place where we say 'It is now' and it is 'now': the place where we are.

Whether 'Fifth Dimension' remains a correct description of 'consciousness' in the eternal realm also is, and must be, an open question. The dimensions – indeed, the nature – of Eternity cannot be plumbed. But 'Fifth Dimension' remains useful, since it describes consciousness accurately, in the space/time cosmos of mortal life, and retains the same function (as focal point of reality) in Eternity itself. Likewise, it is useful because on both sides of the equation, it relates consciousness to time, as central enigmas.

We function in both worlds – the mortal, and the eternal; and we turn the same Janus-faced gaze on both worlds, in our inner consciousness, as time itself appears to do. Likewise, as time flows forwards in one world (the mortal), backwards in the other (the eternal), so our consciousness assumes a differing role in each. In one, we are mortal – dwindling towards decay and death as time moves us forwards. In the other, we are spiritually tested and spiritually growing – 'from glory to glory', if we are in Christ's Kingdom, and trust Paul's splendid words.

We share the onward flow of time, and the unrelenting law of entropy with this cosmos. We share the 'still point' of a present that always goes on, and is always where we are, with Eternity.

This more mysterious backward flow of time (from future, through present, into past) we also experience, in day to day life. It is the 'now' which was explored in Chapter 2.

In our 'now' of consciousness, all we actually 'are' exists. Our 'now' is the place also where free-will, prayer, decisions exist, along with actions; since we are always at home 'here', making choices. It is also, therefore, the place where the dance takes place:

> Except for the point, the still point,
> There would be no dance, and there is only the dance.
> I can only say, *there* we have been; but I cannot say where.
> And I cannot say, how long, for that is to place it in time.
>
> (T.S. Eliot, 'Burnt Norton')

So we face a paradox. The 'still point' is the place of 'our' being, our link with the eternal. And it is here that decisions are made by us, which in large part condition what we become. But the other time, of mortality (clock-time), is the actual sphere of 'becoming'. It is on this scene that our physical and spiritual growth and decay are enacted like a drama – for the whole social world to see, and take part in, and affect.

A further paradox is that the eternal dimension unfolds and encompasses our 'becoming' to the degree that it is, and must be, part of the dance. The heaven or hell which tinges our consciousness, and grows or diminishes there, relates to eternity: as do the

Platonic verities, Goodness, Beauty and Truth; and the Pauline 'Theological Virtues', Faith, Hope and Charity.

For Plato, Goodness is ultimately the greatest of his three, though the three are, strictly, inseparable. For Paul, Charity is the greatest; though again, no absolute division exists between the three. For Plato then, 'Goodness' is the summit of our endeavour; for Paul, it is Love.

IV

On Earth, in our mortal life, we are tested; and it is here, as strangers and pilgrims, that we seek the city 'that is to come'.

But we know that the physical changes we undergo towards decay are part of clock-time, and belong to that side of the equation alone. They happen and, once taken place, there is no reversing them. Prayer may work 'forwards', to influence outcomes still in the future. But it cannot work backwards, to undo illness, accidents, actions, and in the end death.

And even 'forwards' prayer is not simple magic. Requests to God might be answered 'no' as well as 'yes'. I think this is why many people (not all of them consciously 'religious') make one special prayer, one special compact with God, born of love. No doubt, God takes such prayers of the heart very seriously, but they can neither force God's hand, nor alter human free-will. This is an area verging on superstition – sometimes verging on desperation – where no rules are possible; and such compacts have no real place in any rational doctrine of prayer. Our life on earth is a bumpy ride always, and is meant to be. Some, perhaps most of the bumps are ordained or permitted by God, past any appeal.

So what role can we find, for prayer? We must start from basics. First: to surround people with love and blessing cannot harm them; provided that our prayer is purged of possessiveness (a quality which negates any prayer). It may even protect them, in clock-time and beyond. Second: the prayer of blessing which comes from and increases love, without possessiveness, certainly cannot harm us, as we utter it. It may make us more effective instruments for God, in our immediate object. It will certainly build up our general spiritual health.

Here is firm ground, for prayers of petition; but the basic ground rule of life remains. *Prayer cannot break the laws of space/time, or their actual* raison d'être; *it cannot alter the ground plans for a life.*

The purpose of prayer is put, with total clarity, in phrases from the Lord's prayer: 'Thy Kingdom come; Thy will be done in earth, as it is in heaven'. We pray for the blessing of ourselves, and of those we love as eternal beings; we cannot be blind to immediate needs in this life on earth. Prayers for benefits (as we see them) in this earthly life may indeed cause God to alter the course of the future: perhaps, because the prayer can be accommodated; perhaps, because love *is* the ultimate purpose of life. The future is still fluid (one can suppose) as it flows towards us. We should see it not as a film unrolling in predestined order, but as God's creation still in process; still with the greatest of all Creative Minds in control.

But, since God's ultimate purpose is our testing, and our preparation for return to Himself at the end of it, His plans go far beyond ours. There must be times when God cannot be deflected; for reasons that we have to take on trust as good. No doubt, this is what Paul had in mind, when he linked our individual prayers with the whole of creation; a sublime passage, where we are implicitly co-workers with the divine Spirit Himself in the ultimate good:

> For we know that the whole creation groaneth and travaileth in pain together until now.
>
> And not only they, but ourselves also, which have the firstfruits of the Spirit, even we ourselves groan within ourselves, waiting for the adoption, to wit, the redemption of our body.
>
> For we are saved by hope: but hope that is seen is not hope: for what a man seeth, why does he yet hope for?
>
> But if we hope for that we see not, then do we with patience wait for it.
>
> Likewise, the Spirit also helpeth our infirmities: for we know not what we should pray for as we ought: but the Spirit itself maketh intercession for us with groanings which cannot be uttered.
>
> And he that searcheth the hearts knoweth what is the mind of the Sprit, because he maketh intercession for the saints according to the will of God.
>
> And we know that all things work together for good to them that love God . . . (*Romans* 8: 22–8)

The prayer 'Give us this day our daily bread' brings prayer to earth, and to pragmatic necessities; but the supreme prayer is for the spiritual healing of ourselves, and of all creation. Grace is certainly operative in this realm (though it, too, may take time far past our reckoning, in God's true plan). T.S. Eliot, after pursuing the possible *impasse* of determinism through his whole, great poem *Four Quartets*, comes to this marvellous *détente* in 'Little Gidding':

If you came this way,
Taking the route you would be likely to take,
From the place you would be likely to come from . . .
If you came this way by day, not knowing what you came for,
It would be the same, when you leave the rough road,
And turn behind the pig-sty to the dull façade
And the tombstone. And what you thought you came for
Is only a shell, a husk of meaning
From which the purpose breaks only when it is fulfilled
If at all. Either you had no purpose
Or the purpose is beyond the end you figured
And is altered in fulfilment. There are other places
Which also are the world's end, some at the sea-jaws,
Or over a dark lake, in a desert or a city –
But this is the nearest, in place and time,
Now and in England.

If you came this way,
Taking any route, starting from anywhere,
At any time or at any season,
It would always be the same: you would have to put off
Sense and notion. You are not here to verify,
Instruct yourself, or inform curiosity,
Or carry report. You are here to kneel
Where prayer has been valid. And prayer is more
Than an order of words, the conscious occupation
Of the praying mind, or the sound of the voice praying.
And what the dead had no speech for, when living,
They can tell you, being dead: the communication
Of the dead is tongued with fire beyond the language of the living,
Here, the intersection of the timeless moment
Is England and nowhere. Never and always.

(T.S. Eliot, 'Little Gidding')

In the last resort, wills are free, and no power can annul them. God Himself does not override the freedom of will which defines us, as both eternal, and 'His'. None the less, there is a movement Paul speak of, 'from glory to glory'; and this is spiritual growth taking place – through all the 'becoming' of clock-time – as 'eternal life'.

Eternal life grows in, and may (exceptionally) transfigure, men and women who are still growing older, and still perhaps decaying in their body, here on earth. And equally, there is the reverse change, towards anger, cynicism, bitterness, perhaps destruction and evil, which also takes place in clock-time – relating just as surely to the eternal reality that in our actual choices, we become, and so, actually, are.

We have to accept that for some fellow humans in time, negative emotions grow from a very hard destiny, which 'explains' how they form in the first place, and why very heroic efforts indeed may be needed to overcome them ('Deliver us from evil'). What is one to say, to those born to genetic or environmental horrors of the very worst kind? Severely crippled bodies or minds; total poverty or slavery; lack of all aptitude; a home or family that rejects them; a society that hates them; an historical moment where they are hounded for the colour of their skin, their deviation from unyielding dogmas, the colour of their hair, the shape of their nose?

Such savage impediments in life (and many more) 'explain' negative emotions; they define the cards dealt by life which are the stuff of our challenge – the basic rules of the battles to be fought.

In many, they are challenges gloriously overcome, and turned to blessing – which overflows, by its nature, to all who are privileged to see. ('Wherefore seeing we also are compassed about with so great a cloud of witnesses, let us lay aside every weight, and the sin which does so easily beset us, and let us run with patience the race that is set before us'.) In others, they lead to lives hopelessly warped and stunted; where all we can do, looking on, is to pray for grace to be granted; the fruit of which may not be ours to see.

There are some who say they are 'put off' the Christian religion by the Cross (I shall return to this, later); yet in sober truth, could a religion, without the Cross, ring remotely true? The Cross is central: not as a supposed occasion for 'blood-sacrifice' or 'vicarious atonement'; but as evidence that the man who incarnated God most perfectly on Earth could indeed be scorned, and rejected, and tortured to death.

This world is harsh, and the harshness defies understanding. It is more purgatory than paradise in our usual experience of life. At times, it can seem like hell. Yet the 'feel' of our consciousness – the tinge of heaven or hell apparent there – is an index that we dare not ignore. If we feel 'hellish', then we are on a dreadfully wrong path, however we came there; however inexplicable our sufferings, and unjust the fate that seems to be ours. If we sense a growing presence of God, we are far more likely to be on the right path; though we must check, by the effect we have on others, how true this is. It is all too easy to delude ourselves in times of respite, that mere good fortune, or easy good nature, confirm the favour of God.

We must recall also that even the radiance of transfiguration is precarious, in clock-time. It can seemingly fall prey to senility, before life is extinct. Likewise, we must remember that though some types of physical beauty linger into old age, these are not evidence of spiritual fruit in themselves.

Such matters are so highly personal and mysterious, that they are fraught with danger if we apply them beyond themselves. 'Judge not that ye be not judged' is Christ's definitive word. In the social world, criminal actions need to be defined and, when proved, punished; but spiritual judgements are reserved for God alone. For ourselves – and for others, whatever their background – prayer, worship, such healing as is possible, remain our sole hope, in quest of grace.

It is always possible that the highest standards will seem to 'the world' disreputable and even blasphemous – as they did in Jesus, in his time among men. It is possible that the central battle prescribed for our own life will bring scorn, not honour; everything turns on the prevailing *mores* of the time. Yet a bad social reputation is no evidence of virtue. Paul's 'discernment of Spirits' remains the grace we all need.

No wonder Paul urged 'discernment' so often: warning that the devil in person may appear as an angel of light. No wonder, 'Lead us not into temptation; but deliver us from evil' is the culmination of the Lord's prayer, in this arena on Earth where our souls are to be tested, and renewed.

'A vale of misery' was Shelley's reflection on life, from a sombre mood. 'A vale of soul-making' was the truer, romantic resonance sensed by Keats. Keats worshipped Beauty, and mourned its certain passing. He writes in his Odes of clock-time, and plumbs its anguish; but transience could not circumscribe his vision of Truth. 'Beauty is truth, truth beauty' must be enough, as testament from a man who suffered so greatly, and died so young. On his tomb, he had inscribed the melancholy words, 'Here lies one whose name was writ in water'. Like many artists, many saints, like Christ even, he appeared to die very near to despair. Yet his forebodings proved wrong, as they do for some (not all) of us. The Beauty he served was not a lost cause. It was Keats who said, among his axioms for poetry, that great poetry 'should strike the reader as a wording of his own highest thoughts, and appear almost as a remembrance'. The voice of Platonism has seldom sounded in English more powerfully: and Platonism, in the form in which Plotinus finally perfected it, is the philosphy rightly thought most congenial to creative art. Keats had the further grace (like Mozart, a little before him), of a bawdy humour – finding sex funny and sacred in turns, as those near to God most usually do.

There is a temptation, at this point, to explore looming complexitites; but these are, in moderation, for the rest of the book. It is important to keep this chapter clear, and brief.

If consciousness, the Fifth Dimension, is 'in and out of time', it shares its complex nature with time itself. We cannot forget that though our real being is in 'the still point', along with our eternity, we are seriously constrained by clock-time at the heart of this scheme.

I refer to the innumerable data of our birth, genetic and social. Our body, brain, colour, nationhood, gender, social class, sex-orientation, status, temperament, moment in history – these and many more particulars are 'given'; as are our health, powers, aptitudes, in their general scope. Today, the mention of DNA and genetic engineering puts some of this 'simply'. Yet in such notions, lurk problems, and horrors, coming nearer to our social agenda by the day. They can too readily turn into a modern doctrine of determinism; overriding the freewill and choice that is the essence of life. They can threaten to become a base for genetic 'blueprints', allowing human preferences (for a master race?) to take over from the conditions prescribed by our birth, and ordained by God.

I am far from suggesting (the reverse, rather) that we 'accept' social evils; or regard them as anything less than our challenge to find, and serve, God. We have to oppose poverty and prejudice, two giant causes of man-made evil. We have to learn to love, not hate, diversity and individual uniqueness. These are God's special seal, on each man and woman; His particular gift to them. They are also the field where every kind of dogmatist rampages, proposing to impose his or her preferences, wherever possible, on the handwork of God.

The life and example of Jesus might be guidance enough, on these issues; but where in sober fact do we *find* Jesus? Unfortunately, most branches of the post-Constantine church are not the best place. Far better go to a well in Samaria, where a woman is working; and find Jesus engaging in discourse with an alien (and a sinner), to whom he offers eternal life, springing up like a well inside her, as free gift for the asking (*John* 4: 1–39). Or we can turn and return to *Matthew* (25: 31–46) where Jesus offers the clearest guidance, to Jew and gentile equally, of his normal mode of presence, here on Earth.

Social diversity is God's plan; God's creative instinct. Our earthly exile relates to it, not always easily; but we can be sure we shall be more, not less, distinctive when we arrive back home. Diversity is the place for accepting God's will, and acting as Christ did: just as human need is the incentive to let God's Spirit act through us. With this twin perspective, our fifth dimension has its map, for prayer and action.

The questions 'Where Am I?', and their answers, may seem perplexing; but as Eliot's *Four Quartets* shows, the complex and the simple are two sides of the same coin. Eliot's great work concludes with an image of 'fire' and 'rose' unified; and with these wonderful words taken from Lady Julian of Norwich: 'All shall be well and all manner of thing shall be well' (Julian of Norwich: *Revelations of Divine Love*).

For this particular life, this pilgrimage, we have our personal data; which must be accepted as our incarnate *raison d'être* on earth. Our 'becoming' in space/time has its crucial importance, but the decisions made in our 'now', where the dance is, hold the key.

I started this chapter with a quotation from Eliot: 'To be conscious is not to be in time'. If I follow him again, it is because his words cannot be bettered. 'Burnt Norton' is the *locus classicus* now, for all discourse of the kind engaging us. But the speculations had become central to my life many years before I encountered Eliot. 'My words echo/Thus, in your mind . . .' Eliot indeed writes; adding,

> But to what purpose
> Disturbing the dust on a bowl of rose-leaves
> I do not know.

This experience is shared, I believe, by a great many people. But most are deterred from discussing it, for reasons which Eliot also explores. Religious and numinous experience is profoundly important, but it strains language. The ideas are at once familiar, and extremely hard to express. They become too complex, wresting words to breaking point. They are hard to convey even to ourselves, if we want our images to be precise. And they are still harder to convey to others – even when, rarely, people are willing to open up. Ideas and experiences have to come together in partnership, since individual moments of great and radiant intensity, alone have power to flesh out the words.

This is why the famous mystics are often great poets and writers. They can offer images which, defying paraphrase, release profound inner echoes and resonances; relating our own private experiences to the poet's, through this rare gift for selecting and arranging words that reach immeasurably far beyond mere intellect's writ.

Eliot calls our life on Earth 'the dance' (an ancient image, used by Plato; loved by Yeats also). 'The dance' brings together in our minds many interchanging patterns and memories, played out against 'the dark backward and abysm of time'.

Eliot speaks of 'The still point of the turning world', and defines it in images chiefly negative; but the still point is indeed the 'now' of which I speak. Eliot sees it as both 'in and out of time': by which he might mean, as I do, that it has its 'becoming' in space/time, but its reality in eternal life.

Throughout *Four Quartets*, certain numinous moments are captured, and these are symbols and images reaching deep into personal memory – like our own struggles, battling onwards, through language, towards light. There is one passage where both perspectives converge, using Eliot's key images yoked together, and placed in relation to both kinds of the 'time' of which I speak here:

> Time past and time future
> Allow but a little consciousness.
> To be conscious is not to be in time.
> But only in time can the moment in the rose-garden,
> The moment in the arbour where the rain beat,
> The moment in the draughty church at smokefall
> Be remembered: involved with past and future.
> Only through time time is conquered.

I define consciousness as 'Fifth Dimension' for this reason precisely. Like time itself, it relates both to space/time, and to the more real, eternal world beyond.

The fifth dimension alone gives the other four dimensions existence; since it is the only place where they can be real. Yet the four dimensions of space/time provide immeasurable vistas, both for scientific minds like Newton's and Einstein's, and in the 'hints and guesses/Hints followed by guesses' which art, nature, moments of vision, intense perceptions of Beauty and Goodness, all give.

This, I believe, is why mystics have appeared in all races, times and nations; and why their essential insights converge, at Eliot's 'still point'. The notion of incarnation haunts our imaginations, since we ourselves are incarnate in a turning world where we are, and are not, at home. In Christ, Incarnation is a specially rich concept, both in his wisdom of 'The Kingdom' (to which I give absolute precedence), and in his proclamation of divinity coinciding with, and destined for, 'a world not this world'.

In the next three chapters, I shall touch on three obstacles to religious insight, as I see them. Then, I shall turn to three paths of Wisdom, that great men have often appeared to 'know' in their bones. But first, a penultimate section to this chapter on the most important of all errors blocking religion (in my view of it); and then a brief summing up of this key issue.

V

I was glad to recall, when writing the last few paragraphs, the quotation from the *Guardian* which appears as a note, in Chapter 1. The importance of consciousness as central to 'experience' – and also as a function of the immense complexity known to inhere in the human (physical) brain – is now accepted again by a number of modern, scientific minds.

I think that a lot of people are kept from religion by the assumption that space/time is the whole of 'reality'; and that God (if He exists) is either Himself a part of it, or at the least, that space/time reflects (or should reflect) God's own nature and laws. Paul Davis, in *The Cosmic Blueprint*, reminds us that 'the most fearsome result ever produced in the history of science was first announced by the German physicist Hermann von Helmholtz in 1854. The universe, claimed Helmholtz, is doomed'. He continues:

> This apocalyptic prediction is based on the Second Law of Thermodynamics. The remorseless rise in entropy that accompanies

> any natural process could only lead in the end, said Helmholtz, to the cessation of all interesting activity throughout the universe, as the entire cosmos slides irreversibly into a state of thermodynamic equilibrium. . . .
>
> No new process, no mechanism, however ingenious, can alter this fate, because every physical process is subject to the imperative of the second law. (Paul Davis, *The Cosmic Blueprint*, Heinnemann, 1987)

A.S. Eddington later made the same basic point, in a passage where the implication for religion is drawn out:

> The law that entropy always increases – the Second Law of Thermodynamics – holds, I think, the supreme position among the laws of Nature. If someone points out to you that your pet theory of the universe is in disagreement with Maxwell's equations – then so much the worse for Maxwell's equations. If it is found to be contradicted by observation – well, these experimentalists do sometimes bungle. But if your theory is found to be against the Second Law of Thermodynamics I can give you no hope; there is nothing for it but to collapse in deepest humiliation. (*The Nature of the Physical World*, Cambridge University Press, 1928)

Now, as a layman, I am not sure how far current scientific theories will hold water, or be modified, or fail, in years to come. But I can see that Eddington's magisterial edict rules still, and seems beyond challenge – so that those who envisage God as contained within space/time and its laws, rather than understanding Him as their Creator, must assume that God will share in the final giant eclipse, as Entropy wins.

For my present purpose, I am assuming that most of us know Entropy by the more familiar names of transience, or mortality; and I see no reason to doubt the truth of Watts' famous hymn, when we sing with him:

> Time, like an ever-rolling stream,
> Bears all its sons away.
> They fly forgotten, as a dream
> Dies at the opening day.

It seems vital, therefore, for religious people to make clear that they do not subscribe to the view of God underlying Eddington's edict; and that, with the exception of religions which have revolved around ultimately mortal gods, they all agree that the entire universe, marvellous though it is, and long though it still has to run, will eventually run down, go cold, and cease to be. This perception, far from being incompatible with religion, should be an inalienable part of it. Bertrand Russell is a famous example of a man who rejected Christianity for the sole reason that he could not, or would not, accept this crucial distinction:

> All the labours of the ages, all the devotion, all the inspiration, all the noonday brightness of human genius, are destined to extinction in the vast death of the solar system, and the whole temple of Man's achievements must inevitably be buried beneath the debris of a universe in ruins . . . Only within the scaffolding of these truths, only on the firm foundation of unyielding despair, can the soul's habitation henceforth be safely built. (*Why I Am Not A Christian*, Allen & Unwin, 1957)

Russell was a remarkable man, and a very high-ranking philosopher; but he had no concept of the basic nature of religion. And we should recognise that the Christian Church has not, in its various past cosmologies and battles with science, helped in this matter. Indeed, I shall explain (in Chapter 6) why I regard the doctrines of the Fall of Man, and the Atonement, as major errors – one of the several ways in which the historic Church of Christ helps block out the light of Christ. The 'fall of man' seems to assume that the failure of Earth to be perfect and immortal is due to some event in clock-time (whether this is interpreted literally from *Genesis*, or allegorically), and that, without the basic slip-up by the first man (or by angels who fell before him), we should actually be immortal, and in Paradise, here and now. My contention is that this is obviously incompatible with the entire cosmic theory which we live with but more, that it is incompatible with all true Wisdom, and most of all with Christ's doctrine of the Kingdom of God.

As will be seen, my own argument is that this entire, mortal complex in clock-time – Big Bang to Black Hole, or however future generations choose to describe it – is the place of our exile only, not the place where we *are*. The 'eternal now' which mystics, artists, and visionaries speak of, is the place we exist in, here and now (the 'still point') – and links directly with the Kingdom of God where, as R.S. Thomas puts it in a marvellous poem, 'There are quite different things going on'.[1] This 'still point' is the 'now' where we always live, as long as our home is Earth. It is the space which is our direct link with the eternal life we *have* now (though seen through a glass, darkly); and which we return to, fully, after death. We must hope of course, to return in triumph, as by grace we shall do; provided that our deeds and choices on Earth have not gone terribly wrong.

I take the view that intimations of immortality speak of a different, transcendent reality; and this is surely confirmed in Christ's proclamation of the Kingdom of God. The morality of The Kingdom does not belong to time, change and entropy, and has no natural home in it: it is a morality where the poor are blessed, enemies are forgiven, the broken are healed – a morality which in our deepest being we recognise, and greatly rejoice in; but which, in the mortal cosmos we know, flies in the face of all reason and sense.

Any divine progress we make, by God's grace, 'from glory to glory' is in total counterpoint with our mortal progress, through decrepitude to death. But, as R.S. Thomas's poem on 'The Kingdom' also says, 'It's a long way off . . .' – long indeed; not in space/time at all. Yet it is also *near*: right in our inner being; where the Spirit of God, and the Kingdom, also belong.

My belief is that the entire cosmos is a construct made by God, through which we (and God, by way of His immanence in our, and other, consciousnesses) experience mortality, for some necessary end. Call it punishment; call it education; call it refreshment for jaded immortals; call it whatever combination of purposes you think it most likely to be.

After death, we leave space/time and its laws behind us. God has created, but most certainly is not contained by, the Second Law of Thermodynamics, or by any other laws of this cosmos that have been, or are yet to be, named.

Why has God created this cosmos? We know we are here, on planet Earth, in a fleeting portion of clock-time. We know we are having an exciting, often an all-too exciting stay. No doubt, He has made this vast construct for other purposes, also: but whatever these are – whatever other creatures are incarnate within it, for whatever reasons – then the laws of entropy, mortality and death apply to them, too.

As Janus-faced creatures, our eternal self is known in the 'now' where we are anchored. It is known in the God we find here. It is known in the special quality of consciousness witnessed to and lived by Jesus Christ.

Our religion (and our existence) commit us to live, suffer, make or remake our souls here. Our deepest instinct tells us, *this is not our home*. Bertrand Russell was not a Christian, it seems, because he saw the universe to be mortal. He saw what any fool sees – yet how grandly he spoke of it; how powerfully he expressed the tragic potential which creative achievement, and the highest vision, inherit on Earth.

Religious truth is beyond mortality, beyond space/time. All of us, know it or not, are journeying; very near to – enormously far away from – home.

> Thou, Lord, in the beginning hast laid the foundation of the earth: and the heavens are the work of thy hands.
>
> They shall perish, but thou shalt endure: they all shall wax old as doth a garment;
>
> And as a vesture shalt thou change them, and they shall be changed: but thou art the same, and thy years shall not fail. (*Psalm* 102: 25–7)

VI

So: to sum up. Consciousness is not itself 'in time', or to be confused with it. But it does share, with the fourth dimension, a crucial paradox linking the two. The time of space/time runs forwards, and is the stage of our drama; the 'time' which runs backwards is a still point itself. It coincides with our consciousness, as the only place where consciousness is. It runs from a future which does not exist, to a past which does not exist (so thought Augustine): but fleetingly, through a present which is, also, our 'now'.

In my own view (which was also, I think, T.S. Eliot's), the 'future' of this time does in fact exist, in the consciousness of God. This is why I believe it is an active, not a preordained process; and why I think prayer might positively affect it, to the degree I have tried to define. I suspect that the past exists also, in God's consciousness, though judgement on the past exists, effectively, 'now'. Maybe, the past becomes a huge new country, visits to which will be a feature of the wider contours that eternity has.

It was with this in mind that I put, on the tombstones of my grandmother, and of my father and mother, another quotation from 'Burnt Norton' that acts like a mantra for me. Five short, simple words, set apart, as a sentence: echoing, in these great regions of hope, for they cannot be contained or confined:

AND ALL IS ALWAYS NOW

Part II
Three Roadblocks to Wisdom

4

The Linguistic Vandals

'Where Am I? is a question basic to humans, since the three dimensions of space and its problematic fourth dimension, clock-time, are all involved. Further, the Fifth Dimension, consciousness, comes into the equation. The Fifth Dimension shares with the fourth dimension a complex status, which the first part of this book has been concerned to explore.

'Where Am I?' links naturally with other cosmic riddles, 'Who Am I?', 'Why Am I?', 'How Am I', all familiar to those who remain curious about the meaning of life. These questions, which elude scientific answers, are not to be silenced, though there are linguistic vandals who attempt to do just this. They favour a form of psychic repression, based on fear of ridicule, akin to the sexual *tabus* which we have just about managed to shed during my adult lifetime.

Unfortunately, though linguistic *tabus* are less pressingly urgent than sexual ones, they still affect everyone. The damage to basic spiritual words like Beauty, Goodness and Truth, and above all, 'Wisdom', has spread from philosophers in the academy to society as a whole. Our popular culture is formed by the media; and the media are dominated by opinion formers whose language, and vision, reflect the prevailing trends. A further problem is that teachers and academics are affected by a cultural climate. As basic words become suspect and tinged with ridicule, the truths behind them become dark also; and lost to sight.

II

I propose to put the linguistic vandals in perspective. But a few insets on the approach adopted here and on some inherent difficulties, need to come first.

My own religion is independent of and inimical to dogmas, whatever shape and size they assume. Priests, politicians, philosophers, fanatics lay seige to us with their dogmas. Sometimes, these are sweetened with promises: come to 'Christ' (or Marx, or Freud, or whoever), and all your problems will be solved. Usually, behind the sweeteners and soon to move to the foreground, are various threats. These can range from social ridicule and ostracism (a pervasive, and very well tried deterrent), to an eternity of torture in Hell Fire for those who fall by the way.

'I must make my own system or be enslaved by another man's', Blake asserted, in reaction against offensive drivel from all shrunken, dogmatic minds. And again, turning to the particular dogmas most natural to religion:

> The ancient Poets animated all sensible objects with Gods and Geniuses, calling them by the names and adorning them with the properties of woods, rivers, mountains, lakes, cities, nations, and whatever their enlarged and numerous senses could perceive.
>
> And particularly they studied the Genius of each City and country, placing it under its mental Deity.
>
> Till a system was formed, which some took advantage of, and enslav'd the vulgar by attempting to realise or abstract the Mental Deities from their objects – thus began Priestcraft;
>
> Choosing forms of worship from poetic tales.
>
> And at length they pronounc'd that the Gods had order'd such things. Thus men forgot that All Deities reside in the Human breast. (Blake, *The Marriage of Heaven and Hell*)

I would not deny that some dogmatists attain spiritual gifts, and a measure of wisdom. But their dogmas wound them. Their humanity is stunted by false certainties. We do well to hear them with caution and mistrust.

In balance, I would not deny that major oracles and poets like Blake deal in riddles. The last line quoted above requires a powerful counter-truth to balance it; as Blake was the first to agree. But Blake speaks for most prophets and artists in the gist of his argument, which is that dogma flaws religion, and can make it wicked through power.

The greatest of all religious prophets, Jesus of Nazareth, was at serious odds with the political and religious dogmatists who eventually killed him. He is no less so, I shall argue, with the numerous later dogmatists who claim to 'be' his church. He proclaimed the Holy Spirit who would 'lead into all truth' those who accepted God's sonship, adding that such men and women would perform his kinds of works, 'and greater', when he was gone. The famous tests he gave, for true religion, extended to the Samaritans (the 'Good

Samaritan' of Luke's parable; the Samaritan woman at the well, in *John*), and to all who have befriended the poor, the imprisoned, the outcast, since history began. 'The Spirit blows where he will', he also said, on one occasion. He spoke of 'other sheep, not of this fold' when he was among his own, chosen disciples.

Had Christ been able to see 'his' church, after Constantine, what would he have made of it? Bishops, parading as princes, and lecturing the poor from palaces; popes, inventing absolute dogmas, and proclaiming them 'necessary to salvation'. Protestant sects by the hundred, each claiming a corner in salvation, and consigning to outer darkness all who refuse to swallow their brew. Did Christ ever foresee, or fear, such developments? We are told, that he 'knew men's hearts'.

No doubt, Christ would have admired the Salvation Army, for doing his works among the poor, and living simple lives. He would have been at home with the Society of Friends, and with all mystics seeking Truth through love, prayer and quietness. But he might have found quietist tendencies inappropriate, at times when bitter battles present themselves, and have to be fought.

He would have smiled wryly, no doubt, at Dostoievsky's famous 'Grand Inquisitor' parable, offered by Ivan in *The Brothers Karamazov*. Dostoievsky imagines Christ returning to earth to have a look at his church, many centuries later, and nearly being put to death again by the Inquisition. He is told that his 'terrible gifts' of love and freedom were never needed or welcomed by men, and lead only to unhappiness. The Church has returned its ethos to power, authority, dogmatic pragmatism, and has no intention of submitting to its Founder again.

III

At root, if I need my own label, I often choose 'Hellenist', though I like to think that 'Christian' is not out of the question (we'll see). The teachings of Plato and of Plotinus, when I first encountered them, seemed strangely familiar. They came, as Plato would have expected, like an unlocked memory – like a meeting with a very old friend whom one had known in some lost time and place. Somewhat later, when I first read the Greek Tragic Dramatists, Aeschylus, Sophocles and Euripides, I found that my own turmoils and inner contradictions were half-healed by their wisdom and strength.

For twenty-one years, I had struggled with nature, finding 'soul' and 'body' apparently doomed to be at odds. Like too many others, my problems had been exacerbated by misdirections offered as education. First, there had been the mish-mash of alleged 'Christian morality', offered in schooldays as supposed absolutes, and linked with a doctrine of the Trinity at total odds (in its presentation) with elementary maths. Then afterwards, in teenage years, there was the destructive irony of scepticism, encountered in writers like Aldous Huxley, Evelyn Waugh, Lytton Strachey, which seemed skilled in demolition, but devoid of any life of its own. During an entire 'education', the Greeks had been kept from me – this is the only way I can describe it – or presented, if at all, as a pagan tradition now long dead.

Even today, we hear much of 'Christian values', 'Christian ethics' from a British Government determined to restore life to blinkers, and from a popular press finding great mileage, in these concepts, for mockery and hate. No wonder, the youth culture of the 1960s, and the New Age religion that emerged in the late 1970s and 1980s, came as a welcome release from Mammon masquerading as Christ. Whatever their growing pains, such movements reopen the doors of perception. They take an overdue backward look to lost customs and *mores*, and discover possible help, in alliance with modern knowledge, for a new spiritual birth.

I encountered the mystical traditions first in English writers. It is Vaughan, Traherne, Blake, Wordsworth, T.S. Eliot who allowed me to affirm my deepest instincts as true, and gave to them words and images that grow in power with time. These poets will turn up again in what follows, but I am glad to name them here. If readers of this book turn to them (or, surely, turn back to them), my main purpose in writing this will be achieved.

Among oriental teachers, when I later encountered them, the Dalai Lama impressed me, with his evident holiness. Produced by a strange-seeming system, in a closed, once-alien country, he has been fated by history to belong to men and women throughout the world. His own religion, a variant of Buddhism, is often elusive; but his prayerful presence, and radiance, are a specially timely gift. What I know of Hinduism appears to reach farther back in history than other surviving religions, but I find it easier to admire Hinduism than to give it assent. The traditions sprawl, and are rich in legends; the abstract formulae leave me rather at sea. Both Hesse and Jung have been influenced by 'The East', absorbing Hindu writings. But

Jung was right to warn of a gulf, still unbridged and formidable, between East and West. This has to do with a cast of mind and a long tradition, not with basic humanity: yet 'the way' of detachment, and negation, has little to say to me.

The teachers I have learned most from, over a lifetime, are the New Testament Christians: Jesus supremely; then Paul, that amazingly subtle, loving, intuitive, irascible man, whom one must read (first, anyway) in the King James Authorized Version, if only because the prose, and poise, of the English metaphysicals were so close to him. John would come next: author of the Gospel and the Letters and in my view (I am glad to find some recent scriptural scholars, and Jung, agreeing), of *Apocalypse*. The unknown writer of *Hebrews*, from his Hebrew/Christian ethos, creates a strange beauty and throws up many glorious insights, even though they are entangled in arguments that I partly reject. A quotation I use more than once in this book haunts me like a mantra: 'for here we have no abiding city; but we seek one that is to come'. The *Hebrews* writer points to the 'saints' as 'a great cloud of witnesses', all more than half at home in God's Kingdom while still here on earth. Like Paul, this author used 'saints' to mean 'committed Christians'; and, if we include among them all men and women who reveal God's presence in their daily actions and compassion, then the witnesses surround us indeed: our full, best answer to whatever complexities threaten to engulf us, and extinguish our light.

The Greeks came to my rescue, from the ill-effect of the amazingly stupid 'Christian education' already touched upon. I have lasting reservations about the worth of Christ's alleged 'church' (catholic and protestant branches alike) which are at least as deep as the reservations these bodies clearly have about me. But I do not doubt that Christ is supreme among teachers and prophets; and that the doctrine of 'The Kingdom' is our major entrée to wisdom and truth. It is this doctrine which confronts the space/time *continuum* with a truly stunning paradox from which our touchstone for truth will most probably stem, whichever path we take, and however fast or slowly we move.

IV

Now to return to my questions, and their basic validity: 'Where Am I?', and the allied group.

These questions come naturally to children, with the sharp edge of beauty and wonder that novelty and curiosity bring, to a brave new world.

Later, we may abandon such questions as 'difficult'; more difficult than, at first asking, they surely seemed. The lack of clear-cut answers may lead to pessimism. It may point a false way to discouragement, boredom and despair. Yet with luck, we notice this or that signpost, at a major division of the ways – pointing a path stretching far beyond childhood, far beyond life itself. Even so, the mundane world gets its grip on us, as clock-time ticks us relentlessly onwards towards the full measure of common strife. It ticks us on to competition, and worldly engagement; to the basic effort required for survival, and for a niche in life. It ticks us on to the struggle for money, and employment; the struggle to match sex with love, and aggression with achievement; the struggle with 'the world'. It ticks us on to the intellectual struggle between many competing doctrines of 'truth'. Even Wordsworth, a natural mystic of a very high order, could express forebodings the very nature of which bring us up with a jolt:

> We poets in our youth begin in gladness;
> But thereof comes in the end despondency and madness . . .
>
> (Wordsworth, 'Resolution and Independence')

And Wordsworth's famous 'Immortality Ode', from which I quoted in my first chapter, includes elements that we ignore at our peril:

> Heaven lies about us in our infancy!
> Shades of the prison-house begin to close
>   Upon the growing boy,
> But he beholds the light and whence it flows,
>   He sees it in his joy:
> The youth, who daily farther from the East
>   Must travel, still is Nature's Priest,
>   And by the vision splendid
>   Is on his way attended;
> At length the Man perceives it die away,
> And fade into the light of common day.
>
> (Wordsworth, 'Immortality Ode')

Wordsworth was luckier than most of us, in childhood and youth; lucky in his lakes, his natural health, his godlike vision. Not many of us are rooted in such good genetic, and environmental, soil.

I shall argue that we all have our chances – some, perhaps more than they realise. But to be born poor, ill, enslaved, or otherwise handicapped, is no easy send-off. For some, it sufficiently 'explains' crime and violence (as, in part, it does). Yet no one is without the divine spark, the God within; great virtues come from the most heartbreaking lives. However fortunate or the reverse we are, on worldly assessment, what we 'see', or ignore, is a secret between God and ourselves. 'We had the experience but missed the meaning' (Eliot again) is too often the story of most of our lives. One way or another, the great questions become lost, in the mind's dusty corners; along with the great answers which hover around us, seemingly just out of reach when we need them most.

This whole area of life may be filed away under 'pending'. Or it may be prematurely discarded, as 'dead'. It may become subverted by Christian indoctrination into charming, incredible stories; which are then discarded along with clear vision, since the two become too entwined to escape one mire.

V

But also, there is a pressure on us to think of the very questions as 'childish'. Or worse, there is pressure to write them off as a linguistic mistake. These pressures are my concern, in this chapter; *which is intended for those who have been bullied out of religion by being deprived of its words.*

The accusation 'childish' works both ways, like a well-seasoned boomerang. Fortunately, most of us know this in our bones. There is 'childlike' as well as 'childish'; Christ himself made the distinction: 'except you become as little children, you cannot enter the kingdom of God'.

'Childlike' means open to wonder, to the joy of the 'first time'. It is a quality powerfully evoked by Dylan Thomas in many poems, not least, 'Fern Hill':

And then to awake, and the farm, like a wanderer white
With the dew, come back, the cock on his shoulder: it was all
Shining, it was Adam and maiden,
The sky gathered again
And the sun grew round that very day.
So it must have been after the birth of the simple light
In the first, spinning place, the spellbound horses walking warm
Out of the whinnying green stable
On to the fields of praise.

'That very day', 'simple light', 'spellbound horses walking warm' . . . In such phrases, and the poem's iridescent exuberance, we recover and more than half-experience early raptures: the paradise once real, now lost; still beckoning. The Catholic theologian, de Caussard, spoke of 'the sacrament of the present moment': a memorable definition of the 'now' where we really are, even when childhood's wonder has gone. Some very holy people retain their quality of the childlike, and it sustains them in much bleaker periods of their later life. When Pope John XXIII was dying, he was asked with typically modern tact by a journalist, 'how does it feel, to be a dying Pope?' John's answer sticks in my mind, healing and radiant: 'Any year is a good year to be born; any year is a good year to die'.

Great poets, artists, composers evoke the childlike; as did Pope John – not because he was Pope, but because he was a man immersed in God's glory, even as a specially painful cancer killed him.

We come then to 'Wisdom'. 'Wisdom' is the jewel in man's crown in all ages, and in all human conditions; the one sure signpost to 'The Kingdom'. Yet in our age, and for particular, wicked reasons, the very word has become almost *tabu*.

What other words go with 'Wisdom'? Beauty, Goodness and Truth: Plato's trinity; alive in people, nature and art: these qualities stir us to the deeps, to the human profound:

Footfalls echo in the memory
Down the passage which we did not take
Towards the door we never opened
Into the rose-garden. My words echo
Thus, in your mind.
But to what purpose,
Disturbing the dust on a bowl of rose-leaves,
I do not know.

(T.S. Eliot, 'Burnt Norton')

So why has 'Wisdom' been a *tabu* word during much of my lifetime? Why only now – in the wisdom of the young, and of a few older pioneers like Sir Alister Hardy, Kathleen Raine, Laurens van der Post, Carl Jung, the Dalai Lama, Martin Luther King – is the word 'Wisdom' sounding out again, with its promise of liberation into great human vistas that we had almost sealed off?

V

Conscious and serious enemies of Wisdom have been chiefly to blame. The enemies are not all linguists. Stalin, Hitler, determinists and political tyrants of all kinds have used the deterioration of language for their own, evil ends. But it is the Linguists who have given haters of Wisdom and wreckers of greatness a foothold, in the very fortress of 'Truth'. I speak of our actual acedemies: schools, universities and colleges; the trainers of teachers and clergy. These institutions, whose purpose is to pass on and add to human wisdom, have more recently been happy to deny, all too often, that Wisdom even exists.

Among the earliest linguistic vandals were the 'Logical Positivists', as they called themselves. These were followed by kindred academics, both among professional philosophers and spread throughout the humanities and the sciences – all continually refining their labels, to increase obsfucation, and to increase the deep unease they spread.

Is 'deep unease' too strong a description? I never 'believed' them, myself. But my early school years, through to university (late 1930s to early 1950s), were oppressed by the darkness they spread.

They had predecessors, of course. Hobbes's *Leviathan* is a notable seventeenth-century example. But, like most earlier onslaughts on the language of religion, *Leviathan* was in its own period eccentric, and had little impact on cultural life. Words like 'spirit' and 'God' were assumed by Hobbes to derive from metaphors mistaken for entities, and to relate simply to ideas in the history of thought, not to real, objective equivalents. The repeated attempts of humanity to express its greatest realities by extending and refining language were therefore delusions, resting (Hobbes felt) on a false theory of language itself.

Christianity, and paganism before it, has seen such attempts off in the past, without fuss. But the reappearance of linguistic reductionists in our own century is a more serious challenge. It was presented as 'Modern' (a serious misuse of a vital word), and it soon became first established, and then respectable, in the philosophers' own little world. The linguists were powerful at Oxford, and fairly powerful in Cambridge. They were a poison at work, soon, on the whole cultural scene. They came to rule the universities insidiously, since their dogmas were felt to chime in with the science of 'relativity' and with a new, cultural age.

Like other young people, I searched keenly for 'Wisdom', although this was no longer a current word, or a word that I used myself. I felt God's presence in certain religious sanctuaries; in the poetry of Wordsworth and Keats, and in the world of music; in heroic acts, which the war against Hitler highlighted; and in numinous moments, which were always unpredictable but from time to time happened, bringing overwhelming awareness of the presence of God. These numinous experiences were by far my most important initiation (they still are; at the very root of my life). They are marked by joy and intensity – one becomes what one sees, and is lifted with all creation into divinity – and on occasions, by strong, inner peace, that may survive the experience itself for anything up to an hour. I could not relate such things easily to academic language, hard though I tried. Luckily, I did find words, but they were in Shakespeare, Blake, Wordsworth, Keats, Eliot (not propositions, but creative events).

Even so: to speak of God was not easy. While routine worship was performed in school, with straight-faced lip-service, serious religious discourse was most certainly not. The weight of adult consensus against exploratory religion, backed as it was with irony and, worse, puzzlement, was far too pervasive to be ignored.

The real problem was not with the philistine and the indifferent, who are always with us. It was with rottenness in the guardians themselves, the self-styled servants of 'truth'. While it was always clear that dogmatic religious systems would swallow me up happily, if I let them, free religious exploration was far from easy to find. Academic disciplines had become enclosed, in their own assumptions. 'Detachment' and 'rigour' are fine ideals to speak of; but all talk of 'truth', objective and universal, was seemingly ruled out, in their name. The theory of evolution had spread from science to all other disciplines, so that the 'state of debate' was no longer learning's arena, but seemingly, its endgame and goal as well.

It became ever clearer that 'religious instruction' as I had known it had been a façade only, conducted by men whose own convictions were not engaged. The season of Christmas was dominated by angels and Magi and cribs and booze and presents; a 'family occasion', with optional worship thrown in. Easter was gloomier; with talk of God's death and resurrection in history; with empty tombs, angels again, an ascension into Heaven and the coming of the Holy Ghost at Whitsun – and for some, a Lenten fast first; though normal people left this bit out. Clearly, very few people 'believed' in the angels, the Magi's strange star, the post-resurrection meetings – but the pretence of these things, inside the churches, was a social barrier against any other religion that seemed to ring true. The saints in stained-glass windows suited bishops and priests, who hoped they resembled them; but their actual connection with a young man of the first century AD surrounded by fishermen, workmates, a few odd women, tax-gatherers, a hanger-on prostitute, was not a connection that anyone known to me was anxious to make.

The legends had swallowed Christianity, and swallowed religion – since any other religion was pagan, or superstitious, or cranky, by general consent. To call such Christianity a 'myth' gives the word 'myth' itself a bad name. There was no reality here; no pretence at reality of a halfway decent kind. Neither honest religion nor honest sexual teaching (which struck me as parallel) was on the agenda in my boyhood and early manhood (1930 to 1946, let us say).

The linguistic vandals came into prominence when important realities were already largely silenced. Perhaps their offer to rob the 'big' words of meaning was met with a certain relief. They infiltrated my own realm, English Literature, where they remain influential, though in effect more and more stranded, as their tide starts to ebb. 'Linguistics' hived off to a separate world (often described as a 'discipline'; and characteristically, changing its name, every few years). The real writers, like Thom Gunn, Ted Hughes, Sylvia Plath, Wallace Stevens and R.S. Thomas, continued to use words for exploring reality in all its aspects; and critics who followed them started to look for new paths. 'Cambridge criticism' tided literary studies over in the mid-century, and perhaps will retain its power, for another age. For this to happen, however, close reading of major literature will have to remain a central experience, in the humane syllabus of all universities and schools.

But the linguists helped to create an ill climate; a disfigured landscape, imposed on 'reality' itself. Maybe the lack of conviction in 'religious teaching' helped them; along with the phenomenon to which

T.S. Eliot gave a name and an image, 'The Waste Land'. In this book, I concentrate on Eliot's later, positive masterpiece *Four Quartets*; but in 1922, his powerful earlier poem analysed, without healing, a felt spiritual malaise. Yeats, whose own religion was occult, spiritualist, Eastern, pagan – virtually everything but Christian –also offered phrases that summed up the religious vacuum:

> The best lack all conviction, while the worst
> Are full of passionate intensity
>
> (W.B. Yeats, 'The Second Coming')

Reality had become warped, language impotent. Good men and women had not gone away, they were visibly with us, but they were marginalised, in a world where evil, and evil rulers, gained in power.

'Why so powerful, if wrong?' was the question that nagged me, as words like 'beauty' and 'goodness' fell from use. 'Why no positive guidance, from those committed to truth and wisdom as a career? Why their refusal to use the words that all human cultures in the past have been most proud of, and in many great and enduring ways have tried to make real?'

As I write this book (in the mid-1990s), the climate is fluid, and a battle is gathering again. Of this, more later; but whatever the truth of it, I sense that the young are open to religion with a new purpose and drive. The churches will not do; nor will Pope John Paul II's *Veritatis Splendor*: but Christ, and the 'great cloud of witnesses', are a different, more hopeful sign. Perhaps their time is coming again, serious prayer is returning; not for a stranded few, but for a society no longer 'post-modern' but *modern* – in the way that Eliot, Yeats, Kafka and most of our greatest artists have, increasingly, been.

In the linguists' view, all metaphysical questions are childish errors; mere failures to see the limits imposed, on truth, by language itself. Allied to this, and more subtly worrying, is the notion that such questions are unadapted to the human brain. In a sense, of course, this is true; and that is the sting of it. Yet it begs the question (the questions) in a specially stupid way. Why do the questions strike us from birth, and haunt us till death, if they mean nothing?

Is not the search for answers the reason why we are living at all?

It was John Stuart Mill, himself an early victim of his father's extreme rationalism, who pointed out that because a thing is beyond our understanding, we need not necessarily doubt that it exists.

The concept 'God' is so far beyond us by definition, that huge areas of reality must belong to God's consciousness which do not, and could not, impinge on ours. God created, but cannot be contained in, human minds. But what 'is' our human mind if it does not relate to the Beautiful, the Good, the True, which are nine-tenths of life? And what are these realities, if they are not sources of power and remembrance – summoned up by 'life' from deep hidden sources far beyond any writ that discursive language and logic can have? Our human mind cannot function alone, it is *part* of our wholeness. The whole man, and woman, finds God in the signs He offers; in ways attuned to our whole, conscious selves.

I give the Platonic words capitals, as a paid-up Hellenist; or maybe, as a literary critic who is serious about his craft. Is it not strange that, while numerous great artists in this century have been and still are profoundly religious, most academic critics, weighed down by linguistic reductiveness, are not? Is it not remarkable, in fact, that so many of our major composers, poets, novelists, painters have been and are spiritual explorers, while the literary journals and university English schools have been chiefly agnostic and atheist (almost, though not entirely, to an equal degree?).

Well. No doubt, men and women who create beauty, and perceive goodness from their inner ferment of opposites, are less prone to deny words and meanings as the stuff of combat than are armchair philosophers, cosily playing at god from a long way off. 'Without Contraries is no progression. Attraction and Repulsion, Reason and Energy, Love and Hate, are necessary to Human Existence' (Blake, *The Marriage of Heaven and Hell*). R.S. Thomas, a major mystical poet from this half of our century, defines the struggle to reach God in an image that, using wrestling Jacob, relates language and its apparent failure to a mystifying Anti-Logos in God Himself, which may be the other side of the Word Made Flesh:

> You have no name.
> We have wrestled with you all
> day, and now night approaches,
> the darkness from which we emerged
> seeking; and anonymous
> you withdraw, leaving us nursing
> our bruises, our dislocations.

For the failure of language
there is no redress. The physicists
tell us your size, the chemists
the ingredients of your
thinking. But who you are
does not appear, nor why
on the innocent marches
of vocabulary you should choose
to engage us, belabouring us
with your silence. We die, we die
with the knowledge that your resistance
is endless at the frontier of the great poem.

(R.S. Thomas, 'The Combat')

T.S. Eliot also speaks of 'the intolerable wrestle/with words and meanings' as an experience linking creative artists and striving humanity in a common fate. And, towards the end of 'East Coker', Eliot both amplifies this, and puts it in a context of hope that is, in turn, its antithesis. All our lives, we wrestle with words, in often unbearable tension. At the highest level, we are conscious of failure, and this is temptation. The 'truth', as this part of *Four Quartets* offers it, is strenuous, for what truth could not be? Yet Eliot's poetic mastery transfigures the battle, in its very strain:

And what there is to conquer
By strength and submission, has already been discovered
Once or twice, or several times, by men whom one cannot hope
To emulate — but there is no competition —
There is only the fight to recover what has been lost
And found and lost again and again: and now, under conditions
That seem unpropitious. But perhaps neither gain nor loss.
For us, there is only the trying. The rest is not our business.

Home is where one starts from. As we grow older
The world becomes stranger, the pattern more complicated
Of dead and living. Not the intense moment
Isolated, with no before and after,
But a lifetime burning in every moment
And not the lifetime of one man only
But of old stones, that cannot be decyphered.

There is a time for evening under lamplight
(The evening with the photograph album).
Love is most nearly itself
When here and now cease to matter.
Old men ought to be explorers
Here and there does not matter
We must be still and still moving
Into another intensity
For a further union, a deeper communion
Through the dark cold and the empty desolation,
The wave cry, the wind cry, the vast waters
Of the petrel and the porpoise. In my end is my beginning.

(T.S. Eliot, 'East Coker')

VI

I used the word 'Evil' when describing the linguistic vandals. There are worse evils in our century – human violence and genocide; glib acceptance of poverty and prejudice; the growing onslaught on the integrity of our planet itself. But by its nature, evil needs the degradation of language, since wise, creative and beautiful language holds evil at bay.

I have spent my life as a literary critic, and my work has been to keep one high channel of grace open. The world's great writers are men and women who wrestle with complexity, in experience and language, and emerge with new icons for Life. As Professor Brian Cox put it once, speaking of his role as teacher, 'I come as a man bearing gifts'. Whatever our career, there is always God to be shown and celebrated, since God chooses to be known through our human works. But words and literature are specially important channels, to be given, and handed on therefore, as a sacred trust. Language cannot defeat evil unaided, for men and women have free-will, and can override language, as they can all other signs from God. But language at full stretch keeps the highest potential for man available. It keeps us keen in judgment, open to detect deception in depth.

Attacks on language have always proceeded side by side with tyranny. Milton's Satan, in *Paradise Lost* and *Paradise Regained,* is master of the art of confounding words and concepts, as a preparation for traducing and blackening God. Aldous Huxley hit on the manipulation of language as a major aspect in the creation of a seeming-paradise (*Brave New World*) that, in its essence, amounts to the unmaking of man. In *1984* George Orwell perceived that the reduction of language is fundamental to the enslavement of humanity, since great literature is a permanent threat to the totalitarian mind. Because creative art is our conscious struggle to explore and extend meaning, Orwell's Newspeak and Doublethink define themselves as the exact reverse. The aim of 'The Party' is to limit consciousness, until men are no more capable of real communication, and consequent change, than are the brutes. 'Newspeak' is a systematic method of diminishing words: in the first place by pushing them in the direction of orthodoxy; and in the second, by pushing them towards unconsciousness itself. The suggestion that orthodoxy is a halfway house to unconsciousness is developed in the description of Newspeak. Orwell associates Newspeak, through the sinister philosophy of Syme, who expounds it, with murder: and so, with the gloating annihilation of humanity planned by the party itself.

In *1984*, attacks on the past, and on language, are twin aspects of an ultimate onslaught upon *fact*. That two and two make five, if the Party says so, is a principle that O'Brien is determined shall prevail. If we can be made to doubt whether the past did or did not happen, we are already being moved far from sanity. If we can further be made to doubt whether the present is happening as we think it is, the abolition of man as *animal rationnel* is near to being complete.

Orwell, though not confronting the adademic vandals head-on in this terrible fable, demonstrates how necessary their work is to any political tyranny at its ultimate reach.

How much greater the evil, when art and religion are lopped off, in the process; when everything wise is derided: when our basic human questions are denied their actual right to be asked. The best one can call it is supreme academic folly; a Trojan Horse in the city of Athens (Priam's revenge?) and in the centre of all that *Athens still is*. Such vandalism is the apotheosis of minds blinkered to wisdom and blinded in arrogance. Yes, a department of evil; a gateway to evil; fruitfully exploited by many political reductionists in their turn – Marxists, Egalitarians, and Monetarists among them.

Orwell's 'Newspeak' is on the record, and a revisit to *1984* can do no harm. If you think that Newspeak has ceased, why not cast around for a few more modern examples? The 'Ministry of War' became 'The Ministry of Defence', in my lifetime. Try 'Care in the Community' (and half a dozen similar gems) for size.

The diminishing of language, along with onslaughts on its great words and on their most powerful users, is a prime threat to remember, when praying 'Deliver us from Evil'. Deliver us from those who say that those questions are not important, which haunts us from childhood. Deliver us from fools and wreckers who deny that asking, and asking . . . and seeking . . . is the meaning of life.

It is no coincidence that the denigrators of these primary questions, which attest our status, deny the Platonic trinity of values too. Everything that enhances our lives, or colours our happiness, may be written off as 'misuse of language'. I have in mind love, friendship, liking, bonding – everything good in relationships; likewise justice, judgement, compassion, which fall in varying degree victim to all systems that deny Beauty, Goodness and 'Truth'.

'Truth': is it here, that we reach the heart of the problem; the foot-in-the-door for those wreckers, who do so much harm. The quotation marks round 'Truth' suggest doubt; or should we say rather, complexity? Should such quotation marks extend to 'Beauty', and to 'Goodness', as well?

The philosophic route can lead to quicksands, if epistemology is given its head; and later chapters will deal with some practical dangers that then arise. I have written elsewhere on 'art' as revelation, and discussed certain complexities in this arena with specific reference to six chosen texts.[1] Here, I am content with an appeal to common experience and commonsense.

I recall a broadcast discussion, many years ago now, when I was rebuked for using the word 'beauty' in a Third Programme literary free-for-all. The poem in question had a grim theme, I recall; but an undoubted beauty of form was its chief affect. My assailant, the denier of 'beauty', was himself (if I remember correctly) a poet, but he challenged the word as a legitimate critical term. It struck me then and still does, that we had reached an *impasse*. From this point, one can assert with vigour, but not logically prove.

The phrase, 'beauty is in the eye of the beholder', though an ultimate lie, has become familiar; and no one denies that diversity exists, both in perception and taste. Wordsworth, speaking of Nature, made a crucial distinction in this area of 'seeing':

> Therefore am I still
> A lover of the meadows and the woods,
> And mountains; and of all that we behold
> From this green earth; of all the mighty world

Of eye and ear, both what they half-create,
And what perceive.

(Wordsworth, *Tintern Abbey Lines*)

We depend upon sight and hearing for our basic perceptions. If our organs are impaired, we miss at least some of the data. If our senses are untrained, we miss most or all of the finer shades and the essential meaning. If our senses are absent we lack the actual impressions. In any event, we contribute to ('half-create') as well as receive preceptions, as Wordsworth records.

Within this framework, 'taste' differs widely. Ideals of beauty – in humans; in animals; in natural landscape; in the varieties of art – are in flux always, and in a manner not simply 'personal' in scope. We trace major changes of fashion and background assumptions from age to age, along with all matters of judgement that bring about, or result from, such change. Perhaps necessarily, we all have a tendency (one that is very strong, in creative people) to prefer those types of beauty, and experience, that most nourish us. In addition, some are tone-deaf, and respond very little to music. Others vary widely, even when responding to the arts, and to aspects of life itself, that in fact touch them most.

When this is said – and much more, that inevitably follows from it – there is little that is 'relative' in beauty itself. We know that piles of rubbish, passed off as art, is a con-trick. We know that self-styled 'brutalist architects' offer a kick in the teeth to beauty, in the very name they adopt to describe themselves.

All criticism presupposes *close attention*: which, however surrounded with labels or adorned with the technical, is the basic discipline of the critic's art. The canon in literature, as also in music and the other arts, has been built up over a long period: 'classics' from Greece, Rome and the 'ancient world' generally; the Jewish/Christian scriptures, and holy texts from other religions; then, from Britain, a list of truly major poems, dramas, and more recently novels, that offer riches and truths enough to be foundation and touchstones for our cultural health.

Naturally in a multi-cultural world, we enlarge our horizons. Modern travel and media have helped create a 'global village', as those misled by a little learning often call this. We have become aware of the culture, *mores*, nature of far more communities, and earthly environments, than we knew of before 'the media' brought them into our homes. But we are terribly misled if we think that we penetrate their heart, and riches, from mere hearing and sight. 'The global village' is equated with the entire world, its entire cultures, its manifold historical evolutions and powerful achievements: yet too often, we know of it only as TV and other media present such aspects as can be crammed into a half-hour 'slot'. Yet 'the village' still *is* our own native heath for each one of us – if 'village' means the kind of truth that is bred in our bones.

We are now familiar with remarkable writers and artists from most of the world's countries. We enjoy the talents of gifted conductors, violinists, pianists from the Far East and South America and Africa and indeed most countries, who interpret our own European culture with power, as well as introducing us to their own. What this amounts to is no diminution, but addition, to the resources of beauty: a gift enhanced by the many good and heroic people who make news on the world stage in the causes they fight for; or who suffer with dignity when caught in conflicts and wars. Jimmy Porter, in John Osborne's *Look Back in Anger* (1956), ranted that there were no great heroic causes left. This was in the decade after the Second World War, the death-camps, the huge battle against Hiter's evil; it was in the decade marked by McCarthyism in the USA, the Korean War, the Cold War with its philosophy of Mutually Assured Destruction (MAD), escalating racial prejudice in South Africa and parts of the Southern USA States, the adoption of farming techniques based on widespread poisoning of the land and factory-farming; much, much more . . . Jimmy Porter's speech was craven and spineless and despicable (as I hope Osborne meant it to be). His play's huge impact was due not to agreement with its hero, but to Osborne's vibrant challenge to the actual apathy and quietism being encouraged, in our culture, at that time.

VII

To say that 'beauty is in the eye of the beholder' is philistine; and in nine cases out of ten, philistinism is a profound moral fault. At the least, it is laziness, inattention, a squandering of the mind and senses we were given. At the worst, it is a trampling on human greatness, with intent to destroy.

The 'beautiful' shades into the 'good', and both into 'truth': and the amalgam is Wisdom (or part of it): the jewel in man's crown.

Likewise, ugliness challenges us, if it slides towards evil. 'Why have men allowed this?' is our only proper response to tower blocks from the 1950s, 1960s and early 1970s that are hideous to look at, inhuman to live in; and already crumbling to ruin after a short, ignominious life. Some have collapsed; more are now doomed to destruction. The faults of structure were deliberate (a mix of penny-pinching, and alleged artistic sanctions from architectural 'brutalists'); and are of a kind hard to parallel in any other society, however far back into history we look.

Such ugliness is evil, and we should face this squarely. When ugliness is 'natural' (through genetic data or faults; through illness, accident and disfigurement), the proper response is compassion and healing, allied to an attempt to see beyond mere surfaces to the inner soul. The work of medical men, against illnesses, is a proper example of the healing of ugliness. So is the nurturing of all that is good and beautiful in everyday life.

When we turn to 'goodness', the matter is even simpler (and I say this, knowing that 'the discernment of spirits' is indeed a gift we all need). Good and evil mingle in all of us, and we learn to discriminate between them and to encourage the good.

In saying this, I touch on the deepest roots, and potenial, of our humanity. But I allow for multivalence as a good-in-itself, naturally. I allow, too, for the inevitable and painful and atrociously funny confusions caused by puberty and menopause; as well as by intervening episodes of shame that we bring on ourselves. I allow for widely differing social environments and genetic specifics; and for diverse moral attitudes on issues such as consenting adult sex. I take account (what literary critic could not?) of those deeper complexities, affecting us individually, which make works like *Anna Karenina*, *Middlemarch*, *Great Expectations*, *The Wings of the Dove* such stunning mirrors of life, in the medium of art.

As usual, I reject all dogmatists and mistrust all judgementalists. We need law in our society (as Greeks and Hebrews knew); but we need Christ's understanding and forgiveness in our human hearts.

Once more, however, the extremes shape a map for me. If the centre confuses, the outer features are clear. Hitler, Stalin, Myra Hindley and all other serial murderers were and are deeply wicked; who doubts it? The Dalai Lama, Martin Luther King, James Baldwin, Nelson Mandela are forces for good. The good are diverse, as any further extension of the list would further emphasise. The evil meet, in a terrible sameness; a fog or miasma of horror that can only be passed over, by human tribunals unable to face it, to the private dealings, and the judgement, of God.

Do we deny that certain moments of beauty catch up with us, and transport us? We can only be indulging in cant, if we do. Such beauty is not in our eyes, as beholders. It comes to us, as a gift. And now consider, 'goodness is in the eye of the beholder': a phrase less often used, but a natural twin to the foregoing lie. Can we assent to this, as a proposition; and leave things at that? Naturally, some of us find some people conditionally 'good', but are wary of them. (I am a great admirer of Richmal Crompton's William, but am glad to meet him safely at bay in his books.) But few of us would write of God's Kingdom as if it were merely 'our way of seeing'; or be prepared to discuss it as our (or even as Christ's) personal quirk.

The word 'True' is uniquely difficult, as I originally acknowledged by giving it quotation marks denied to Beauty and Good. Not only is 'True' multivalent; but it also has a great many different frames. In philosphy, in science, in mathematics, 'true' acquires special meanings: it may be described as correct observation, then as correct deduction, prescribed by known postulates or rules. Such 'truth' does have the nature of a game, a chess-type construct (though mathematics is thought by many to transcend human systems, and to reach towards things-in-themselves – much as music does). In ordinary human affairs, we distinguish truths from falsehoods; but again, this system works to chiefly pragmatic statements, and rules. In the Platonic Trinity, 'Truth' is always distinctive. Unlike Beauty and Goodness, it is not incarnate in people and things. It is not incarnate even in a system of philosophy or religion. Such systems aspire to 'Truth', but do so abstractly; in ways prescribed for themselves.

'Truth' is best thought of as an attribute of the Good and Beautiful; or as a witness that the Good and the Beautiful come from, and belong with, God. Truth is a quality we attest, therefore, wherever Goodness and Beauty are found. 'What the Imagination seizes as Beauty must be truth' (Keats). This insight accords with much that we find in Romanticism; and, extended to 'Goodness', we find it in the mystics as well. The *locus classicus* and full sufficient word, is the opening chapter of the Gospel written by John.

We apply 'tests of truth' to society, in specific contexts; but encounters with Beauty and Goodness are 'Truth' finding us. Platonic and neo-Platonic images are darkened reflections, in time, of the eternal; the Christian religion finds the eternal fully incarnate, in one,

God-filled man. 'I am the Truth', said Christ, on trial before Pilate. 'What is Truth?' pondered Pilate – surely more than half-responding to Christ, and more than half comprehending; even though, in his harsh role as judge, he could only harden his heart.

For Christians, Christ may be not only the fullest, but the only, 'incarnation'. If they go this far, they risk imprisoning a universal concept in their view of one man. Christ's qualities were indeed noble and manifold. But they are not exclusive; and this, indeed, is the whole point of them. We are all sons of God, as Jesus often attested. We are all eternal – but doomed to fight here, in mortal exile, against evil. Eternal life is the wine, the well of pure water, that Christ came to reveal.

Incarnation extends to all Goodness, all Beauty, that is christened and cherished as Truth.

> The hint half guessed, the gift half understood, is
> Incarnation.
> Here the impossible union
> Of spheres of existence is actual,
> Here the past and future
> Are conquered, and reconciled
> . . . .
> And right action is freedom
> From past and future also.
> For most of us, this is the aim
> Never here to be realised;
> We who are only undefeated
> Because we have gone on trying;
> We, content at the last
> If our temporal reversion nourish
> (Not far from the yew-tree)
> The life of significant soil.
>
> (T.S. Eliot, 'The Dry Salvages')

5

Insubstantial Pageant

The first objection to religion came from wreckers. This second strikes me as noble. For some, it may seem not so much an objection to religion, as its true summation; the answer to all our questions, pursued to the end.

I refer to Solipsism, in its several varieties; siren-like voices, to which many are drawn. I respond willingly to them myself in certain moods, more than half-hypnotised. The appeal of oblivion! A final return, to non-being; expressed often in Swinburne: nowhere more powerfully than in 'The Garden of Proserpine', with its tug towards cutting loose, and drifting to rest. I suspect that most readers of reflections like these will know the appeal of it, at times when their dearest wishes could ask no more.

In my view, solipsism has two main forms – the high, and the low, as I shall call them. The 'low' comes first: the view that we, ourselves, are dreaming the world. Then the second, the 'high': a deep suspicion that some slumbering deity is dreaming us.

II

In modern Western thought, most 'low' solipsism is an off-shoot of Locke's empiricism, and was arrived at, through Berkeley, by Hume, in a series of adjustments to Locke's severely rational plan.

Locke was a Christian, not a deist (or so he tells us), in the controversy that raged between these two as 'the Enlighenment' matured. But for later readers, it is hard to see that Locke differed greatly from the deists. His 'argument from design' puts a Great Intellect in place, as 'First Cause' of creation. Then, his offered proofs of human immortality and of rewards and punishments after death, ratify 'rational' human morality; adding up to a religion which explicitly excludes instincts and emotions, in favour of purely rational belief.

Locke's aim was to achieve an epistemology adequate to the science of Newton. And like Newton, who was also a Christian, he found in 'discursive reasoning' a conclusive and sufficient base for religious life. In *An Essay Concerning Human Understanding* (1690) he postulated that we receive our entire knowledge of the world through our five senses, and that our brain, assembling impressions, passively perceives things 'as they are'. The brain then makes deductions, using rational faculties, among which all necessary religious truths can safely be placed.

A little later, however, Bishop Berkeley stressed that our 'senses' are fallible. We have ideas and images in our minds, which the five senses bring us; but how are we to know that they correspond exactly to the world 'outside'? The nervous system, which transmits impressions to the brain, must also modify; besides, the taste of an orange may relate more to the mode of 'our' taste-organs than to the orange itself. It is apparent that Berkeley spoke of the human senses, and their perception, in the Locke tradition; and assumed that all five senses were functioning well, for his typical case.

Berkeley, considering such problems, found his own religious solution. The chief matter at issue, he came to consider, was how to 'prove' that external things continue to exist when no human senses receive them and when no human mind attends. God is called in: not merely, as in Locke, as a deduction made by correct human reasoning; but also, as the Creator whose unwavering attention keeps all Creation intact.

It was left to Hume, a little later again in the eighteenth century, to question the 'logic' of believing in an external world – and therefore, of God – at all. For Locke, the 'argument from design' had been fully sufficient. If we come across a watch in the desert (he thought), and have not seen one before, we shall observe a design in it, and correctly deduce a (human) creator with a purpose in view. In a similar way, observing the 'order' in the cosmos that Newton had discovered and codified, we deduce a Maker, as the First Cause that logic demands. Design does not happen by chance, in human artefacts. How much less can it have happened, unplanned, in Creation itself?

Hume, following the perception that we 'know' only our sense-impressions, could find no certain way of relating these to 'reality' at all. All we can say, is that a flux of impressions occurs; and we assume that there is also a 'self' inside us, observing them. But both the 'self', and therefore all deductions made by this 'self', are not subject to rigorous proof, in Hume's judgment. How can we know that a 'self' exists, in the flow of impressions? Or, that an ordered, created cosmos can be correctly deduced?

The odd result of Locke's quest for a 'God' rooted firmly and solely in 'reason' was, therefore, an unruly flux, as envisaged by Hume. This tradition – though extremely provincial, and related to the strictly Western scientific ascendancy (circa 1650–1950) – had a very high profile in my own, formative years.

It was as well for Hume, a man of charm and serenity, that he could regard his own solipsism as little more than a game for the mind. When out of his study, he resumed normal life as a cultivated landed gentleman, taking for granted that the world he moved in was actually there. His atheism was more than a game, however, since he held it deeply. He died serenely, surrendering himself back to non-being when his flux of sense-impressions had reached their end.

Hume was not himself unduly bothered by his thinking; but he had left a terrible stumbling-block for rationalists still to come. Most were clearly obliged to take Hume's reasonings on board, and try to refute them; but this has proved singularly difficult to do. Bertrand Russell himself admitted, in his *History of Western Philosphy*, that on his own premises, Hume cannot be disproved. So solipsism remains possible, even now, to a purely rational mind. Even worse, our normal belief in 'reason' rests, in the end, on an act of 'faith'.

I call this 'low solipsism' not in disrespect to Hume (one of our greatest and most distinguished thinkers), but purely because it makes 'us' the sole centre of life. This is equally true of Locke's starting point, from which Hume reached his own conclusion; but with Hume, we have not even 'us' in the centre; merely, a flux we call 'us'. The result of such excesses of reason is unreason, of a distinctively dizzying kind.

Famously, Dr Johnson 'disproved' Hume, from well outside. He kicked a stone which moved, as stones will when assaulted; so, stone, and Johnson, were both 'really there'. In this way, eighteenth-century 'commonsense' rode to the rescue of its own god of 'reason', when reason was carried, by its greatest exponent, so beyond the pale.[1] (Perhaps it is worth remarking that Johnson had an almost pathological fear of death, and especially, of oblivion; and that he could not forgive Hume's untroubled death as an atheist, at a moment when he should have been screaming repentance, Johnson thought, and shivering with fear.)

Johnson's gesture with the stone is amusing, but not specially convincing; though my own 'answer' is of a similarly instinctive kind. I call this 'low' solipsism because 'we' are its centre. The dream of life, if it is one, is 'ours', and comes from within.

My own objection is that the dreams we do in fact have are random; their substance, imaginary. They are the product of our subconscious mind, playing games of its own. Some dreams are so vivid that we do not 'know' we are dreaming when we are engulfed in them. But, when we wake, the 'feel' of waking is impossible to mistake. One twist in nightmare is that we can think we have wakened, when we have merely passed into another, perhaps worse, dreaming disorder. But the real 'waking' reveals this, too, for the illusion it is.

The people in our dreams, though sometimes founded on real people, have no existence; and our dreams affect no one in the 'real' world outside our minds. The events in dreams, though chaotic, soon fade on waking, returning to plague us only if we are traumatised, and in need of help. Their *raison d'être* is best left to prophets, oracles, psychiatrists, or to our own honest and searching reflections. My own guru, Jung, has much to say on dreams, and can be alarming. In this area, I reluctantly prefer that dogmatic old unbeliever Freud (*The Interpretation of Dreams*). He keeps dreams wholly as 'our own' in substance, allowing no prophetic intimations from the 'Collective Unconscious' to find a way in.

But to assume that waking life, too, is a dream, on a higher level, has an arrogance which I cannot, and will not, accept. Not only does it relegate all other people, all the rest of the cosmos, to my own 'invention'; it assumes that all music, all books, all nature are created by me. It assumes that 'I' am god, or the only god needed in my universe. It obliges me to have written Schubert's Piano Sonatas, Beethoven's Symphonies; to have made Heaven and Earth.

The simple fact is that if one trusts Beauty, Goodness and Truth as real revelation, one trusts them as greater, more real, more mysterious than 'oneself'. We assume that the world existed before we came into it, and will survive our departure. We recognise that Evil, too, is more real than our dreams; even the horrible ones. As solipsists, we should not merely have to imagine, but to consent to, the deeds of Nero, Hitler, Stalin and the rest.

My own rejection of 'low' solipsism is therefore an act of faith (should one call it so?). Certainly, it features among my strongest instincts, backed up by any hopes I have of being 'sane'. For, if I believed myself the author of the whole external world, I should not only be blasphemous; I should, without doubt, be raving mad. Certain delusional states are frightening for this very reason; they lock their victims in a stifling, fantasy world, with no apparent way out. As Chesterton once acutely remarked (perhaps taking anguish rather too lightly): 'The madman is not the man who has lost his reason; he is the man who has lost everything but his reason'.

For my part, I regard my cat as infinitely mysterious and almost supernaturally beautiful; if I believed I had 'dreamed' her, I should finally give up. The answer to 'low' solipsism is to be found precisely in the wisdom which Plato and his pagan school expounded, and which Christ defined as the Kingdom of God. We need, and we have, 'a great cloud of witnesses'; men and women so outstandingly good, whether they are personally known to us or recorded by history, that we should be lucky indeed to follow in their path and hope, one day, to join their ranks. We have not framed or created these in our imaginations, and for this, profound thanks to God. The lesser cannot contain the greater, in any circumstance. The lesser cannot contain the greater, even in dreams.

III

The 'high' form of solipsism may be less easy to answer; though once again, an act of faith can perhaps do the trick. This 'high solipsism' is the view that we are not the dreamers, but the dreamt; part of 'God's dream': or at the least, part of a dream of some being vastly greater than ourselves. In oriental mysticism, the idea is seldom far from the surface: or so it seems; but perhaps we easily get this wrong? For a Western mind, trying to engage with the orient is our chief problem: trying to assess, for example, precisely what degree of 'reality' the dream-idea has, when applied to our lives.

In the West, we find the dream-idea of high solipsism expressed less often, but when it is, it can shake us: for some, it is a continual sub-text in Shakespeare himself. The Duke's 'Be absolute for death' speech, in *Measure For Measure,* breaks through his Christian 'act' (as a friar), to thoughts of a strangely non-Christian kind:

> Thou art not thyself;
> For thou exist'st on many a thousand grains
> That issue out of dust. Happy thou art not:
> For what thou has not, still thou striv'st to get,

And what thou hast, forget'st. Thou art not certain;
For thy complexion shifts to strange effects,
After the moon . . .
. . . .
Thou hast nor youth, nor age,
But, as it were, an after-dinner's sleep,
Dreaming on both . . .

(Shakespeare, *Measure For Measure*, III. i. 19–25, 32–4)

Hamlet's approach to such thoughts in his most famous soliloquy (the 'To be or not to be . . .' speech) is now embedded in most of our minds. In *The Tempest*, Prospero uses words which, to many, sound like 'Shakespeare himself' speaking: a fact that tells us much about Shakespeare, whatever its 'truth' to the play:

You do look my son, in a mov'd sort,
As if you were dismay'd: be cheerful sir:
Our revels now are ended: these our actors,
As I foretold you, were all spirits and
Are melted into air, into thin air:
And, like the baseless fabric of this vision,
The cloud-capp'd towers, the gorgeous palaces,
The solemn temples, the great globe itself,
Yea, all which it inherit, shall dissolve;
And, like this insubstantial pageant faded,
Leave not a rack behind. We are such stuff
As dreams are made of, and our little life
Is rounded with a sleep . . .

(Shakespeare, *The Tempest*, IV. i. 146–58)

Prospero refers to acting (Shakespeare's art) and, beyond that, to magic. In my view, it is Theurgy (white magic) which he chiefly practises, though Peter Hall, making heavy weather of Prospero's one, shocked reference to 'raising the dead', suspects Goety (black magic), too. But beyond art, and magic, Prospero refers, it seems, to reality. The whole feel of the piece belongs with a mystical vision of life.

There are many Shakespeares; he is a man for all readers; yet a note, like Prospero's, can be heard, as an echo, in all his *genres* and works. It is not to be wondered at that he appealed greatly to Borges: the greatest solipsist of our age, whose short prose comment on Shakespeare, entitled 'Everything And Nothing' (*Labyrinths*) is a wonderfully sensitive and resonant salute.

The other piece I continually return to is in *Alice Through The Looking Glass* – where Lewis Carroll does not spare Alice a fine taste of solipsism, among the events in *her* dream. Alice has just been entertained with 'The Walrus And The Carpenter' when she and her hosts find the Red King snoring, and all gather round:

> 'He's dreaming now', said Tweedledee: 'and what do you think he's dreaming about?'
>
> Alice said 'Nobody can guess that'.
>
> 'Why, about *you*!' Tweedledee exclaimed, clapping his hands triumphantly.
>
> 'And if he left off dreaming about you, where do you suppose you'd be?'
>
> 'Where I am now, of course', said Alice.
>
> 'Not you!' Tweedledee retorted contemptuously. 'You'd be nowhere. Why, you're only a sort of thing in his dream!'
>
> 'If that there King was to wake', added Tweedledum, 'You'd go out – bang! Just like a candle'.
>
> 'I shouldn't!' Alice exclaimed indignantly. 'Besides, if *I'm* only a sort of thing in his dream, what are *you*, I should like to know?'
>
> 'Ditto', said Tweedledum.
>
> 'Ditto, ditto!' cried Tweedledee.
>
> He shouted this so loud that Alice couldn't help saying
>
> 'Hush! You'll be waking him, I'm afraid, if you make so much noise'.
>
> 'Well, it's no use *your* talking about waking him', said Tweedledum, 'you're only one of the things in his dream. You know very well you're not real'.
>
> 'I *am* real!' said Alice, and began to cry.
>
> 'You won't make yourself a bit realler by crying', Tweedledee remarked: 'there's nothing to cry about'.
>
> 'If I wasn't real', Alice said – half laughing through her tears, it all seemed so ridiculous – 'I shouldn't be able to cry'.
>
> 'I hope you don't suppose those are *real* tears?' Tweedledum interrupted in a tone of great contempt.

> 'I know they're talking nonsense', Alice thought to herself: 'and it's foolish to cry about it'. So she brushed away her tears, and went on, as cheerfully as she could, 'At any rate, I'd better be getting out of the wood'... (Lewis Carroll, *Alice Through The Looking Glass*)

In actual fact, the Red King, Tweedledum and Tweedledee are 'sorts of thing' in Alice's dream, and duly vanish, when she later wakes up. But the dream is very vivid and very logical; and its arguments are not really dispelled by tears.

In my view, the notion that we are dreamed by some God, or by some other great being, is as little subject to disproof as is Hume's rational thesis, in his elegant prose.

We have to grasp, I think, that waking consciousness is different in kind from sleeping consciousness, as Alice surely finds when she is awake.

In fact, our own consciousness persists, except in sleep or under drugs, and resumes with waking; and the people, things, scope of the entire world is not rooted in us. The very vertigo induced by my first two chapters – the scale and insecurity of the cosmos – is reassuring, if we think how very different it is, in the end, from a very long dream. So indeed are the questions we cannot answer, yet cannot stop asking; we know in our bones that they point in the direction of truth. So, most of all, is the basic ground of Greek, Christian and mystical wisdom (to which I shall soon turn, now). The pursuit of Wisdom lifts us up, to a greater intensity; it belongs to a greater, not a lesser truth, than waking life. I am prepared to believe (or want to believe in some moods?) that we may come from and return to oblivion; but not to conclude that we are part of some troubled, cosmic dream. Our encounter with reality is too sharp for this; so is our struggle. So are the demons we fight, and the goals to which we aspire.

If all these things are accidents, it is surely unfortunate, but crying would not help (fortunately, we have Borges, as well as Carroll, at hand to read). It seems far more likely that we *are* real, along with our struggles; and that Plato's Trinity, Christ's Kingdom, are realities surrounding our lives.

There is no way, in logic, to make such opposites balance; but an act of faith comes naturally, to humankind. The problems of solipsism need not detain us.

The possibility of oblivion remains, perhaps, a key part of our test.

The human mind has no experience of a Being who Is, and Who had no beginning; and Who creates beings like us, for a destiny far transcending 'this life'. But again, we have no experience of Everything coming out of Nothing. This second idea seems marginally the harder of the two to engage with – if we consider the Kingdom; if we listen to Schubert; if we take time off to commune with the cat.

Yet 'Everything coming out of Nothing' *is* the postulate of Hawking's cosmos; it is a dogma for scientists who say: 'Everything came from Big Bang'. ('What happened before Big Bang?' – 'Where did Big Bang Come from?' – 'meaningless question', say some scientists; 'meaningless use of words', say the linguists: 'don't even ask'.) But try to imagine Big Bang coming from nowhere; expanding in the ways science depicts for us; producing Milky Way, Sun, Earth, life on Earth; dinosaurs first; us. At the very least, it is harder to do, than some seem to think it? As a dogma – which it is – it is hard to take whole.

But if we turn instead to our 'Now', and its Fifth Dimension, we discover the territory where all great religion and art find their soil. We discover the territory where we all live, including the scientists. We can balance changing theories and fads, in man's brief, brief history, against the stupendous, irrefutable reality of Now.

> Make a joyful noise unto the Lord, all ye lands.
> Serve the Lord with gladness: come before his presence with singing.
> Know ye that the Lord he is God: it is he that hath made us, and not we ourselves; we are his people, and the sheep of his pasture.
> Enter into his gates with thanksgiving, and into his courts with praise: be thankful unto him, and bless his name.
> For the Lord is good; his mercy is everlasting: his truth endureth to all generations.
>
> (*Psalm* 100)

'It is he that hath made us, and not we ourselves'. Does the Psalmist not express, in these marvellous words, the quintessence of Hebrew Wisdom; and of all traditions of Wisdom, Eastern and Western alike, that are based in high Truth?

6

Original Fallacy

I come now to a main reason for the disrepute into which religion has fallen. For historial reasons which have ceased to be valid but which linger on in assumptions, we pretend that Man, and 'this' world, were created perfect. God intended it to be Paradise, and placed the new-minted race of humankind here, as a proper home. It is then assumed that subsequent ills were due to 'The Fall of Man' (the Eden myth, whether treated literally, or as allegory); or maybe, to a prior Fall of Lucifer/Satan, which led to Satan's successful tempting of the first woman Eve and, through her, of Adam.

This view of the Fall grew in importance in the early Christian centuries, and was specifically linked by Augustine with human sexuality. Augustine's view had its opponents both at the time and among some medieval theologians later. But today, especially by those who consider themselves 'post-Christian' but pick up their ideas of the church by hearsay, it is often mistaken for 'the' orthodox belief.

'The Fall' undeniably has many Pauline texts to support it, and it gained ground among austere ascetics, long before Augustine gave it his special weight. One way or another, it has come to dominate most 'Christian' views of man's place in Earth's history; and even, of the actual origin of Evil. Most of us will not fail to notice links with the accounts of Satan's memorable temptation of Job; and still later, of Satan's temptation of Christ in the Wilderness. On these great occasions, as also seemingly in Paradise, Satan carried out his temptations with God's overt, or tacit, consent.

The major crux must be that this prevalent view of Earth's creation, and 'purpose', squares neither with normal moral values, nor with our scientific understanding of the world. It seems clear that this Earth is part of the space/time continuum working to laws so far removed from 'Love' in the Christian sense, that no supposed slip-up by humans, or by any other cosmic beings, can account for their basic nature, from Big Bang onwards. Like many other moderns, I take the Earth to be either a prison (Plato's view for the most part); or to be a very severe education or re-education of immortal spirits in exile; or at the very least, to be a necessary if painful episode in the lives of immortals, carried out in a place with far more resemblance to the catholic doctrine of 'Purgatory' than it has to any simplistic portrayal of Paradise. We are at present exiled in a situation that is, and was meant to be, a place of suffering and mortality. Luckily, it is shot through with 'intimations of immortality' which many religious people have charted; and with that glorious seal of divinity which Jesus of Nazareth called 'The Kingdom of God'.

On the first view, that Earth was 'meant' to be Paradise but has been wilfully dislocated, we have somehow to account for 'the problem of pain'. But this 'problem of pain' (or 'problem of Evil' as it is sometimes called, surely misleadingly) is a Christian obsession, and very likely a Christian invention as well. Why should we see pain as a strange anomaly, in a system that Hawking describes as running from 'Big Bang' (its beginning) to 'Black Holes' (its putative end)? This 'world picture' is our current one, of recent origin; but from the earliest times, humans knew that their world was a mix of good and bad experiences, ending in death. Early gods were appealed to for blessings, and propitiated in times of outstanding disaster; but neither they, nor humanity *per se*, were naturally 'blamed'.

For many centuries now, the mental gymnastics of theologians who assumed that Earth was meant to be Paradise, but was wrecked by human, or Satanic sinfulness, have enjoyed an ascendancy. Dissenting voices were often deterred by stern measures, including persecution and death. It is hard to decide whether catholics or protestants worked harder in this fraught area. By and large, protestants were cruder in their analysis and more vociferous, perhaps because they so strongly attached the doctrine to texts from Paul. But anyone who knows Milton will be familiar with the labyrinthine ingenuity with which the doctrine can be defended against all the many problems that it is seen to entail. Milton did not link the Fall with sex, of course (far from it), but with 'Disobedience' – which is to say, with Pride, the deadliest of sins. And, though a fanatical Puritan himself, his arguments present the most sophisticated catholic, as well as protestant, insights on 'The Fall'. *Paradise Lost* is wonderful poetry – and wonderful rhetoric to try one's wits on – but it probably provides an inevitable *reductio ad absurdam* for the doctrine itself. It is doubly ironic therefore that our own century, which has very largely ditched the theology on which Original Sin was erected, continues to act as if God's very being, as Love, is cast in doubt by Evil; by War; by Suffering; even by Transience itself.

My thesis here is that if we return to the perspective I have so far been outlining, we shall see that 'the problem of pain' (or the problem of 'Evil', in this traditional setting) simply does not exist. The problem we face on Earth, rather, is the Problem of Goodness. Where does it come from? Why do we feel it so normative and somehow deeply familiar, despite its evidently alien quality, in the Big Bang 'world'? How did it get into the cosmos described by Hawking – the clock-time life of continual change, decay, violent upheavals, where entropy rules?

And why does the reality, and indeed the pre-eminence of Good, continue to convince us – both in the pagan version of Beauty, Goodness and Truth chiefly associated with Plato; and in Christ's amazing paradoxes of the Kingdom of God?

The true position is that we live in a world where God's love and care are not the ground rule, but continual intruders – though intruders marked with a total authority, rooted in our own human depths. They remind us of a 'city' we are exiled from, and are now seeking as the main purpose of our mysterious, open-ended sojourn here. Though we were born in this world, and undeniably belong with it, we are not 'of the world' in our truest selves.

The resonance of Paradise of course attests this, also; which is why the *Genesis* myth is so powerful, even if we leave aside 'Original Sin'. For me, the truth of Paradise is the truth of a lost world, infinitely present, yet not located in the space/time continuum at all. It belongs among the reminders of eternal life we bring with us, from some quite other home: the Kingdom of God, from which we came here; and to which we hope to return.

The misunderstanding of the Eden myth has had other disastrous consequences for religion, culminating in doctrines abhorrent to most men and women today. It assumes that God punished the whole human race, for the sin of the 'first' man and woman; and continues to do so, to the end of time. It further assumes that God was half-appeased, once, by the blood of slaughtered lambs and animals – and then, was 'fully' appeased by the blood-sacrifice on the cross of His son (or, if you think this, of Himself).

Beyond this, 'salvation' has been made impossible for humans to achieve by their own love, and sacrifice; and has been made to depend on blind belief in the 'one sacrifice' offered vicariously, in history once, by one man for all. Even worse, the fruit of this 'sacrifice' can be appropriated only by the kind of faith that swallows it whole, asking no questions: in lieu of which, our unpleasant experiences on Earth will be followed by an unending experience of torture, in the flames of Hell.

The 'problem of pain' is an error, in my view, by its actual nature, since Earth's basic 'laws' (or should one say, the basic laws of the cosmos to which Earth belongs) are not those of God's Love *per se*, but of God's testing: (God's Love manifested through testing, as we shall no doubt find). My belief is that most of us, with the church obsessively pushing us, are looking at the chief *data* of religion the wrong way up. We should not be seeing Earth's basic and natural laws as a 'special problem'. Rather, we should be pondering God's Kingdom of Love and Healing as an amazing mystery: 'not of this world', as Christ definitively told us, yet 'in' this world, becaused rooted in our own profound.

Our evidence points to a 'true home' where we really belong; where Beauty, Goodness and Truth flourish, and Love rules supreme. And accordingly, it suggests that the Earth, though a beautiful lodging, which we should cherish as stewards and by no means despoil as we are currently doing, belongs in essence to a different order of creation; designed by God for sterner ends.

I set out the contrast starkly in this manner, so that readers will be clear about the nature of what is to come. But I shall now 'start again', with the aim of amplifying; and with the risk of using material that properly belongs elsewhere. This sixth chapter is about the block to religion arising inside traditional Christianity, including the two major creeds, and many other dogmas, of the professing church. For some, these probably prove the biggest roadblock of all.

II

'Original Sin' is based on literal (or certainly allegorical) views of the opening of *Genesis*, and upon famous New Testament passages, in Paul especially, which may be taken altogether too literally. *Genesis* was written by the Jewish people, long before Christians came on the scene and chose to include it (after a stringent selection process) in their own scriptures. But the Jewish people never did camp out on the misfortunes of Adam and Eve, and on supposed long-term consequences, to anything like the degree that Christians do.

I believe that since 'Original Sin' is a notoriously untenable 'explanation' of the origin of human pain and waywardness, its total identification in Christian theology with a scheme of salvation by blood-sacrifice, and even with the basic fact of mortality, is a standing obstacle to serious religion, and to a proper understanding of the Kingdom of God.

The blood-sacrifice aspect ('Atonement') is the doctrine that God's supposed wrath against the whole human race was appeased, once and for all, by Christ's horrible death on the Cross. This links back to a recurring theme in the early Old Testament Books, of appeasement by blood-sacrifice: a practise not unique to the Jewish religion, but featuring largely in its earliest chronicles. For most races, God's wrath was deduced from the many natural disasters and other ills that afflicted them; and by the intuition that penitential worship, including differing kinds of sacrifice, is required by God or the gods, to quieten them down. But the Jewish system was attached to the Jews' altogether special consciousness, that they were a people chosen by God uniquely, and bound to Him by special contracts dating from Eden itself. Moreover, this consciousness of election was counterpointed by awareness that they continually sinned against their True God by the very worst fault in His Book. This was idolatry: the worship of 'false gods' in place of Jehovah (or 'Yahwey) – a sin against the very principle of their being, 'Thou shalt have none other God but Me'.

In somewhat later periods, the Ten Commandments which Moses brought down from Sinae were treated fairly selectively, as the records show. Great heroes and kings, like Solomon and David, were sexually promiscuous, and disregarded even the prohibition against adultery at times. Though displeased, God did not discard them from His favour. Solomon retained his reputation as the 'wisest of men', and David his place as the favoured King from whose line the Messiah would be born. Later still, other prophets began to stress, again, the need for sexual purity. Throughout Old Testament history, a string of prophets was sent to rebuke the Jews for their wanderings; and to recall them, to the One True God. It was the fate of the prophets to be scorned, ignored or martyred in their lifetimes, but to be revered (like the Christian saints later) when they were safely dead.

But in the early days, when idolatry loomed large, blood-sacrifice flourished as the prescribed path back to grace, by way of the Law. One major instance of this pattern was Abraham's proposed blood-sacrifice of his own, precious son Isaac – a deed demanded by God, against all Abraham's basic instincts (and in defiance of the scheme of salvation in which Isaac was supposed to have a key role). In the nick of time, God sent a ram to be sacrificed, instead of Isaac; and Abraham was let off the hook. But God still commended Abraham for his intention to proceed as commanded. In much later Christian theology, this came to be seen as a 'type' of the sacrifice of Christ on the Cross. God, who spared Isaac, did not spare Christ – whose whole purpose was thus seen to be to die, in this manner, in 'atonement' for human sin. This doctrine was embraced by catholics and protestants; it is found in the Creeds and has pride of place there; it features for 'fundamentalists' as the very heart of Christian religion to this day.

Let us turn to Abraham and Isaac: a vivid episode, by any reckoning: and bound up with much subsequent reflection on religion in the Jewish and Christian faiths. Whatever God's purpose, Isaac was spared; and Abraham was tested. The 'test' is of a kind to make any easy view of God, as Love, hard to sustain as a *simple* idea. Later in the Old Testament, blood-sacrifices were rejected, by several influential prophets. They announced that God had become sickened by the smell of burning lambs and other flesh rising from altars; and that pure hearts, and pure worship, were much more to His taste. The matter of Abraham and Isaac remained, of course, pending. It was indeed Christians who returned to it, and to the agenda of blood-sacrifice in its starkest form.

I think it safe to say that very many people have left the Christian church, or been deterred from joining it, by the doctrine of Christ's death as blood-sacrifice, and by the theology of 'Atonement' as a religious 'salvation' wholly related to this. In our own century, revulsion against bloodshed has increased, along with its practice. It is well worth remembering Wilfred Owen's savage mutation of the theme, in a powerful poem – which is now at the heart of Britten's *War Requiem*, written for the rededication of Coventry Cathedral after its rebuilding (1962), and one of the most haunting works in modern music:

> So Abram rose, and clave the wood, and went,
> And took the fire with him, and a knife.
> And as they sojourned both of them together,

Isaac the first-born spake and said, My Father,
Behold the preparations, fire and iron,
But where the lamb for this burnt-offering?
Then Abram bound the youth with belt and straps,
And builded parapets and trenches there,
And stretched forth the knife to kill his son.
When lo! an angel called him out of heaven,
Saying, Lay not thy hand upon the lad,
Neither do anything to him. Behold,
A ram caught in a thicket by its horns;
Offer the Ram of Pride instead of him.
But the old man would not so, but slew his son, —
And half the seed of Europe, one by one.

(Wilfred Owen, 'The Parable of the Old Man and the Young')

Britten's searing juxtaposition of this (and other) poems by Wilfred Owen in the context of the Christian Requiem came from a 'believer', but tested every resonance of the Abraham story to near destruction. Britten was not alone in singling it out, as a modern crux for religion. Bob Dylan's resonant 'Highway 61' made a great impression on me, and still does. The 1960s opened many radical new channels back towards recovered wisdom, which we must once again strive to return to, if the nightmare legacy of the Thatcher/ Reagan years is to be rolled back.

The life of Christ is known to us chiefly through his early Jewish disciples; and it is not surprising that they were influenced greatly by the Old Testament when attempting to make sense of the Cross. Jesus himself 'searched the scriptures' to discover his own destiny; but blood-sacrifice had no place in his parables and 'signs'. The emphasis was on works of forgiveness and healing; on respect for the poor and downcast; on denunciations of pride and corruption among contemporary religious leaders – all reaching summation in his vision of the Kingdom of God.

The references to his coming death and resurrection, towards the end of his short ministry, we have to interpret as we can. The resurrection imagery probably referred to great, general insights, which Paul finally offered in *I Corinthians*, 15, and elsewhere. The resurrection narratives in the four Gospels (Mark's added later, and all of them curiously at odds, in tone and detail) most likely reflect oral traditions, akin (in modern examples) to Fatima and Lourdes. The literal resurrection of Christ, as a sign from God, would not have been impossible, and might indeed have happened – given the demoralisation of the scattered apostles; and the unique closeness of Jesus to his Father, God. But the religious truth of Christ's victory is stronger, and surer in ground, if we understand it, chiefly, as a myth.

Christ taught that we are all sons of God in exile; put here on Earth, to refresh and build up the 'eternal life' which is in us, as it was in him. His teaching presupposes a general salvation, when we pass back, at our death, to the place where we truly belong.

The forebodings of Jesus's own death ring true enough, to an earlier framework. Jesus knew the risks he was running, given the path that he followed, and would not renounce. The prophets before him had gone to their death, for the truth's sake. How should he be exempt, coming from the same line, sent directly by God? The parable of the householder vainly demanding the fruit from his vineyard, bears directly on this. His servants were savaged; his son was killed. This parable occurs in *Matthew* (21: 33–9) and is in *Mark* and *Luke* also. This suggests that it made a deep impression; and was probably used by Jesus, in his teaching, more than once. We find in Jesus a growing foreboding of coming betrayal; a personal foreboding, touching the human heart. Though most of us recognise the truths of the Kingdom, and even rejoice in them, we may yet as humans turn savage – and how clearly Jesus understood this – if too many stern and pragmatic demands are made upon us in their name.

It is therefore especially unfortunate that the Cross came to be seen by the Church as blood-sacrifice and not as the triumph of duty, and life, that it actually was. The sacrament of the 'breaking of bread' speaks of shared suffering; and of God's identification with His creatures up to, and safely past, their moment of death. In place of this spiritual insight, several times offered to us, we find a reversion to the primitive Old Testament pattern; and at precisely the point where this most blocks out the light. It is as if the God who rescued Isaac (not, surely, on 'second thoughts', but for the testing of Abraham?), is now accepting blood-sacrifice from the most pure of all men (his special son or, in Trinitarian theology, Himself). He does this, in 'vicarious satisfaction' for a doom universally brought on mankind, by His own savage reaction to Adam and Eve's first fault.

The concept of 'justice', in this, has always been offputting. In the 1990s and in the century to follow, it is even less likely to attract civilised minds, loving hearts, to the church. If we are supposed to believe that 'the gospel' – the good news – brought by Christ actually *is* this scenario, then the entire thrust of the Kingdom is distorted, and lost.

Unfortunately, the pattern of 'Original Sin' and 'Atonement' matured, in the very early centuries; and was incorporated into the growing baggage of dogma that formed the post-Constantine years. It is centrally part of the Orthodox, Roman and Anglican creeds now – however mellowed towards mystery by good, holy disciples in pulpit and pew. For fundamentalist Christians, it is at centre stage always; eclipsing most that Christ is, and surely must be.

My own view is that the historical church's understanding of God was knocked off course by 'Original Sin'. The doctrine became a definitive 'explanation' of an unreal dilemma. It was compounded by 'Atonement' as a supposed 'solution', devised by a wrathful God. Yet we do indeed need forgiveness. We have grieved God's spirit, and cannot live without assurance that God still loves us. We need God's Spirit in our hearts, to sanctify us; in our souls, to bring assurance that, somehow, God will bring good, even out of past sins. The gospel of forgiveness, of healing, of slow but certain sanctification, precisely is that unique coming of God which the first disciples saw, and touched, in Jesus. It is the 'good news' exuberantly grasped, and explored, in the Epistles of Paul.

The most lasting casualty of a false scheme of 'vicarious atonement' has been *the coming of the Kingdom* – however happily a great many churchgoers redress this lost balance in their own lives and works. The 'truth' of Christ's death is surely that this Earth is not 'Paradise'; and that neither Earth, nor the giant cosmos containing it, was meant to be. A further truth of Christ's death, writ large now, at the dead centre of history, is that human goodness is most often scorned by worldly men and women and – when seen as threatening – driven to the margins of life; or put to death.

The most important truth, however, concerns 'eternal life' as our actual here-and-now possession, even though we are God's sons in exile, in an alien land. Eternal life is with and in us, hourly tested, by twin forces; by mortality (which belongs with clock-time, and is truly inexorable); and beyond that, by Evil – a real and terrible mystery, against which we can only pray, expecting God to hear our prayer. Eternity is experienced in the 'now' where we live, our

'Fifth Dimension'. Its quality (whether close to God; reasonably close; somewhat, or even terribly distanced), can be tested against the Holy Spirit, and against God's gifts of love, joy and peace, left by Jesus himself.

Jesus of Nazareth reassures us that our own suffering, however terrible, and our own alienation, are not outside the reach, and the healing, of God. He demonstrates that death is the common lot of humans, and that the Cross is always possible. It even seems (and here, we look back to Job also?), that great virtue makes the Cross more, not less likely, as a portent of death. We know that those who love most also suffer most, from bereavement. We observe that those who follow closest to Christ are those most likely to be scorned in life, and honoured (if remembered at all) only when dead.

My suggestion is that if we drop the notion of 'Original Sin' and face the cosmos without it, we shall bump into the far more hopeful, and promising, problem of 'Original Good'. We shall notice that, even in a universe weird and alien in its nature, ruled largely by selfishness, we encounter Beauty, Goodness and Healing at every turn of the way. The witness to these great realities is common to pagans and to Christians and to all religions, and to some of no religion. It is the presence of God, alive and radiant; even though it is seen 'as in a glass, darkly' – as wise men from all traditions know.

We find, in short, a Kingdom whose roots are not in this cosmos; yet whose gifts, fruits and imperatives are deeply at home in our hearts.

III

I shall take up this main thread again later; but need now to look more closely at two specific problems, to which the notion that Jesus's death was a blood-sacrifice give rise. The first concerns the nature of our life on Earth as we currently know it. The second returns us to the part played by the doctrines of Fall and Atonement in the subsequent theology of all parts of the church.

From the doctrine of 'Original Sin', the crux of Atonement follows – to the degree that all men without exception are deemed to be 'dead in sin'. Adam's fatal fault became a kind of HIV of the spirit, passed on at birth to all of our race. God doomed humankind to death, for the first human error; and had then to find a way round

His own wrathful decree. Here we have the basic *datum*, on which a vast theological edifice now rests.

All men are 'fallen'; all are doomed to Hell by God's Justice: no surviving virtues, in any particular men and women, can help their cause. So vicarious help must be given, to some (even to all?) human victims, if God's Justice is to be trumped by His Love.

St Paul was the first theologian to equate Jesus with a 'second Adam', come to refight the original battle, on behalf of all humanity, and to emerge this time victorious from the fray. One could say, that just as one man, Adam, brought death on the race universally, so another man, Jesus, reversed the curse, and all it entailed. In his dying agony, Jesus 'cured' inherited Evil, by 'satisfying' God's Justice; and returned humanity at large to its first, intended state. The logic is that of Paradise Restored by Jesus's sacrifice; and this, because he was not one exceptional man only; but also, uniquely, 'God'.

This, I take to be the basic formula, as we know it now in major creeds, and in the presentation of 'The Gospel' by the Church. Yet it seems that several riders must be added, to this simple scenario, if it is not at once to collapse. Death was not in fact abolished in clock-time by Christ's death; death happened to him, and it will certainly happen to us. Earth is still nothing like Paradise as depicted in *Genesis*, and no expectation that it ever will be again exists. The process of ageing and decaying has not stopped: indeed, Jesus spoke of these things as a basic aspect of life in 'the world'. So restoration of the status quo ante was not Christ's purpose, or his achievement. A role of 'second Adam' too literally interpreted, cannot have been what Paul had in mind.

The deeper problems arise with later theology, where most of the divisive complications set in. First, the second Adam was man, yes; but he was supposedly God also. He was God uniquely among men, in Trinitarian theory; 'at one' with the Father as no other man or woman can ever be.

Whether Jesus of Nazareth had any such notion of himself must be conjectural; though the force of his most usual teachings suggests the reverse. But, to bolster this later and now orthodox view held by most of the churches, mythic accretions to the Gospels have become central to Christian life. In effect, the birth narratives in two Synoptic Gospels have become central to theology, even though they play an introductory role only *in situ*, and have no counterparts in *Mark* or *John*. From *Matthew*, we have one half of the vital early narratives – Herod's savagery to the children; the adoration of the Magi; the symbolic gifts of gold, frankincense and myrrh; the angel's two visitations of Joseph and the flight to Egypt; Jesus's childhood in an alien land. From *Luke*, the other half of this picture comes to us – the angel's visit to Mary; the Annunciation; the link between John the Baptist and Jesus; the shepherds in the fields, visited by angels; above all, the conception of Jesus by the Holy Ghost, and Mary's virginity. Following Luke, the Roman Church has embellished Mary to just this side of divinity, with Mary's Perpetual Virginity, Immaculate Conception, and Assumption, the crowning touch. Christ's 'brothers and sisters', clearly so designated, have been explained away as 'cousins'; Joseph has been shunted away into the background, even in his role as a saint.

This is the dogma. How, then, does it compare with our actual records? Christ's 'reported' references to his family are few, and not especially flattering. They have been tacitly conjured away, in most sermons and doctrine, in favour of an idealised version of 'the Christian Family' as a middle-class ideal. I have heard very few attempts to preach sermons on Joseph; the material is meagre, but does exist. *Luke* 3: 23 must be one of the least quoted (and recollected?) verses in scripture: 'And Jesus himself began to be about thirty years of age, being (as was supposed) the son of Joseph, which was the son of Heli . . .'.

If the birth narratives have loomed too large in the church, in its usual thinking, the same could be said of all that follows Jesus's death. The accounts of Jesus's physical resurrection, of his ascension into Heaven, and his promised Second Coming in Judgment at the end of history, now form, along with the birth narratives, the main body of the historical creeds. Jesus's life, ministry and teaching is passed over, in favour of these two areas; around which the main events and drama of the church's year revolve.

A major problem lies in the nature of the narratives, in these crucial areas. Are they intended as literal truth, or are they essentially visionary? And, if they are supposedly historical, on what sources do they rest? The final chapter of *Mark*, from verse 9 onwards, seems oddly tacked on (as scholars tend to think it was). *Mark* is a superbly vivid gospel, factual and challenging; and amazingly powerful in its depiction of Christ's crucial years. Mark's Gospel surely concludes with the mystery surrounding Jesus's death, and the reported amazement of three women (Mary Magdalene, Mary, mother of Jesus, and Salome) at the sight of the empty tomb, and the words of a strange young man – or an angel in the form of a man.

The accounts in *Matthew, Luke* and *John* are suggestive of numerous oral sources, garnered in the years following the crucifixion, and with precisely the mix of piety and credulity, homeliness and oddity, that traditions of the kind usually have. In our own century, we have oral stories about the Angels of Mons and other First World War mysteries; we have appearances of the Virgin at Lourdes, at Fatima, in Ireland, in Yugoslavia (as it then was) – a whole crop of recent appearances, one of which, in Ireland, now has an International Airport marking the spot. Some of these were attested by saints (often children or young people); some by large crowds of ordinary and diverse people (Fatima has already come to stand out, in this aspect).

The resurrection of Jesus as a physical event may or may not have happened; if it did, it was clearly an exceptional event, to hearten the scattered apostles; and not a 'type' of the 'eternal life' we possess on earth, and hope to possess far more fully after death. In this context, I am considering the similarities and differences between Adam and Christ, as the church depicts them; and I shall concentrate on these.

The 'first Adam' doomed the whole race irreconcilably, and with no exceptions; this is the datum on which 'the Atonement' is built. The 'second Adam', if such Jesus was, 'died for all men': but here, we find more exceptions to prove the rule than rule itself?

Did Christ indeed die for all men and women who had lived before him, Jews, pagans, and all others who had walked the Earth alike? Not if the early church could help it: and to assert 'universal salvation' (*pace Romans* 11: 32) is still rejected as heresy by most visible churches, catholic and protestant, to this day.

Well: did 'the second Adam' die, then, for all men co-existing with him, and with all coming after, as long as the Earth endures? By no means as clearly as we could hope or expect. If you ask most Christians, they require baptism as the rite of entry: and preferably, baptism by the right not the wrong person, or sect.

Many churches practise 'conditional baptism' on adult converts, if there are any doubts about a previous baptism they may think they have had. The unbaptised are still often thought of as 'the ungodly' or 'the heathen'; and no non-Christian rite they have received can lift this reproach. The exclusiveness of baptism appears to restrict those who were 'saved' personally by Christ in his years of ministry, to those whom he baptised himself, or allowed his disciples to baptise, in his later years. Possibly the followers of

John the Baptist are also included, since John was specifically sent to 'make straight the path' for the Christ.

Later, you had to hear about Christ, and believe, and receive Baptism from his appointed apostles as these gradually spread their presence through the gentile world, if you were to be 'saved'.

We remember, however, that the early Church developed a growing habit of deferring baptism to the death-bed. This arose from its belief that sins committed after the rite had been accepted might undo the Atonement itself. A new, adverse record of sins might accumulate, of a kind which even the Cross could not reach. It seems that the early church had not yet discovered the 'sacrament of penance', whereby confession to a priest, followed by absolution, allows the Recording Angel to delete as you go along. This wheeze more than half 'solved' the problem of sins committed by the faithful after baptism; just as it comprehensively assisted the build-up of priestly power.

In the Orthodox and Roman churches, and much later in the Anglican, Baptism has remained ritual initiation to the religion (an age-old notion, shared with all mystery cults). Soon, the habit of baptising infants became customary: clearly, because the rite remained essential to salvation – even to a new-born child, in the event of death. It was the Baptist sect and its forerunners, and certain other dissenting bodies, who reverted to adult baptism, by 'total immersion' following upon 'conversion' – the model of John the Baptist, and of the baptisms performed by Jesus himself. In the catholic churches, the new rite of 'Confirmation' was devised, whereby at 'years of discretion' churchgoers could reaffirm the baptismal vows, taken for them as babies by others, by their own free-will. Confirmation includes an episcopal laying-on of hands, and a new infusion of the Holy Spirit (as at Whitsun?). Copious credal 'instruction' precedes Confirmation, attuned to the dogmas demanded by the sect which presides.

From very early days, 'No-Salvation-Outside-The-Visible-Church-As-Defined-By-Us' became a rule. The Roman sect makes this claim exclusive, at least as far as its own flock is concerned. It does 'recognise the Orders' of Orthodox Christians, albeit reluctantly (a concession less handsome than it sounds, in that the Orthodox descend in fact from the Apostles, while the Romans were the first true protestants to break away). The Romans do not, however, recognise Anglican orders as 'valid', defining Anglicanism as one of many late protestant sects outside the fold. Anglicans usually prefer to think that their Orders are 'valid' (under a 'Catholic but Reformed' label): but Anglican evangelicals reject the very notion of 'apostolic orders' as a popish deceit. Episcopally-minded Anglicans in Britain are encouraged by their uninterrupted possession of pre-Reformation cathedrals and churches: a marvellous heritage, with the 'feel' of holiness that buildings long prayed-in most often acquire.

Catholics (or priestly churches) throw their stress for 'salvation' on valid baptism, on regular 'confession', and on membership of the correct visible church. Protestants, in contrast, see adult 'acceptance' of Christ as the real turning point, with baptism following, as a social seal that a new human soul is safely home. The pattern of salvation starts with hearing a preacher; then follows 'accepting Christ' formally; then, repenting sins in one's heart (or sometimes openly in a congregation); and finally, being immersed in the water of baptism. The order of priorities throws 'salvation' back from objective priestcraft to subjective dogmas; imposed by whichever sect the new convert has had the fortune to join.

The huge stress put by protestants upon preaching ('evangelism') followed from this, in most churches that opted for non-catholic paths. Christ's own promise of a life inspired by God, and naturally flowing from the Holy Spirit as its true source and witness, has been displaced by the notion of hearing sermons, deciding for Christ, testifying to the whole congregation in baptism; with a huge public hubbub sometimes thrown in.

From this point, however, the protestants were divided. Some offered salvation to all who followed this process; others (the Calvinists chiefly) reserved it for those already 'predestined to salvation' by God. Either way, protestant churches have gravitated towards exclusiveness, in much the same way as did Orthodoxy, and the Roman sect. It became fashionable to refer to protestants as the 'invisible church', to distinguish them from priestly ritual; but chapels are visible enough to most eyes, along with their ways.

Most protestants exclude those not of their own denomination from salvation, finding that abounding heresies cancel the work of the Cross. From their viewpoint, other kinds of protestant are as badly off as catholics; and perhaps even worse off than beyond-the-pale pagans, to the degree that, as professing Christians, they appear to be taking Christ's name in vain.

In time, catholics of the Roman sect defined 'salvation' as a matter of valid baptism, followed by an ability to believe everything propagated as faith by a whole sequence of popes. In addition, there had to be an occasional Holy Communion, and regular penance and mass-going; with a 'good death' to round things off. For protestants, salvation was 'having Christ in your hearts' – being 'born again', after succumbing to some fiery ranter; and then, confessing sins in personal prayer to God as one went along. The essence, for some, was to proclaim oneself 'the greatest of sinners' on every possible occasion, while remaining impeccably respectable in social reputation (or undetected, in any actual sin). In these ways, believers could become assured of their own salvation, through Christ's 'one sacrifice'; with the caveat that for Calvinists, Jansenists, and others drawn to 'predestination', there were lingering fears lest God's lottery had gone against them before the start.

The damage inherent in such views is widely documented; especially, when vivid accounts of the eternal torments of Hell were thrown in. James Joyce's *Portrait of the Artist As A Young Man* includes a classic Hell-fire sermon – in this case catholic; though protestants can compete, in the hell-fire stakes, on very even terms. We have all come across biographies which record fear of Hell engendered in childhood; and then, a life permanently alienated, perhaps, from Jesus himself.

What, then, is a provisional verdict? Christ as 'second Adam' does, for Paul, have the power of striking metaphor, conveying the exhilarating sense of liberation into here-and-now eternal life on Earth, even in exile, which Jesus's good news of The Kingdom can bring. 'You must be born again' was Christ's own word for it: offered to a prominent Pharisee, Nicodemus, who 'came to Jesus by night' to affirm belief and to probe further these amazing new truths (*John* 3: 1–21). The life of Jesus was 'God-with-us', Emmanuel, the Word Incarnate; all those who knew him, and saw the light there, experienced The Eternal alive, and triumphant, in mortal flesh. It took his death, however, to seal the final glory; which is, that no power on Earth can quench Christ's light, or make him subject to death.

The entire gospel depends on Jesus's true manhood. His great prayer starts 'Our Father' not 'My Father', for we are asked to join him: accepting the Kingdom as he did, and bringing its values to Earth.

In our days, we have witnessed the power of evil testing human lives very terribly. Millions of Jews and other victims died in Hitler's concentration camps, and in the purges of Stalin, Mao Tse Tung (and of far too many more dictators since). We have likewise witnessed the lives of individuals following Jesus's pattern, from many traditions – Martin Luther King, Steve Biko, the Dalai Lama, Nelson Mandela, and a gathering throng. I would personally wish to include Laura Davies, the little girl from England, whose short life was a very special witness to the Kingdom, for modern times. By modern medical techniques, she suffered amazing transplants, in a vain attempt to prolong her earthly life. Through it all, her courage, tenacity, joy even, shone unquenchably; along with a positive, unique identity that no suffering, no surgical changes of bodily organs, could affect.

How could a child suffer so, and be allowed to? How could her parents have to endure it? 'And Simeon blessed them, and said unto Mary his mother, Behold this child is set for the fall and rising again of many in Israel; and for a sign that shall be spoken against; (Yes, a sword shall pierce through your own soul also), that the thoughts of many hearts might be revealed' (*Luke* 2: 34–5).

Many sensitive people shared this brief life and death of Laura Davies with helpless empathy, as a world audience watched, on TV, the agony and triumph of a child. This, for me, is Christ's last victory over death, in stark reality: God-with-us at the last extremity, for all humans born. If the resurrection of Jesus did happen, it did so once, for historical reasons; but that unique resurrection would be a wonder apart. Christ's death on the Cross, and its manner, was the real *truth* of The Kingdom: 'The light shineth in darkness; and the darkness cannot swallow it up' (*John* 1: 5).

To turn Christ's death into a once-for-all blood sacrifice, to calm God's wrath, is to diminish all that he taught, and *is*. By all means let us see him as 'second Adam' if, in doing this, we see that all men, from those first born on Earth until the last, belong with an eternal power that nothing worldly, nothing mortal, can quench. Let us by all means pray 'But deliver us from Evil', with all the power we can muster. Let us recognise that some exceptional people are chosen to proclaim God's kingdom at the extreme, in every age.

Blood-sacrifice is an early intuition, that had its purpose; in later times, a higher law has been found. 'But the hour cometh, and now is, when the true worshippers shall worship the Father in spirit and in truth: for the Father seeketh such to worship him. God is a Spirit: and they that worship him must worship him in spirit and in truth' (*John* 4: 23–4). Jesus did not come to put the Earth back to some imagined Paradise. How could he, when immortality is not on offer, in the cosmos we have? He came to proclaim the eternal life that is in us; a transfiguring glory that all who live, suffer, die as he did, also proclaim.

Original Sin; Blood-Sacrifice; literal 'second Adam': all these are distortions of great truths, which we have to understand in our hearts. In this section, I have looked at the consequences, affecting the church adversely, of too literal a reading. Considered as dogma, literalism is still, for many, a stumbling-block to faith.

IV

I turn now to the second of the two specific problems I spoke of, at the start of the last section. This is the part played by 'Original Sin' and 'Atonement' in the total theology of all parts of the church.

I have sufficiently indicated that the post-Constantine church departed widely from the New Testament. But the doctrine of Original Sin has permeated Christian history since the first Christians, with texts in Paul often cited (though Paul is far more subtle in his use of them, than most Christians realise to this day).

The Christian God, unlike pagan gods, is One, not many. 'The Trinity' obviously complicates the 'Oneness'; but in theory it does not cancel it out. In its credal form, the doctrine of The Trinity was influenced perhaps by the great, late pagan philosopher, Plotinus. Plotinus's tripartite god, in *The Enneads* (2nd century AD), is a final flowering from Greek thought; and remains far more resonant, I find, than the doctrine of 'The Trinity' now taught by the Christian church.

The New Testament provides all the texts used by Trinitarians; but they do not necessarily point to this, now orthodox, view. Jesus called God 'his' Father and 'our' Father, making little difference between the two. In many encounters, he offers the same sonship that he has, and the fruits growing with it, to any of us who accept the 'eternal life' that is, by right, ours. The 'Holy Spirit' most often signals God's immanence in creation; a force always waiting to be recognised, sole agent of 'sanctity'; yet elusive also; moving 'as He will' in the world.

> Return, O Holy Dove, return,
> Sweet messenger of rest.
> I hate the sins that made Thee mourn,
> And drove Thee from my breast . . .

In His full power, the Spirit 'Blows where He pleases', the scripture tell us. It is human experience that for long periods, He may be or seem to be absent, when we need Him most.

At Burrswood, the Anglican centre of healing near Tunbridge Wells, Kent, there is a 'Breakthrough Cross' crowning the Chapel. At first sight modest, it draws the eye to it – perhaps the shifting sky, and the exceptionally beautiful landscape, help to hold our gaze. The Breakthrough Cross is not specifically linked with the Holy Ghost's 'coming' at Whitsun; but it holds the Spirit, and Christ's last agony, in one, striking icon. Christ is crucified, but the space where his body should be, on the Cross, remains empty. The Spirit is free to pass, through this amazing absence. The sky – blue, or clouded, or at times red as blood – is what we *see*. Emptiness is the space offered by Christ, in death, for the Spirit's coming. We can gaze on it, through the absent body of love.

The Spirit is with us, we know, at times of suffering, of tempting; at such times, the emptiness of 'breakthrough' may be all that we feel. R.S. Thomas writes of the elusiveness, the caprice of the Spirit, in his lovely poem, 'Sea-watching'. Yet the Holy Spirit seals us, always, as sons and daughters of God.

God the Father is God the transcendent: the God Who made space/time, but is so far beyond it, that always and everywhere He eludes our minds. Clearly, in no crude sense is God 'up there' or 'in here' (to use terms much bandied about, in our own mid-century). God is beyond Creation – inaccessible; incomprehensible. But God's Spirit blows through Creation. God is incarnate in Christ, in Christ-like humans, in all goodness and beauty. God can be seen and touched and handled – to the degree that we catch His passing, each time that our spirit discerns. ('I greet Him the days I meet Him, and bless when I understand'.)

From these perceptions – all true; all of vital import – one can imagine how Trinitarian theology evolved. But God transcends the dogmas, and may be blocked out by them. We need the space of breakthrough, not the blockage of riddling; as the Cross at Burrswood very simply depicts.

We have One God, Whose nature is loving; but Who is known to men also in pain, grief, fear. We are indeed alienated. Jesus said that 'all sins can be forgiven, except the sin against the Holy Ghost' – and is this sin in fact ours; beyond redemption? 'Grieving the Spirit' is an open concept; but it surely includes all that is most foul, most loathsome, interposed by sin between ourselves and God.

For most of us, the problem is daily and personal; if we seek to woo the Spirit, He is not far off. Jesus also said, when asked by amazed disciples 'but who then can be saved?'; 'With men this is impossible; but with God all things are possible' (*Matthew* 19: 26; also, *Mark* 10: 27).

In what sense do such doctrines relate, then, to Jesus himself? Jesus gladly proclaimed himself Son of God, and Son of Man, the alternative title. But he proclaimed 'Son of God' as a discovery that all humans could discover also, and make real for themselves. He did say, in some versions, that he came 'first for the Jews', but that was natural, since he was a Jew himself. This did not stop him meeting and talking with a sinful Samaritan women, to whom Eternal Life was promised, with no strings attached. There are few signs that he thought of salvation as a personal gift, except in the sense that he could offer his own complete assurance, and awareness of, God. He did not associate salvation with preaching, especially; and he did not exclude anyone close to God, whether they lived alongside, before, or after, himself.

The reverse is true, rather. He chose to accept John the Baptist's baptism, despite John's doubts about whether Jesus should receive gifts from himself. It was at this baptism that Jesus received further assurance directly from God of his personal mission. His own baptisms, performed later, no doubt continued the tradition of John the Baptist that he now belonged with himself.

Again: when Jesus was asked about The Kingdom, he said little about preaching, or about verbal profession. He asked for complete commitment – or, sometimes, he spoke in parables, or offered 'signs'. Those whom he defined as 'his' in the famous *Matthew* passage (25: 31–46) were not people who have heard a rant from preachers and yelled 'Amens' in return, but those who at any time or place in history have done God's works.

In this aspect, it is the key to all Jesus's teaching of The Kingdom – where a recurring symbol is of valued things lost, and then found. These varied from a poor person's coin, and a farmer's sheep, to a straying son. 'Eternal Life' is being part of the True Vine, as Jesus is; it is drinking of God's cup, if grace is given; it is being in the same boat with Jesus, when the going is rough. It is living as a hidden but precious ingredient of the world around us; it is helping the poor, wretched and imprisoned, when they come our way. It is being a 'witness', in ourselves and in our normal daily actions; and then by word of mouth, if the occasion calls. Paul was right to say, that we need preachers, to spread Jesus's gospel; but the work of bringing the 'good news' home is chiefly achieved in actions, not words. Following Jesus is like becoming a city set on a hill that cannot be hid. Personally, it is following the light one has, sure that more light will come.

I do not for a moment believe that Jesus wanted to start a specific sect around him; though his chosen twelve, and his other close friends and associates, were a nucleus of faith. When asked about discipleship, the terms he set for it were high (almost impossible?). The 'rich young man' went sorrowing away, since he was unable to meet them; yet Jesus saw good in his heart – indeed, loved him; and we cannot suppose that the rich young man was lost to the Kingdom of God. When Jesus picked on Peter's sudden insight 'Thou art the Christ, the Son of the living God' as the 'rock' to build his church on, he was identifying the right track to take, in our time on Earth.

This precept again stretched backwards and forwards; it concerned all recognition of and delight in the holy, the good, when these are encountered, and not surely, some quality peculiar to Jesus himself. It seems especially strange that 'the rock' should have been associated with the man, Peter, rather than with the insight which called out this change of name. And it is even stranger that a whole sect should have risen on it, claiming absolute power over Heaven and Hell for one, chosen man. Peter the man wobbled, especially at the crucifixion; but he turned up trumps when the disciples reconvened, after Jesus's death. In no sense whatever, though, does he foreshadow the line of 'popes', proclaimed by the Roman sect as his 'successors' to this day.

On the afternoon of the crucifixion, three people are picked out, as somehow making Peter's great discovery for themselves, and being 'unlocked' by it: a centurion in the crowd; a crucified thief (if Luke is right); and Pontius Pilate, in that he put the famous written sign on the Cross, at some personal risk to himself (if John is right). In essence, the church was given one strong and enduring symbol, by Jesus himself, for its 'worldly' presence; the simple, solemn ritual of the bread and the wine.

From here, I return to the major stumbling-block of 'exclusive salvation'; and to 'The Atonement' (Christ's supposed blood-sacrifice) as the supposed entry to this. Among other things, this doctrine obscures the truth that Jesus's life, not his death, was the heart of his mission. It obscures the fact that his doctrine of 'eternal life' was a truth he revealed, and lived out to the end, as a truth for us all.

The doctrine of 'The Atonement' also assumes that blood-sacrifice, far from being superceded as it had been in the later parts of the Old Testament, was a mere forerunner to Human Sacrifice, planned for the centre of time. Abraham's proposed sacrifice of Isaac, as a test of blind obedience, had been aborted by God. But in a deeper sense, if we follow the story, God *had* to abort it, since Isaac was the child conceived in deviousness, and destined to be Abraham's true heir in God's long-term plans for 'His People'. Even so: we cannot be sure in what manner God actually 'spoke' to Abraham; and how far the sacrifice was a sick fancy aborted, when God's truer inner voice came through.

The human sacrifice of Jesus is a different circumstance; since, if the doctrine of 'The Atonement' holds, Jesus's agonising death by torture is the actual purpose of 'The Incarnation', and God's ultimate plan, in fulfilment, for the whole human race.

I suspect that more people wrestle with these notions than one normally imagines; perhaps finding in them some mystical sense of God's presence in all pain, including their own. If truly religious people can remain inside dogmatic systems without harming themselves, or others, by doing so, it is little to my purpose to attempt to unsettle their faith. Yet I suspect, too, that very many people wrestle with these enigmas, and cannot cope with them. The complex twists and turns of doctrine tend to obscure Truth itself. People who feel that Trinitarian theology defeats them, and that blood-sacrifice sickens, should be free to follow their own path to the light, without feeling blocked out of Christ's Kingdom by the edicts surrounding 'atoning sacrifice' inside the church.

The further notion that Jesus's physical resurrection confirms God's acceptance of sacrifice, merely compounds the distancing effect that all dogmas have upon Jesus's vivid parables, and his rich, vibrant life. What we can hold to, for certain, is that Christ proclaimed a Kingdom 'not of this world'; a Kingdom with its upside down laws of healing, forgiveness, and unconditional love. We can also be certain that he reaches a depth of reality in ourselves that responds to this teaching, despite all 'reason', and because *it is touched with remembrance of a truer, fuller life than we currently have.* We see, too, that Christ lived out his values on Earth, in a way *fully* human – so human indeed, that man's divinity transfigured him, and could not be quenched, even by betrayal and death.

Jesus taught 'eternal life' first as a here-and-now reality; and then, as a final fulfilment after death, to which this world is at best only partially attuned. But he also taught the value and integrity of each man, woman and creature. Even a fallen sparrow, worth half a farthing is noted by, and important to, God (*Matthew* 10: 29; and also *Luke* 12: 6 – where 'five sparrows worth two farthings' is the market price). The doctrine is specifically linked with the assurance that *every hair of our head is numbered*: a phrase I italicise, since its implications are stunning, especially in the context which Jesus provides. We are in territory of the utmost delicacy, and also immensity.

The beauty of this passage is that it moves backwards and forwards, and ignores all churches equally. It does not link salvation with having seen, or heard of, or accepted, Jesus himself.

The lost son, the lost sinner, the lost (or confused) Samaritan women – all these mattered to Christ. He did not promise them 'survival' nor (as some religions do) reabsorption in 'The One' after death. He offered them 'life more abundant' for the asking, for the *realizing*: 'life eternal'.

I am suggesting, then, that it is time to recover the Cross from notions of blood-sacrifice, and restore it to the central mystery which it truly is, in religious lives. Perhaps it is no accident that the most striking of all poets of the Cross has come in our own lifetime (R.S. Thomas); and that the sheer physicality of the nails, the dereliction, is his sombre theme. Blood-sacrifice can repel, and drive away converts; but a religion without the Cross would also repel, by not ringing true. Let us recall Christ's vibrant life as our most usual memory of him – as we seek to recall the life of our own loved ones now passed over, and not the final time of dying, vivid though it was. The dedicatee of this book died, while I was writing it; his last words to me, as it happens, were 'Fear not'.

We should also recall Christ's promised gifts – peace, love, joy. These are 'not as the world gives'; they are 'beyond understanding': they are not the simple delight a hedonist might crave. They are a divine resource, for good times and for ill times also. They are 'in' but not 'of' this world, in the strict sense. They belong with the reality from which we – like Christ when he spoke them – are exiled 'now'.

Christ must be Lord of the Dance, Conqueror of Death, Prophet of Wisdom: Supreme exemplar, for all creatures born; Supreme for ourselves.

V

'Original Sin' can bog us down in the problem of suffering; and the further problem, that all events supposedly part of the space/time continuum have the Second Law of Thermodynamics to account for, in a rational way.

But if we allow that suffering is normal on Earth, and mortality certain; can we not let Christ amaze, and exalt us, with Original Good? All human Wisdom converges, on Divine Incarnation: the God felt in the world, in all things holy, in all our love, in 'every common sight' that we truly 'see'. Wordsworth found in small, unnoticed acts, a summit of goodness. He celebrated grandeur, in mountains, lakes, and 'spots of time' shot through with the numinous. His *Immortality Ode* culminates in Incarnation, as the summit of all:

> And oh ye Fountains, Meadows, Hills and Groves,
> Think not of any severing of our loves!
> Yet in my heart of hearts I feel your might;
> I only have relinquished one delight
> To live beneath your more habitual sway.
> I love the Brooks which down their channels fret,
> Even more than when I tripped lightly as they;
> The innocent brightness of a new-born Day
> Is lovely yet.
> The clouds that gather round the setting sun
> Do take a sober colouring from an eye
> That hath kept watch o'er man's mortality;
> Another race hath been, and other palms are won.
> Thanks to the human heart by which we live,
> Thanks to its tenderness, its joys, and fears,
> To me the meanest flower that blows can give
> Thoughts that do often lie too deep for tears.

(Wordsworth, *Immortality Ode*, conclusion)

One thing remains to address. If I regard 'Original Sin' as a wrong-headed doctrine, misdirecting our attention, what do I make of the great myth of *Genesis* myself? How do I respond to the fall; and to the expulsion of Adam and Eve?

I hope it is not cheating to say that my response is expressed, to perfection, in the first section of 'Burnt Norton'. This poem which, with Eliot's other *Quartets*, I regard as my fifth Gospel, captures the essence of the lost garden as nothing else known to me – not even *Paradise Lost* – quite does.

The *Genesis* account is itself poetry, of a very high order. The story is amazingly compressed, yet its echoes are endless. The whole action is vivid, and dreamlike: pared down in detail, with no word or image redundant; yet elusive as an oasis or mirage, one can hardly tell which.

The one 'explanation' offered, for the fatal prohibition, is God's naked authority; along with whatever the name of the Forbidden Tree might evoke. As to the Fall – we hear or overhear the exchanges; but there are no explanations: or none that makes sense. The Serpent calls God a liar ('Ye shall not surely die'), and impugns God's motives ('For God doth know that in the day ye eat thereof, then your eyes shall be opened, and ye shall be as gods, knowing good and evil'). Eve then examines the fruit, and finds it 'good . . . pleasant . . . to be desired' – and she eats it. She then gives it to her husband; and he eats it too.

Then they know they are naked. They make aprons, to cover themselves. When they hear God, walking in the garden, they are ashamed; they attempt to hide. God's interview with them is brief and business-like. He establishes that they have disobeyed; curses the serpent (whose form Satan has invaded, and used); and pronounces His doom – exile from Eden; the woman's subjugation to her husband; a life of sorrow, thorns and thistles in place of gardening; and a return in death to the dust they were made from; for them, and for their seed, to the end of time.

The details following are, if anything, still more pregnant. God confirms that 'the man has become like us, to know good and evil', and therefore exiles him; lest he should now eat of the Tree of Life, which grows nearby, 'and live for ever'. The close of the passage is amazingly clear, and endlessly teasing:

> Therefore the Lord God sent him forth from the garden of Eden, to till the ground from which he was taken. So he drove out the man; and he placed at the east of the Garden of Eden Cherubims, and a flaming sword which turned every way, to keep the way of the tree of life.

Reading this, one is with Kafka's Joseph K. in *The Trial*; or with Henry James's haunted Governess in *The Turn Of The Screw*: everything is clear, heightened, intense; and wholly obscure. Explanations crowd in (of course), and are totally useless. The truth is incontestable, and part of our lives. Those Cherubim wielding the sword 'every way' are at their posts still. The Tree of Life is barred, this side of our death.

Many cultures have Creation myths, with their own resonances. Most hark back to a Golden Age that, somehow, has been mislaid. Even Tolkien, a staunch Roman Catholic, made his own myth for Middle Earth ('Annul in dale', from *The Silmarillion*). The uncanny power of *Genesis* is its total truthfulness; and its avoidance of any hint of questions unasked. The whole of *Paradise Lost* lurks here (and many of us know Milton's version). Milton wove a huge, complex poem, of great power and beauty. But in the end, *Genesis* is far more resonant; and far more complete.

I suppose that we all 'fit' the myth to views which evolve, in our life and probing; but we do well to recall how much greater than this, the myth is.

I have come to see it as the story of our truly original exile: the occasion of our entering a womb, and being born naked, here on earth. 'Paradise' never did exist in space/time, it is too real to do so; its essence is different, and so is its home. We ourselves truly belong to Paradise, but are truly exiled; the sword still guards it, against our return. The Tree of Life is elsewhere wholly; it does not impinge on Big Bang and Black Holes, and the Cosmos between. No scientists will find it in their test-tubes, however they look there. The worst they might do to us is torture us for a while, on 'life-support machines', if we are unlucky in dying. They cannot keep us from death, and the glory beyond. It is fitting, and right, that the one path to life (as *Genesis* tells us) is through death, and a return to the dust where we began. 'Ashes to ashes, earth to earth, dust to dust' – the law of clock-time.

God does not say in *Genesis* what lies beyond that. Very possibly, the myth concerns our actual reason for coming to live here, in exile. But that is part of the mystery 'of good and evil' – which we 'know' now; but wholly fail to understand.

Opponents of Christianity often claim that God 'meant' men and women to remain as children; that the Devil was right, and the Fall is better than perpetual life without 'moral knowledge' would have been. But this is to tear the myth, in our own direction: not Milton's direction: but then – like Milton's – not the direction, either, of the myth as it stands.

For me, 'The Fall' speaks of 'remembrance', *par excellence*; the doctrine that Plato believed in, from his pagan stance. The myth says we are displaced; we are not where we should be. We are in a harder, dangerous place; and we have a course now to run. We know we are not at home. We know that we are somehow responsible. We know that God Who willed the exile is also with us, inside it; as He was with the fallen Adam and Eve.

This is the part of 'learning' that really is 'remembering': Eliot's 'Hints and guesses/Hints followed by guesses' from *Four Quartets*. It is what Paul had in mind in his grand, simple formulation 'for here, we see as in a glass, darkly; but there, face to face'. Paul knew, supremely, that Christ 'was' the answer to the mystery. In him, 'We behold God's glory' – but God's glory finally reduced, and raised, to a Cross. This is what the writer of *Hebrews* was surely speaking of when, adapting the Old Testament experience of exodus, he called us 'strangers and pilgrims'. For here, we have no abiding city; but seek one that is to come.

This is the thought haunting Keats, I would hazard, in a famous letter written to John Taylor on 27 February 1818, when he related his own art of poetry to the reality underlying all art:

> In Poetry I have a few axioms, and you shall see how far I am from their centre. First, I think Poetry should surprise by a fine excess and not by singularity – it should strike the reader as a wording of his own highest thoughts, and appear almost as a remembrance. Second, its touches of Beauty should never be half-way, thereby making the reader breathless instead of content: the rise, the progress, the setting of imagery should, like the sun, come naturally to him – shine over him, and set soberly though in magnificance, leaving him in the luxury of twilight . . . if Poetry comes not as naturally as the leaves to a tree, it had better not come at all. (John Keats, *Collected Letters*)

Since we do indeed come from afar, our memories washed as by Lethe, Eden is the great archetype remaining. We are to respond to Wisdom, wherever we find it, as pointer to all that is truly of God. In 'Burnt Norton', the 'moment in the rose-garden', a profoundly numinous moment perfectly caught in poetry, is presided over by the courteous, ghostly presence of Adam and Eve. Eden is every numinous moment, every intimation of holiness: every encounter with Plato's 'Beauty, Goodness and Truth'; with Paul's 'Faith, Hope and Love'. In his greatest poem, *In Memoriam*, Tennyson conducts us through a triumph of love over grief, from the depths of bereavement. Towards the end of his life, he dramatised himself as Merlin:

> *I* am Merlin,
> And *I* am dying;
> *I* am Merlin
> Who follows the gleam . . .

For my part, I find the truth of Eden, and its loss, at the heart of my being. It is the centre of the Fifth Dimension; the heart of the Dance.

The heart of Christ's teaching 'is' Eternal Life: here with us, in Earth; but known here in sorrow. We know 'eternal life' now, outside Eden; we do not understand, as we should at home. For us to be 'as gods' must be ironic, a sick joke of Satan's. But God endorses it: at least, up to a point. We know enough of Good and Evil *to fight a life here, as we have to do.*

'Deliver us from Evil'. Who will not pray this? If one should elect to ignore it, the signals show 'Danger: Danger Ahead'. Christ lived his life, died, and came through triumphant. In or out of 'his' church, his beauty continues to hearten us, his 'Fear not' to inspire. We sense our eternity in the fact of our consciousness: the double timescale washing over us, as we live. We know that eternal life, after death, will answer our questions: or if not answer, give us all the knowledge we can, as humans, receive.

My next three chapters turn to three different routes to Wisdom, each treated personally; and so, each treated very partially, to a degree I am bound to regret. This second section has concerned roadblocks, that might keep us from wisdom. No doubt, some readers have other blocks to cope with – but I hope that these three might open new and useful paths for some, who have seemed to themselves to be almost lost.

Let me end this section with another quotation from Paul: where the 'entire creation' is linked with each one of us, in Paul's amazing vision of the stakes surrounding life:

> For I reckon that the sufferings of this present time are not worthy to be compared with the glory that shall be revealed in us.

For the earnest expectation of the creature waiteth for the manifestation of the sons of God . . .

Because the creature itself also shall be delivered from the bondage of corruption into the glorious liberty of the children of God.

For we know that the whole creation groaneth and travaileth in pain together until now . . .

And we know that all things work together for good to them that love God . . . (*Romans* 8: 18–19; 21–2; 28)

Part III
Three Paths to Wisdom

7

The Wisdom of the Greeks

If you could go back for a jaunt in history, where and when would you choose? I should be tempted to hear Mahler, conducting the first performance of his Fifth Symphony. This was not a triumph. The orchestra was sceptical; the music was fifty years ahead of its audience, as Mahler knew. But to hear the music which, in its organic unity most nearly expresses 'me', as the composer first realised it, would be a great experience. It is a moment when I would catch coming into historical time, after the long visions and revisions of orchestration, a work which reaches me as 'a remembrance'.

To journey back to any point in the life or ministry of Jesus is out of the question. The assured *tabu* is a further reminder of the special awe surrounding that special life. Whatever his status, in our credal formulae, he is unique among humans, and not really anchored in time. 'The kingdom of God' belongs very specially to 'here and now' consciousness. If we do not find it with us today, no journeying in space or time would help.

If pressed, I should choose to be in Athens on that day in the sixties of the first century AD when St Paul arrived in his wanderings, and encountered an altar inscribed 'TO THE UNKNOWN GOD' (*Acts* 17: 15–28). It would be splendid to watch the amused sceptics, mainly Epicureans and Stoics, gathered round him; and their courteous interest in his amazing, predictably thunderous response.

Paul was a highly intelligent, complex man, from a deeply Jewish background. His own wisdom transcends the Greek, in a final reckoning, but on this occasion, I would have felt torn between the two. Luke called the Greeks flippant, which they might have been, in a certain urbane irony. But their altar embodies its distinctive, timeless wisdom, much needed today. God's own name for God is God's secret; the Greeks sufficiently reverenced their gods to use their own, provisional names for them, and not venture beyond. The phrase 'He whom men call Zeus' is used by Aeschylus. It could be paralleled in Sophocles, a profound religious visionary, for all his heightened sense of life's tragic irony.

The altar in Athens 'TO THE UNKNOWN GOD' was eventually displaced, by Christians; but not before Constantine had captured their leaders in the fourth century, and twisted their religion away from truth and towards worldly power. As I write this, John Paul II is making dogmatic pronouncements, far more inimical to Jesus, than was that altar where Paul proclaimed to Athenians 'the God and Father of our Lord Jesus Christ'.

Perhaps, estranged from the Church as I am in the 1990s, the altar TO THE UNKNOWN GOD is the place of worship most suited to me? Yet it will not wholly do, now. Inside or outside 'Christendom', the 'God and Father' revealed in Jesus is the reality beyond all others, the God to whom I pray, and always will. When I further accept that no consideration on earth would take me, on my historical jaunt, to meet Jesus, I realise that 'thou shalt not look on the face of the living God' is in my mind.

On Mars' Hill, Paul proclaimed God's name, and His clear identity. For his part, he despised Greek wisdom, and he had come to teach, not learn. In this, the Church has officially followed him, and is unlikely (in any of its branches?) to change much now. Yet Greek ideas were smuggled into Christian thinking from the first – without acknowledgment; but with chiefly happy results. In my next chapter, I shall explore why, for me, Christ is pre-eminent; and why Paul's letters bring me closer to God than Aeschylus, Sophocles, Euripides or Plato ever quite do. This chapter concerns the Greeks – but, to balance their altar, I remember another symbol, that has taken root in my mind. On a high point in Cornwall near St Ives, with the ocean below it, there is a memorial steeple; with the one word, RESURGAM, inscribed.

How perfect Latin is, for this grand proclamation – one rock-hard word, virtually holding in stone the meaning it guards. But in any tongue, 'I will rise again' (and its declensions) takes me to Paul, and his letters: their baroque rhetoric tangled with passion, and overflowing with love.

And the Greeks? Though less certain than Paul, and more pleasurably receptive of novelty, they remained at all times open to offers of 'truth'. They listened to Paul, in these one-way exchanges. But they did not abandon their own well-tested, hard-learned truths.

In this brief chapter, I shall touch on two distinct but complementary forms of wisdom which, from a culture which ran also to Aristotle (who is not my concern here), have continuing power and refreshment for modern minds. I say 'modern' advisedly, since I have in mind the early twentieth-century writers who chose this word to describe themselves. The contemporaries of Yeats, Eliot, Joyce, Kafka, Auden and the others belonging with them, registered 'modern' as a very total break with their immediate past. But looking back now, from the end of this century, I am struck by their strong affinity with the fifth century BC. Perhaps for the first time, in the 2500 years that have passed between them, minds truly akin to Aeschylus, Sophocles and Euripides are back on the scene. Whether they would agree with this themselves, is an open question. But I offer a few further names, to chart my line of thought – Dostoievsky, Henry James, Hardy, Wilfred Owen, Ibsen, Chekhov, Jung, Pinter . . . there are many others also, who are both 'modern' and 'ancient'. Perhaps, 'half-timeless' is the most handy word for such writers? (it would allow a few others, like Shakespeare and Blake, to slip in as well).

I propose to turn now to the gods, and to the Olympians especially; then more briefly to Plato and his tradition, with Plotinus (second century AD) as a great, final peak.

II

But a word first on Heraclitus, a somewhat irascible mystic. He was a believer in war, in confrontation, in creation from Fire. Perhaps the doctrine which makes him most interesting is his perception that opposites always and everywhere mingle, since life is a perpetual flux. 'Men do not know how what is at variance agrees with itself', he writes. 'It is an attunement of opposite tensions, like that of the bow and the lyre'. And again, 'there would be no unity if there were no opposites to combine; it is the opposite which is good for us'.

Like most Greeks, Heraclitus employed questionable metaphysics. But typically, his doctrine was a construct less of arguments addressed to the mind than of sensitive intuitions writ large. 'The way up and the way down is one and the same', he wrote – so earning later immortality, as the motto-author used by Eliot for *Four Quartets*. 'You cannot step twice into the same river' is another of his sayings. This would fit perfectly into the central (third) section of 'The Dry Salvages', Eliot's great Quartet about 'such permanence as time has'.

Much pagan thought and religion worked in just such a frame.

It is no accident that twentieth-century psychoanalysis, and art, cannot be detached from Greek myths and archetypes; which are as natural to us now as they were in Athens, five centuries before Christ.

Because the Olympian gods pre-dated men and lived incalculably longer, they expected and received the homage of men. They were often attached to basic human attributes, and to specific places or elements – attesting man's instinctive awareness of beauty, and his natural gravitation towards worship and awe. There was propitiation and some fear in religious compacts, but order and vitality, in unison, were the main perceived fruit. The Greeks never forgot the mortality surrounding all ideas and achievements, and they had a heightened sense of the complex ironies of fate. But, in contrast with certain other cultures, these never became with them a morbid obsession. It was an added spur to creativity even; and seems therefore more youthful than elderly – as most things pagan still do.

Fairly early in Greek thinking, the 'Elements' were perceived as forces so basic and powerful, that they were clearly akin to gods themselves. For Heraclitus, Fire was the primal energy, underlying all things. Today, he would have found little to surprise him in our current myth of Big Bang. But other elements than Fire – Earth, Air and Water – contended for supremacy; since some mix of these could be found in all known cosmic effects. It was Empedocles who finally made them a natural foursome, and as such they were (and are) yoked together, to this day.

By some commentators, these attempts are written off as mere primitive guesswork: a lame attempt at the 'understanding' not achieved until our own 'Renaissance', fully two millennia after the flowering of Greece. But in truth, much that was understood by the Greeks is of universal importance; and has since been mislaid, to the very great peril of our world. The Greeks functioned not only through rational theorising, but by 'natural religion' felt and practised at the centre of life. This helps to account for the reverence for nature ('the environment') which characterised paganism, and which bore fruit in history long after Apollo's last Oracle was closed. As Robin Lane Fox has shown (*Pagans And Christians: From the Second Century AD to Constantine*, Viking, 1986), it was the early Christians who attacked holy groves, and took saws to trees in wanton destructiveness. They did this in their zeal against paganism as a system, which they saw as a demonic threat to their own one, true God. While the pagans would gladly have found room for the Christian God (one, two or three, as the arithmetic veered), the Christians could bear no other God but their own. In this same spirit, it was Christians who first replaced living, diverse gods, with their own lifeless dogmas and abstractions. And it was Christians who declared animals to be 'without souls' – thereby severing animals from the gods (a fearful impertinence), and equally, severing them from men (a serious and continuing impoverishment for both).

Perhaps I can insert here that if by God's grace I do arrive in the afterlife at some suitable 'mansion', I shall expect four greatly loved cats to be in residence – or at least, familiar visitors – and several hundred more to pop in, from time to time.

From the first, 'nature' has been denuded of gods, and in the end deadened, by the Christians' amazing notion that the Greek gods were fallen angels, up to no good. In the long run, their distant successors made 'nature' fit for the mechanical rationalism in Newton and Locke that was to pass as 'Christian'; and eventually, for the unleashing of technology, usury, greed which is 'Christian' today. Christians helped to initiate earth's rape by their desecration of nature (perhaps 'de-sacralization' is better, if such a word exists). This process results from a certain iconoclasm apparently endemic to the religion – though why so negative an attitude should appear so soon after Jesus of Nazareth, and in his professing followers, is beyond my power to grasp. (One must suppose that the monotheism inherited from the Jews had to be defended; and that accusations of polytheism, arising from trinitarian stirrings, made the early church highly touchy, at this point. Reverence for the Earth is, however, Jewish; and clearly, Christ strongly endorsed it. Iconoclasm against the natural world – as also against human art later – must be an aberration; of the kind that psychotherapists should perhaps study in depth.)

In the 1990s, as we survey a wrecked environment, and a headstrong rush towards world catastrophe, the Greek reverence for Earth, Air, Fire and Water must seem an all too recklessly discarded and savaged belief. Our best hope is to revive it along with much other lost wisdom, just as soon as religiously-minded scientists and artists, and environmentalists, and spiritual explorers generally, can link their insights, and set about making some new consensus prevail.

After Thatcher and Reagan, and currently Major, our cities could do with civic temples, raised by public and private funds and basic human dedication, to whatever gods – apart from Mammon – we still *de facto* honour and accept. As I revise this (1 February 1994), I read that the City of London proposes to put most of its great churches in mothballs, because they are no longer 'economic' to run. This includes great buildings by Wren, and many survivors of the great fire of 29 December 1940. The congregations have dwindled (Why? Do they ponder this?). Even the tourists are no longer able, it seems, to prop them up.[1]

Greek religion was chiefly intuitive, not systematic. It sprang from recognition of great and more lasting powers than man. Rooted in civic pride, custom, love of structure and beauty, it branched and varied according to the gods and attributes favoured, by different cities, and men. Later, the Romans would turn great men into gods, their own Emperors chiefly. But this flattery of politicians was a fall from pagan idealism. Perhaps it was Christian influence seeping back, to deprave the pagan world?

Religion has many tributaries, some of them mystical. There were Oracles on offer from Apollo, for divination and help. But truth is manifold, and the prophets reflected this. The Priestesses of Apollo spoke always in riddles, sometimes in signs. No clear distinction between religion and poetry was formalised, since suggestions released through symbols strike far deeper than creeds conceived by the mind. Homer was the nearest that the Greeks ever came to 'scripture' and, as Heraclitus noted: 'The Lord whose is the Oracle of Delphi neither utters not hides his meaning, but shows it by a sign'.

The gods of a city were at one with its aspirations and culture. Great temples were raised, to serve the citizens, and to please and impress all travellers passing through. Influential citizens would donate an altar as their personal tribute, and civic life would combine with religious faith. Each year would be marked by ceremonies, some for local deities, some for the great seasons and changes of the Earth. Domestic life moved towards household gods, and small works of piety. Art, philosophy, heroism all came within the sway of an appropriate god.

It is true that the grander philosophers would sometimes disparage this 'popular' religion. Even Plato found the Olympians lacking in weight. But, for exceptional men in their intricate by-ways, exceptional philosophy: for most mortals, religious piety, celebration and solace sufficed, in the arena of life.

The gods required gifts for their shrines, in return for which they were usually open to petitions and prayers. If neglected, they were apt to turn nasty, as is always the way of gods. But they could be appeased; and their anger seldom led to slaughter on too grand a scale. What one had to remember was the *tabus*, and the darker areas; if you were a king or a father, take special care before uttering a curse. The gods took more notice of meanings and acts than they did of motives; if once engaged by humans, it was too late to try to make them withdraw. Life's many ironies found echoes in the Oracles; and the gods were at home with irony, perhaps in ways blocked off from human minds. But generally, the picture was lighter. The gods focused reverence – that vibrant quality, which makes paganism perennially attractive; and which we could indeed do with, again, as Christ's second millennium moves to its close.

If you ask, 'How did the pagans believe in their gods?', the answer is hopelessly difficult to phrase. But then, religious quest is always like this. Not by dogma or priestcraft; not by logical discourse; not by enshrined revelation: yet traditions grew up, which wise men took care to treat with respect. The gods were part of life's richness; their rites and their forms were a duty, and a solace. They were beacons of light, in a largely harsh world. Beyond that, they gave men wisdom, and a spur to creativity. The Greeks would not have polluted the Earth as we moderns do; even if they had been given the means.

III

My own encounter with the gods came at Cambridge (through the Tragedy paper, in Part 2 of the English Tripos) and their voices reached me at a crucial time. In the turbulent teenage years they would have been a (literal) godsend; but I had always understood that paganism was a system of errors, long since dead. In my early twenties, the Greek gods rescued me from the last lingering enchantments of 'Victorian Honest Doubt', and from the last lingering confusion of Victorian lies, and evasions, about sex. They even rescued me, in the nick of time, from the Christian priesthood; for which I was accepted on the morning when I finally decided that I had 'lost' Christian faith for good. With one bound I was free: what a glorious rescue! I suppose the church can be mildly thankful as well.

Without the 'Greek Paper', I might have remained a sort of Christian, and a sort of priest. I knew I was religious, and always would be; so what else, but Christian, was there to be? But the major problem of early manhood would have remained, insoluble and crippling. How reconcile a 'religious nature' with impossible dogmas? How live with a moral system which split me into several warring parts that could never be joined?

No doubt, those three great Tragic Dramatists of the fifth century BC are in no way 'typical'; they present the gods through the medium of visionary art. We could as easily generalise about the Norse gods from Wagner's Ring Cycle, as about the Greek gods from the three outstanding creative minds to concern us now. (Yet when this is said, Wagner's Ring is indeed a work of genius with great truths on offer. It is not Wagner's fault that his Norse gods are truly hopeless cases; and Wotan's Valhalla a shambles that the Greeks would have filed away amongst their own worst dreams.)

Aeschylus's *Oresteia* is the one great Trilogy that survives for us; and it is teasing to ponder the riches that are lost.

Aeschylus's *Prometheus* is a wonderful play but, torn from its context, we have to guess how the second, and third, plays might have been. I imagine that the pattern of thesis, antithesis and synthesis might have recurred there, but Shelley's *Prometheus Unbound* would very clearly not have found a place.

The three plays of *Oresteia* are in effect one artistic experience. Though each could exist independently, and could be produced as an entity, Aristotle's 'beginning, middle and end' clearly spans all three. And, though many tragic theories (including Aristotle's) have revolved around them, they are more like a symbolist structure than like 'tragedy', in total effect. There are tragic ironies enough, but we do not rest with these. We end with celebration, as a tragic cycle is broken in a 'reconciliation' that has proved at least as important for our European political and legal development, as it has for art.

The first play turns on Agamemnon's homecoming, after the Trojan Wars, and his final trials at sea. It explores the condition that had come to exist in Greece during his long years of absence; and centres on the welcome prepared for him by his wife, Clytemnestra, who has effectually ruled in his stead.

At the opening, a Watchman sights the beacon which says that the wars are over, and that the heroic victors are safe, and about to land. His magnificent speech establishes a high vitality, which later finds echoes in Clytemnestra's very different elation, and in Cassandra's half-crazed prophesies of doom.

The main action of the play is carried by the Chorus, which consists of the City's 'Elders'. These are men who were too old to go to the war at its beginning, and are now too cowed by age and tyranny for heroic words. They convey deep unease about their city, which is sick with a malaise that has long been growing, and which they cannot check. They fear Agamemnon's homecoming as a signal for deeds of horror, which they are too demoralised so much as to name. A tangible web of fear, spun by the Chorus mainly, builds through long exchanges, pregnant with concealment, and evasion, and impotent guilt.

In *genre*, this is a 'revenge play' (as is the Trilogy) – but to say this is to skim the surface, and more than slightly to distort. The Trojan War was 'caused' by the elopement of King Menelaus's young wife, Helen, with Paris; a blow to Greek pride that only war could assuage. Or perhaps we should say, this was the 'immediate cause' – or even, the pretext? (much as the assassination in Sarajevo was the 'cause' of the 1914–18 war). The Greeks resolve to be avenged on the Trojans who have wounded them. They embark on a war destined to last for ten, terrible years.

At the outset, the gods are divided in sympathies. They are involved with Agamemnon's affairs (the House of Pelops) already, through much earlier deeds – which we hear of only as the play unfolds. This new war, though heroic, will clearly be grim, of necessity. It will be tainted with *hubris*, that most basic of all human sins which displease the gods. Young men will suffer and die, and to what purpose? To avenge the exploits of Helen; who is always perceived as a whore.

To a degree that modern readers might find surprising, the war is represented as a great evil throughout. Heroic people and deeds abound, as is to be expected, but the cause of the war is tainted, and its end is all grief. There are speeches that readily remind us now of Wilfred Owen (though this similarity was either missed or glossed over, in my 1930s childhood, *entre deux guerres*). Aeschylus conveys 'the pity of war' in striking images of slaughter, rape, murder and civil decay. Perhaps the wrong done to Agamemnon's brother, King Menelaus, 'had' to be righted, or Greece would have lost all claim to respect in the world? But perhaps the cause is too trivial for major bloodshed: perhaps false pride is the true cause, a lack of proportion not pleasing to the gods? Confusion among the gods (or men's perceptions of this) is a reminder that any simple 'blessing' of soldiers or weapons has no place in a truly serious religious scheme.

Artemis – a militant goddess herself, though chiefly associated with chastity – comes close to aborting the war at the start. Given the sin against chastity which is the immediate pretext, her support might have been expected by the Greeks. Yet the test she initiates, far from confirming this, can plausibly be read in more than one way. The winds are unpropitious, and remain so. Can the Greek fleet hope ever to sail, on its deadly mission to Troy? The soothsayer Calchas foretells that the Greeks will eventually triumph, under Zeus, but that Artemis will keep the winds unfavourable unless a sacrifice is made.

This sacrifice is to be of Agamemnon's daughter, Iphigenia. Only if Iphigenia is brought or lured to the waiting fleet and then killed ritually, will Artemis relent, allowing the fleet to sail.

Already, the complexity of the issue is apparent, in searing images. Is Agamemnon truly bound to this war by honour; or is he impelled by false pride? Should he retreat from the war, given the chance provided by Artemis? Or should he sacrifice his daughter in the terrible way demanded, so as not to lose face? The scales come down against Iphigenia – who is bound and gagged, lest her dying words should be a curse on the enterprise; and an innocent child's blood is firstfruit of Helen's war. The Chorus half exonerates Agamemnon, in classic fashion: 'Then he put on/The harness of Necessity'. Yet their description conveys the scene's horror, beyond such reasoning; 'blasphemy', 'Impiety' are other words they use. The two perspectives are balanced by more general reflections, though they cannot be finally reconciled. These lines, placed a little earlier in the scene, link Zeus's own will, and enigmatic purpose, with the human confusions:

> Zeus, whose will has marked for man
> The sole way where wisdom lies,
> Ordered one eternal plan:
> *Man must suffer, to be wise.*

Iphigenia dies; the winds change; the fleet sails. After the ten bitter years described in *The Iliad*, Troy is sacked and punished. The strategem of the Trojan Horse ends the war, by a final Greek treachery. Helen's elopement is avenged in rape, fire and plunder.

Helen herself is changed, into myth and legend, where she now belongs.

Aeschylus's *Agamemnon* is 'about' the hero's homecoming; but the whole war comes with him, in the city's consciousness – along with family horrors stretching back still further, and not at rest. Clytemnestra has ruled 'like a man' (which is to say, unnaturally; tyranically) in the true ruler's absence. She has taken Aegisthus (Agamemnon's cousin) as her lover, while protesting her chaste fidelity to the world. The ageing Chorus of Elders are too demoralised to speak out openly, but their endless nods and winks, and sombre set pieces, are the stuff from which tension grows. Their reaction to Cassandra's wild prophesies, which is one of sheer terror, suggests that, despite all their evasions, they have suppressed their fears to the verge of repression (in Freud's usage of this term).

Clytemnestra greets the news of her husband's return with exhilarated rhetoric, burning with a personal intensity that bodes no good. She blazes in images, like one of the hilltop beacons, as the ships bearing Agamemnon come closer to land.

In the event, Agamemnon has a part in 'his' play that is brief, and far from attractive. Clytemnestra tempts him to enter his home walking on purple carpets; an honour exclusively reserved for the gods. After token resistance, more clearly marked by pride than by reverence, he succumbs to pressure, and commits the blasphemy in full, public view. Clytemnestra's cries of triumph, as he is murdered in the house by herself and Aegisthus, mingle with Cassandra's still unheeded and increasingly frenzied warnings of doom.

The play's chief event is Agamemnon's murder. He is ensnared in a net, and stabbed to death. The hysteria of Cassandra is matched by growing fear in the Chorus – who still pretend to think her raving, and mad.

When the murder is revealed, the whole city is in terror; but ambivalence pervades the play's entire mood. The gods are at strife, as so often, and only partly attentive. They intervene among humans, but humans are small part of their care. The war is an enigma: heroic, certainly; but a bitter tale of youth, innocence, culture betrayed and destroyed. We never do discover whether Artemis's demand for Iphigenia's sacrifice was made to deter the war; or whether she wished to add to its horror; or was following omens best understood by herself.

Not unnaturally, Clytemnestra proclaims that the killing of her husband is in essence revenge, for her murdered daughter. For good measure, she lures Agamemnon to a blasphemous act on his homecoming, which further 'justifies' her action, and dramatises the arrogance which caused Iphigenia's murder ten years before.

But Clytemnestra's other daughter, Electra, passionately hates her mother; while her son Orestes is in exile, having fled for his life. We sense that Clytemnestra and Aegisthus have been exulting in adultery and tyranny, and that the terror they caused is rooted in themselves.

This plot is complicated by an older feud, in the house of Tantalus. Atreus (Agamemnon's father) had lured his own brother Thyestes (Aegisthus's father) to a terrible death. He had proclaimed a feast, apparently honouring his brother, but had served for meat the body of Thyestes's murdered son. When Thyestes realised the horror, 'vomiting murdered flesh' he fell. In dying, he put an inexorable curse on the entire 'house of Pelops': (Pelops was the father of himself and Atreus; the house is usually known as 'The House of Tantalus', from further back).

Clytemnestra's lover therefore has his own cause for revenge against Agamemnon – a murdered father, in classic line for the further shedding of blood. In this complexity, Aeschylus is true to his sources, which he makes continual use of, for the profound and distinctive vision that his *Oresteia* is to become.

The theme of blood-feud passing from father to son through the generations is profoundly Hellenic, though we now know it better (perhaps) from the parallel Old Testament belief. Characteristically, Israel's God decreed visitations of 'the sins of the fathers upon the children, unto the third and fourth generation of them that hate me'. For the Greeks, these chains of vengeance were a mixture of pragmatism, psychological insight, and social *mores*. All three strands link with their own society; and with their own, very different, gods.[2]

The second play of the Trilogy, *Choephori*, has Orestes as hero. But the bitter hatred of Electra for her mother Clytemnestra is the driving force. In this play, the Chorus is made up of Clytemnestra's women attendants (her slaves), who are bound to serve her, but are deeply torn between duty and hate. As they say, they 'Obey because I must/And as I can, control/The bitter hatred of my soul'. But their fear and hatred, both played on by Electra, become far more openly partisan and threatening than the different role of the Elders, in *Agamemnon*, had allowed. They share Electra's hatred of her mother, but strive fitfully to dampen it. Their greater fear is that madness will again be released, through the great, doomed house. Electra's hope centres wholly on Orestes's return, to exact vengeance. But Clytemnestra's spies are alert. If he comes, Orestes will be killed instantly.

And – if Orestes should come – would the killing of a mother by a son really appease the gods, and end the cycle? Or would it merely prolong it, adding a new, still greater sin, to the terrible list?

Choephori is more concentrated as a drama than *Agamemnon*, more pared down to one vision and action (no doubt, Aeschylus relies on the knowledge of the full situation that his audience will have gained, from the first play). Fear and hatred of Clytemnestra (and by extension, Aegisthus), intense and fanatical in Electra, is diffused but growing in the nation they rule.

Orestes does return, in disguise. He passes Clytemnestra's guard successfully, by a stratagem which includes bringing reports of his own supposed death. But first, he has encountered Electra who, when convinced of his true identity, greets him with blood-chilling ecstasy, and total, near-demented, support. Orestes has indeed come back to avenge his father; but he is more appalled than Electra by the deed to be done. On the positive side, he is not only supported by Apollo, but urged on by the god, with dreadful predictions of his fate if he fails in the task:

> The word of Apollo is of great power and cannot fail.
> His voice, urgent, insistent, drives me to dare this peril,
> Chilling my heart's hot blood with recital of threatened terrors
> If I should fail to exact fit vengeance, like for like,
> From those who killed my father. This was the god's command:
> 'Shed blood for blood, your face set like a flint. The price they owe no wealth can weigh'.
> My very life, he said, would pay in endless torment for disobedience.

But this is balanced by hints of torments on the other side, if he does kill his mother; backed by the suggestion that he is caught between a rock and a hard place. Apollo's 'Oracle' has hinted that the worst tormenters – the Furies – will finally back Agamemnon's avenger; but Orestes must have sensed ambiguity, or something uncertain, at this point:

May I put my trust in oracles like these? or not?
Even if I cannot trust them, yet I must do this deed.
To this one end my will is urged by many motives . . .

As this speech continues, many critics have seen a foreshadowing of Hamlet – in the *task* of vengeance; in the numerous (too numerous?) reasons assembled by Orestes; and in doubts surrounding supernatural omens, as he allows his mind to brood. But Orestes has Electra to steel him – and, also, the Chorus, who are the first, now, to greet his hesitant speech with a very clear reply:

Hear now, you powerful Fates!
Receive our prayer, and send
By Zeus our Father's hands
Fulfilment of that end
Which fervent hope awaits
And our just cause demands.

The deed is achieved. Clytemnestra and Aegisthus die, at the hands of Orestes – avenging his father chiefly, yet caught up, too, in the unfolding horrors of his House.

In the event, Orestes finds only mental torment; and it begins to appear that The Furies are wholly on Clytemnesra's side, as perhaps Orestes had feared. In this play, Orestes alone sees his dreadful pursuers, in the closing pages; he recoils from them in the utmost horror and panic, leading the Chorus to fear that he must have gone mad. The Chorus rehearses unfinished business – new horrors – in the stricken House.

The third play, *The Eumenides*, is the tale's consummation. Here, horror yields at last to reconciliation as we witness, against all expectation, the end of the curse. This time, the play takes its name from a Chorus which is also a protagonist, 'The Furies', who drove Orestes distracted, even before they appear. It is said that at the first performance of *The Eumenides* many spectators fainted and some had miscarriages, when the dreadful hags at last came into view.

The Eumenides are Earth Goddesses, older than the Olympians in origin, and with an authority as awesome as any we shall find. They belong with the elements, with the original stuff of any known creation. Their names mean 'The Kindly Ones' and in this, deep truth is hidden; as this play exists in part to make clear. But first, they are hideous beings, hounders of matricide – 'The Furies', defending the oldest, most sacred of human *tabus*. Very naturally, Orestes is now their prey, and they propose to kill him – whatever Apollo or the other Olympians might do, or say.

Very probably, their role as avengers was originally wider, and rooted deeply in blood vengeance itself. In this play, the sanctity of motherhood is their object – a relationship they single out from all others, using arguments which sound odd now, but still have power to stop us in our tracks.

The play opens outside Apollo's Temple at Delphi. The god is present in person, receiving Orestes, who comes for sanctuary and help. The Priestess, unaware of the god and his suppliant and of the still-sleeping Eumenides, arrives at the Temple, expecting a normal day's work. Her first speech is full of interest. 'Loxias' (Apollo) is 'fourth successor' to the line she serves, at Delphi. The young god, now in charge under Zeus, inherits an older, more basic tradition than Olympus. The Priestess's opening invocation 'First in my prayer of all the gods I reverence/Earth, first author of prophecy' starts a daily ritual, but reminds us that Earth – to whom the Eumenides belong – is the moving power. She next salutes 'Themis, Earth's daughter', the second ruler of the Oracle; then 'Phoebe', another 'Titan child of Earth' – who yielded power to her 'young namesake, Phoebus'. Phoebus (Apollo under another title) was appointed by Zeus personally; and the Oracle (which had lapsed somewhat?) was re-established at Delphi, after feats of engineering performed under the guidance of the gods themselves. The Priestess, rehearsing the ancient nature of her role and its abiding sanction, prepares for a new day of prophecy. But, entering her Temple, she cries out in fear, struck with horror by the sight she sees. Orestes, still polluted with his mother's blood, is prostrated at the altar: and beside him are the monstrous women – Harpies; Gorgons; 'Black, utterly loathesome' – whom the Priestess can in no way identify with the gods, or with nature itself. But Loxias is there also, 'Priest, Prophet, Healer; powerful': and wisely, the Priestess retires, leaving the god to deal personally with his violated Temple. Presumably, she fails to notice the ghost of Clytemnestra, which arrived hard on her heels, to awaken the Eumenides and spur them into action.

First Apollo speaks, offering help to Orestes: 'I will not fail you, Near at hand or far away, I am your constant guardian and your enemies' dread'. But, when the Eumenides wake and confront Apollo (a marvellous episode), Apollo himself seems shaken by what he hears. The murder of Agamemnon by Clytemnestra is important to

Apollo, but the Eumenides regard it as a small affair. Husband and wife are not blood-relations (this is a major theme), so the murder of Agamemnon cannot compare with murder between parents and children. Matricide is the supreme horror, 'blood calling for blood'.

Soon Orestes has fled again, and Apollo has proposed a proper adjudication, with Athene as the goddess most suited to let justice prevail. The Eumenides, unimpressed by Apollo, brush Athene aside also. 'I will never let Orestes go', is their simple riposte. Apollo replies 'He is my suppliant; and I will stand by him and save him if I can'. This final clause strikes a new note, ominous for Orestes; Apollo withdraws into his Temple, nominating the judicial proceedings under Athene, in Athens, as next port of call. The Olympians are indeed 'new gods' for the Eumenides, though their power over men is now, in theory, complete. But can the Olympians truly cope with darker, deeper elements in creation, representing power that their new order cannot yet contain?

The action is a confrontation between the older powers, the Eumenides, their origins lost in antiquity; and the new young gods ('upstarts', to the Eumenides), now constructing an order where reason and instinct will, with luck, balance and hold.[3]

Apollo is naturally presented as a youthful, urbane, talented, immensely attractive figure, a shade slippery in reasoning, but backed with his status as god, if the charm fails to work. For the duration, he is involved with Orestes, as his champion, and his whole power as a god is staked on this. Any slight doubts he feels will, if justified, threaten the entire structure of Olympus – indeed, the peace and order of Greece, which stands or falls with these gods, as the first audience knew. The stakes, for Greece as well as for Orestes, could not be higher.

The Eumenides are true hounds, with a licence to kill Orestes. They are The Furies (the Kindly Ones), to be deflected from Clytemnestra's revenge by no loopholes or tricks. It seems that the curse on the House of Tantalus is to continue further; that as Iphigenia and Agamemnon and Clytemnestra and Aegisthus have died, so now must Orestes. Against this old law of revenge ('It will have blood they say, blood will have blood') stand the Olympians; and with them the Greeks, seeking a new, better way.

The Eumenides is the play about man's invention, with some help from the gods, of civil law. It is the prototype of the system we now know as 'Law' in most western countries: an early, public instance of blood-feud handed over from the participants to impartial arbiters who will, therefore, not share the blame. Offenses against citizens up to and including murder are no longer to be avenged by the immediate family (or more recently by vigilantes, or terrorist groups); but by due social processes, conducted by an institution of state. The instinct for gut-revenge is embodied in The Eumenides – oldest of goddesses and, should the processes of Law once again fail, newest as well. The vesting of 'justice' in impartial advocates, impartial fellow citizens, impartial judges bound by custom, will remove punishment from the realm of instinct to reason (if it works; and to the degree that it continues to work). In this way, the trap of unending chains of vengeance can at last be ended. Likewise, individual anger can be satisfied (or quieted) by a process taken out of 'our' hands.

Athene becomes, with Apollo, the obvious agent for this new order – the goddess of Wisdom, joining with the god of Structure, Harmony, Music and Light.

At first, refusing to accept the trial and scorning all compromise, the Furies seem set to abort the proceedings, and continue on their ancient, tried path. 'Cruel to be kind' underlies their own name as 'Kindly Ones'; and there is much to be proved, if this name, and its role, is to be set to one side.

Athene proceeds to the trial even so, meeting hate with persuasion; the Eumenides remain wholly impervious to the process, secure in their repeated litanies of blood. Their ferocious indictment of the court, the judges, and not least the claim that it does contain justice, keeps dramatic tension at a pitch seldom achieved.

The trial itself is indeed a strange affair. It verges at moments on the comic, on pure nonsense even, as it was surely intended to do? Athene, as Judge, is about as convincing as Shakespeare's Portia (in a much later play). Apollo, defending Orestes, uses arguments which sound slippery not just to modern ears, but surely to Aeschylus's absorbed, first audience of Greeks? The culminating 'argument' involves the Judge herself – weirdly and uniquely; but before this, the whole presentation is odd. It is asserted by the Eumenides that whereas husband and wife are not 'blood-relations', mother and son are, in the highest degree. A murder of husband by wife is therefore far less serious than matricide. This later crime cries to heaven for vengeance, in a way that no pleading of Agamemnon's case can affect.

Apollo agrees, in theory; but urges that Clytemnestra's vindictiveness, and mode of murder, set her apart. He goes on to argue that the child is the seed of his father, not of his mother; and that this is defence enough against the Eumenides' main claim. On this view, the mother borrows the seed from the father, for its nine-month fruition, then delivers it back to the true parent – the father – as if in trust.

Other arguments sound equally bizarre, as the trial progresses (or are they just unfamiliar? – might our own standards of judgment be far less universal than we think?). I would stress that the play's extraordinary power depends upon no continuities or discontinuities between Greek culture and our own; but on its probing of basic issues of vengeance, and relationship, that go to the roots of life. It is legitimate to recall Shylock's trial before Portia in *The Merchant of Venice*, and other strange Shakespearean 'trials' in his comedies, tragedies, histories, and his symbolic 'last plays'. The trial of the Knave of Hearts in *Alice In Wonderland* is pertinent; as are the trials of Darnay in *A Tale of Two Cities*, of the hero of Camus's *L'Etranger*, of K. and Joseph K. in Kafka himself. In all these and many other major literary instances, a yoking of social realities to compelling religious, psychic and 'power' undercurrents, takes us very directly back to the Greeks, in method and mood.

In *The Eumenides*, the crowning 'argument' is that Athene herself was born fully grown from the head of her father Zeus so that, uniquely among the gods, she was without a mother herself. In this way, she is persuaded that the mother's claims to unique sanctity are indeed exaggerated; and her casting vote appears to rest on this ground.

Christians will recall that Christ who, according to the Church, had no human father, had also a half-human mother (Mary was conceived 'without sin', and so was uniquely unfitted to pass humanity on to her child). Yet the cult of the Virgin (and 'The Family') have been central for catholics, for a long time now; and similarities between Christ and Athene have long been apparent (Yeats did not get there first).

If we think Orestes' trial odd, the Olympians slippery, the archetypes more intuitive than rational, then this is all firmly based on Aeschylus's text. The Eumenides are no more convinced by the arguments used by the Olympians than we are ourselves. When, for all their ferocity, they finally yield to persuasion, a subtler process is at work.

The trial, flawed as it is, offers to the House of Tantalus escape from the fatal *impasse* of unending revenge. It produces a judicial system (a remarkable model) to replace the older justice of 'an eye for an eye, a tooth for a tooth' (to use the familiar, Jewish, words). It passes the fate of Orestes over from the revenge meted out by ancient, implacable goddesses, to selected peers, impartial and honest (to the degree that these things are possible in flawed, blinkered men). The process includes the presiding and participating gods, with Eumenides as Protagonist, to underline a religious and ultimate seal, on so profound an event.

Why are the processes so odd? I imagine, because Law is odd, and always must be; however strongly a pretence at total reason and fairness is maintained. Ancient custom, occasional prejudice, sheer human unpredictability, cannot be phased out in any known world. As I write this, Israel and the Arab world are attempting a move towards 'justice'; Bosnia and Ireland behave as if plays like *The Oresteia* do not exist. Organisations like the UN and the European Court of Justice struggle with harsh intractables, and we do ill to condemn them too harshly for imperfections along the paths they are forced to tread.

Greek wisdom was to use reason as far as possible, while acknowledging the prime power of instinct, and the practical limits set against all merely social ideals. Why do the Eumenides submit, at the last? Again and again they denounce the proceedings and it is hard for us, as their audience, not to see the point. But they are old. They are ancient gods, in need of rest, and acceptance. Their time has come to merge themselves with new, younger powers. They are gods who can be integrated, if someone has the Wisdom of Athene, in a manner that incorporates basic honour, and understanding, for all.

While Apollo berates the Eumenides, exchanging insults with them robustly, Athene treats them with a respect they deserve, but perhaps no longer expect. Her flattery is in no way idle; it is based on reality. She does not have to go back on it later, as mere pragmatists might.

Rather, she offers a new home for the older gods, in the caverns beneath Athens; a permanent, honoured place, at the heart of Wisdom itself. When they finally accept, the whole action turns to celebration, and procession. The Kindly Ones are not finally exiled, but fulfilled.

For indeed, though justice is constructed on 'reason', or our best attempts at it, its roots are in passion and instinct, not excluding revenge. It is part of Greek poise that the older order survives, underpinning the new one; slumbering not dead; since the Eumenides are not beings who will die while humans and other gods live on. Justice remembers the profound, the abyss, on which it has its foundations. And, if the time should come when it forgets the Eumenides, then it is Justice, not they, which will wither, or die. In such time, the Eumenides will awake once more, refreshed by their slumber, and roam as immortals at large in the world overhead.

The Oresteia, which includes two purely tragic plays, and is our one remaining complete Trilogy, ends in celebration of problems solved and of civilisation making one great move ahead. It ends not as tragedy but as triumph, as the two gods of Tragedy (Dionysus and Apollo) are reconciled. The whole drama spills over from art, to the world of society, where great art belongs by virtue of its Beauty, Goodness and Truth.

IV

The two great Oedipus plays of Sophocles are not part of a Trilogy, though if *Antigone* is placed after them, it may wrongly seem that they are. *Antigone* was written first and stands apart as one tragic archetype: the situation when two strong wills, convinced of their rectitude, collide and destruct. It is one action, complete in itself, somewhat resembling Shaw's similar but inferior *St Joan*. We can understand it best as an absorbing, self-contained drama, offering no 'reconciliation' to the Oedipus plays that they do not already have in themselves.

Oedipus Rex was also conceived alone, as a single action; and is profoundly tragic, since that is its basic plan. But, by the accident of Sophocles's longevity, *Oedipus At Colonus* now exist alongside it; and inevitably, the second play interacts with the first. Taken together, they transform 'tragedy', much as *The Oresteia* does, to a different area altogether of religious drama, where healing is possible; and even Oedipus's fate can be seen as blessing, not curse. In Sophocles, however, this is the effect of a happy accident: and he and Aeschylus have little in common, apart from profound reverence for the gods.

Sophocles is sometimes thought of as 'the most religious' of the Greek tragedians, but all three were profoundly religious in differing modes. In *Oedipus Rex*, when Jocasta assures Oedipus that he 'cannot' be the guilty man since her own child perished, at her command, shortly after his birth, the Chorus is shocked not (immediately) by the hideous ironies still unfolding at the heart of the play, but by Jocasta's 'A fig for divination!'. This precipitates the great Chorus starting: 'I only ask to live, with pure faith keeping/In word and deed the Law which keeps the sky' . . . It is a cry of horror at Jocasta's immediate blasphemy, in denying the truth of oracles that have come to her direct from the gods. Some Victorians found this akin to evangelical hymnology (and the translation I have used might reflect this view). But Sophocles' gods are wholly other than those of the Victorians, and his reverence is quintessential paganism of an age-old, personal (even domestic) tone:

> Zeus! if thou livest, all-ruling, all pervading,
> Awake; old oracles are out of mind;
> Apollo's name denied, his glory fading;
> There is no godliness in all mankind.

Sophocles' gods are, at root, the Olympians; but the Orphic mysteries also colour his plays. This strain of Greek religion belongs to areas of mystery religion that pervade the pre-Christian centuries in many countries, and are in no sense connected with the Olympians and their whole, special world.

Like Aeschylus, Sophocles must be read and reread carefully. I cannot provide here even a reliable map. What I want to point to is the amazing insight which transforms Victim first to Saviour; then to Polluter; then, to still more exalted Saviour: thereby anticipating an essential paradox later gathered around the figure of Christ.

The tragic pattern of *Oedipus Rex* is famous, and archetypal. Many later writers have approximated to it in their greatest dramas (Shakespeare, Racine, Ibsen, Chekhov, Eugene O'Neill spring to mind). There is an irreversible flaw in the past – something already done, and therefore unchangeable. The tragic pattern forces the past back into the present relentlessly and terribly, where its only possible effect is to destroy. Every apparent discovery that seems, at first, to evade disaster, it yet another step in its epiphany.

Before his birth, it was foretold of Oedipus by oracles that he would break basic *tabus*, killing his father and marrying his mother. In this terrible manner, he would be a polluter of himself, and of his whole social world. His parents, appalled by the prophecy and trying to avert it, sent the new-born infant, as they thought, to his death. But human compassion saved the infant, when the agent hired to kill Oedipus chose to abandon the helpless baby instead.

Oedipus was found by strangers who, taking pity on him, nurtured him as their own natural child.

When in due time Oedipus himself learned of the curse that was upon him, he took his own steps to avert it turning into truth. He left and fled from his parents (as he thought them), again to make sure that the curse of the gods could not be fulfilled.

The part played by the gods in this is strange, and inexorable. It is their decree that arbitrates the fate of Oedipus, but their motives are never explained or explored. Perhaps the Oracle sees into the future, and speaks without equivocation. Perhaps the god predestines Oedipus's fate; or Sophocles discovers it, as a god-given myth for exploring his own mind and art.

In attempting to avert the decree, Oedipus's parents are 'blasphemous'. Jocasta's 'A fig for divination!' gives deep offence to the Chorus, who see it as subverting reverence, on which all order in Earth and beyond earth depends.

In the pattern of the play, the foretold destiny always rules Oedipus. Like his parents, he attempts by drastic measures to avert it, when the details become known to him. His rise to kingship as Thebes' saviour must seem propitious: surely a man fitting this role is favoured by the gods?

Possibly a man fated, as he is, should not be hot-tempered; should not kill a man 'old enough to be his father' in a fight. Possibly he should not marry a lady 'old enough to be his mother'; even though, as Queen of Thebes, she is part of his prize, when he lifts the curse of the Sphynx. We wonder if Oedipus does indeed 'contribute' to his destiny; and if so, whether this at all 'absolves' the gods? Such moral questions are natural, but we are not led to explore them. We register simply, that the 'pollution' of Oedipus is far from his own conscious acts or wishes; and has no place even in his subconscious designs.

At the start of the play, we meet Oedipus at the height of his fortune; saviour of Thebes, and widely respected King. This is the moment, however, when a further curse threatens the city. The murder of the previous husband of Jocasta, King Laius, appears to have roused the wrath of the gods. A plague is sweeping the city, 'beyond all telling':

> Beyond all telling, the city
> Reeks with death in her streets, death-bringing
> None weeps, and her children die,
> None by to pity.

Oedipus, saviour of Thebes already from the Sphynx's oppression undertakes to seek the cure again, for this new and unlooked for event. He seeks divination from the Oracle of Apollo, and receives, through Creon, the guidance he needs. 'There is an unclean thing/ Born and nursed on our soil, polluting our soil, which must be driven away, not kept to destroy us'. The guilty man is the killer of Laius, Jocasta's first husband. He will infect Thebes with his presence until 'the payment of blood for blood'.

Upon hearing this, Oedipus solemnly undertakes to seek out this guilty man, and expel him. Then, he utters his famous curse on the polluter of the land. The man is to be expelled; he is to go wandering friendless thereafter until his life's end; he is to wear a mark of shame (like Cain?), so that no home or place will receive him:

> Nor do I exempt myself from this imprecation:
> If, with my knowledge, house or hearth of mine
> Receive the guilty man, upon my head
> Lie all the curses I have laid on others . . .

It is an ancient tradition, at the centre of several Greek plays and used later by Shakespeare, that a curse once uttered cannot be retracted. The gods have heard, and registered; there can be no recalling the words on any grounds. If they are spoken on false assumptions, wrong information, treacherous misdirection, the intention matters nothing: the curse is all. The gods hear and accept such human petitions – with special note for those uttered by a Father, or a King.

It is often suggested that this play represents the moment when 'intention' entered Greek morality: as a challenge which, in this play, is starkly clear. Oedipus curses himself, though he cannot know this. Does his own implacable lack of pity or concern for motives somehow endorse the sternness of the gods? Are the gods mocking ever more ruthlessly, as they sport with Oedipus, forcing him to take on, by an act of his own will, the horror ordained by themselves? Or is a moment like this the one foreseen by the first Oracle, when conveying to Laius and Jocasta the fate that surrounds their child? We note that Oedipus does use the phrase 'If, with my knowledge' . . . Not much is made of this; yet it lies in this play, as a potent undercurrent. Years later, it was a seed for *Oedipus At Colonus*, written by Sophocles in extreme old age.

Oedipus Rex becomes a relentless march towards its predestined 'Ecce Homo!' It is as useless for us to attempt to judge Oedipus, as it is dangerous for us to judge or question the gods. The various episodes in which Oedipus, expecting good news, finds only new horror hidden in it, generate dramatic intensity which has often been imitated, never surpassed.

Ibsen's use of the pattern in *Ghosts, Rosmersholme, The Wild Duck* and many major dramas, is bound to stand out for us, now. Hardy also uses the pattern in his tragic novels – where it involves a human indictment of the Victorian God (or perhaps, of belief in any God).

When Jocasta finally arrives at the truth – just before Oedipus – she cries out in horror; and kills herself. Oedipus puts out his eyes, as a reflex action of horror, and in doing this, compounds the blasphemies which the Chorus perceive. Then, he confirms the curse on himself, and departs into exile. In this way, be becomes Thebes' saviour for the second time: but in how different a way, from the first.

Is the 'sin' of Oedipus a sin at all? This question rests at the heart of the plays. His fatal deeds are done in ignorance; and after many steps have been taken to avert them. Are these attempts to thwart an Oracle still further and worse sin, in the eyes of god? These questions represent a major crux, for Greek culture; and their resonance remains, in ever new forms, for ourselves. Did Bacon remotely foresee nuclear bombs and lethal global pollution, when he hailed the 'new science' as a certain saviour of mankind? Did the farmers who embraced mechanised and technological methods as 'economic progress', foresee the wholesale sacrifice of animal, and human, welfare this would later entail?

The one thing we can know for certain, is that Oedipus does not kill his Father or marry his Mother by *conscious intention*. Likewise, no *subconscious intention* (*pace* Freud) is possible, in the frame we find present in *Oedipus Rex*.

Some modern readers blame the gods, perhaps naturally. We have Shakespearean echoes haunting our minds, from deeply wounded characters ('As flies to wanton boys we are to the gods/They kill us for their sport': *King Lear*). We recall the last savage stroke in Hardy's *Tess of the d'Urbervilles*:

> 'Justice' was done, and the President of the Immortals, in Aeschylean phrase, had ended his sport with Tess.

When I ponder this, I do not feel it especially Aeschylean (though no doubt, some trigger for it comes from Aeschylus's work).

Sophoclean, yes: just so long as we ignore the tone of Hardy's irony; which seems to block out Sophocles's whole religious vision, with a blasphemy at which most pagans would have quaked.

Other commentators prefer to blame Oedipus. The killing of Laius, the marriage to Jocasta, were his deeds, whatever their contexts. The curse was his. Perhaps the gods simply foreknew, and offered the truth?

But other readers pursue the notion that the *Oedipus* plays mark (perhaps, indeed, help to bring about) a great 'modern' discovery: the importance of 'intention' to morality, and to judgments made by men (and even, by gods?) Before the fifth century BC, this view was rejected. By now, it is taken for granted; and how did it make its cultural way?

Oedipus himself does not draw self-exonerating conclusions (not explicitly; and not in *Oedipus Rex*). He accepts his 'pollution' when he knows it, as *fait accompli,* and take the 'guilt' fully on himself. Perhaps, in one sense, *this* is the play's major 'moral discovery'? – though, if so, it points an especially fateful parallel, for hindsight to note. Five centuries later, Christ was to bear the burden of sin, in orthodox Christian thinking; while being 'a man without sin' himself. This action was then to become the world's salvation: though virtually the whole world had seen it, at the time, as the richly deserved end of a blasphemer on the Cross. Oedipus nowhere, in this play, laments himself as a victim. But he does intuit that some *meaning for good* might lurk behind the horror; some suggestion that he is 'marked out' by the gods for a special, and unprecedented, design.

The relevant words come towards the play's ending, and are not picked out for special emphasis. Yet, given Sophocles's long life, with *Oedipus at Colonus* towards the end of it, we may justly pause over them; a great seed planted, perhaps, in this terrible soil?

> No longer let my living presence curse
> This fatherland of mine
>
> . . . .
>
> And yet I know,
> Nor age, nor sickness, nor any common accident
> Can end my life; I was not snatched from death
> That once, unless to be preserved
> For some more aweful destiny . . .

Is this Oedipus 'cheering himself up', in the only way possible? Hardly that; he has dealt with himself, and still does, harshly enough. 'Aweful' is, as always, a word combining awe with terror. The very idea of 'the holy' revolves around the close conjunction of the two. Against all hope, Oedipus utters a hope (more than a hope; a prophetic conviction) that the gods are not sporting, but are indeed working out a great, if dark and terrible, design.

Other readers have seen *Oedipus Rex* as a Kafkaesque drama, prefiguring modern man's doubts about his status (if any) in an apparently random world. Some have modified this towards a scheme which allows the gods to work out, justly, their own meanings and purposes, despite the total failure of human minds to discern what these are, or could conceivably be.

Children invent *tabus* (we know) and become obsessed by them (one must walk on the paving-stones only, never on the cracks between). All superstition supposes rules in the universe which seem 'irrational', but which we still guard against, with help from any oral traditions we have. How many of us turn over our coins, if we see a new moon through glass first; or try any strategem to steer critical interviews, or surgical procedures, away from Friday the thirteenth?

Even those of us who are 'above' such ordinary superstitions may make private compacts with the gods, at times of great need. Or we might adopt some trivial ritual, designed by ourselves for obscure reasons, which we observe (or avoid) as if all our luck were at stake.

Is life itself a chess-board; perhaps in several dimensions – with pieces whose rules are unknown to us, and whose end is predetermined in the lottery of birth?

Is life snakes-and-ladders on a board whose features are hidden; and whose moves rely on dice that we cannot control? Should we keep to the white squares of life only; avoiding the black, for dear life itself? Or does 'morality' toy with us, as we half-see yet also half-intuit it; the blind leading the blind? (a controlling image, of Oedipus's later life).

If we deviate from a pattern, does nemesis inevitably take us? – akin to the law which says, if we step off a cliff we die; whether we choose to take this step, or not?

Let us face this directly, and try not to flinch from it. The gods exist. They are great. They must be worshipped. Sophocles is as pious a pagan as we shall find, and tells the truth. To blame the gods is futile, as well as wicked. Where is our power-base? What are our sanctions, to offer against them? (even supposing, that we judge ourselves to be 'without guilt'). The gods will hear our curses, and record them; they will hear our supplications, and may or may not choose to help. They cannot be expected to bear with our merely human judgments, upon their far-off, Olympian decrees, and their own reasons and needs.

Fittingly, *Oedipus Rex* finishes with a speech from the Chorus which, distancing the action, becomes a general 'truth' for us all. No doubt, this is a supreme example of catharsis: that deep, psychological cleansing, which Aristotle thought of as the major, tragic effect:

> Sons and daughters of Thebes, behold: this was Oedipus,
> Greatest of men; he held the key to the deepest mysteries;
> Was envied by all his fellow-men for his great prosperity;
> Behold, what a full tide of misfortune swept over his head.
> Then learn that mortal man must always look to his ending,
> And none can be called happy until that day when he
> carries his happiness down to the grave in peace.

Much later in life, Sophocles wrote *Oedipus At Colonus*. In the event, it offers new perspectives upon the earlier play. Whether we ascribe this to old age in Sophocles, or to organic development, may depend upon our reading of the penultimate quotation I gave here from *Oedipus Rex*.

Oedipus, now blind and old, arrives in Colonus; where he is received at first with kindness, because of his plight. But when he becomes known by name, he is feared. Men shrink from him, and he is pursued by enmity. Much of this is fermented by Creon, whose malice is poisonous; but Oedipus has added his own self-curse to the curse of the gods.

As the play progresses, we become conscious of a profound change in Oedipus. The moral question left pending in *Oedipus Rex* as, at best, a mystery, is confronted now by Oedipus, and by the play itself. Oedipus has come to believe, in his exile and sufferings that, since he sinned unwittingly, he is *not truly guilty at all*. His anger remains (indeed, it has deepened in exile). But he is conscious that the deeds which pollute him cannot be laid at his door.

For some, this supports the view that 'motive' enters morality definitively, in *Oedipus At Colonus*, making Sophocles an important innovator in the distinction between 'intention' and 'act'. Oedipus does indeed feel that he has been reviled too long, and unjustly. He asserts, in the face of Creon, his accuser, a fierce and defiant defence:

> The gods so willed it – doubtless an ancient grudge
> Against our house. *My* life was innocent,
> Search as you will, of any guilty secret
> For which this error could have been a punishment,
> This sin that damned myself and all my blood.

Such insights are evidently important; but a deeper moral mystery unfolds, at the play's heart. In *Oedipus Rex*, Oedipus cursed himself as polluter of Thebes (and the Oracle confirmed this); and he decreed that the curse must follow him all his days, and wherever he goes. But in judging himself this harshly, as in the self-blinding, did grief and anger derange him; did 'punishment' loom in his mind, blocking out more complex and god-guided truths?

Now, he asserts a new understanding with the gods, acquired in exile; going beyond the tragic madness of the former play:

> Do you not think I read the state of Thebes
> With clearer eyes than yours? Surely, and why?
> I have more certain guidance, the true word
> Of Phoebus, and his mighty father, Zeus.

He has discovered that correct understanding of *what he is* requires another word: the word which, in another tragic crisis two and a half millennia later, Rudolph Otto would also assert, as perennial truth, discovered often in terror and fear:

> To 'keep a thing holy in the heart' means to mark it off by a feeling of peculiar dread, that is, to appreciate it by the category of the numinous. (*The Idea of the Holy*, 1917)

In all religions, even the Christian (or perhaps, especially the Christian), 'holiness' includes the awe, fear, terror of special selection by God. As Otto also remarks, it can be the fate of those who are denied the route to God by way of the Good, Beautiful and True (all of them very important to me, as will be apparent), to encounter, rather, that 'Mysterium Tremendum' which is at the heart of the strangeness, and the truth, of the wholly unshielded divine.

The missing word that Oedipus has discovered *is* holy. In the eyes of men he was cursed, with pollution and danger. But, alone with his sufferings, in his years in the wilderness, Oedipus has discovered something far deeper than a terrible but meaningless sport. He has been set apart by the gods, for a truly exceptional but also, a truly healing fate.

The cynics may call this 'rationalisation', and so it could be. But the action of the drama turns another way. As events unfold, Oedipus passes into the realm of mystery. He is destined to be not a curse, but a saviour, to the land where he is fated to die. Taking aside Theseus, the King, he reveals a mystery – a holy truth, to be told to the King alone. Later, it will be passed on by the King to his own heir, at the time of *his* death, and again as a secret – a mystery destined to protect the land which received Oepidus to the end of time.

This great play is no tragedy, after all. Against all expectation, it is the initiation of a mystery religion. It is Sophocles' exploration, in drama, of a pre-Christian religion, apart from, and transcending, the Olympian frame. The mystery initiated here has amazing resonances, for many who interpret Christ, to this day, in a similar sense.

Alone with Theseus, Oedipus passes on the secret. Then, to those standing by, a sign from the gods at last comes. 'It was wonderful', says the Messenger, upon whose report we depend. 'They wept, and clung together. And when they ended, there was a silence; until suddenly a Voice called him, a terrifying voice, at which all trembled and hair stood on end. A god was calling to him. "Oedipus, Oedipus!" it cried, again and again. "It is time. You stay too long". He heard the summons, and knew that it was from God'. And the account ends with the parting of Oedipus, the nature of which concludes the Messenger's tale:

> In what manner Oedipus passed from this earth, no one can tell. Only Theseus knows. We know he was not destroyed by a thunderbolt from heaven nor tide-wave rising from the sea, for no such thing occurred. Maybe a guiding spirit from the gods took him, or the earth's foundations gently opened and received him with no pain. Certain it is that he was taken without a pang,

> without grief or agony – a passing more wonderful than that of any other man.
>
> What I have said will seem perhaps, like some wild dream of fancy, beyond belief. If so, then you must disbelieve it. I can say no more.

The final chorus to this play contrasts strikingly with the end of *Oedipus Rex*, and in no sense points towards *Antigone*:

> This is the end of tears:
> No more lament.
> Through all the years
> Immutable stands this event.

The exact tradition (if any) behind this is a matter for search. A Christian will be struck by the story of Christ's final ascent 'in a cloud' to Heaven: and, though Sophocles is writing fiction, not history, his account makes my spine tingle, as the puzzling New Testament narrative never does. But far more deeply, the disparity between Oedipus's social reputation and his final destiny must appeal to Christians; along with the paradoxes of 'holiness' that set this play apart from others by the Greeks.

I have stressed that though Aeschylus and Sophocles are rightly called great and seminal Tragic Dramatists, both went beyond tragedy, in their greatest art. *The Eumenides* ends in celebration – older gods reconciled with new, social justice created; the 'Kindly Ones' led in triumph, at last, to a final home. *Oedipus At Colonus* ends with the apotheosis of Oedipus in a manner pointing tragedy itself towards the highest reaches of religious truth.

The Olympian gods, as we know, are not man's creators; they were by no means always his friends. At least once, in their earlier years of power, they were tempted to wipe men out; seeing human beings as experiments of the Titans that had turned out none too well.

The gods were immortal when compared with men, but not immortal absolutely. Like men, they 'bow to Necessity' in their own, larger scale. The Chorus in *Agamemnon* charts three known orders of gods, culminating in the present. 'The first of gods is gone, Old Ouranus, once blown/With violence and pride/His name shall not be known' . . . 'His strong successor, Cronos, had his hour,/ Then went his way, thrice thrown/By a yet strong power'. 'Now,

Zeus is Lord; and he/Who loyally acclaims his victory/Shall by heart's instinct find a universal key'. And they add:

> Zeus, whose will has marked for man
> The sole way where wisdom lies;
> Ordered one eternal plan:
> *Man must suffer to be wise*

V

What kind of reality, then, did the gods have? Were they 'poetic tales' at first, who were later 'abstracted' for dogmas? No. They were real powers. They required man's worship, intervened in men's lives, ruled men's affairs.

Consider, for instance, the chief gods of love. Both were women, both were huntresses: Aphrodite, the goddess of sexuality, and Artemis, goddess of the chaste. Both were beautiful, sweet, cruel, sometimes hideously destructive. Both could bring delight or torment, happiness or death.

Aphrodite demands that we acknowledge the erotic as power touched by divinity. Artemis demands that the erotic acknowledge other powers, touched with divinity, at the ground of our love.

But the Greeks knew that the gods 'really exist'; in the sense (among others) that sex, and chastity, are not mere aspects of any one 'self'. Aphrodite and Artemis are true powers, not expressions of allegory. They presided when our parents begot us (with luck, in harmony); just as they preside in what we lamely call 'our' sex-lives, today. They are not confined to any one man's psyche, nor are their laws special to his own little world. We encounter in them powers independent of us and free from our moulding, powers which moulded us, rather, and actually brought us to birth. Such powers, the Greeks believed, must be recognised, and reverenced fittingly. They must not be mistaken for quirks of 'our' inner life. Of all races, the Greeks best evaded the snare of psychic entrapment and reduction, to which post-Freudian psychology too often points its followers today. As deities, both Aphrodite and Artemis had a claim on man's loyalties. To withold dues from either was to risk madness or death. At one level, their power has its base in human nature, which can deny them only by attempting to deny itself. To deny Aphrodite is (in modern jargon) sexual repression. To deny

Artemis is compulsive addiction to sex. Aphrodite insists that we know ourselves as men, not as angels. Artemis insists that we know ourselves as men, not as brutes.[4]

The gods are real, and the Greeks had their names for them; they paid them dues, built them temples, lived in their sway. They also knew that their own names for the gods were their 'own names', precisely. For the Greeks, Zeus as head god was the ultimate father-figure. Athene, goddess of Athens, was chosen for her attribute, Wisdom, to inspire all Greece. Other nations might have their own names, and this mattered little; since the gods were themselves, and sought the best names that men could give. It is apparent that this approach bypasses the curses of most religion – dogma and sectarianism – and suggests that Athene is always an excellent goddess to woo.

As we have seen, the gods loved and guarded the Earth. There were gods for the household, gods for the cities, gods for every wood, grove, lake and natural place. There were gods associated chiefly with the elements (Poseidon with the Sea, Ceres with the Earth – corn and fruitfulness) just as there were gods associated with the great instincts, and with the great ideals. As long as worship was given, the Earth would be cared for; the inner life would be protected from chaos and harm. In normal times, the cities would know peace and the harvest would flourish. In war, the gods might help or hinder – though to their own plans, naturally, before those of men. The entire spectrum of political and psychic life was therefore encompassed, in a system which was religious at root, and pervasive through all human life.

Above all, the gods were true gods and must be truly worshipped. It is *a right balance between them* that brings order and wholeness to men. The great gods in particular are jealous and, if neglected, revengeful. You cannot deny Aphrodite or Artemis their dues, without inviting their wrath.

This system was understood chiefly as religion (it is religion): the lives of cities were in every way enriched by religious events. Great Temples were built, each reflecting order and beauty. Successful citizens might give an altar or even a Temple, to adorn their town. The gods were honoured in turn, the great gods at festivals; gods of the cities, the household, local cults, as their season came round. The god's image would be carried through the streets and through the assembled people, to be honoured with flowers, gifts, and whatever sacrifice tradition decreed.

The turning of Emperors and of certain 'great' men into gods was a later debasement; a sign that the inner genius of paganism and its customs was becoming diluted and lost. Still later, these great pagan instincts passed into other religions. Catholic processions, on saints' feast days, are the nearest we are likely to come now, to pagan 'holy-days'. Happily, the great cathedrals and arts of (mainly) Catholic and Orthodox Christianity, produced great palaces of beauty – where God's presence is experienced by many, through this wise and happy consecration of art.

The beauty of paganism was its comprehensiveness. It is this which we find in the great tragic writers, rightly calling them 'wise'. In Aeschylus, insights drawn from the gods led to great social discoveries; in Sophocles, they led to amazing psychological insights (as in *Electra* and *Philoctetes*), as well as to the mystical territory underlying the Oedipus plays. We cannot be surprised that our own century has rediscovered the Greeks as guiding spirits – putting their gods, and archetypes, to extensive and various psychic, and artistic, use. It is to be hoped that Greek wisdom will become increasingly important, to all who are trying to save our ravaged planet from destruction at this very late hour. The destruction was unleashed by iconoclasm, by greed, by human self-aggrandisement, all sanctioned by gross trends in the Christian Church. If Christians will return to Christ, we shall have a very immediate improvement. But pagan wisdom, though taking second place to Christ's Kingdom of Heaven in our personal quest for renewal, offers healing insights to all true friends of the Earth.

Perhaps the most distinctive impression made by the Greeks, on our century so far, is in the realm of psychology. Among the Tragic Dramatists, it was Euripides who was most acutely aware of this 'level'; and who left works that have been a major inspiration to Yeats, and Jung, and many poets, novelists and dramatists of our time.

VI

I still recall encountering Euripides in a Victorian version, which equated him with the Victorian agnostics, as a man rejecting his own pagan religion much as 'honest doubt' was, in their day, rejecting Christian 'faith'. As a supposed mocker of the gods he was even alleged to run in some subterranean tradition; culminating in figures like George Bernard Shaw.

From the earliest reading, it was clear to me that Euripides is as profoundly religious as his two great contemporaries, and differs chiefly in his dramatic technique. Possibly he brought to bear a youthful panache that can be mistaken for levity. Some of his own contemporaries found him 'cynical', too. If we require a modern parallel, I tend to look to figures such as Dean Inge, Bishop Barnes of Birmingham, Bishop John Robinson, and the (now retired) Bishop of Durham, David Jenkins. All these strike me as profound and courageous Christians, who have borne honest personal witness to Christ, despite the various dogmas flung around him by the Church. They have been suspected of heresy by those more concerned with the lies of the Church than with the truth of its Founder – and to this degree, fit the pattern of prophets who are more likely to be canonised 'outside' the Church than 'inside'. Among twentieth-century figures they rank among important Christian witnesses, scarcely less controversial than directly committed (politicised) figures such as Steve Biko, Martin Luther King, Bishop Desmond Tutu, Bishop Trevor Huddlestone, James Baldwin (and many more, most of whom we shall not even know by name). Euripides – an artist of genius, as well as a prophet – was a similar witness to pagan wisdom, in his time.

It is sometimes objected that Euripides' gods are cruel, and unhuman; as if such a depiction showed unbelief in itself. Is the reverse not true, rather? Aphrodite 'is' sex and sex is not kind, not 'human': the goddess is ecstatic and violent, she is bringer of sweetness and death. All true gods are ambivalent and must be, in a world made as ours is. The gods of Aeschylus and Sophocles have the same ambivalence as those of Euripides: readers of the plays we have already looked at, will not need reminders of this. (And would the Christian God ring true – to 'the world as it is', again – if one left out Christ's betrayal, mockery, crown of thorns, and Cross?)

Any problems the Victorians felt are post-Enlightenment problems, rooted though they may be in the ancient doctrine of 'original sin'. Why indeed do or should we expect 'good' as a norm for our instincts, and so for our gods, and their actions, and even for our own personal fate at their hands? There is little ground for this expectation in the real universe: and in seeing this, Greeks and moderns join with the truly clear-sighted, in all places and times.

The 'Where Am I?' questions, explored in my opening chapters, found us whirling in space, on a minor planet, bound from Big Bang to Black Holes. There is no 'law of love' apparent, in the Hawking universe – any more than there is in 'the survival of the fittest' which Darwin discerned as a general condition of life. The real problem, one must insist, is 'the problem of goodness'. To address this, we turn first, these days, to Christ's great teaching of the 'Kingdom of God' – to the wisdom of Christ and of his earliest followers, as we know them in New Testament Books. The Greeks offer much, but not this level of wisdom: how could they? In the main, they were highly sensitive pragmatists, inhabiting a universe where one cannot get past the Second Law of Thermodynamics ('Necessity', as they called it; 'change and decay', in still more homely terms). One needs a creation where our immediate universe is an inset in a wholly other larger reality, if one is to find laws 'in', but not 'of' the world, as Christ did. (We have seen that Sophocles approached such areas in *Oedipus at Colonus*, breaking past the Olympians. There are strong intimations of some ultimate transcendence in the Orphic mysteries, and in Plato also – whom I continue to leave aside, for a while.)

I have mentioned Aphrodite and Artemis as examples, of Olympian polarity: Euripides' *Hippolytus* comes aptly to mind. In this play, Hippolytus, the hero, worships one goddess exclusively. He chooses Artemis, and becomes her close disciple and friend. Both hunter and chaste, he is fanatically close to her cause. Unfortunately, he not only ignores but shuns Aphrodite – who accordingly, opens this play in person (as most Greeks might fear). Her ominous Prologue includes the general rule guiding her:

> Over all that see the light of the sun my rule extends.
> To those who reverence my powers I show favour,
> And throw to the earth those I find arrogant and proud.

This general programme she expands, with precise details of the plan she has chosen to be avenged upon Hippolytus, for his blasphemous stance. The plan involves the destruction of the totally and highly virtuous Phaedra (wife of Theseus, King of Athens, who fathered Hippolytus out of wedlock), who is to be the chief instrument in Hippolytus' disgrace and death. The plan also involves great suffering for Theseus himself, who is a secondary agent. It also involves a harsh fate for Phaedra's Nurse – a well-meaning, earthy character, rather new in Greek tragedy, whose last comments are a half-detached perspective with its own, wry pain: 'I tried to find a remedy for your trouble, and I was unlucky. With better luck, I would have been called a wise woman. After all, wisdom is only happening to guess right'. H'm.

Aphrodite has involved all these in her strategy, since she needs human agents: and the gods are not sparing, when deeply enraged.

Some critics have found this opening 'undramatic', because it removes the element of surprise (at least, from the basic plot). It serves, however, to underline the inexorable will of the gods; and the rules of harmony, which men cannot ignore without reaping the whirlwind to come.

Artemis, who is an off-stage presence at first, as Hippolytus' protector, takes no steps herself to thwart Aphrodite's revenge. Solidarity among the gods (even opposed ones), invariably overrides loyalties forged between a particular human and a god.

In modern terms, we might analyse Hippolytus as a rigid puritan, in whom sex is both repressed and reviled. As Artemis's 'favourite', convinced of his rectitude, he is a true fanatic, and open to the likely fate of such a temperament in all cultures and times. Shakespeare's Angelo in *Measure For Measure* lurks in the wings. Not unnaturally, Artemis accepts her disciple, and is proud of him. He enjoys the peculiar graces (cold, swift, haughty, noble) that she gives.

If Hippolytus expects the goddess's approval to extend to protection, he makes the mistake that all fanatics do, whatever their creed. Artemis allows Aphrodite's programme to unfold without any hindrance. Aphrodite's Prologue is wholly familiar to her (it could easily be her own also; and, in that she might avenge Hippolytus 'later', it actually is – as the unfortunate Theseus, and the dying Hippolytus, later hear from her lips). The Prologue is not a 'surprise' to her fellow gods, or to an alert Greek audience. The element of 'surprise' lies in the human psychology of the goddess' other victims (the Nurse, Theseus, and Phaedra herself). It is this psychology which Aphrodite first calculates, and then uses – in a way wholly unknown to them; but in no evident manner violating their sovereign freewill.

So Phaedra, who deserves no punishment and is guilty of nothing, is drawn in and destroyed – very simply, because she is there. To be in the wrong place at the wrong time is a classic formula for human misfortune; just as the reverse has sometimes been seen as the secret of all great human success. Aphrodite inspires Phaedra (not Hippolytus) with uncontrollable sexual desire – for her stepson: a horror that, starting in incredulous self-loathing, ends in disgrace and disaster, when the well-intentioned Nurse betrays her secret to Hippolytus, and so to the world.

The Nurse is a timeless portrait of a fairly normal human type. She is shocked at first by Phaedra's sickness, then intrigued by it; and in any event, determined to help. The thought, 'Why not? – such things happen' quickly takes over. Like many goodnatured, bossy, stupid people she interferes, with the best of intentions, and with no notion of what truly complex people are apt to be like.

Phaedra, finding herself betrayed, kills herself; but not before taking revenge on the unwitting object of her love. She leaves a note falsely accusing Hippolytus of dishonouring her. Theseus, devastated by his wife's suicide, reads and believes the note. Without further enquiry, he utters a curse on Hippolytus – the curse of King, and Father (like that of Oedipus). By the time Theseus has learned the truth and repented, it is too late to act; but what action could help, when the curse is once put into words? Hippolytus, attempting to flee into exile, has been fatally wounded in a fearful chariot incident – brought about by the gods (we know), in answer to Theseus' curse.

Hippolytus lives long enough to have a final, affecting reconciliation with Theseus, in a scene which balances whatever colder impressions we have formed of him, before. Theseus has been told of his son's impending death by Artemis, who now enters in person, when her major role is past. Artemis speaks not with compassion or even with sorrow but in a manner emphasising Theseus's threefold guilt, and her own, neutral role, as a god.

The play ends with praise from the Chorus for the 'nobility', both of Theseus and Hippolytus; a view echoed by Theseus, though he is himself broken by this strange drama stagemanaged by the gods.

What judgements do we make on the humans; are judgements possible? Are they mere puppets, in a drama they cannot control?

The obvious answer is that the humans are free; and exalted; and noble; moral judgements are therefore appropriate, and must be made.

The most treacherous deed is undeniably Phaedra's, when she falsely accuses Hippolytus of rape. Is she a woman scorned, or a woman distraught; is she mad, even? The lust is 'entirely' her own; even though it fell on her, outside her seeking. Her own reaction is horror and self-loathing, a fearsome self-judgement which is merely compounded by her total failure to control the passion. Her attempt to confide in the Nurse is basic therapy; the Nurse's fatal meddling leaves her exposed, and with no option but to die.

But why does she not die nobly; is she not truly responsible for her treachery? To accuse Hippolytus (of all men) of rape – and that falsely – is revenge against her unfortunate victim, of a monstrous kind. Is she desperately attempting to exonerate herself, posthumously; exchanging her reputation for his, in a final throw? Or does 'love' turn to hate, turning her murderous, as Love unrequited and shameful is apt to do? Whatever we feel, her 'nobility' is buried with her. All the virtue she strove for is wrecked, beyond redress.

In a similar way, we weigh our judgement of Theseus: should he have uttered his curse, without pondering at least on possible errors or maybe, even consulting a god? His love of his wife – of her beauty and virtue, up to their ending – convince him completely. (Did it also cross his mind, that Hippolytus' chastity had been too good to be true?)

The Nurse offers a perspective of great interest: her 'classless' instinctive reaction would be nodded through, by many, in all centuries; and seems 'common sense' in a major battleline still, as I write. Should we see her as normal; honest; loyal – sweeping hypocritical cant away, when her mistress needs love, and only convention says 'no'? Or is she totally blind to the higher morality of sensitive people; to the degree that 'honour' must rule such higher natures (and, for some, very naturally, crosses all boundaries of class and of change?). What is clear is that she has no understanding of Hippolytus, or of Phaedra. She meddles and wrecks, as such people are destined to do. In some moods, we might wish she were right, and that life could be 'solved' by her. More normally, we are glad to place her as wrong.

Yet that other perspective: the one that is 'higher' than human: what are we to say of the part played, in all this, by the gods? For Aphrodite, the action – and judgement – involves only Hippolytus. He has defied her divinity, and must suffer; along with whatever agents are most appropriately to hand.

A perennial fascination is to be found in Aphrodite's planning: which is why the Prologue, thought undramatic by some, 'is' the drama itself. Touching her power, the goddess has no special problem. She can invade and destroy whom she will, since this is her right. But she also calculates the free reactions of Phaedra; and presumably gambles (feels certain?) that Phaedra will be broken enough to act as she does. She calculates also the free reaction of Theseus; and, again, assesses that his curse will, duly, be made. We have to assume, I think, that Aphrodite is not predestinating; and that a power such as that is not hers to use. Rather, the calculation is that of Euripides. In offering these intuitions to Aphrodite, as human artist, he reveals to us, surely, much of himself?

We ponder again the 'truth': *is* the outcome inevitable? Might Phaedra have died, taking the blame, letting Hippolytus off this baited hook? Might Theseus have reacted more wisely ('acted in character', even?): or was his curse, too, a virtually certain affair?

Before the play is through, Artemis makes one further contribution, another turn of the screw in Euripides' distinctive world. Artemis has already explained the primary cause of her own inaction, in words which, to Theseus, can come as cold comfort at best: 'Your sin is great. Yet even you may still find pardon for what you have done. For it was Aphrodite who, to satisfy her resentment, willed that all this should happen; and there is a law among gods, that no one of us should seek to frustrate another's purpose, but *let well alone*' (my italics). 'I tell you', she goes on, 'but that I fear Zeus and his laws, I never would have submitted to such dishonour, as to stand by and see Hippolytus go to his death; for he was dearest to me of all mortals.'

The 'well' that has been left alone includes the fate also of Phaedra, Theseus, the hapless Nurse even; but these do not come into Artemis's tale. We find, before we are through, that Artemis does promise an act of vengeance on behalf of Hippolytus, in a manner that confirms some in the view that Euripides is, indeed, 'a mocker of the gods'. Though there was nothing that Artemis could do to help on this occasion, she promises a future 'revenge against Aphrodite' when she finds the chance. This will come when some other unsuspecting (ill-advised?) human worships Aphrodite, with the same exclusiveness that Hippolytus herself offered to Artemis. Then, it will be Artemis (presumably) who appears, to speak a similar Prologue; and another victim, and his or her closest family and associates, who will bear the brunt of Artemis's psychological calculations and her planned attack. 'You need not curse' she assures the broken Hippolytus, and Theseus, (surely belatedly?) . . .

> Not even the black depths
> Beneath the earth shall thwart the vengeance due
> For this cruel wrong that Aphrodite's rage
> Wreaked on your body for your pure soul's sake.
> I will requite her: with this unfailing bow
> My own hand shall strike down in just return
> The man her heart holds dearest in the world.

In the course of the play, our sympathies will have veered between the characters; though our attention is chiefly absorbed in events themselves. Have the two goddesses been agents of vendetta, thereby sporting with mortals; or have they been prophets of human psychology as it is, and always will be? The 'inevitability' felt in any human work of art is partly technical. But beyond that, we award the accolade of 'greatness' when the artist's plot corresponds, as we sense, to deep and abiding truths.

It would be shallow to suggest that the mechanism of 'justice' which humans evolved, and Aeschylus celebrated, has yet to spread back – according to Euripides – to the gods themselves. The gods *are* the powers which create; they are not 'moral' agents. Their truth, for our purposes, is their 'truth' to the human scene, as we know it ourselves. We are aware, I think, that *Hippolytus* embodies a universal human truth, in the great Greek tradition. The gods are powers who must all be worshipped as gods, none neglected or slighted. Here, lies the path of harmony. Elsewhere, there are many abysses, and a certain fall.

It is equally true that the innocent suffer, as well as the 'guilty', when a whole situation rides out of human control. The human psyche is complex, the pitfalls innumerable. Our judgements on this or that agent are necessary and inescapable; but they are not, and cannot be, of the essence. Judgements come to a mire and may sink, along with ourselves. Wisdom alone can guide us, in times of chaos; but wisdom comes from watching and heeding the ways of the gods.

It seems clear to me that, by challenging towards an adverse view of the gods (even among his first audience), Euripides forces a precise and disturbing reappraisal of 'psychological' truth.

In Aeschylus's dramas, the gods have a profound part to play in social balance; however odd their ways may seem, if we miss this fact. In Euripides, they have a central role in psychic cohesion – and their 'cruelties' are a perception of truths which very specially link 'our' century with the fifth century BC. Both of these dramatists explore great truths, of unchanging relevance. Both are healers: though Euripides is the more zany (the more youthful?) of the two.

Later, in his pseudo-classical play *Phèdre*, Racine rehandled the story of *Hippolytus*, to throw tragic emphasis on the afflicted heroine, and her fatal *'flamme'*. Euripides' basic plot turns up also in numerous modern dramas; sometimes, with the classical references explicit, more usually not. For some of us, the truths are chiefly 'psychological' and social, in some deadly conjunction. If religious enigmas are not part of the equation, other forces of determinism or irony (genetic; medical or the like) may feature instead.

A man like Hippolytus is bad news for all of us. Chastity, with fanatical rectitude and highly developed egotism allied to it, cannot make for social ease. We may call it 'repression', finding the hero part-victim, and foreseeing for him some massive explosion of the kind Aphrodite wills, yet also foresees, in Euripides' play. Likewise, a passion like Phaedra's is inherently destructive and tragic. If it gives rise to pity, this is our human reaction. What is certain, is that it will end in chaos, and fear.

Euripides offers the spectacle of two excesses clashing, in a context where the gods not only rule, but also heal, if men can, by some miracle of virtue, also be wise.

Hippolytus is a play for all seasons as, too, is *The Bacchae*. The two plays are similar in structure, and both achieve universality in truth. Possibly *The Bacchae* has a special, added relevance, to the decade we are now living in; and indeed, to our whole troubled century from 1914 onwards: with Sarajevo as a strange, current link.

In *The Bacchae*, Apollo and Dionysus frame the action, but Apollo is felt, not seen, as the tension builds. The 'dark god' speaks the Prelude (as Aphrodite did, in *Hippolytus*). He wants vengeance for personal slights he has variously suffered; and proposes an apotheosis of himself, as god, through an unleashing of chaos that, in the Prelude, he broadly outlines. Then, disguised as a human, he becomes an actor himself, in his own drama – where the victims are to experience his power, most fully, in their own, hidden depths.

Dionysus is older, in legend, than the Olympian ascendancy, but this is an aspect that need not detain us here. He has come among the Olympians, in the manner we hear of; and his credentials are to be asserted inside the Olympian system we have come to know.

He has come to Thebes 'first' since the women there, his mother's sisters notably, have dared to question his mother's account of her rape by Zeus, leading to his own birth. They have scandalously suggested that Semele 'lost her virginity' is the normal manner, and threw the blame on Zeus to get herself off the hook. We must bear in mind that these women also, and not only Pentheus, are marked out for punishment, and a terrible fate. Their doom is to become Dionysus's own most fanatical followers and, as 'Bacchae', to exemplify his worship in quintessential and wholly unbalanced excess.

At the same time, Pentheus, the present King of Thebes (and

grandson of Cadmus, who was Semele's father) is conducting a defiant assault on the Bacchic cult in his land. Dionysus's prime purpose is to 'prove' his godhead beyond any further doubting. His plan is to concentrate a show of strength against Pentheus personally, but in doing so, to punish his present followers for their libels once spread against his mother and against his own divine birth. The centre is, therefore, to be found in these words:

> Thebes must learn, unwilling though she is, that my Bacchic revels are something beyond their present knowledge and understanding; and I must vindicate the honour of my mother Semele, by manifesting myself before the human race as the god whom she bore to Zeus.

The main target is to be Pentheus – who, though not explicitly a worshipper of Apollo to the exclusion of other gods, is a man whose puritanism takes the form of obsessive mistrust of instincts, in favour of order and form.

> And this Pentheus is a fighter against God – he defies me, excludes me from libations, never names me in prayer. Therefore I will demonstrate to him, and to all Thebes, that I am a god.

The instrument of punishment will naturally be his own followers – who have become so totally enslaved to his revels, that they have lost all saving perspective; in the manner that Pentheus, also, is now fated to do:

> my mother's sisters said – what they should have been the last to say – that I, Dionysus, was not the progeny of Zeus; but that Semele, being with child by some mortal, at her father's suggestion ascribed to Zeus the loss of her virginity; and they loudly insisted that this lie about the fatherhood of her child was the sin for which Zeus had struck her dead. Therefore I have plagued these same sisters with madness, and driven them all frantic out of doors; now their home is the mountains and their wits are gone . . .

Though Apollo does not appear in the play, he is Dionysus's natural opposite: the god of Light, Structure, Order, Music, against the 'dark god' of Instinct (dreams; inspiration; intoxication; infatuation;

hallucination; madness; excess). The presiding god at the Greek Tragic Festivals was in fact Dionysus; but Apollo was honoured also, as the twin god of art.

As with Aphrodite and Artemis, the opposites might, again, be mistaken for twins. Both Apollo and Dionysus are handsome, sweet, cruel, sometimes hideously destructive. Both bring delight or torment, happiness or death. Both are closely associated with creativity and the creative process, since they 'are' the polarities between which creation occurs. There must be craftsmanship, structure, technique, dedication in artistic creation; there must be power, passion, the fullness of 'life' in all its aspects, light and dark. Since great art must be the marriage of these opposites, their gods are interdependent, though polarised. Both must have libations and reverence equally, in the true Greek way.

Perhaps if Apollo sought revenge, it might be my making men pedants; by creating places like Dickens' Coketown, in *Hard Times*? In this play, our attention is focused intensively on Dionysus. If Apollo is also palpably present, he exists at least as much in Euripides' own art – the dramatic structuring – as he does in his Olympian status as Dionysus' polar twin.

The action concerns the god's homing-in on Pentheus. For this purpose, Dionysus is disguised as a young man of Bohemian charm, of precisely the kind whom Pentheus most mistrusts. 'Not one of us; away with him' is the gut-instinct; Pentheus goes further, determined to root out the upstart himself, and his whole scandalous cult.

We recognise Pentheus's age-old, puritan reflex; but the dark god is not easily displaced. Relentlessly, Dionysus probes the 'dark-side' lurking *in* Pentheus – the god's own 'home territory', to be found as much in his enemies as in his friends. He tempts Pentheus insidiously, posing as a half-ally; no doubt, Pentheus will want to see 'near at hand' the things he abominates, further to stir up his own, righteous rage? Certain long-repressed desires and fantasies are conjured up, in more lurid detail. Pentheus is played on first through 'disgust', then through 'curiosity' (a very near neighbour); finally, by compulsions long pent up, now stirred and coloured by Dionysus in person; who well judges that the deeper Pentheus's original repulsion is, the more useful as a 'thin edge' it is certain to be. Pentheus is worked on by an expert, with basic powers of hypnosis; he little thinks he is in the hands of the 'true god' himself.

The unfortunate Pentheus is lured to walk the streets, disguised as a woman: supposedly, to spy on the Bacchae, to attain full knowledge; and so, both to increase, and assist, his own natural disgust. Inevitably, the plan, once agreed, takes hold of him. There is a seminal direction in the text, reading: 'From now on, Dionysus gradually establishes a complete ascendancy over Pentheus'.

It is not my purpose to recount the events in detail. This is a play that readers of a book such as this cannot fail to read, or reread. We must keep in mind that the Bacchic women are as much the god's victims as is Pentheus – for, though his worshippers now, they slandered him earlier; and therefore, they are to be led into typical, yet specially terrible, excess. Their acceptance of Dionysus as a true god, rightly worshipped, tips over into a mirror-image of the exclusive devotion paid to Artemis, by Hippolytus, in our previous play.

The apotheosis, described by a Messenger, is truly terrifying. Pentheus and the Bacchae alike pass under the hypnotic spell cast by the god; and from there to madness; and to the appalling denouement, of which we hear. Pentheus is torn limb from limb by the frenzied women (including his own mother's sister, Agaue). It is only when the frenzy abates, along with the illusion of their own godhead that goes with it, that the women discover what, in fact, they have done. They had supposed themselves to be caught up in a state of joy and innocence; they had imagined they were dismembering a sacrifical beast. At the last, the wretched Pentheus pleaded with his aunt for mercy, but she did not know him. She was immersed in the all-consuming ritual of ecstasy, which was also death. 'Agaue was foaming at the mouth, her eyes were rolling wildly. She was not in her right mind; she was under the power of Dionysus . . .'.

In this manner, Dionysus has a complex revenge, and achieves his epiphany: his own comment is 'Behold me, a god great and powerful, Dionysus, son of Zeus and Semele!' Thebes, the city which has 'mocked his divinity', is punished: 'The royal house is overthrown; the city's streets are full of guilty fear, as every Theban repents too late for his blindness and blasphemy'. The present king is also singled out for a peculiar punishment (the details here are obscure, harking back to Dionysian traditions predating the Olympian frame of the play). Dionysus rubs in his victory, saying that 'they have left recognition of him too late for repentance', and adding: 'If you had chosen wisdom, when you would not, you would have found the son of Zeus your friend, and would now be happy'. The play concludes with a brief, enigmatic Chorus which both distances the play, and passes it on from its own age and culture to 'all time':

> Gods manifest themselves in many forms,
> Bring many matters to surprising ends;
> The things we thought would happen do not happen;
> The unexpected God makes possible:
> And that is what has happened here today.

The central truth of *The Bacchae* needs little exegesis. We have seen the rending excesses of released repression, when the power by which it held finally snapped. When I was young, Hitler's youth set out on an adventure, some in joy and innocence; the denouement in the gas-chambers followed all too soon. The mix of military goose-step and manic rhetoric at Hitler's rallies, is an image that grows more, not less vivid, with the passing years. I speak for myself: the events were in childhood years, at the time half-registered. The denouement was in my schooldays, when much knowledge came under pressure, along with the bombs. Those younger than me know these events, if at all, as history. It is to be hoped that Dionysus does not have to produce similar epiphanies for every new age.

In the 1960s, 'youth culture' and (briefly) 'flower-power' were a splendid episode. They swept away repressions and hypocrisies long due for nemesis. On this occasion, Dionysus came as saviour (in Euripides' words, he was 'a friend'): and the restoration of balance was achieved, this time, from the 'dark god's' side. Even so, a culture of drugs and excess entered the pattern, bringing its own foreseeable nemesis, for those going too far.

Our century has speeded up, and lost its directions; the 'Greek' checks and balances happen, but we reduce them to 'trends'. A great mind like Jung's could (more or less) ride the tumult – uniting 'light' and 'dark' in complex myths resembling the Greek (and often, closely akin). But for most of us, and for much of the time, the pattern is hidden. We veer from acceptance to denial. Victims of excess, in whatever direction, become new stumbling-blocks, new signals for another dramatic change. That basic Greek instinct for poise, embodied in so much buoyant wisdom, gives way to an endless veering – from repression, to excess, to repression, as new 'trends' appear.

Apollo and Dionysus – both gods; both requiring worship: in harmony giving art, giving peace, giving happy relationships; in disharmony, giving all that negates order in life. Are such great simple insights – won by the Greeks in art that has the power of scripture – really as elusive to our 'leaders' and 'opinion formers', two and half millennia later, as they currently seem?

The Greek wisdom should be easy to grasp, and for long periods has seemed so. It requires no great virtue or intellect, to find the sense in it. We have an ancient wisdom – evolved by the Greeks, refined by great artists and philosophers, long proved in practice – which has the advantage of according, also, with quite simple 'common sense'.

We do not need the Greek names for their gods, the Greek system as a whole, to help us. The matter does not hinge on nostalgia for some supposedly golden period, lost in the past. It is a perception that all basic instincts and elements are holy, and must be respected; that they must balance each other, and not run, through loss of proportion, out of control. Pared down in this way, we have at least a formula; which culture and civilisation can build on, and keep in repair. If we further adopt the Greek principle of reverence, and some awareness of the complex, we shall be inside the mainstream of European culture at most subsequent times.

The Greek wisdom addresses very practical questions. How are we to avoid the trap of self-destruction lurking in too rigid order (repression; bureaucracy; tyranny . . .), without tipping over into the self-destruction of total abandon – without rules, without love? To deny Dionysus is to risk being like Pentheus and, one way or another, dwindling in rigidity, or exploding, if the repression finally fails. To embrace Dionysus wholly, without the dues proper to Apollo also, is to fall into complulsive sexuality, or drug addiction, or gambling, or any other compulsion – or, like the Bacchic Women in the play, into madness itself.

In *The Bacchae,* Euripides achieves a perfect image, in that we see those who court one fate (Pentheus) destroyed by those courting the other (the Bacchae themselves). The Greeks knew that there are times and seasons for instinct, times and places for restraint, in an ordered whole. The alternations are similar to those in Christian feasts, and fasts. They knew further that both sides of the equation are divine, and must be judged so; and that balance is the secret of civilised wholeness and health. This applies equally to the body politic, and to the inner balance which we now call 'psychological'. Its *fons and origo* is and must be religious – whatever 'names' for the deities we give them, or they accept as their own.

Only a continual balance of opposites can produce health and wholeness. In art, it is always a union of technical excellence with the deepest passion and instinct, that produces the works which, in whatever medium, move us most. Their fashions and styles vary greatly, and this is natural and vital; but any failures of structure, or of passion, and art will fail. In personal life, our deepest love goes always with structure and discipline: perhaps, with a social model, like marriage – perhaps with a personal model, appropriate to ourselves.

I am amazed to hear so much talk of 'sex and violence', as though these two states were in some way destructive, and linked. Sex goes ideally with love, with shared lives and destinies, with mutual sharing and happiness; if it joins with violence, it is clearly doomed from the start. 'Violence' is a true evil, the denial of order. But it kills not only sex: it kills and corrupts all it touches – our social politics and economics and whole system of values; our inner world, whether that be of psychic turmoil, or of stasis.

In daily living, we rightly mistrust both negative chastity, and restless compulsions that give their victims no let up or rest. We know that some union of opposite powers is required, above all for marriage; but also, for friendship, for neighbourhood harmony, for smooth relations at 'work'. We know that these frameworks bring joy in themselves, and relief from the loneliness that so readily follows when the basic structures of society crumble and fall.

All of this is available in Greek Tragedy: the two great plays most recently looked it, bring the truths home, to our inner lives and hearts.

Yet regard our society: and I speak now of Britain; and the years of my own adult life, since the Second World War. Our educational system has veered backwards and forwards between repressive discipline, insensitive to individual needs and aptitudes; and a progressive free-for-all, insensitive to structure and to the cultural disciplines themselves. The correct balance – obvious as always, to all 'natural' teachers – has eluded our politicians, bureaucrats, 'experts', with disastrous results.

Then consider our economy itself, in its very essence. It has veered from an idealistic social vision of 'equal opportunity', to an amazing monetarist reaction and free-for-all. The former ideal mutated to 'egalitarianism', leading to denials of talent, and to penal taxation (over 90 per cent at worst) levied on the very people most needed to make the system work. The reaction against it has been unrestrained greed, seen as sole motive-force for 'expansion'; and then, to the emergence of a reverse-Robin-Hood state, where the poor are plundered, to give to the rich.

Such excesses (paralleled in the chaos of social life, with its similar switchbacks), would have left any normal pagan gasping for breath. Not every member of the audience in Athens would have understood fully; but the main drift of their great tragic drama, with its truth and importance, would have been to most spectators very clear. The Olympian worship was not perfect in its long centuries, any more than the Christian now is. Both tolerated evils that we today find amazing (slavery; a low role for women; many others): yet the Greeks had the seeds of civilised living at their core – and the power to achieve harmony in their body politic which extended, also, to every aspect of life. We have seen Aeschylus charting, and perhaps assisting, the momentous shift from naked blood-vengeance, to a system of Justice administered impartially, by Law. We have seen Sophocles charting the point where 'intention' became recognised, and important, in moral judgments; and then intuiting religious mysteries where polluter and saviour might merge in high, and transcendent, truths known to the gods.

And what are we to say, today, of our unfortunate planet? Wrecked lives, wrecked social institutions, yes; but a wrecked planet? – Can this really be true?

I shall return to the implications for Earth later; and to the wreck that its present stewards – ourselves – have made of it.

But I cannot exonerate the Christian Churches from blame, in the whole wrecked spectrum. They were told to leave 'the things of Caesar to Caesar': they were not told to allow Caesar to rule the Church in place of Christ. When sexual actions are still judged by arbitrary rules, devised by priests and prelates, it is small wonder that happy relations between adults can be denounced as 'sinful' simply because they exist in other, often needed and natural, frames. Nor is it odd that disastrous marriages, loveless liaisons, once these have been sealed with priestly blessing, may be applauded as 'good', irrespective of the misery they cause, and the social sourness they spread. The radical failure of the Christian Church to be rid of Pentheus, has its fated nemesis in distorted, bacchic patterns that emerge, in our general society, instead.

I shall return again, to certain wider implications; but these reflections come insistently to mind, in the context here. We cannot revisit the Greek Tragic Dramatists without reflecting, that they have seldom spoken more urgently and relevantly, than they do, in the 1990s, to our own, stricken world.

VII

Such reflections return me to my own theme, for a moment: the kind of 'reality' in which the Fifth Dimension, human consciousness, exists.

The Olympians offer wisdom on various levels, but they belong to the realm I am calling 'clock-time'. The Olympian gods are not the creators of everything; and they are not truly immortals. Their power is real; but it is encompassed by death and decay.

The Second Law of Thermodynamics is relevant, in a modern assessment of the place their great wisdom has. The gist of the Second Law (for which I go yet again to Hawking) is that 'one can create order out of disorder (for example, one can paint the house), but that requires expenditure of effort or energy and so decreases the amount of ordered energy available'. The result is 'that in any closed system disorder, or entropy, always increases with time'.

From this, Hawking reminds us that time as we know it in the space/time continuum moves only forwards. We 'remember' the past, not the future – as we should do, if time were reversed. So: when you drop a cup and saucer it smashes, and this is irrevocable. The broken thing is lost for good. In a reverse flow of time, broken objects would fly together, creating the original; as they seem to do if you run a film backwards, of course. Hawking goes, from here, to speak of 'the arrow of time', or 'time's direction':

> The increase of disorder or entropy with time is one example of what is called the arrow of time, something that distinguishes the past from the future, giving a direction to time. First, there is the thermodynamic arrow of time, the direction of time in which disorder or entropy increases. Then, there is the psychological arrow of time. This is the direction in which we feel time passes, the direction in which we remember the past, not the future. Finally, there is the cosmological arrow of time. This is the direction of time in which the universe is expanding rather then contracting. (Stephen Hawking, *A Brief History of Time*, p. 145)

The wisdom of the Olympians belongs with that of other religions (is Buddhism among these?) which are ultimately compatible with the extinction of all things made, including ourselves. 'Even the gods bow to Necessity' marks an utmost limit. In English poetry, perhaps Pope's brilliant invention of 'the goddess of Dulness' in *The Dunciad* comes closest to the thought. Much of the poem is dated, on account of its satire; but the conclusion is a brilliant image of Necessity (Entropy?) reaching its very last gasp:

> Lo! Thy dread Empire, Chaos! is restor'd;
> Light dies before thy uncreating word;
> Thy hand, great Anarch! lets the curtain fall;
> And Universal Darkness buries All.

We can find much that we need, today, from the Olympians. Our environmental crisis cries aloud for pagan resurgence, if only to bring reverence for Earth, Air, Fire and Water to the front of our minds.

But what we cannot find in the Olympian Hierarchy is any answer to the original questions, which our very deepest intuitions crave, and in times of crisis need. Who are we? Where are we? Why are we? Where are we heading? Except in vague nods towards Hades, the Olympians are silent on these.

I am arguing that the 'now' in which we live is a major mystery; and that though it is 'in' clock-time, it is not 'of' it, when rightly appraised. At any given moment, as we move towards death, following the arrow of Entropy, our attention might switch from one Janus-face of time to the other, in our mysterious dance towards a city we have lost, and are endlessly striving to find.

Inside clock-time, we indeed move forwards – from conception and birth, and on through as many of Shakespeare's 'seven ages of man' as we survive. Mortality is the inexorable rule in this progress: but, when we ponder our 'now' as the still point of our consciousness, we encounter a dimension not inside the space/time continuum at all. Here, time does flow backwards – from the future, through the present, into the past.

Augustine pointed out, however, that the future does not exist, the past does not exist, and the present is so fleeting that it cannot be said to 'exist' either, in any true sense. What he was saying – and T.S. Eliot explores it in *Four Quartets* with unparalleled resonance – is that 'this' time-scale is outside space/time, and so outside its laws. 'We' remain in the present, never leaving it. As I pointed out in Chapters 2 and 3, there is no more possibility of getting 'five minutes into the future', than there is of getting 'five minutes into the past'. We remain in the present as long as we are conscious and, inside this present, our entire consciousness, and reality, exists.

For light on this, we need prophets, artists, mystics, psychic and paranormal explorers; and so, we must turn to oracles differing from those which have engaged us, here, with the Greeks.

But the Greeks do have a mystical tradition, running parallel with the Olympians, and criss-crossing with more ancient traditions, half-surviving alongside them, it sometimes seems. *Oedipus At Colonus* has been our closest encounter, in this chapter, with this other more shadowy, and inaccessible, world. The Orphic mysteries are at the heart of them; but certain of the great philosophers are also congenial, to those of us drawn towards the mystic path.

I shall come in my next chapter to Christ's 'Kingdom of Heaven', which I regard as a revelation apart. It is the greatest revelation mankind has ever received, or ever can receive; since it concerns a Kingdom wholly outside space/time – outside space/time's 'worldly' human laws, and its cosmic 'laws' of thermodynamics – yet intimately at home; and eternal; and healing *in our own human hearts*.

But first, there must be a brief note on the Greek philosopher, and his great second century AD follower, without whom this discussion of paganism would rightly seem like *Hamlet* without the Prince. I make no attempt to discuss Plato at length, since this is well-trodden ground, and far less important to our present situation than Olympian wisdom. Plato does contribute, however, to Christian thinking, both for good and evil; and it is to this aspect that I turn.

VIII

Plato was scornful of Olympus and its deities, as dialectic philosophers often are. His own god belonged with 'Reason', in the definition which he gave the word; and with the 'eternal intimations' that Reason contains. Luckily, the Orphic mysteries influenced him, with their transcendental deities, and their intimation of a human destiny not confined to 'this' world.

Plato was a seminal philosopher, who has proved happily irrepressible. Of all the Greeks, *pace* Aristotle (and Aristotle's late disciple, Aquinas), he has had the most influence upon general Christian tradition, in the two millennia that the religion (the religions?) attached to Christ have so far survived.

I am not a theologian, and steer clear of the worst tangles; but I should be surprised (let me put this moderately) if John, and Paul, and most of the New Testament writers were not cross-fertilised by Plato, whose ideas were in the air. Unless we assume this, several major insights must have originated simultaneously, in parallel cultures. This is not impossible, but direct influence seems much more likely, among literate, widely travelled contemporaries, living in the same part of the world.

The Christians called Greek wisdom 'folly', severely playing down pagans; but this was most likely a mixture of Pauline paradox, and the sheer weirdness of 'early Fathers' and 'desert Fathers' shortly to come. By the time that the Greek gods had been turned into devils, and the pagans consigned to hell as a job-lot, little sense could be expected from the Christian camp.

The influence of Plato was no unmixed blessing; but it was mainly beneficial at the start. I have in mind Plato's conviction of a divine stamp on the world, and on humans particularly; his belief in the human soul's eternal origin, and nature; and the intimations of immortality which he found in creation. St John's Gospel is based on The Word made flesh, come to dwell among us: this high perception (Incarnation; Logos) centres in Christ, but has clear affinities with Plato's 'Beauty, Goodness and Truth'. These great attributes are specially found in Christ, as unique Incarnation – yet their power spills over, by the Spirit, to all who are grafted 'in' him. For the church, the 'grafting' became exlusive, and linked to Baptism. But, as I have said already, Christ's own view was wider, embracing all those, both before and after him in human history, who did 'the Father's' works.

In addition, Plato emphasises the supreme value of discipline, of purity, of steadfast pursuit of spiritual knowledge; and here, he is in entire agreement with Paul. No doubt, he would have agreed unreservedly with the great text in *Philippians*, which is the definitive charter for any and all education worthy the name:

> whatsoever things are true, whatsoever things are honest, whatsoever things are just, whatsoever things are pure, whatsoever things are lovely, whatsoever things are of good report; if there be any virtue, and if there be any praise, think on these things. (*Philippians* 4: 8)

If these words had been inscribed on every university, school and educational institution in Christendom; and if they had been faithfully followed (as they still might be?), we should have been spared the appalling shambles that education currently is.

It is unfortunate, therefore, that Plato's gnostic division of man into two parts – one 'good' (the soul), the other illusory (the body) – was far less healing in its cultural effect. This severe divide encouraged that excessive fear of the body which Christians, from the later first century onwards, fell prey to; and which led by seemingly inexorable steps to the austerities of the 'desert Fathers' and other ascetic loners of their kind. It either infected, or intensified, the early church's tug towards puritanism; and has persistently damaged every branch of Christendom since. I can find no evidence of such an attitude in Jesus himself, in any gospel account. There is much to suggest that Jesus enjoyed laughter, good fellowship, drink and feasting in their proper seasons, even attracting the reputation of a 'wine-bibber', a friend of prostitutes, a sabbath-breaker, from the religious leaders who conspired his death.

It seems encouraging that St Paul was largely untouched, also, by negative moralism – though one admits that sex was not his *forte*, and that numerous women (and some men) could get gratingly on his nerves. In *I Corinthians* 15, he asserts the inalienable unity of soul, mind and body, as an entity coming from God, and returning to God. This unity asserts not some amazing juggling trick on the 'last day' to bring ashes, dust, bones and the rest together in a huge spectacular, but the *unique individuality* of humans, sealing each one of us as eternal, precious and irreplaceable, in the sight of God. It is a union which places the body, as we know it on earth, in relation to our eternal destiny, 'in and out of time'.

Naturally, the defects of the body (genetic or environmental) will not be 'resurrected'; nor will its ageing, and the other depradations of time. But our body, however grotesque, is a 'casket' now holding us. And, however far removed from our 'real self' it may be in this earthly exile, it does bear some true resemblance to our eternal being. Paul gives the assurance that the resurrection will be of 'we' ourselves, as 'we' fully are and as others have known us; and that, to the degree 'we' are inwardly glorified in this life by grace, as the body ages, God's 'great weight of glory' will fully and finally transfigure us, on our last coming home. When 'Glorified', we shall for the first time truly 'know' each other, in glad recognition – not 'as in a glass darkly' as now, but 'face to face' and 'as we are known by God':

> But some men will say, How are the dead raised up? and with what body do they come?
>
> Thou fool, that which thou sowest is not quickened, except it die:
>
> And that which thou sowest, thou sowest not the body that shall be, but bare grain, it may chance of wheat, or some other grain:
>
> But God giveth it a body as it has pleased him, and to every seed its own body.
>
> All flesh is not the same flesh: but there is one kind of flesh of men, another flesh of beasts, another of fishes, and another of birds.
>
> There are also celestial bodies, and bodies terrestial: but the glory of the celestial is one, and the glory of the terrestial is another.
>
> There is one glory of the sun, and another glory of the moon, and another glory of the stars: for one star differeth from another in glory, So also is the resurrection of the dead. It is sown in corruption; it is raised in incorruption:
>
> It is sown in dishonour; it is raised in glory: it is sown in weakness, it is raised in power;
>
> It is sown a natural body; it is raised a spiritual body.
>
> There is a natural body, and there is a spiritual body . . .
>
> And as we have borne the image of the earthly, we shall also bear the image of the heavenly . . .
>
> For this corruptible must put on incorruption, and this mortal must put on immortality.
>
> So, when this incorruptible shall have put on incorruption, and this mortal shall put on immortality, then shall be brought to pass the saying that is written, Death is swallowed up in victory . . . (*1 Corinthians* 15: 35–44, 49, 53–4)

For Plato, the 'body' is a prison, to be endured on Earth, and after death transcended. For Paul, it is rather a tabernacle; our prison on Earth while we fight our fight here – but beyond this, the living seed of our eternal life hereafter. In both views, it is 'at one remove from reality', involved with confusion and corruption. But in Plato the body is incidental, a temporary lodging, largely known as a hindrance to the spiritual life. In Paul, the body is the image of our true selves, to the degree that exile in space/time and the particular conditions of exile can make it so: an essential and eternal part, as an acorn may be to an oak, of our whole, true self.

IX

The Orphics (to return towards Plato) were associated with the ancient legends of Dionysus. They believed in the transmigration of souls, a form of reincarnation which allows men to reappear in animal or non-human bodies. They also believed in judgements between lives, affecting our transmigration, so that we reap rewards or punishments for our actions here.

Their association with Dionysus has led to accusation of orgies, or of exclusiveness; all of them wide of the mark. John Burnet, in his *Early Greek Philosophy*, points out that the Orphics who became powerful in Greece in the sixth century BC are close to genuine mystical sects in any age. Their pursuit of ecstasy was spiritual, not sexual. They formed communes devoted to purifying the spirit by worship, in preparation for its release from the body at death. As their name implies, their doctrines were closely linked with Orpheus. Orpheus had decended into Hades to seek his loved wife, Euridice, and, though the quest had failed, he returned to tell the tale. He could be regarded as a natural guide to the perils of the underworld and to the journey we might each encounter between death, and our next new life. Burnet points out affinities between Orphic and Hindu beliefs of the same period, while doubting that any direct influence took place between East and West. The Orphic word 'orgy' meant 'sacrament', and was a deep spiritual cleansing of the inner self. Orphic beliefs were open to 'anybody', without distinction of race or sex. Admission was by initiation, performed when disciples were individually ready, as such ceremonies are. Bertrand Russell, placing the Orphics broadly in more recent perspectives, chose an analogy that probably amused him, but seems to be near the truth:

> Broadly speaking, those who were of a religious temperament turned to Orphism, while rationalists despised it. One might compare its status to that of Methodism in England in the late eighteenth and early nineteenth centuries. (Russell, *A History of Western Philosophy*)

I have mentioned Heraclitus, a philosopher who might have been more in tune with the Olympian system than with the Orphic, in that he believed in perpetual flux, and the precarious balancing of opposites that prevails in the world. Parmenides, in contrast, asserted that, properly understood, nothing changes. The only true being is 'The One', which is infinite, invisible, and the ground of all life. This 'One' was not equated by Parmenides with God, or with Orphic or mystical religion, yet Parmenides has been seen as the father of 'metaphysics', for two reasons he could not have foreseen. One was his use of a form of dialectic that became characteristic of Socrates and Plato. The other, was his doctrine of 'changelessness', which bordered on mysticism, and led to the possibility that learning is not an empirical process *ab novo*, but a 'remembering' of truths always known, because truths never change.

Bertrand Russell correctly points out that Parmenides' logic is baseless; but he makes an extremely significant comment, which I want to quote. He refutes Parmenides with the aid of his own linguistic theories, but allows that, if Parmenides were here to answer back, he might accuse Russell himself of 'superficiality' in return. He imagines Parmenides saying, for example: 'If memory is to be accepted as a source of knowledge, the past must be before the mind *now*, and must therefore in some sense still exist'. Russell goes on:

> I will not attempt to meet this argument now; it requires a discussion of memory, which is a difficult subject. I have put the argument here to remind the reader that philosophical theories, if they are important, can generally be revived in a new form after being refuted as originally stated. Refutations are seldom final; in most cases, they are only a prelude to further refinements. (Russell, *ibid.*)

This links directly with my own Chapter 4 here, as well as with the mystical tradition that Parmenides did not belong to, but influenced in various ways. Russell assumes that such theories are based on erroneous logic, but keep reappearing: Hydra-headed monsters, always ready to bedevil clear thought. My own view is the practical reverse of this, as will be obvious. I believe that all 'important' truth (to keep Russell's word) is in essence intuitive, deriving from real contact with the transcendental and, to the degree that this is so, enduring. The relative aspects of truth (including logical defences of it) belong with the culture, the use of language, the general public assumptions available to given people, in the segment of history where they happen to be. There is a perennial human striving to clothe deeply felt truths with 'arguments' that, supposedly appealing to 'reason', are apt to stand or fall by this often inappropriate test. But the greatest truths are felt in the heart, on the pulses, in our consciousness (the Fifth Dimension), and these truths are in images, icons, resonances, that pierce to our depths.

Our logical attempts at 'proof' are understandable, and logic is an admirable faculty in its proper place. The last thing I intend is to sanction every whim, delusion or caprice that can clutter our human brains. But the truths Parmenides was offering – and *a fortiori* Plato, Christ, and all great prophets – belong to a religious order where 'mind' must be known as one ingredient, only, of body/mind/soul. 'Logic' belongs with observation and deduction in the empirical sphere, and has to be kept in its rightful place. It overlaps with, but cannot swallow whole, the great religious perceptions. This is what St John meant, in his famous proclamation at the opening of his Gospel. I have in mind the first fourteen verses of the first chapter: and, in this context especially, verse 5: 'And the light shineth in darkness; and the darkness comprehended it not'.

My whole quarrel with the linguistic vandals rests on this contention; that words, like music, can and must strive towards transcendent insights, and at their best half-realise them; but that the insights transcend our structures, and are uncompromised by our failure after failure with *words*, in the high quest for truth. Tennyson expressed the nature of the quest in *In Memoriam*, the fifth section of which puts one important aspect memorably:

I sometimes hold it half a sin
To put in words the grief I feel;
For words, like Nature, half reveal
And half conceal the Soul within.

But, for the unquiet heart and brain
A use in measured language lies;
The dull mechanic exercise
Like dull narcotics, numbing pain.

In words, like weeds, I'll wrap me o'er,
Like coarsest clothes against the cold:
But that large grief which these enfold
Is given in outline and no more.

Tennyson was charting the traumatic experience of love, and bereavement. He was concerned (inevitably, we readily see) with the difficulty inherent in words (even words as fine as these) to reach anything approximating to the heart's felt, precious states. T.S. Eliot, one of the greatest mystics of this or any century, confronts the issue several times, in *Four Quartets*. I have already indicated that *Four Quartets* is a major port of call for all my likely readers, a work to which one returns at every new stage of life. Let me quote two passages here, of direct relevance to explorers of Wisdom in every tradition and time:

> Words strain,
> Crack and sometimes break, under the burden,
> Under the tension, slip, slide, perish,
> Decay with imprecision, will not stay in place,
> Will not stay still. Shrieking voices
> Scolding, mocking, or merely chattering,
> Always assail them. The Word in the desert
> Is most attacked by voices of temptation.
>
> (T.S. Eliot, 'Burnt Norton')

and then again:

> So here I am, in the middle way, having had twenty years —
> Twenty years largely wasted, the years of *L'entre deux guerres* —
> Trying to learn to use words, and every attempt
> Is a wholly new start, and a different kind of failure
> Because one has only learnt to get the better of words
> For the thing one no longer has to say, or the way in which
> One is no longer disposed to say it. And so each venture
> Is a new beginning, a raid on the inarticulate
> With shabby equipment always deteriorating
> In a general mess of imprecision of feeling,
> Undisciplined squads of emotion. And what there is to conquer
> By strength and submission, has already been discovered
> Once or twice, or several times, by men whom one cannot hope
> To emulate — but there is no competition —
> There is only the fight to recover what has been lost
> And found and lost again and again: and now, under conditions

That seem unpropitious. But perhaps neither gain nor loss.
For us, there is only the trying. The rest is not our business.

(T.S. Eliot, 'East Coker')

Profound, and heartening.

For the religious, Plato is and always will be central, for his analysis of existence, and for the mystical cast of his mind. He made a famous distinction between 'Understanding' and 'Reason' that remains useful, through all changes of fashion and taste. 'Understanding' is the sphere of logic, of rational discourse and argument. It is concerned with the evidence received by our five senses, and transmitted by way of the nervous system to the brain. 'Reason', in contrast, is a direct perception of Beauty, Goodness and Truth, the soul's own 'knowledge'. These spiritual data overlap with 'understanding' – they mix with its analysis and merge with its thinking, so that 'rules' of aesthetics, and morality, have one foot always in this material world. But in themselves, they are revelation: our closest and primal encounter with 'Truth'.

Plato believed that the realm of Ideas is the 'true world', of which our human world is an imitation, at one stage removed. The nub of the doctrine is that Beauty, Goodness, Truth are 'Ideas' which pervade all divine creation. Unfortunately, however, Plato tended to identify 'The Good' with the soul, and with the soul's ideal attempt to transcend the body, and return to its proper realm. The world of the senses, and the body, he thought of mainly as snares for the spirit, luring it to prolong its exile in 'time' and to darken all proper awareness of itself. Our senses are tinged with illusion, as life itself is; and can be transcended only by purification – with the Good as goal, and very stringent disciplines as 'the way'.

Virtue, in this guise, becomes the quest of the philosopher; and eternal life the goal to which he is set. Like the Orphics, and the Eastern mystics, Plato seeks to transcend the material, and to achieve eternal bliss by way of achieving the Good.

Plato believed that our soul goes through many incarnations, not all of them human; and that our ascent, or descent, will depend upon our progress or lack of it 'this time round'. For these reasons, he argues that the way to escape from the cycle of incarnations and to achieve the Good lies through philosophy. It is unfortunate, but perhaps inevitable, that he regards mathematics as the highest form of philosophy (our nearest approach to the eternal), and gives the impression that only those expert in maths, as well as advanced in asceticism, can be more or less certain of returning to bliss.

We might suppose that music, like mathematics, is a universal language. Both escaped the curse of Babel, because their language is symbols. Both bring beauty and knowledge to all humans who are skilled in their modes. Mathematics is reserved for a few, however, to conquer; while music, though revelatory to many more people than are versed in its written symbols, is a closed book also to some (the 'tone deaf'). It is a matter of record that while mathematics has led many famous practitioners to belief in a rational God (Newton and Einstein, for instance), it does not have this effect on everyone (as Hawking again shows). Moreover, Senior Wrangler status would be a severe hurdle to jump, on the way back to Heaven – even if advanced mystical insights always went with it hand-in-hand.

Another unfortunate deduction made by Plato is that art is not at one, but at two, stages removed from the 'Real'. Since the realm of nature, and body, is already at one remove and best seen as a prison, this leaves men's highest creative achievements in the deepest dungeons – a disconcerting reversal of all common sense. For this weirdest of reasons, Plato exiled 'art' from his Body Politic – though as many have noted, he had much of the poet's temper himself.

It was left to Plato's late and greatest disciple, Plotinus, to put this error to rights. Plotinus lived in the second century AD, when Christians were already active but the final Christian victory over paganism, under Constantine, was still a far-off (and surely unlikely) event. For Plotinus, all beauty is revelatory, despite its tinge of illusion. Man's art – like his goodness – is an overflowing of God's presence in man. Our works of art, far from being a further step backwards from reality as Plato asserted, are fruit of the indwelling life of God in our human souls.

Plotinus is recognised by many as the 'artist's philosopher'. His famous Trinitarian God, though different from the Christian Trinity in structure and function, has had a greater influence for good on Christianity (I would say) than had Plato himself.

A note on Plotinus is all I have room for; but he was a singularly good, and attractive man. His work is not wholly original, since his Trinity is foreshadowed earlier; perhaps in Plato himself; certainly, in lesser philosophers spanning the two. To what degree it was influenced by Plotinus's contact with Christians must be conjectural (as must the degree to which the Christian doctrine of the Trinity, in the form we now know it from a later period, gained something from Polotinus's *Enneads* and the tradition in which this great, pagan treatise itself stands).

Plotinus's God is made up of three, unequal deities. They are not called 'persons' but two of them could almost bear that word. The greatest God is transcendent and wholly unknowable – at least to creatures like men, bound to their five senses, and to time. The central god, 'Nous', looks up to the transcendent God, and then looks downwards, transmitting much of what is seen to the deity below. This third god is immanent, in every part of creation as well as also being its creator. He is the transient world of ever-forming, ever-changing beauty – from moment to moment revealing new and fleeting configurations of the Good, the Beautiful, the True. The 'forms' of beauty are in constant play, like waves of the sea gathering, shaping and breaking: a constant diversity of particular moments, all returning then to the deeps, the One, just as particular waves return to the whole, unresting sea.

In this sense, though Plotinus does not 'affirm' us as eternal beings, he does affirm the divinity we bear, and the fact that it cannot be lost. But we have indeed to turn to Jesus, and to John and Paul following, to find the doctrine of *the eternal integrity of each unique, individual self*. In this sense, Christ not only goes further than the pagans, in affirming our eternity; he brings a new and shining perception, differing in kind from everything going before.

Perhaps scholars will instinctively wish to controvert this. Much in the *New Testament* is prefigured, of course. We can point to The Wisdom Books in The Old Testament and in *Apocrypha*; and to marvellous verses and images scattered throughout the Old Testament (perhaps also to Essene texts recently discovered, or still to come to light in the future; certainly, to 'hints and guesses' in pagans like Sophocles, and the Orphics, and many other prophets from the earlier world).

Yet Christ's teaching of The Kingdom has compelling power, that makes searches for 'influence' beside the point in my experience of it, as well as fruitless. Its witness is *in itself*; and its witness is deep, also, *in those hearing it*. Not a single human being is unmarked by God, or put on Earth without a purpose – however wretched, hopeless, obscure, his or her life might seem to be. Not a bird worth less than a farthing falls to earth, but God marks it. The entire creation exists, and is held, in His gaze. Christ is the prophet of creativity, of uniqueness, of 'individual identity', of God-given diversity – of much often thought of (in recent times) as 'romantic', but in essence Christian (and profoundly non-puritan: as one must assert again and again, in a context like this).

Plato's emphasis on divine witness in the Good, the Beautiful, the True, is a high point of mystical awareness, among the Greeks. It links well with the teachings of Jesus, as the *New Testament* presents these; but it still basically, and crucially, differs. From this dance of similarity and differences, touching God's incarnation, comes the criss-cross of influences between the two.

In general, the Church has been influenced for good by Plato; but there is a negative side to the account. Plato's downgrading of the senses, and of human creativity, offered a foothold to iconoclasm, and puritanism, which crept into the Church and has greatly damaged it – from the earliest days of development, in the late first century AD, right up to the 1990s, when I write.

X

Plato offered various 'proofs' of human immortality, several ascribed to Socrates as their source. None has stood the test of time, in the original setting. The one that most fascinates me is his theory of 'recollection'; a view that accords with my own experience, from childhood on.

Plato knew (who better?) that human learning involves hard work, much memorising, strenuous moral discipline; and in this, that it very much belongs with our 'this worldly' life. But beyond this slog, which we must all submit to, he believed that the greatest of all truths may come to us as 'a remembrance'. Teachers and discipline belong with our basic learning, but the awareness that comes as remembrance is eternal truth erupting into time.

I have several times mentioned that this has been true to my own experience; and that poets who also feel it (Vaughan, Blake, Wordsworth, Keats, Eliot among others) offer far more resonant and stirring evocations than I ever could.

When I first heard Mahler's Second Symphony, it went home to me as a very deep part of *myself*. I could not imagine that these sounds had ever not existed, or that I was hearing them for the first time myself. As it happens, I did not encounter the work until my twenty-third year, which was about sixty years after it was composed. It is a matter of record that it was written with labour and sweat and with at least one major hiatus, even though it appears a seamless, and inevitable, whole. Likewise, it has its place in Mahler's complex, wayfaring development as an artist, and in the eleven symphonies (including 'Song Of The Earth' and the unfinished Tenth) that charted an amazing spiritual exploration in his lifetime (a fifty-year span).

It is obvious also that it 'belongs' with its period: and that, though Mahler was an innovator well ahead of his time and destined greatly to influence later music, his roots were firmly in the great Romantic period before him, as well. The relationship between 'clock-time' and eternity is dramatised, in the resulting paradox; this symphony is 'in and out of time' as numinous moments are ('in' but not 'of' the world, to use Christ's words). I am led to believe that it relates to a profound experience, located in Mahler's eternal being; and that it was brought into clock-time, in this form, as part of the incarnate work he had especially come here to do.

T.S. Eliot's *Four Quartets* is a poem with a musical structure, and it, too, bears very directly on this great theme. His own words are chosen for their power to work like music, as he says in his opening ('My words echo/Thus, in your mind). Later, in 'Burnt Norton' there is a passage to which I return often, and which is perennially relevant to the matter in hand:

> Not the stillness of the violin, while the note lasts,
> Not that only, but the co-existence,
> Or say that the end precedes the beginning,
> And the end and the beginning were always there
> Before the beginning and after the end.
> And all is always now.

The central two *Quartets* explore the impermanent and the permanent respectively, in their main tonality; but the mystery of the eternal existence of things 'before the beginning and after the end' always recurs. Towards the end of 'East Coker', there is a passage that acquires differing echoes for me, as I grow older, always enriching and deepening its confessedly elusive truth. As more and more friends pass through death and are temporarily lost to me, I find it profoundly 'true' as an expression of bereavement, deepening with time. But it is a passage rooted in our lifelong exploration of 'history': in essence, a raising of 'learning' to the higher wisdom of love:

Home is where one starts from. As we grow older
The world becomes stranger, the pattern more complicated
Of dead and living. Not the intense moment
Isolated, with no before and after,
But a lifetime burning in every moment
And not the lifetime of one man only
But of old stones that cannot be deciphered.
. . . .
Love is most nearly itself
When here and now cease to matter.

(T.S. Eliot, 'East Coker')

Towards the end of 'The Dry Salvages', with its pervasive sea-imagery floating the truth 'time is no healer', a further passage, in the key tonality, arrives:

But to apprehend
The point of intersection of the timeless
With time, is an occupation for the saint —
No occupation either, but something given
And taken, in a lifetime's death in love,
Ardour and selflessness and self-surrender.
For most of us, there is only the unattended
Moment, the moment in and out of time,
The distraction fit, lost in a shaft of sunlight,
The wild thyme unseen, or the winter lightning
Or the waterfall, or music heard so deeply
That it is not heard at all, but you are the music
While the music lasts.

(T.S. Eliot, 'The Dry Salvages')

As I grow older, certain chamber music acquires for me this magic, as never before. The final String Quartet of Schubert, and his great String Quintet; the major Quartets and Quintets of Mozart (the G Minor Quintet especially); the Archduke Piano Trio and the final String Quartets of Beethoven; almost all the chamber music of Brahms – all these experiences, and many more, take me 'back to childhood'. I use that phrase, but it is not even approximate: 'long ago and far back' ('not in time's covenant') is nearer? Such resonances are not of this earth.

Literature and certain other arts approximate to music; always, it seems, when the mystic power of God's presence is most nearly approached. Occasionally a whole city like Venice turns to an icon; certain pictures (Titian's 'Assumption') or sculptures (Michaelangelo's Pietà) hold the same, astonishing power. In literature, much of Wordsworth, and most of Eliot, are virtually music. Then, Lady Julian's amazing 'Revelations of Divine Love', given on the night of 8 May 1373, is a work to remind us that Jesus may appear again in the visions or person of certain transfigured humans – as well as through his more normal meetings with us in the broken figures of the imprisoned, or the poor.

All these things are the central truths of my being. Either that, or they are my life's central delusions: a view of them which I do not, and could not, believe.

I am not dealing with statements or theories, or idealised memories. I include these things with no intention to persuade or entice. Simply, they are the place where 'the dance is' when I near it; they are 'non-negotiable', as some of my students in the 1960s used to say. If you find this true of yourself, you need no persuading. But you may find in it also a useful reminder of the eternal life that can all too readily *escape your attention*: for months, or even for years. 'We had the experience but missed the meaning' . . . (Eliot's context for this phrase is too long to quote; but is wholly appropriate if this rings a bell: the Second movement of 'The Dry Salvages'). It is a reminder that such moments *need* their witness; and the witness should, and must be, ourselves.

Plato's doctrine of knowledge as remembrance is a seminal insight. It is wholly independent of any 'arguments' that he, or any others, offer to give. His words 'crack and strain . . .' like all words, and his meaning is well beyond logic: it belongs with Truth.

XI

At times, I have called myself 'a Neo-Platonist'; and this is useful shorthand for rejecting the linguistic vandals and all their works. But I am ambivalent about Plato, though a sort of part-time disciple. These too brief comments cannot be omitted, from a book with this theme.

His very core doctrines are the assertion of his three great Absolutes; and of his understanding that we do not 'belong' to 'this world'.

It is here that he has his happiest meeting with Christian tradition, since his core beliefs come tantalisingly near, at times, to Christ himself. No wonder I have gravitated so naturally towards Christ, or Paul, while trying to speak of Plato: yet the great Greek dialectical intellect seems poles apart from Jesus (except, as a natural tease?).

By great good fortune, the Christian doctrine of Incarnation added substance and credence to Plato: offering the divine glory *fully* manifest in one, human life. The Fourth Gospel, attributed to John, and almost certainly by one of the original twelve disciples, expounds Christ as *Logos*: the Kingdom of God come among us, in flesh and blood. The words are familiar, but why not repeat them? They are the true heart of Christmas – beyond the tinsel and the myth-making and the now all too commercialised mists. They catch up the myths, surrounding them in a transforming radiance – so that the poetic tales from Luke and Matthew shine again with beauty; and a Midnight Mass of Christmas lifts priests, and pious mortals, and closing-time drunks, beyond the church, and back to the miraculous, 'uncomprehended' truth:

> In the beginning was the Word, and the Word was with God, and the Word was God.
>
> The same was in the beginning with God.
>
> All things were made by him: and without him was not anything made that was made.
>
> In him was life; and the life was the light of men.
>
> And the light shineth in darkness; and the darkness comprehended it not . . .
>
> That was the true Light, which lighteth every man that cometh into the world.
>
> He was in the world, and the world was made by him, and the world knew him not.
>
> He came unto his own, and his own received him not.
>
> But as many as received him, to them gave he power to become the sons of God, even to them that believe on his name.
>
> Which were born, not of blood, nor of the will of the flesh, nor of the will of man, but of God.
>
> And the Word was made flesh, and dwelt among us (and we beheld his glory, the glory as of the only begotten of the Father), full of grace and truth. (*John* 1: 1–5; 9–14)

John is a difficult gospel. There is so much of love in it, yet so much also to puzzle us. This opening is amply fulfilled, however, in John's personal and translucent portrait of Christ. Jesus does shine, in John's account, with peculiar radiance. And most of the material used is unique to John. There is a mixture of inwardness and light that is hard to analyse, but utterly pervasive, from the first sentence to the last. Though the Transfiguration is not recorded (in this Gospel alone) as a separate episode, one feels its quality permeating the whole. The very heart of John's narrative is Christ's great prayer (the 'other' Lord's prayer), made directly to the Father (Chapter 17). On the very brink of his betrayal and arrest, this amazing prayer, along with the discourse to the disciples which precedes it (Chapters 13–16), takes us as near to God, and to God in man, as we are likely to be.

Twice in my life, I have called myself 'a Christian', and had great joy in it. Prayer in Christian churches – offered alone, at quiet times, in the silence, is the experience of churchmanship I am saddest to miss. Twice I have felt bound to leave the church, in a lifelong quarrel, which is and must be crucial; since the natural direction of my love is directly involved.

For those who have no such quarrel – or who live honestly in the church, whatever the tensions – I do not doubt that the church is a good place to be. It offers healing and grace, beauty of worship, a check on compulsions; along with many priests, laymen and bishops who are true men of prayer. The great buildings of the church acquire sanctity, a palpable sense of the holy, peculiar to places set apart for prayer. The sanctuary, the side chapels, often the churchyard, are a serene focus for meditation in the presence of God. I would not seek remotely to foist my personal quarrel off on to others; unless they feel that the church's dogmas actually obscure their own full access to the Kingdom of God. Then, they are on their own, as I now am, with the support and order of church worship lost to them. This may be a price God demands and needs, for some special purpose. One must hope that it is a choice not too tainted with human pride.

At present, I am split. I should like to attempt a third 'return'; but could it be more successful (even if welcome) than the others have been? The basic problem remains, and will do, for my lifetime; I see no honest way back, particularly since it is the church buildings, and the liturgy I miss – not the people, not the followship: aspects that were, and always would be, mainly a strain. Besides: I find the creeds themselves among the most difficult affirmations to join in. They appear designed to make peripheral things central; to make them, even, a test. The birth and death narratives loom large and portentous, so that the Kingdom, even the Spirit himself, seem somehow contingent on these. Trinitarian formulae, and the doctrine of 'atonement', become explicit: emphases which were, in fact, worked out after several centuries of Christian worship had already passed, and to satisfy warring factions for whom the *minutiae* of dogma loomed larger than Christ's universal love.

Perhaps the Church might realise that many people are put off – repelled – by its credal statements, and kept from religion itself (or from direct access to worship) by them. Perhaps it should consider that its chief problem, for many of us, is not a 'failure to communicate', but a lamentable success in communicating far too well.

Perhaps I could settle for being a Christian in exile; or hope for the right to be called 'Christian', without any need of stretching the truth.

However this might be, I am still supposedly concerned here in part with Plato; whose major insights are surely fulfilled, corrected, and transcended, in Christ's vision of The Kingdom of God.

XII

So I come to Christ next; but must, first, add a postscript. I wish that the Church at the end of the first century AD and in the period before Constantine, had been more like Jesus, Paul, Luke and John, than Robin Lane Fox (and others) make it appear. The great fear and rejection of sex which dominates most of 'the Early Fathers' is not found in Jesus himself as a central concern. His 'good news' is of love, and the eternal life springing up inside men; and all else is brought to the test of *this*.

Touching sex, Jesus expected order and reverence; as is clearly natural. Few religious leaders would differ, on this. We must ask ourselves: is sex allied to love, joy, peace, and freedom; or is it allied to violence, compulsions, degradation, leading to destruction; to actual murder, or spiritual death?

The test is simple, and starkly comprehensive. It is hard to understand how it has been surrounded with the rules, restrictions and priestcraft, that now so distort and obscure it. But human nature and diversity have been overriden by precepts so rooted in puritanism, that phrases like 'sex and violence' can be mouthed unchallenged; as though Christ, or any wise man, ever had seen them as one.

Jesus's teaching on sex includes repentance, and forgiveness. Paul defined sin as 'falling short of the glory of God' *in any particular*. The moment we detect such 'falling short' inwardly, in our striving for wholeness, we need to offer the flaws to God to be annulled, and healed. Paul, and Jesus himself, held beliefs about sex in common with their culture – but 'love' was seen always as the solving test; as it is in all aspects of life. Jesus's teaching is vivid and resonant, but short on dogma. Paul's *I Corinthians* 13 is a universal touchstone of love.

Paul spent his whole ministry in action and controversy, and his letters to the churches are an extension of this. Often, he was coping with particular crises rising in his new, young converts, as the major paradoxes of love veered from their centre in the Kingdom in opposite ways. The Galatians were lured back towards legalistic notions, and this called for a restatement of the total liberation brought about by love. But the Corinthians were tempted to confuse their new 'freedom in Christ' with occasional licence. They had to be reminded of order, and recalled to the Kingdom's pure, moral ideals.

In effect, these twin errors, and the vigilance they call for, are very close to the balance which the Greek Olympian system also existed to check. They are the core of morality for 'the religious' of all traditions; and perhaps, for the most basic moral insight of humankind. The closer we come to 'the mind of Christ', 'God's grace', or whatever true light we live by, the less such errors are likely to bemuse us. We shall readily understand, and even naturally celebrate, both the dramatic insights of Aeschylus, Sophocles and Euripides, and the splendidly incandescent rhetoric of Paul.

I believe that the Church was right to appropriate many pagan myths and symbols, even if it did this stealthily, and with no acknowledgment to the pagan wisdom they often contained. I wish that the Church could have assimilated the Olympian, not the Platonic, view of 'mind and body', and the needful tension of opposites that Greek Wisdom has at its core. Though the Olympian system is not transcendental, and is therefore more constrained than Plato's, its pragmatic insights are universal in scope.

The Christian vision soars to the 'city' we seek here; it proclaims the prime power of Love, and of the holiness open to all. It avoids Plato's elitism – his stress on mathematics and philosophy – rightly seeing that this path is falsely exclusive (and far less certain in direction, than Plato believed).

The Church was well guided, at the outset, in its positive insights; Paul, John and Luke (these especially?) all served it well.

But the pagans were better as stewards of this world we live on. They saw that it reflects God's glory in a manner that calls for reverence; and that it is our current home, to be fittingly cherished – even if we do know that our true home is as yet 'far off'. The pagan gods of the groves, woods, lakes, mountains were no mere superstition; they were true recognition of divinity abroad on the earth. The Greeks received the earth from God, and treated it rightly. They assumed – if for different reasons from us – that it is adapted to humans; and that it is the only dwelling, under the Heavens, we are likely to have.

In the final decade of the second Christian millennium, we recklessly drive to destruction every element – Earth, Air, Water, Fire. If the Greeks had found the power needed to do this, they would have renounced such power with horror. Unless the Church wakes up, and says something (starts shouting; starts yelling from the rooftops), then those most concerned with the Earth's sanctity will never be drawn to the church's way.

The Church has, in its liturgy (still tucked away, somewhere?) the *Benedicite*: an amalgam, largely from Old Testament sources, of praise for the Earth. It used to be prescribed for Anglicans in occasional usage: an alternative on chosen Sundays to the 'Te Deum' (and a very welcome relief, it always seemed). In the *Benedicite*, good Christians and true praise God for all parts of creation; they 'bless and magnify Him for ever' for the wild and diverse beings He has made. They exhort the creation itself to join them, in their fervent singing: 'O ye Whales, and all that move in the Waters, bless ye the Lord: praise him and magnify him for ever'.

Is this still heard, rising from some congregations? Does the congregation keep a straight face, when singing it? Do the church men and women go out, when worship is over, to look God's Whales and all that move in the Waters frankly and fully and joyfully in the eyes?

More and more people in all generations are luckily taking some action for these – and the many other – creatures, that the *Benedicite Omnia Opera* lists for praise. It is late in the day – a mopping up of evils already committed; a battle entered upon too late, perhaps, to save the Earth. But it is a battle that must be fought, by all living people. How are we to face the 'mansion' Christ has gone to prepare for us, in the promised Kingdom, if we first have to look back, at Earthly lodgings fouled-up? How are the churchmen who fulminate against vandals and hooligans and graffiti, going to face these charges levelled far more terribly at themselves?

This chapter might end with a word for the Whales and Dolphin Society; for Friends of the Earth, WWF, Greenpeace, the National Trust, the Woodland Trust, the RSPCA, RSPB . . . a growing number (not forgetting the National Society for the Prevention of Cruely to Children, which belongs in the spectrum). All these would come as balm to the pagans – watching those who came after them – and to Christ, casting an eye, as ever, on those who are doing his works. 'O All ye Works of the Lord, bless ye the Lord: praise him and magnify him for ever'.

The Church of course does have St Francis, a saint in the canon; does he still have a 'day'? I suppose that he must. Is is possible that St Francis is honoured, but with a touch of embarrassment – a bit of an eccentric? Is it possible that he has joined the Christmas crib – Virgin and child splendidly clad, Magi and Shepherds kneeling – in a corner reserved for the children, and drawing the Christmas crowds for an odd, happy tear?

It is good to know that growing numbers are turning to 'ecology'. They may not be 'religious', but they would have pleased the pagans; and no doubt they please Christ. I began with Paul on Mars' Hill, addressing the pagans on their altar 'TO THE UNKNOWN GOD' with ringing confidence; proclaiming in the city of Athene, to a half-amused audience, the Name that would replace Athene's – as indeed it did. Might one end with a reminder to the Church of Christ, in the 1990s, that the Mars' Hill rhetoric seems far less relevant and spiritual, just now, to most of us, than it manifestly did to Paul?

Perhaps the church should let sex and gender ride for a bit, and look more closely at violence. Perhaps it should reread its *Magnificat*, and take to heart Mary's view of riches. Perhaps it should sing its *Benedicite*, and then prepare to take it seriously, on this amazing planet we have all been given to guard.

I turn next towards an all too brief look at Christian wisdom; then, to the numinous and holy as 'signs', whenever they come. This third section, on Wisdom, is the imperative driving me to write this book – in an 'annus horribilis' with a vengeance; and with time running out. I cannot write as a fit exemplar of Wisdom. Perhaps my only plausible role is that of a 'disturbing element'? – as my grandmother long ago thought.

8
The Kingdom

When Jesus was asked by his disciples for a special prayer, he gave 'The Lord's Prayer'. It has been used by Christians of all denominations and by many non-Christians, and was first known to me in the wording I shall use here. As a prayer, it is best applied inwardly, to day-to-day needs. It has, through its very austerity, ever differing applications and depths. I am not a theologian or a minister, so I shall use a rehearsal precipitated by my mother's death. The reflections are more coloured by my own cast of mind than by universals. I shall begin by saying a little about my mother, as background.

II

All her life, my mother had looked for faith, and failed to find it. Either she had really failed, as she thought, or she had found faith enough for her, but failed to recognise it as the genuine thing. She had been baptised as an infant, and regarded baptism as crucial, in some highly personal way, not easy to grasp. I think she felt it was indispensible to any kind of religious hope there might be, notably to hope of an 'after-life'. The intense need for this loomed large for her until well into her eighties, when it ran out of steam. Perhaps it went underground; perhaps she thought she had solved it. Perhaps she decided that I could no longer help.

Her life in this world was hard; full of frustrations, and punctuated by illness and by chronic unease. As a baby, she had had eleven operations for a growth on her neck, one each month in her first year; and the scars remained all her life. In her thirties (my childhood) she worked hard, for two pounds a week at Selfridges, one pound as wages, one pound (roughly) as commission on the goods she had sold. The post was supposed to be half-time, but since the hours ran from midday to seven in the evening, this stretched the term rather far. My father had been gassed in the war, and was in hospital for several years in the 1930s, for mysterious lethargies.

Until the start of the Second World War, he belonged with the unemployed. My mother seemed always tired, and suffered from severe migraines, with fits of vomiting that were alarmingly severe. Often, she looked deathly in colour and lined with suffering: 'not long for this world', as my grandmother would say. I sometimes dreamt of her death. In one dream, she was dead on the hearth, her feet in a musty, little-used cupboard, her face turned towards me, dangling upside down. I noticed three green Everyman Volumes in place, on the bookcase, and my vision seemed drawn to these, then back to her. The next day I took these books – which existed in fact – and disposed of them. It was my first attempt at sympathetic magic, I suppose.

Throughout my childhood years, my mother was torn between fits of sternness, and natural kindness, or inward withdrawal, whichever it was. She passed on to me the gift of reading, and some writing, in pre-school days, and for this I have been profoundly grateful all my life. On my first day at school, a teacher rebuked her for doing it; and said that I should have been taught these things after coming to school. I recall thinking angrily, that the woman was a fool; my mother seemed nonplussed. Luckily, this first encounter I had with the poison of 'progressivism' was too late to prevent her from passing on to me her truly priceless gifts.

My mother's kindness was apparent to everyone who liked her. Many of these thought her 'sweet' (a very basic mistake). A great many neighbours and colleagues wanted to know her and to form a friendship. But she found personal relationships an unbearable strain, and warded them off. She felt that people expected from her more than she could give them. She believed that she was happiest on her own, and so, for the most part, she was. Her family strained her enough; so did her work to keep us. She was determined to 'keep us respectable', and she did. Luckily, the house we lived in had been bought on a mortgage and belonged to us. This was assisted by my father's father – a successful but erratic businessman from the mid-middle class. He was churchgoing, conservative, respectable, with a very large family; but his fortunes fluctuated – from suburban villas, to rented rooms in very varied back streets of London. Like most of my uncles and aunts, he was hearty and affable, but given to fits of anger of a half-crazed kind. Like them too, he was 'in the money' or not 'in the money'. We were lucky that a former phase coincided with the chance, for my parents, to buy their house. It is lucky too that he initiated the purchase and dealt with the lawyers, since my father was chronically unable to carry decisions through. The house was on three stories in Warlock Road, Paddington – a district built for small, middle-class families with one or two servants in the 1850s, but soon left behind by them as London expanded outwards and the class structure shifted. In the 1930s, the house was in a street mainly 'let-out' in flats and rooms (middle-classes going down, retired 'gentle-folk', a large Irish community just south of Kilburn, assorted eccentrics, some genuine working-class enclaves). Most houses were on 99-year leases, but ours was peppercorn: the 999-year leases that were virtually freehold, apart from ground-rent.

The house meant that my mother could let rooms to lodgers – a pair of upstair rooms for 13/6 a week, and two separate rooms for 7/6 each ('No service', of course). This money, along with my father's war pension (or was it the dole?), and my grandmother's 'widow's pension' was enough, always, to see us through.

My mother always yearned to be 'on her own', but seldom could be; so friendships really were beyond her needs. One or two people she was fond of, and 'knew', but always on a distant basis. She 'could not bring them home' because of the non-stop warfare, between my father (when he was there) and my formidable grandmother, who had her 'room' downstairs. My grandmother kept the lodgers in order with a rule of terror – which was just as well; since some were decidedly strange. The only two people my mother really needed were her mother (until her mother's death, considerable later), and then, her largely absent son – myself.

Her main obsession was with 'life after death', as she called it – or still worse, as it seemed to me, 'survival'. This was essential, because she longed to meet one or two people after her death, notably her brother (who had been killed in the war), and her mother; but more, because she wanted to live beyond death herself. Desperately she needed 'answers': (Why are we here?; Where do we come from?; What is the Meaning?); and still more, she deeply feared oblivion (Just imagine! Nothing ever again . . . Nothing . . . Nothing!). Had she read Yeats, she would have been fascinated by his quest for 'someone to answer all my questions'; fascinated, too, by Yeats' choice of oracles: 'some old tramp in Sligo', or 'some medium in Soho', 'some long-dead craftsman in the golden age of Byzantium'. Had she read Philip Larkin, 'Aubade' chiefly, but any of his gloomier musings, she would have found her inner refrain sounded back to her, with daunting power. In later times, I tried to keep copies of journals with Larkin's poems away from her. She was disturbed enough with religious fears, without further treadmills thrown in. Though Larkin writes finely, he is exceptionally negative and depressing, in a way that major artists, by definition, cannot be.

My mother continued to hope that I might 'answer all her questions'. Had I not been to Cambridge – by her considerable sacrifice; and was I not supposed to be a don? She assumed that education would have given to her the entrée to 'answers', if she had had it; and her real reason for letting me go to university (against many other instincts) was that I would make the discoveries, and share them with her. She had left school at fourteen (by courtesy of Balfour). This coincided with the outbreak of the Great War, and her first job at Whiteley's. Her own mother had left school at ten (by courtesy of Forster) – and, though literate and highly intelligent, was so entirely different from my mother (a boisterous, happy extrovert, who dominated my childhood) that my mother's 'questions' seemed not greatly to bother her.

I say 'seemed', but this is not true, really. My grandmother had once been an Anglo-Catholic, but her devotion had lapsed. Unhappily, her son William went to the war and was killed in 1916. This left my grandmother angry with God – angry, bitter and unforgiving – and she lived on without religion; though in her heart there was a core of belief. She was a true-blue person, in the Disraeli tradition: poor and working-class, yet in her instincts aristocratic, and totally free. The royal family, the British Empire, Winston Churchill belonged to her; and she ruled the earth, freely and fiercely, with total independence of heart and mind. Her belief in justice was absolute, and even frightening; she was amazingly like Hermione Baddeley's depiction of Ida Arnold in the film of Greene's *Brighton Rock*. She would have met the Eumenides as an equal, and readily joined them. She once confided to me her image of happiness: she would love to be a gypsy, travelling round the country at will, totally independent: and it struck me that this dream of liberty was very like Eliot's numinous moments in *Four Quartets*.

But me? I was the lucky one, for education: born in 1928, when the ladder of opportunity was at last in place. So, with my mother's sacrifices (real enough, though she did make them sound exceptional), I managed an Exhibition at Cambridge, after a wartime schooling in London (Blitz; Doodle-Bugs; then V2 Rockets; and excellent, elderly teachers, too old for the war). I admit that I left home with huge relief, even though my childhood and schooldays as I recall them were mainly happy, and I was bound to my grandmother with ties of affection that remain strong and vivid, thirty-seven years after her death. My mother was an anxious area: I couldn't be easy with her, and I certainly couldn't, and wouldn't escape her for good. My father, sadly, I never got to know.

My mother suffered many frustrations, but the chief of them were, I am sure, intellectual. If she had been given 'my' chances, she would have taken them; if her intellect had been trained, she might have lived a fruitful, though never an untormented, life. She would have discovered that her doubts and fears are shared by most sensitive, innovative people, and she would have enjoyed wandering among the many attempts on them by philosophers, artists and seers. Like everyone else, she would have realised that the riddles are unanswered, but she would have stuck with them, in a more hopeful way. She would never have thought them childish or meaningless questions, however well educated she had become. She was never a fool. She might have added to the world's store of wisdom; and even found some of the peace that eluded her (though this I doubt).

As it was, she remained uncertain and uneasy; and I fear she thought sometimes, that I really did know 'the answers' – especially after Cambridge – but was deliberately keeping them from her; a truly wounding idea. My own excursions into and out of Christianity (first in pre-university and university days, 1947–54; then later, from 1966 to 1978) cannot have helped matters. Nor can the fact that I am basically a religious person, just as she was. I tried to explain this to her very variously, but with little success.

Another problem had been her weird attitude to the Church, to which I tried on and off to entice her. The Church meant the Christian Church of course, because of Baptism. It also meant the Church of England, since she had been baptised into this, and so had I. Besides, other sects horrified her, for a number of reasons. She had met catholics at work and they were all the same: confessing one day, doing the same things the next. She had met dissenters, and found most of them stuffy and humourless. She did admire the Salvation Army and as a girl, had apparently briefly joined it; but this episode was closed.

All of this sounds and perhaps was prejudiced; it demonstrates the extreme confusion between religion and morality which existed then for a great many people, and I fancy still does. It took me a great time to disentangle the two myself, and I was saddened to find that Professor Basil Willey, whom I greatly admired, was entangled also; though at a far more rarefied level, I suppose. We are talking of the 1940s and the 1950s, and luckily, my mother would never have dreamed of coming out with her feelings in a hurtful way. She spoke of religious groups from her own experience, but when she heard belatedly of Hitler's 'final solution', I noticed that this kind of prejudice lapsed. She found Hitler impossible to grasp, and this was 'before television'; but the evil, and its roots in prejudice, got through to her.

For her, my enthusiasm for the Labour Party, and for liberalism in general, were highly perverse. Like my grandmother, and the Dyson clan (a sole point of agreement between the two), she was deeply conservative, and an English/London partisan through and through. The centrality of the Church of England was confirmed by its (then) association with conservatism; and it had earned the general approval of everyone in the family, except me, for its treatment of Mrs Simpson and King Edward VIII. (Rather interestingly, my father stood out from our home, and from his family, by supporting Attlee's Governments and voting for them. He knew that I agreed, but we did not discuss it: this does seem a terrible missed opportunity.)

Why then did my mother shy away from Church buildings; and regard them with an odd mixture of dislike and fear? As far as I know, she went to church worship only six times in her life. Once was to be baptised (at St Augustine's Kilburn, where my grandmother then worshipped. I was glad to secure the Vicar of St Augustine's for her funeral). Her marriage was in a Registrar's Office; but she did have me 'properly baptised'. This was at St Peter's Church, Paddington; and the all-important certificate was over her bed, framed, to the day of her death. Then, I more or less forced her – by what arguments I forget – to hear Brother Edward, the Village Evangelist, preach in St Marylebone Parish Church during Bishop Wand's 'Mission to London' (around 1950). As I had gambled, she sensed his holiness; but she was 'not convinced'. Why not? 'Well, I felt uncomfortable'. And it all 'seemed so odd'.

When I chose to be confirmed (in 1947) she refused to come to the service, and was actually furious; apparently, the Baptismal Certificate did not need a sequel like that. Perhaps it was that she knew I had discovered sex, and this disturbed her; perhaps she thought me odd, like the Church. No doubt, she thought me a 'hypocrite' (on sex, she would in those days have found John Paul II too liberal by far). But I think it was more than this. There was a fear of church worship of any kind; along with a fear of my making a commitment in the realm where her 'unanswered questions' ought to have barred the way.

Perhaps she also went to baptisms, marriages, funerals out of politeness; I have counted the funerals of my grandmother and my father, and her own, in the six church visits. But if so, she would have been extremely uncomfortable, while appearing to others more than usually 'sweet'.

Finally, she very much wanted a Christian burial, and for some reason feared that I would deny her this wish. She even feared that I would have her cremated, and her immortal soul utterly destroyed in consequence, as she thought I meant to do for myself. There were also occasions in earlier years when she wanted me to marry, on the grounds that unless I had children, there would be no-one in whom she would be able to 'reincarnate'. This was encouraged by my grandmother's periodic conviction that I was a reincarnation of her dead son William; though what sort of a belief this was, would be hard to make out.

I think that my mother did trust me, finally. In her later years, we got to know one another very much better; and the TV, to which she became addicted, broadened her views to an amazing degree. It certainly fed her long-starved longing for knowledge, and made her more liberal, in some areas, than I am myself. In the end, she was buried in my father's grave, as was always intended when, just before her ninety-first birthday, death caught up.

The poor church attendance remains a mystery. There were not even token Christmas or Easter attempts at it. The reasons appeared to fall into two groups, with a third in the background, if I try to recall the recurring themes. 'She was not good enough to go to church'. I pointed out that the place was full of sinners, or of people vigorously claiming to be such. She found this 'terrible'. If they were sinners, how could they go to church in the first place? And if they weren't, why did they say they were? Outside church they claimed to be 'respectable', and were the first to censure others, for any public sins. Did they know what they were talking about, and could they be serious? For a long time, these arguments maddened me, but I could not counter them. Now, I fancy that she did understand the word sin, very shrewdly, and suspect that she was more than half right. The upshot, anyway, was that she was 'not good enough herself'.

Secondly, she had a horror of the cross, and still more, of the crucifix. She could not see why such atrocities were shown, and made central features, and even worshipped. The whole atmosphere of the church 'appalled' her and 'made her uneasy'. She didn't feel at home there, and never would. Later when I encountered William Empson in full flood on 'torture-worshippers', I recognised exactly the position she described. By a piece of good luck, Empson's splendidly perverse piece on Coleridge's 'Ancient Mariner' came our way, for *The Critical Quarterly*. Brian Cox and I even decided to have a specially designed cover to celebrate it. I am sure my mother read this (she did look at the journal, and for a time helped to administer it). I know that she read Empson, and various other pieces that would have interested her. Unfortunately, she did not open up on the essay to me. But finally, and here was the rub, she was 'out of place' in the church (or would be, if she went there). People would talk to her, expect things of her: they would try to 'draw her in', and make her life a misery.

All of this I let pass, though I see the point, on home ground. My own excursions into church life have been marked by attempts to evade people of the type she mentioned, and to do things (such as pray), rather than have things done to me by priests and evangelical ranters and the like. Though my tastes are Anglo-Catholic, I never went to the confessional, and disapprove of this wholly as much as my mother could have done. I deeply suspect the motives of most (not quite all) of the priests who practise it; and am convinced that many lives have been wrecked by them.

On the whole, most of the people I have liked and trusted best have been non-churchgoers, and I know that churchgoing can seriously damage the heart and mind. So, perhaps I have more in common with my mother than I admitted to her (well I know I did; and so did she). We shared certain recurring dreams among other things – uncannily similar in feel and in imagery; and in certain tones which we recognised when we talked of them, though these have never, to my knowledge, been conveyed in words. But I very much wish that my mother had let herself hear a few more holy preachers; and I wish she could have liked church buildings, and prayed in them on her own.

Perhaps I am wrong, at least about my mother's last years. She did take to looking into churches in her tours of London on her buspass. She mentioned Waltham Abbey with pleasure. Also, she had a side which she usually kept from me, though it slipped out sometimes. In early days, she had taken part in seances with the Dyson family, and shown unusual psychic and mediumistic powers. Once, she had a session with the Ouija Board which scared her, and 'everyone else'. Apparently, fearsome things had 'come out', about almost everyone, and my mother felt that the Dysons, used as they were to more 'trivial' disclosures, looked on her as dangerous, after this. She was certainly clairvoyant (as were most of the Dysons also), but she steered clear through fear (fear, that is, of the supernatural; not of the absurd English 'witchcraft' laws of the time).

One odd thing is, that the Dysons (at least), though they regularly experienced table-turning, lights going out, spirit noises-off and messages and the rest of it, appeared never to connect this with 'religion', or with 'life after death'. My father saw his dead sister all night at the foot of his bed 'dressed in that old brown dress she used to wear as a girl', and told us about it. But two days later, when her sudden death that night near Brighton was confirmed, he appeared to subsume the vision to his capacious, pedestrian hold-all, 'common sense'. Several times, my mother went, on her own, to seances, especially after the death of her mother, and she received signs that were 'really convincing' (she was on her own, in a back street church chosen at random, and was told things that 'no-one could possibly have known'). Alas, in her personal quest for 'survival', they were not convincing enough.

Her boast was that she had 'never done any harm to anyone', and this gave her comfort. Though the form was negative, I tried not to make too much of a point of that. It was naturally untrue, as it is of all of us but, as she understood the claim, there was truth enough. She had never intentionally caused harm to anyone; and this, I am sure, is completely so. Few people can claim it; and indeed, she did have an instinct for healing; a capacity, somewhere, for love. It was these positive things, and the strength they brought, that drew people to her. She was not 'sweet' but she was, by intention and willpower, consistently good. Certainly, she was better than I could remotely hope to be, and this sometimes annoyed me. It put me at a huge disadvantage when her ceaseless 'questions' couldn't be met.

I did not encourage my mother to 'try' spiritualism, and have always steered rather clear myself; and I have few psychic gifts. When editing *Christian* in the 1970s, I came across explorations of healing and of the supernatural side of the Church of England, and was profoundly impressed by many of the people and places I encountered (Burrswood stands out). But these aspects of the Church have some dangers, and are usually 'hidden'; Christ's own instinct was to hide, not proclaim, a fair number of his supernatural deeds. There is a measure of unavoidable danger, since healing is bound to attract forces of Evil. Our normal witness is meant for the Kingdom itself, as Jesus lived it, and not for personal visions or consolations which God may sometimes grant. I have come across dangerous misuses of psychic power several times, and early realised that T.S. Eliot (for example) regarded this realm with fear. Yet many outstanding men and women explore the psychic and the supernatural without notable damage, and some of them are among our greatest creators (Yeats and Jung surely head this list). I have noticed myself that the personal 'signs' from God which many people receive (far more than one hears of) are of a kind that would be unlikely to 'convince' anybody else. In fact, they are of a kind which often could be coincidence; though some appear to be altogether convincing to the people concerned.

I reassured my mother that her 'dabblings in spiritualism' (as she called them) could not have harmed her; and I hope I was right to keep her from pursuing a religious quest in this way. Curiously, she did have a total belief in 'being watched over' – a benign idea, that went deep, though it did not touch her doubts about 'faith'. She mentioned it many times, and perhaps I wrongly ignored it; in earlier years, I found it superstitious, at best. But I recall that when the Cabinet were attacked by the IRA at Brighton, my mother was oddly disturbed by a phrase that Mrs Thatcher used. The Prime Minister was on the eve (I think) of a birthday, and she said 'This is the day I was not meant to see'. My mother was convinced she had intended to say the opposite: 'But she must have been "meant" to see it; she was saved'. It struck me then, that my mother's conviction on this point was deeper than I had realised – to a degree that made it impossible for me to sort out the crux. The Prime Minister 'could not' have been saying that the IRA did not 'mean' her to see her birthday – since she had put a strong emphasis on the word 'meant'. For my mother, 'meant', in this sense, referred to a divine intention – and survival was, simply, the 'meaning' of the powers that 'watch' us on earth.

The Dyson clan had also used this phrase, with apparent conviction; and, though it did not 'go' with religion, for them it clearly expressed deep-felt beliefs that I failed to understand.

I can well appreciate the impatience most people feel with such ideas and word usages, but have come to think they are not illiterate; rather, they are a very approximate attempt to express a belief. My own problem is that I cannot see how the belief is detached from 'religion'; and to this extent, I may be somewhat tone deaf. The reality of the supernatural became very clear to me, in the 1970s, along with the correct reasons for keeping it a low-profile thing. It seems that 'private' visions are meant for the individuals who have them; that they are sparingly given, and are not meant to loom large. If unleashed they can merge with delusion, and with a huge field of the charlatan; they also go closer to evil than one normally likes. I take for granted that Christ came to earth in essence to proclaim 'The Kingdom'; not to work miracles. In this book, I try to keep to the wisdom and witness that belong with normal and general experiences of the divine.

My mother outlived most of those who had corresponded with her affectionately – always at Christmas; and usually with invitations, which she always refused. She often thought of them and I expect prayed for them. Five or six are still alive, in their nineties. It seems that ladies born in 1900 were a tough breed; with the Queen Mother a splendid flagship.

Some deep violence in my mother, deeply repressed, was always clear to me. I was often scared by the sheer will-power she expended, on daily poise. Did she know it herself? She was often frustrated and downcast; too often, for reasons in which I had a part. However: whether she allowed herself to know it, is another matter. Her hatred of violence, and its symbols, were part of a lifelong attempt to keep the peace at home, and find some peace for herself. Very nearly, she made it to the end; but in 1987, following a cancer operation, a violent psychotic illness occurred. She had asked a doctor to tell her the truth – meaning, to tell her that she had not got cancer. Unfortunately, he or she took her at her word (this area is difficult; but why are many doctors so blind, or foolish, in their phychological dealings with patients?). I suppose that my mother was then faced with somehow accepting the answer (impossible), or discovering that everyone in the world was an enemy, telling lies. She had managed the precarious balance of tensions for a very long period; this was the point at which she snapped. Her subconscious chose the second option, and her dark side got loose. She alarmed everyone, even the professionals; and very certainly, me. She retreated into a terrible, small world of conspiracy against her; where there was no air to breathe, no apparent escape-door to unlock. The hospital was a BBC conspiracy to murder; I was to be murdered along with herself. Two or three times she created terrible scenes, trying to stop me leaving, when I visited her ward. On the other side, the doctors learned that I was in some sort of conspiracy against them, in which cats were wailing all night in the hospital and people, including Peter Sellers, Lord Soper and others, were visiting her in disguise with dreadful warnings, not to be disclosed.

For some reason, the hospital discharged her, in the middle of this episode, to the house where she lived alone, with only Brent Council social workers to help. These latter were excellent, and I cannot praise them too highly. They enabled my mother to spend her final years at home, as she desperately wanted, by doing precisely the things (shopping; a daily delivery of meals on wheels) that, given her reasonably active body, and razor-sharp mind, were the needed links.

But at home, in her psychotic breakdown, she refused to eat; and behaved and spoke threateningly. One experienced worker said that she had 'totally changed', and might do anything at all. She turned her house, a life-long pattern of order and neatness, into a shambles, during one night that had been spent overturning, smashing, breaking in every room. Several scores of sharp-edged things had been collected, beside her bedside; one could only conjecture why.

On the following morning an ambulance crew, at the urging of myself and her doctor but against her will, took her back to the hospital. Theoretically, she ought to have been 'sectioned', to avoid the legal hazard of removing her. Luckily, with further encouragement from her home help – who became a friend of hers, and who stood by her in this turmoil – the short ride to the hospital was achieved and sectioning, which would have wrecked her for good, did not occur. Her consultant, an expert in mental illness, told me that, however alarming, her illness might pass in six or seven weeks. Though it would have been incurable and lifelong if it had happened earlier, it seems that, at 87, the illness can burn out and disappear. By great good fortune, this was a correct prognosis. By late August she was home again, and returned to her 'sweetness', and habits of spotlessness. For her last four years, things remained this way; and I was extremely glad that she broke a lifelong habit, to take the daily drugs that were given. Did she remember the episode? She had to have a quarterly check-up, but she seemed entirely convinced that 'there had been nothing wrong with her', and luckily, nothing happened on these visits (which I dreaded) to disrupt this view. On one occasion, when she was managing her financial affairs with her usual efficiency, she did say, 'I suppose I am lucky that you didn't have me certified'. I was able to turn this into a joke; and that was that.

I mention these details because this rehearsal (or use) of the Lord's Prayer is based on a two-hour session I had with my mother's body, on the day before burial. Every use we make of this prayer is a new one, with different things uppermost, and it is as well to let the one (or several) important things of each day have a natural place. I know of no form of works so austere in form, yet so subversive in context; no prayer, or wisdom, that so totally brings into focus God's world, and this world, and the infinitely varied and infinitely important interactions of the two.

R.S. Thomas's poem 'The Kingdom' had been teasing my mind, but my mother's needs and my own were the focus, that day. More than anyone I know of or have known, my mother embodies the 'strangers and pilgrims' theme from *Hebrews*. I felt a great relief, that she had at last passed to her real place, and that the questions would no longer trouble her in the way that they had. She was back where she belonged and being received gladly. Her guardian-angel, in whom she believed, was no doubt especially happy, since he must have had an exhausting, if rewarding, ninety-one year stint. I half wished that she might give some sign, before leaving completely (and I feel sure that she did, about a fortnight later, in a highly characteristic way). For her tombstone, which is also my father's, I chose words from 'Burnt Norton' which she had been fascinated by (along with the whole poem): AND ALL IS ALWAYS NOW.

While I used the Lord's Prayer, in my last period with her earthly body, I half wished, too, that we could reverse roles, and that she could answer my questions. But in the marble of death, cold as ice, her face bearing life's scars still and just a trace of humour, she was as unattainable as a far galaxy. I hoped that I hadn't seemed as inaccessible to her, in life. Who is to know?

III

(1) Our Father
(2) Which Art in Heaven
(3) Hallowed be Thy Name

(4) Thy Kingdom come
(5) Thy will be done in Earth, as it is in Heaven
(6) Give us this day our daily bread
(7) And forgive us our Trespasses, as we forgive them that Trespass against us.
(8) And lead us not into Temptation.
(9) But deliver us from Evil. (Amen)

(1) Our Father

'Our Father' addresses a God who is our Creator, and always approachable. This goes greatly beyond anything envisaged by the Greeks. It goes beyond the Jewish Yahwey who, though all-powerful and all-present, was concerned with his chosen race only; and often dealt alarmingly with them. Jesus of Nazareth was naturally influenced by the Old Testament (as we now call it), and perhaps by the Essenes and others of whom we are still learning as research goes on. But he stands out as a religious prophet unique in greatness, whose prayer actually starts with this amazing *datum* for prayer.

'Father' is a word of conscious relationship – real on our side, real equally on God's – since otherwise, why should we use the term in this natural way?

We know our earthly father of course; or we know that we had one. The analogy helps, as far as it will go. Unfortunately, my own father was hidden from me, in early life, by the dominance of my grandmother. His long illnesses, and perhaps his natural remoteness, gave her the chance to move me away, in her exuberance, from the shadows he cast. There was clearly some terrible lack in myself, that I let this happen; yet it struck me as natural; or it happened, without any awareness (how could this have been?).

I never could or did relate to my father; though I recall one or two intimate moments with him, when I was young. We would walk in the alleys behind the Edwardian flats in Maida Vale, narrow walls rising well past my head, with shrubs and trees topping them; and I remember surges of pleasure, connected with him. There was one rainy morning on the railway bridge beyond Westbourne Park station, when he said, 'Never mind; soon the clouds will be rolled away'. I knew he meant several things, most of them hidden; but for me, the words spoke of promise and life. Some Sunday mornings he would take me to meet neighbours; sombre, respectable people, who awed me, and kept me dumb. These visits too I loved, because I was with him; but whether he knew this, I doubt. I didn't tell him, then or ever. Perhaps he thought I was bored.

We seldom spoke; when we did, there was usually anger. We quarrelled about many things; most topics went sour on us. The end was often bitter, very close to violence; yet I remember no single trigger, no clearcut beginning, middle or end. Most often my grandmother was there, just in the background. They abused each other; and, as he knew, my heart was with her, though I often knew she was wrong. We did not find the key to being intimate and, if ever he wished it, he failed (was it my fault?) to find a door. I liked him (I think), and sometimes felt strong pleasure; momentary impulses, which he could never have guessed. On the whole, he was shadowy, not fully real; yet he was widely liked (I know), and had depths I guessed at; and he was kind by nature, when safely away from his home.

He would open up on the trenches, and his war-time memories; which went deep, and had scarred him beyond healing (he had been very badly gassed). These stories did not grip me; in fact, I was bored by them. They were 'before I was born' and unreal, as I remember: yet, my grandmother's stories I loved, because they were fun.

When I now read Ted Hughes's early poems, based on his father's memories, I am appalled by my former failure to hear my own father, or respond. The lack of imagination, of sympathy, was mine surely; it is a real defect, shared with my mother (I suppose). I have often failed to 'hear' people I do not feel close to; no amount of vividness easily crosses this gap. Literature is different: there, the words work, unimpeded; fiction adds the ingredient I need, for a total response. Yet I did feel close to my father, in odd small spasms; or did he touch off some response as a catalyst? – I really don't know.

My father loved my mother, and even revered her; but he could not get close to her either (nor could I, then). The photographs of their early married years were happy; they dressed stylishly, laughed together, seemed wholly at ease – all this, before I was born. What went wrong? Was it my birth; or my grandmother's apotheosis; or my father's ill-health (the wartime gassing catching up, in long, mysterious illnesses); or unemployment in the 1930s – the lodgers; the fight to be 'respectable' which succeeded, but at too high a price? I suspect that my mother didn't enjoy sex; and she wanted no more children. And then, there was her inner withdrawal, by instinct, in all relationships, which I already half understood, because I shared it, but it bewildered my father; took him, perhaps, by surprise.

What did my mother think of her own father? This is, for me, a really strange blank. Neither my grandmother nor my mother ever spoke of him, though he had died only shortly before I was born. I suppose I would have known he existed, had I thought of it; yet I felt no gap, and never missed or mentioned him, while still a child. In later years, I tried to question my mother, but she evaded all probing, with sadness, unease, but no sense of any traumatic rift. Perhaps my grandmother had blocked him out for her, as she later blocked my father. Though my grandmother's lost son William dominated her thoughts, and her conversation, her own husband might never have been. Though I admired my grandmother, and recall her with love and happiness, I realise that her presence, living with my parents, was a huge classic mistake.

It seems to me amazing that I did not get to know my father later. I was nearly forty, after all, at the time of his death. By then, my mother ran the house, and looked after things; and I left home at eighteen, for good, with no little relief. I suppose that my father and I could not find common ground, even later; and by then, I sensed he had written me off completely (this had lurked from the start). Near his death, he did say to me 'Look after your mother. She is a wonderful woman'; and he appeared to have something urgent to add; but it didn't arrive.

He did have a great will to live, perhaps naturally. One odd fact, is that I prolonged his life with a lie. In 1966, after several strokes, and with terminal pneumonia, his doctor told me 'This is it; he can't last the week'. When I went in to him, he grasped my hand feverishly, and asked, 'What did he say?'. 'He said the antibiotics are working', I told him, 'and that, if you pull yourself together, you'll be perfectly all right again, soon'. He relaxed, reassured; recovered, and had two more years – though as a helpless invalid, with scarcely any quality of life. But my mother was with him, and nursed him devotedly; as she had my grandmother, in a similar last illness, a decade before.

Why did I lie? Perhaps cowardice; perhaps a sense of his will to live, which was always strong in him; perhaps a general belief in antibiotics that the 1960s brought. Why did I use the phrase 'pull yourself together'? In my early life, he had said this to me often; it was a phrase I had cordially learned to hate. I cannot have used it (for the first and last time) on this occasion out of revenge, surely? No: why should I? I think that I remembered it as a phrase meaning a lot to him, and sensed it was the best form of words to do the trick. I had also come to see it as, to a high degree, valid and important; though on that occasion, I didn't expect it to work.

Water under the bridge . . . I hope that getting to know my father will be one of the pleasures that the afterlife brings. I see that he had at least as difficult and frustrated a life as my mother, and that the First World War experience of the trenches, which wrecked his health, left a permanent scar on his commitment to life. But I did not identify with him as I did with my mother. It really seems that I did not identify with him at all.

So 'Father' has a limited use for me, as analogy; and I wonder about Jesus himself? His human father, Joseph, plays a small role in the New Testament – and is naturally embarrassing to the church, in view of the theology it has later dreamed up. Jesus no doubt thought of Joseph as his father, and his brothers and sisters as siblings; but no closeness to them (or to his mother) is clear in the texts. His gravitation towards the Temple, and towards learned discourse, appeared early; and the psychology of a 'loner' is clear to read. He apprenticed as a carpenter, and would in the normal course have followed Joseph. But when he started his ministry, he adopted his disciples instead. He pointedly referred to them as his 'mother and brothers and sisters' when the family tried to claim him; and 'leaving father, mother, family, wife' for the gospel made part of his theme. We know that the word 'Father' was used exclusively by Jesus of his Father in Heaven; and that 'his Father's business' had precedence over his natural father, and home. Yet clearly, he was a good son, through most of his lifetime, and one can assume that he and Joseph would have been on easy terms.

It remains true that Jesus's 'Father in Heaven' is the Creator of all life; and a new name for Jehovah. Yet Jesus speaks of Him with an intimacy totally new, and even seemingly personal. No wonder the scribes and pharisees were alarmed and shocked. This is the Father he prays to, and taught us to pray to; as we do, in this extraordinary prayer we are using now. We have to recall all four Gospel accounts of Jesus's life (and *John* 17 especially?), to grasp the amazing intimacy that existed between Jesus, and his Father God. It is clearly crucial that while 'Father' remains an authority figure (as is natural, in a patriarchal society), Jesus puts much of his stress on 'love', but the rest on 'fear'.

Though I might want to substitute for 'Father' a different word, to evoke true intimate closeness, I have no doubt that the role, as well as the person, is extremely important in Jesus's choice of the word.

The word 'Father' is especially important now, when 'our' universe is by and large the Hawking model and, as my first chapter suggested, far removed from a family, or a personal, mode. Hawking finds no room for a god, or a creator, in the cosmos. And, though other scientists differ, a creator who could (and should) be called 'Father' is not likely to come back, to the human race, from them. Newton's 'Law of Gravitation' abolished 'Father' pretty effectively. 'Rational Christians' have gone easy on familial language ever since.

The main problem with 'The Enlightenment' was, precisely, in this area. While Newton's laws and Locke's epistemology were thought to be 'reuniting science and religion', and strengthening religion, the effect was to transform God from a person ('Abba') into an abstract, logically demonstrable Idea. Perhaps the eventual mutation of our culture towards godlessness was a natural evolution, after this first step to depersonalise (*not* 'demythologise') God had been made. As we know, recent history has found more and more people asking where God is when we need Him. The Great War dramatised this for my grandmother, in her son's death, which struck her as senseless; and for my father, in experiences that wrecked his health, and dimmed his pleasure in living and his fitness to work. The atrocities of Hitler, Stalin, Mao Tse Tung straddle our century; few parts of the world are free from famine and war. Very clearly a great many people have written God off, as a 'Father'; hence the reason (though not the excuse) for atheist vicars, for religions without a God 'outside us', and the like. In a similar and even more damaging development, we have complacent Christians who turn from liturgy to dancing, and imagine that clap-happy dogmas arouse anything, in most of their fellows, but amazed disgust.

In this (and any) context, Jesus's prayer confronts us with 'Our Father', as a prelude to collecting ourself, in God's presence, for life. In calling God 'Abba' – 'Daddy', as it may be translated – he asks us to to feel close to God daily, as he did himself.

It is clear that Jesus was not equating God simply with the creation of the space/time *continuum*. In his own ethos – different from ours in customs, very close in essentials – he knew that God's home, like his own, and ours, is quite elsewhere. He fully knew that the world ruled by death and decay, subject to Imperial Power and pervasive sin, and peppered with figures like Herod, was no place to find his 'Father' in any full sense. He knew that God's prophets had been killed, by God's own people; and that his own teaching set him on the same, certain path. Jesus continually proclaims a different, more lasting 'order', where he goes to 'prepare a place for us', when our own race is done. The place of The Kingdom has its own rules, apart from 'this world' and in large part alien; except that, the laws of The Kingdom find a remembrance, a home, a call, in our own, stirred hearts. The Kingdom: where the poor man is king and the rich man is outcast; where forgiveness and healing truly are natural laws. In The Kingdom, God rules, His love reaching each one of us. God's will 'in Earth' is to test us in exile, far away from 'The Kingdom' in fact, but with its resonance haunting us; then to welcome us back, with a final 'Well done'. So: 'Father' as head of a family, made for His and our glory; seen 'face to face' at the last, if and when we can bear this; for the moment, seen in Jesus's works, whether done by him personally, or by any other man or woman born on earth. A 'Father' Who is our earthly creator, and our daily protector; yet Whose apparent absence may be a chief rule of the test.

The word 'Father' brings this great truth home, almost shockingly; no one can say and mean it, without some sense of a world upside-down. It shocked the Jews, whose Yahwey was a mystery (and his real Name a secret): the God of Abraham, Isaac and Moses – far off and stern, even to those great founding fathers of old. It shocked the Greeks, who had nothing remotely similar: not in the Olympian circle; nor in the best their philosophy could devise, in more abstract terms. It proved shocking to Eddington, whose God must 'survive the Second Law of Thermodynamics'; and to Bertrand Russell, who was 'not a Christian' precisely because space/time must have an end. Undeniably, it shocks all who are destined for special sufferings; whether under Herod, Nero and Caligula, or under Kaiser Willhelm, Hitler, and a large range of 'world leaders' still in power as I write.

The Father we address, in Jesus's prayer, is *not* inside the Laws of Thermodynamics. He made these laws as part of a separate cosmos. The Father is not destined to have an end, nor are his creatures – despite their sojourn on earth, where 'the sense of an ending' is both our cross, and our spur. Yet the Father, though not destined for an end, is at home in His creatures; He is incarnate in all, experiencing the rules and the suffering of mortality (most nearly, in the life and person of Christ). The entire creation groans and travails together, waiting for (Paul tells us) 'the glorious liberty of the children of God'.

On this present occasion, sitting beside my mother's body on the eve of her burial, I ponder all that my relationship with my own father might have been. I wonder (remotely) what my mother's relation with him was, through a lifetime: good I am sure; but with awful rents, that Heaven will mend. I wonder what the word 'father' meant in fact to my mother: why she never spoke of her own father, to me, to the very end.

'Our Father'. Can we with conviction, with sanity even, presume to address such a term to the universe, and expect a response? This is what the Lord's prayer assures us, in its opening. All the rest follows, only if we pass this point.

(2) 'Which Art in Heaven'

This second clause advances us. In my version, the word is 'Which'. Modern versions prefer 'Who', usually. But 'Which' strikes me as right. It is in immediate tension, for one thing, with the personal 'Father': a reminder that God, though not less than Father, is certainly more. It removes gender problems, allowing us to accept that God is more, not less, then *human* – and so, not really a power we can simply call 'Who'. (Certainly it bypasses all local inanities; such as the 'politically correct' urge, just now, to try 'Our Father/Mother God'.) It is a needful corrective to Father, even – since this opening term, because it is so profoundly 'personal', jumps the really huge gap between an amazing, half-chaotic universe (this playground for scientists), and the approachable God who gave us and is 'our' life, and the life of all whom we love.

Then, 'Which' removes the temptation to imagine a God who is interested in us solely; or is even 'made' by us (or scaled down, maybe, for our special use). If we want an image of God (as we do, being makers of images), then we had best not invent a huge old man sitting up in the clouds. We can best think of holy and special people – and of the people closest to us (whichever side of death they now are) – and, of course, of Jesus himself, as the New Testament records shape him in our minds. The combination of 'Father' and 'Which' is a rich one, since it dares use 'Father', but then puts a check on possible reductions lurking in 'Who'.

God 'Art' in Heaven. The word 'art' again gets retranslated, on account of its supposed archaism (or even, its association with other meanings of the word?). But neither 'is' nor 'are' sounds right, to my ears. Both verbs, singular or plural, limit the godhead. 'Art' belongs, rather, with the mystical frame which God used when He was asked for His name by Moses, and replied 'I AM' (*Exodus* 3: 18). According to John's Gospel, 'I AM' is the phrase Jesus applied to himself, under hostile questioning – to the immense and predictable scandal of fellow Jews. 'Verily, verily, I say unto you, before Abraham was, I am' (*John* 8: 58).

The force of both 'Art' and 'I AM' is to suggest a reality unconnected with this space/time world, and belonging with the Eternal. Jesus's application of God's most sacred name to himself has been debated endlessly, and I do not want to tangle with the dogmatist's games. It seems likely that Jesus was contrasting Abraham's location in history (which is the matter at issue) with the other scale, far beyond clock-time, where God's 'I AM' links with humans in His, and our, 'now'. If so, then the phrase 'Which Art in Heaven' refers, like 'I AM', to the eternal nature of God, and to the Kingdom of God. It unites our ultimate destiny with the eternal divinity which belongs with our 'present'; and which gladly receives and remembers 'The Kingdom', even though we are now so irrevocably immersed in 'the world'.

It refers in short to the nature of consciousness, at the point when it is united with God: 'In Heaven', indeed. It was John Smith, the great though currently neglected seventeenth-century Platonist, who wrote 'Heaven is first a state of mind, and then a place'. The Cambridge Platonist was speaking of that purification of our consciousness which, by inviting the divine to dwell in us, acclimatises us, even on Earth, to our true, lasting home. Purification brings Heaven in, to our innermost being, transforming the life we live daily. It is likewise the perspective we learn to develop towards our destined return to God, upon death. This purification is the centre of Christian life, uniting all its aspects; and the prayer Jesus gives us belongs at its very heart.

We are reminded also that Hell is a state of mind, in its essence; and that it bears, uncomfortably, on the alien values which Christ meant by 'the world'. We could say that Hell is first a state of mind and then a place (like Heaven); recognising, that here too, we speak of our daily life and our Eternity, at the place where they link. In *Paradise Lost*, Milton explores 'hell' as the Satanic consciousness – strayed beyond God's range and so beyond even God's healing, by an ultimate act of rebellious free-will. Satan carries hell with him, in his being, 'though in mid-Heaven'; a torment of alienation, for which no end can be found. Marlowe's Mephostophilis makes the same truth known to Faustus (who can no longer grasp it) in a passionate outburst, occasioned by questions put by the victim he himself has damned:

> FAUSTUS. And what are you that live with Lucifer?
> MEPHOSTOPHILIS. Unhappy spirits that fell with Lucifer,
> Conspired against our God with Lucifer,
> And are for ever damned with Lucifer.
> FAUSTUS. Where are you damned?
> MEPHOSTOPHILIS. In Hell.
> FAUSTUS. How comes it then that thou art out of Hell?
> MEPHOSTOPHILIS. Why, this is Hell, nor am I out of it.
> Think'st thou that I who saw the face of God
> And tasted the eternal joys of Heaven,
> Am not tormented with ten thousand hells
> In being deprived of everlasting bliss?
> O Faustus, leave these frivolous demands,
> Which strike a terror to my fainting soul.
>
> (Marlowe, *Dr Faustus*, Scene 3, 69–82)

God indeed 'is' Heaven, as well as being 'in Heaven': Heaven is God's consciousness, and the place where God 'Art'. In so far as Jesus, or we, are godlike, we are 'in Heaven' (we could add, considering our here-and-now sufferings, 'though in mid-hell').

For most of us, such knowledge is shadowy at best, and far from attainment; rather, it is a supreme intimation from God, which we strive to make real in our lives. Yet no other truth or intimation is more vital to our life, and our daily awareness; hence, the primary place Jesus gives it, in this prayer. Jesus stands out, as a man transfigured, in all his actions; uniquely close to 'The Father'; speaking 'as no man spoke before'. 'Art' implies the godlike reality of heaven, as Jesus fully knew it; as we too know it in part, and seek grace to know it in full.

When we say the Lord's prayer, we are bringing 'this day', with its usual (and special) complexities, into line with the grace and *being* of our Father God. On this occasion, praying beside my mother's body, I am aware of a final difference, in the prayer, for my mother, and for myself. After very nearly ninety-one years, 'the world' is finished: her 'becoming' over, she passes more directly to the realm of true life. 'Art in Heaven' means for her, I hope, that all perspectives are new, and all old questions taken up into truth. For my part, I remain 'in Earth' for a while longer: my exile continuing; my own 'becoming' facing, for me, one major moment of truth. By her death, my mother has crossed the line, leaving me. Both she and her 'questions' are lost, till I pass that way too. Yet in the deepest truth, this petition is still the same for us: God 'Art in Heaven', calling us to be with Him. Jesus gave us this prayer, after all, during his human lifetime; which is to say, from 'my' present side of the great divide.

'To be conscious is not to be in time' (Eliot: 'Burnt Norton'). Here is the essence of God, and from God to us, 'Which Art in Heaven' to the degree that we will to be and can be united with God.

My relationship with my mother no longer 'belongs' with blood-relationship – the aspect which has been so problematic as well as inescapable, up to now. My mother is no longer 'my mother' and never now will be (even though a genetic inheritance stays deep, as I very well know). Just as 'in Heaven' there is no marriage or giving in marriage, so there is no family there, of the earthly kind. Jesus's acceptance of his disciples as 'mother and brothers and sisters', while on Earth still, surely pointed to this. Of our body, Paul tells us the truth, in divine perspective: it was sown in corruption, it will be raised in incorruption: Behold, I show you a mystery: we all shall be changed.

Yet marriage and blood-relationship are great realities. They forge deep, lasting connections – as do all friendships and all earthly relationships, for good or ill. Naturally, we hope that in Eternity those dear to us here will be dear still (more properly: that we shall resume with them a totally real relationship, which was dimly mirrored and too often spoiled, in our time and role here). Of course there will be no possessiveness: that ultimate taint on love; whose purgation is a major lesson to be learned, in this hard ride on earth. But we are told also that every encounter on the road – with an employer or employee, with a neighbour, with a stranger seeking shelter – could be a moment on which our eternal nature hangs. Perhaps it is so swift and seemingly trivial that we scarcely notice; perhaps we are so far still from the nature of heaven, that things central to Jesus remain, as yet, on the periphery of 'this day'. But the heaven or hell within us changes, moment by moment: that 'which Art' is 'the sacrament of the present moment', when the prayer is finished, and normal daily action resumes. This pregnant phrase of de Caussade ('the sacrament of the present moment') is the heart of the matter: the truth of Paul's 'pray without ceasing', as our words pass 'upwards' to God: and 'inwards' to us.

(3) 'Hallowed be Thy Name'

'Hallow' is extremely unusual, as a verb with no associated noun or other part of speech, and with one meaning only. Very rarely does any 'big' word exist without multivalence.

This third petition follows on in the prayer, very naturally. Hallowed ground is ground devoted to sacred and special purposes. It is a natural home of awe, prayer, praise of a solemn kind.

God is 'holy' Himself, and single in Being; we cannot add to God's nature, except in the one form given us; an act of celebration, freely made. It is we who 'hallow' God's Name, truly affirming it: asking grace to move in the hallowed ground, as God's agents ourselves. In a similar way, we 'affirm' individual men, women and creatures, when we seek to love and strengthen the 'hallowed' in them. To rejoice in friends; to seek to forgive and build up God in aliens and enemies; this is a secret power, released by 'hallowing' God.

I am puzzled by those who see praise of God as 'degrading', imagining that it demeans human suppliants to the role of slaves. Praise is our natural response, to things good and lovely. These things fulfil us daily: how much more, the Creator of all loved things Himself?

Yet this crux is of vital import, for many people. It may lurk as a trigger for actual aversion to prayer. Or it may throw people back on purely private prayer, with its danger of indulgence, in place of a formal structure, like this Lord's prayer itself.

I imagine that people who object to praise, in any formal expression, may also find a stumbling-block in God's 'Omnipotence'. If God is 'omnipotent', what can He need, that we give Him? If He insists on our praise, must this not be an abuse of His power? The strange gift of free-will is forgotten, or seen as too nebulous to account for God's need of our Love. We fail to find in it the source of our *reality*, as divine, autonomous beings; or the source of that mutual joy that we have in so many loved creatures of God.

The previous paragraph opens up vast questions; which I merely note here, before passing on. Theses on free-will are many and complex; most of us have no urge to engage with them, and expect no joy if we do. For me, the nub of the matter is 'in' human outgoing; the impulse that leads to any and every variety of creation and love. Let Siegfried Sassoon suffice, in a simple poem, that finds its way into his poetry surrounded by his more normal, grim images of warfare and death:

Everyone suddenly burst out singing;
And I was filled with such delight
As prisoned birds must find in freedom,
Winging wildly against the white
Orchards and dark-green fields; on – on and out of sight.

Everyone's voice was suddenly lifted;
And beauty came like the setting sun:
My heart was shaken with tears; and horror
Drifted away . . . O, but Everyone
Was a bird; and the song was wordless; the singing will
never be done.

(Siegfried Sassoon, 'Everyone Sang')

The truth must be that all virtues have travesties, all light needs discernment. Earthly tyrants exact 'warship' through fear. Is it odd that the highest and most splendid truth, in this simple petition, should have a hellish counterpart, and endless shadows cast by 'the world'? The actual word 'hallowed' is simple, as I began by mentioning; but we need the Lord's prayer daily, and the gradual growth of grace in us, if we are to see God's 'simplicity' for the ultimate glory it is.

Let us recall that Jesus and his early followers lived with Roman power, and with tyrants; and that Jesus often confronted the religious leaders of his day in anger, till they put him to death. Jesus was born in a working-class family, living as carpenters. The grand genealogies set out now in *Matthew* and *Luke* would not have hung in his house, or often been mentioned; both his friends and enemies were puzzled by a certain lack in him of – well, 'background'; 'class'? How come this comparative nobody, berating Scribes and Church Leaders; attracting deference from Roman Centurions by his works and his stance? Jesus 'spoke with authority' as he went his rounds among disciples and sinners; yet more and more openly, he flouted some parts of the Law. We can recall that this prayer we now use was given to Peter, John and other core disciples, when they asked in bewilderment, how he thought they should pray. John the Baptist had guided his disciples, as had other revered leaders; did Jesus have some form of words they, too, could start to use?

The prayer arrived simply enough, on a working day, alongside the parables; no doubt, it must have *seemed* simple, at first. It is very pared down; very sparing of polysyllables. It is very much not rooted in values which Jesus grouped as 'the world's'.

The crux about 'praise', though real, should be seen in context; if we do this, most misgivings fall away. Let us start with our own situation – alone with God; our 'worldly' status, or lack of status, left to one side. We are equal in this prayer, as we are on our deathbeds. We are in God's hands wholly (as I see that my mother is now).

Best start with delight in friends, or in happy events, or in needs pressing on us; best start with a total dependence which has no slightest hint of anything not in 'our hearts'. Let us think of Christ with his friends, with his enemies, with the woman of Samaria, with the thief dying beside him. Then . . . deference? fear? tyranny? – Holy people, things, places – loved people – have nothing, in their nature, of these. Loved people and things are the breath and joy of the soul, they surprise and elate us. . . . 'truly the Lord is in this place, and I did not know it . . . How awesome is this place! This is none other than the house of God, and the gateway to Heaven'. In 1917, Otto pointed out, in his great book *The Idea of the Holy*, that even if we have no experience of angels or visions, no revelations to remember, we still have eyes and ears to see the holy all around us, every day of our lives.

The wonder of childhood fades quickly, as Wordsworth recorded; like Christ, he believed that remembering and recapturing wonder, whenever possible, is vital to life. 'I tell you, except you become as a little child, you cannot enter the Kingdom of God.' So: 'Abba' (Daddy) if one wishes; some days we 'feel' this; all days, we need its truth. Emotions vary from day to day and are usually absent. Emotions are not, in essence, the point. We need a fixed point, a mantra, adapted to western traditions, stamped in our consciousness; potent with power remembered, and with power meeting the day.

On normal days, we start from things and people to whom we flow naturally; riding a tide that is directed and purified by the very austerity of Jesus's prayer. We might progress to the Earth, and its innumerable beauties; to sensations of heartsease, that catch us, for fleeting moments; to the God in all things, creating and sustaining, which we see if God wills it, and which depends not a jot upon us, or our praise, or our life.

I think of Mahler's symphonies, culled from a lifetime's questing; and of one special moment, attuned to this solemn day. It is the last of the numbered Nine, and most of all, I recall its final Adagio, Mahler's amazing 'farewell' to the Earth which he had loved so well. Here is Beauty, known with special keenness at the point of leavetaking; here is vision, moving towards mirage in the gravitational tug, dust to dust.

We lift off from earth, still looking back raptly. The whole surface becomes clearer, smaller; seas, woods, mountains cohering, as Earth perceptibly shrinks, rounds, and starts to recede, in its intricate dance. The moon appears, held in bonds to the Earth and by the same bonds removed from it; the order and strangeness of space-time hold, for a moment, science and magic in one. Then, our back to Earth still, we drift out farther, endless dark behind us, the planet lovelier and smaller, a home we are leaving for good. In the music, the fading of earth merges with the fading of consciousness. One section of the orchestra after another falls silent, as the strings court their drawn-out tryst with silence, still seconds away.

In my 'rehearsal' of the Lord's Prayer, between 10.00 a.m. and noonday on 17 January 1991, in the presence not of my mother but of my mother's body, I ponder her too, for the last time. The beauty of her life, mostly clouded but constant; her sufferings and resilience; her amazement at evil; her longing for a love that eluded her always, as a central law of her life. Over ninety years of looking for a safe place, for her treasure; doubting the treasure; unsure that the place to house it could ever be found. Encompassing and controlling it all, the good and the bad of it, her knowledge that Earth was the wrong place for her, not the place she was 'meant' to be. I trust that, doubts at rest, she now finds glory approaching – the glory that neither she, or anyone on Earth, can know as direct experience this side of death.

I hope she is meeting her mother and her brother; and of course her cats, who ought to come first. She loved cats dearly, though she understood them selectively; never allowing experience to stand in her way. She believed that she could teach them not to kill birds if she continued to nag them; she believed she could stop them clawing her furniture to bits, by imposing her will. She knew that they loved her, and hoped this meant they would please her. The death of two cats, at very different periods, were the only occasions on which I have known her to weep.

Perhaps she is now meeting my father, or perhaps that comes later. They loved each other, but there are repairs to be done.

Do the trumpets sound? My mother 'hated a fuss' in her lifetime. But now? . . . This is the Lord's prayer: 'Our Father, Which Art in Heaven; *Hallowed be thy Name*'.

(4) 'Thy Kingdom Come'

So, here is the heart of the prayer. This pragmatic daily rehearsal, given by Jesus, is rooted in the Kingdom of God. Only Jesus has offered 'eternal life' as one speaking with authority. It is life here on Earth, real in the 'now' we live in: remembering 'heaven'; here to do battle with 'hell'. It is the full life we return to after exile – a life resumed then, purified, by this hard spell of weather we battle through.

Other religions have spoken of 'life after death', or of reabsorbtion into the godhead. Only Jesus meets our individual life, and destiny, with God's 'fatherly' love. The Orphics, the Platonists, other Eastern and Western mystics, have seen 'individual self' as a stumbling-block, which the 'spirit' seeks to escape and transcend. The 'ego' has been placed as a transient obstacle; not as a creative centre, loved for itself alone. It was Jesus who lived, taught, healed, making life a victory; and then, on the Cross, confronted death itself with the triumph of life. For most other religions, we are the waves on a sea, briefly forming; returned, when brief beauty is finished, to the deeps which are 'God'. Only Paul, alight with Christ's vision, proclaimed the full glory. In 1 *Corinthians* 15 he compresses the truth in great images; but it suffuses his Letters, which in essence *are* the 'good news of Christ'.

Jesus alone bases his assurance of human divinity (an assurance which is shared by most mystics) upon positive warmth and humanity as we experience it daily – riches beyond numbering, from God reaching down.

God is the God of Abraham, Isaac and Moses: He is God not of the dead but of the living, as Jesus often said. On the Mount of Transfiguration, Jesus spoke with Moses and Elijah, his glory unveiled for Peter, James and John. This unique apotheosis was granted to Jesus, and to three close disciples, just before the ordeal they would be forced to share, and make sense of, with him. Jesus asserts that God loves all He has made; that He cares for each sparrow. Jesus adds colour, substance, particularity and above all variety, to the hope he gives of fulfilment through death.

Were it not for Jesus, we should have many of the splendid texts that I quote from: yet would even they (Julian of Norwich's *Divine Revelations*, Wordsworth's *Tintern Abbey* lines, Eliot's *Four Quartets*, and the many others post-dating Jesus's lifetime and records), have come to us in the words and structure that their authors' achieved? We should lack the prophet who said 'I am', with divine authority – and who left with fallible, chiefly humble followers and witnesses, the inspiration to mediate him through their own lives and works. We should lack the prophet who, believing in prayer and purity as the 'way' to wholeness, could laugh, weep, eat, drink without inhibition, lifting Earth's pleasures back, to their normal place in the good things of God. 'Ye are they which have continued with me in my temptations, and I appoint unto you a kingdom as my Father has appointed unto me; That ye may eat and drink at my table in my kingdom' . . . (*Luke* 22: 28–30). 'Verily I say unto you, I will drink no more of the fruit of the vine, until that day that I drink it new in the kingdom of God' (*Mark* 14: 25).

The perceptions of Plotinus and Augustine, and of Vaughan, Blake, Wordsworth, Keats, Eliot and a host of such rare humans, achieve a focus and image, in this greatest of all men born. Jesus, too, found God in 'the meanest flower that blows', 'in a grain of sand', 'in the fall of a sparrow': in 'every common sight' of all and every human kindness and hope. He found and charted a progress, 'from glory to glory', to challenge and conquer our progress, through ageing, to death.

Many of the parables recorded in the first three Gospels use homely things, to hint at the things of God. A sower scattering seed, and the ground it falls on; the tiniest seed which grows to become the greatest of trees. Finding things that are lost, a coin or a sheep; or a son who has gone astray. There are odder parables also, like the 'unjust steward': are successful crooks really a model for workable saints? The equal payment, given to workers who have slaved all day, and to those who joined very much later: how do equality, democracy, fairness, square with this?

The fig-tree, blasted for bearing no figs *though out of season,* is a very strange story: presented in one gospel as parable, and in another as 'sign'. Do we find Jesus acting in anger, without reason, and without repenting his action; and if so, where does this fit, in the Kingdom of God? Jesus says he taught in parables partly to subvert understanding; and often, neither friends nor enemies could make much sense of his words. Yet with simple sinners and suppliants he could be patient and kindly; healing their ills, and answering their questions with rare directness and skill.

The 'laws' of forgiveness and healing are complex and difficult (I return to this later, since few matters loom larger in the gospels, or in everyday life). Jesus did not simplify, but he gave no impression of muddle. When he spoke of the fate of the 'prophets of old', and the fate coming towards him, he scandalised some, and left his own followers confused and dismayed. There were many things he knew, but could not speak of; there were other things too dark for our minds to grasp. Evils must come, but woe to the people who bring them. Woe to those (above all) who violate childhood, and innocence. Woe to Judas: who 'must' betray him; and must be one of the twelve. . . .

The mysterious areas are needed, to make Jesus credible; without the dark corners, the Cross, where would we be? If we opt for dogmas, there are many eager to teach us. If we ask for truth, we need 'The Truth' himself, in one, whole life. There are many valued insights, attached by Jesus to particular people, and place. Opposites balance often, in Jesus's teaching; as they do in the sayings of all wise men.

The Kingdom is outside us, before and beyond us, it is not 'our invention'. It is not ours to plumb to the depth, or mould to our minds.

The Kingdom is at hand, it is 'in' us, and in all whom we cherish. It lies all around us, open to all eyes that see.

The Kingdom is the place Jesus departs to at death, to prepare a place for us; a glorious reunion, sealed in the drinking of wine.

The Kingdom must be earned, by 'giving up all', taking up one's cross daily; persevering in the things of each day.

The Kingdom is given so gently, it comes beyond hope, as a last, long-planned surprise:

> Love bade me welcome; yet my soul drew back,
> Guilty of dust and sin.

But quick-eyed Love, observing me grow slack
    From my first entrance in,
Drew nearer to me, softly questioning
    If I lack'd any thing.

'A guest', I answered, 'worthy to be here':
    Love says, 'You shall be he'.
'I, the unkind, ungrateful? Ah, my dear,
    I cannot look on Thee'.
Love took my hand and smiling did reply,
    'Who made the eyes but I?'

'Truth, Lord; but I have marred them; let my shame
    Go where it doth deserve'.
'And know you not', says Love, 'Who bore the blame?'
    'My dear, then I will serve',
'You must sit down', says Love, 'and taste My meat'.
    So I did sit and eat.

(George Herbert, 'Love')

In John's Gospel, parables for the most part are missing. We witness rather meetings between Jesus and a variety of people, which more than make up for their lack. This is a different view of Jesus from the Synoptic portraits. It is inward and searching, as if pondered by a friend, over many packed years. We are told by scholars that the linguistic style of John's Gospel is far from distinguished yet, from the noble opening, through all its record of meetings and discourses, to the strangely personal closing, the whole texture glows, as if transfigured within. Jesus is Love incarnate and his 'good news' is love *in excelsis*; but there is much also of darkness, and fear. The motif of 'sheep and goats' is in evidence (as it is in *Matthew*, also). We might feel that these two accounts, different as they are in content and in their intended audience, both pick up the reality of hell as the other, dark side of all love.

Like the late Bishop John Robinson, Carl Jung, Robin Lane Fox (*The Unauthorised Version*, Viking, 1991) and others, I sense that John's Gospel is indeed by 'the beloved disciple' – or at least, by one loved disciple from the twelve. It must have been put together throughout a long life of prayer and witness, with final touches added in extreme old age. The author's personal vision is easy to detect and discount, if we wish to; what is certain, is that we are uniquely close to Jesus, seen with love's eye. There are episodes like Jesus's simple, beautiful encounter at Jacob's well with the woman from Samaria; and the account of the woman taken in adultery, brought before Jesus by his enemies in an attempt to trap him, at the unhappy woman's expense. (This second story is an interpolation, or a lost section later restored, which scholars argue about; of its authenticity, there can be no shadow of doubt.)

These two women, both sinners, one a political alien (the Jews and Samaritans were estranged), called out Jesus's personal concern for each of us, just 'as we are'. From the Samaritan woman, he asks a gift. He is tired, and for the moment alone. He is thirsty, and needs water, which he cannot draw. The woman gives what he asks, but is amazed that he speaks with her. A man speaking to a woman, a Jew to a Samaritan? And, as she discovers, a profoundly pure man, speaking with a woman who has had several husbands; for Jesus 'knew her heart', though she could not suspect this at first. But Jesus is wholly natural, one human in need with another; even though she is not 'of his flock', and never likely to be. It is to this woman however that he offers back, in return for her kindness, 'a well of water, springing up to eternal life within her' – the pearl without price for all seekers of wisdom, offered *if she wants it*, with no strings attached. The matter of her irregular life is touched on, not in wrath and judgment, but in a quiet, honest exchange. Their shared cultural values were sufficient context. The woman's responses cross all cultural changes, and would ring true today. Total absence of formality, strain, urgency is the feature we notice; along with the apparent chance nature of their meeting in this time and place. Jesus goes on to make a prophecy which, addressed to this woman, has given hope to countless hearers, ever since. 'But the hour cometh, and now is, when the true worshippers shall worship the Father in spirit and in truth; for the Father seeketh such to worship him. God is a Spirit, and they that worship him must worship in spirit and in truth'.

When the disciples return, the woman goes off to spread her wonder (and conviction?). She has had her great moment (*John* 4: 5–30) and she is not heard of, in history, again. The returning disciples are hungry, they too have been working. To them, Jesus says 'I have meat to eat that ye know not of'; and again, 'My meat is to do the will of him that sent me, and to finish his work'. A little later, Jesus offers the 'bread of life' to the multitude; an episode that all the Gospels recount, in their differing ways. Elements of the Eucharist permeate the imagery (wine and bread, meat and water – basic bodily needs, with their parallel in the soul). These gifts make men equal, as life and death do; they turn into symbol, but start in simple encounters, in daily routine.

Later in John's Gospel we hear of intimate discussions between Jesus and his closest followers, mediated through deeper, longer reflection than we find in the Synoptic accounts. We are allowed to overhear, uniquely, another Lord's prayer – direct from Jesus to the Father. This prayer springs from intense and personal anguish; and spans the entire future of life, here, on Earth. It is for us to 'keep in our hearts', as evidence of Jesus's prayer life; it offers nothing that we can attempt to use ourselves. It is the most sacred moment in all the records and, perhaps naturally, no two readings of it ever seem to lead in familiar paths (*John* 17).

The Lord's life is full of The Kingdom, in teaching and living. This is why, for many of us, it is Wisdom's *sanctum sanctorum* – the known centre, containing secrets we feel, and live by; yet never quite see. Many of us, like the Samaritan woman and the woman 'taken in adultery', are Christ's 'other flock'; we are 'under judgment', but can meet judgment only as our life and nature allow. Close disciples who jockeyed for power were rebuked, gently and firmly. The one certain way of missing The Kingdom is through rejection of love.

There are sins to be faced by us all, some tawdry and sickening. Sex, though a joy and an art when healthy, is no joking matter, when mutual love is lost. Sometimes it is one of seven 'deadly' sins, as the Church lists them, that can lead us away from God, into the dark.

Shakespeare seemed to know everything, almost as Christ did – though evidently, purity was not Shakespeare's given path to truth. Sonnet 129 in his famous, very shaded sonnet sequence, compresses much that we know to be true from the dark side of lust.

> The expense of spirit in a waste of shame
> Is lust in action; and till action, lust
> Is perjured, murderous, bloody, full of blame,
> Savage, extreme, rude, cruel, not to trust;
> Enjoyed no sooner but despised straight;
> Past reason hunted; and no sooner had
> Past reason hated, as a swallowed bait

On purpose laid to make the taker mad;
Mad in pursuit, and in possession so;
Had, having, and in quest to have, extreme;
A bliss in proof; and proved, a very woe;
Before, a joy proposed; behind, a dream.
  All this the world well knows, yet none knows well
  To shun the heaven that leads men to this hell.

Do you want to argue? Go ahead; it is highly fashionable. Much of our culture belongs with the closing couplet. Christ's parable of 'the prodigal son' addresses these matters; which he understood perfectly, but chose not to define, as Shakespeare does. One has to hope that readers who are still inwardly arguing, at this moment, against sonnet 129 ('No, I have never lusted like this' . . .) will not revert too suddenly, if deflated, to revulsion – or choose to vent any new found revulsion on others, instead of themselves. ('Back to basics' is a phrase in the news, as I write this. 'Alas, what fools these mortals be' as Shakespeare's Pan said – enjoying himself.)

Shakespeare's sonnet may 'convict us of sin' if the cap fits; and if we are in the mood to try it, for size. It assures us also that we are not alone in sin: Shakespeare spoke for himself, very properly, and allowed us to hear. (May I add that I am writing now outside my profession as critic, and know that any fellow critics who have strayed here may be dancing with rage. I do deal with literary arguments elsewhere, and have made a career of them. But in a serious prayer session, they amount to very little. This particular sonnet's meaning is simple, and clear.)

With sin, of whatever kind, we need compassion; and this is the mark of Jesus with people, when he has them alone. Charles Wesley put it marvellously, as he often did: 'Show me, as my heart can bear/The depth of inbred sin'. I have heard an eminent psychotherapist praise this for its intuitive wisdom, at a point where many of his medical colleagues go terribly wrong. Without the rider 'as my heart can bear' certain visions from the past might rise, and overwhelm us. They could lead to suicide, or settled despair. Their sheer magnitude might cut us off from God finally (and there are stern texts, in scripture, to feed all fears). Jesus did offer forgiveness, without fuss, as Wesley well realised; and with only one, implied condition: which is precisely that we do not deny truth simply because it seems too hard to bear. The poem by Herbert, which I recently quoted, is calm in appearance, but springs from a lifetime's turmoil and doubt. Jesus himself was 'led by the Spirit into the wilderness to be tempted by the Devil': and, whatever the Devil tried, in those forty days, it was certainly tough.

Another Charles Wesley hymn comes to mind; an amazing poem, with power to calm, or elate. Perhaps it is best used at moments of high dedication; but just before a burial, it pierces, too, like a sword.[1]

O Thou who camest from above
  The pure celestial fire to impart;
Kindle a flame of sacred love
  On the mean altar of my heart.

There let it for they glory burn
  With inextinguishable blaze,
And trembling to its source return
  In humble prayer and fervent praise.

Jesus, confirm my heart's desire
  To work and speak and think for thee;
Still let me guard the holy fire
  And still stir up thy gift in me.

Ready for all thy perfect will,
  My acts of faith and love repeat;
Till death thy endless mercies seal,
  And make my sacrifice complete.

(5) 'Thy will be done in Earth, as it is in Heaven'

The previous petition has fixed our spiritual centre in the place it came from and hopes to return to, the Kingdom of God. This petition explores our personal part in the drama. God's will is known, to the degree that Jesus's life, and words, proclaim it. Our 'will' must be conformed to the Kingdom if the prayer is to work.

The contrast between 'Heaven' and 'Earth' is pivotal. Heaven and Earth are different orders of being, often polarised. But both are present in our consciousness (our 'fifth dimension'), and need to be merged. When we hear Jesus speak of 'the Kingdom', he tugs at us. The Kingdom relates to truths we remember from far, in the depth of our being; yet to truths we fail to find operative in history, or in much that we do.

The challenge is to bring our being 'in Earth' back nearer to Heaven – a hugely difficult business, to be attempted in the whole of a lifetime, *yet essential 'today'*. Our nature has to be re-formed to the instincts of love, by difficult, only half-natural, will-power. The search for grace to achieve this seems, in a nutshell, to 'be' the purpose of life.

If we are alienated from God to the tormenting but very normal degree envisaged in Shakespeare's Sonnet 129, the Lord's prayer is incremental healing, handed to us by Jesus as one of his gifts. We need to say it daily, in and out of season; and this petition of 'will' can give special hope, it we let it, in very bad times.

If we are alienated from God beyond Sonnet 129, there is certainly danger. The willed discipline of saying and pondering the prayer, when all instinct rejects it, is a lifeline to cling to, for our very soul's sake. Christ's teaching and living threw a continual light on the kingdom, both in its boundless scope, and in its stern reminder of the price to be paid. If the words of the prayer mean nothing to us 'today', or are simply an irritant, then our job is to say them; and leave them, along with any shred of hope we have left. If we have no hope, then our job is to say them and leave them.

In a profound way – and even at the best of times – this petition, following the previous one, brings us back to our daily burdens, and to 'Earth', with a bump. Praising the people and things we love and seeking their welfare will most likely, for many, be our natural way 'in'. But our own part confronts us next, and for this we need cleansing: since our 'will' must turn into action, and reshape to the day. If God is to answer our prayers He needs agents; so let us face it. The most natural agent, or, the most total obstacle, may be ourselves.

At a time of bereavement, face to face with my mother's body, the last practical chance for me has gone. For sixty-two years I have had daily chances, a long enough period; now all that is 'past'. Everything comes down to God's power of healing the past, which I judge, in my own life, mostly failure. Our life before birth is lost to our memory ('hints and guesses, only'); the line beyond death is effectively sealed. Between, we assess our possessions, make our souls. The possessions of Earth, if we had them, come and go, transient baggage for pilgrims. The treasure that matters? Jesus said, 'Where your treasure is, there will your heart be also'.

If Jesus was mistaken; if the mystics imagine things, building hopes on mirages; if the linguistic vandals are right – all treasure is gone. For many, this 'is' the truth, and they try to face it. Of the two ultimate possibilities – return to God, or return to oblivion – they test which they find easiest to imagine, or to believe.

I am not sure what religion (if any) e.e. cummings had, but one poem haunts me; perhaps it links us all, if we love. There is a great egalitarianism in the first and last things; those lovely bubbles of life, where religion sets up its stall.

anyone lived in a pretty how town
(with up so floating many bells down)
spring summer autumn winter
he sang his didn't he danced his did.

women and men (both little and small)
cared for anyone not at all
they sowed their isn't they reaped their same
sun moon stars rain

children guessed (but only a few)
and down they forgot as up they grew
(autumn winter spring summer)
that noone loved him more by more

when by now and tree by leaf
she laughed his joy she cried his grief
bird by snow and stir by still
anyone's any was all to her

someones married their everyones
laughed their cryings and did their dance
(sleep wake hope and then) they
said their nevers they slept their dream

stars rain sun moon
(and only the snow could begin to explain
how children are apt to forget to remember
with up so floating many bells down)

one day anyone died i guess
(and noone stooped to kiss his face)
busy folk buried them side by side
little by little and was by was

all by all and deep by deep
and more by more they dream their sleep
noone and anyone earth by april
wish by spirit and if by yes.

women and men (both dong and ding)
summer autumn winter spring
reaped their sowing and went their came
sun moon stars rain

(e.e. cummings: 'anyone lived in a pretty how town')

For those reading this book, religious instinct burns, and wisdom stays constant; but areas of doubt (are they fear?) most likely remain. We are speaking of precious treasure, far beyond rubies. On most days our treasure is laid before God, in thanksgiving or anguish; if He does not understand, this is not through fault on our side. At the time of death, the treasure is gone from our keeping. We no longer have it to offer. It is back with the Giver; and in what sense if any is it 'ours' now at all? How handle the words, when their meaning alters so strangely? Should we try, 'Thy Will be done in Heaven, as it is in Earth'? The final prayer at the graveside comes very close to this; but the symbols test our faith to destruction when we need it most: 'Earth to earth, ashes to ashes, dust to dust; in sure and certain hope of the Resurrection to eternal life . . .'

To someone of my temperament, praising God through His works comes naturally. Enough has been said, to make this clear. I recognise that for some, the path to God lies through renunciation. But from this, I shy away, by conviction and instinct: though of course, at the graveside, and in all such places, I have to submit. It is possible that some are forced to the path of renunciation by a different temperament; or because they see certain dogmatic *tabus* as 'really' godgiven, and not as an accumulation of lies told by priests. Some find themselves on the *via negativa* by choices made for them, or by choices made by themselves and then irrevocable – as poems like Hopkins' 'Terrible Sonnets' seem to show.

The wars of this century are thrust on us, along with its other horrors – accumulating out of control, perhaps, as the 1990s advance. My grandmother was far from alone, though she clearly felt so, when her son was killed in action, and she bid God farewell.

For these reasons, we know that Earth is not Paradise; and was never meant to be. The drama of life can bring this home with trauma; but however sheltered, no life evades its final moment of truth. God's Kingdom must be elsewhere, at least in its fulness; it lies behind us (no doubt), but we have no approach to it now by a backward march. The way back is guarded by angels with swords, exactly as *Genesis* tells us. 'Shall a man enter a second time into his mother's womb and be born?'

We must be 'born again', Christ says, 'born in the Spirit'. Yet still, our new life on Earth, will lead to the Cross. Our treasure must lie beyond the Second Law of Thermodynamics, and must be safe from it. The time comes (has come and gone, at the graveside), when our own prayers can hope to reverse the nature of things. We need God the Transcendent truly present and truly with us, if we can say, with hope: 'O Thou Who changest not, abide with me'.

As God is loved in his works, so is He praised in them: here, the spirit of Hellenism and the inspiration of Jesus of Nazareth unite in me, linking much in Plato with still more in Paul. 'I thank my God upon every rembrance of you, always in every prayer of mine for you all making request with joy . . . For God is my record, how greatly I long after you all . . .' (*Philippians* 1: 3–4; 8).

In daily life, praise comes naturally in the rhythms of duty. A doctor heals, a teacher passes on learning and, ideally, wisdom. All this must be chiefly of God. A lawyer safeguards justice, and this is of God also; just so long as he doesn't take years to do it, and charge ten times too much.

My own vocation has been the passing on of great literature, and, as my old friend and fellow editor Brian Cox once put it (himself, I think, quoting), all teachers come as 'men bearing gifts'. The basic formula for teaching is Paul's, which I shall quote yet again, since the truth about teaching has never been better put. Paul's insight extends far beyond formal education, in which it is rooted, to take in entertainment, culture, politics, and every corner of life. 'Whatsoever things are true, whatsoever things are honest, whatsoever things are just, whatsoever things are pure, whatsoever things are lovely, whatsoever things are of good report: if there be any virtue and if there by any praise, think on these things'.

Paul does not say that these things will guarantee virtue. The reality of free-will remains, in all of our lives. What he does say, is that their natural tendency is to affirm, and build up, all that is good and beautiful. Indeed, just as depraved or ugly things degrade, when they surround and absorb us, so created beauty is exemplary and conducive to good. Wordsworth believed that his life lived amongst lakes, mountains and scenes of wild, natural beauty was an active blessing, which had helped to build his creative and spiritual powers. It had brought him, with time, empathy with all human suffering; and healing closeness, in this, to the living God.

This petition of the Lord's prayer is practical, and active. But its reservations must be returned to again. Earth cannot 'be' Heaven, though it can aspire to it. 'Heaven' and 'Earth' are separate, the one God's home, the other His transient creation – even though in prayer, and action, they can and must be linked. The Kingdom has its foothold in our hearts and in the Good we aspire to, but the daily tug of life is towards smallness and death. We shall not be delivered from change and decay, and from the laws of our earthly testing, this side of our return to fullness of being after death. But we can be strengthened by 'comfortable words' (words that 'build up and toughen', as the Prayer Book usage signifies). The Lord's prayer is designed, very specially, for this daily end.

Some religious people find great peace in suffering; most are plunged into misery and doubt. What Jesus offers is his own sure sense that God's will 'Art' in Heaven; and that it *can be* 'in Earth': just so long as we make this prayer a true programme for life.

I suppose I am underlining again the prayer's startling austerity; its notable lack of emotion generated from within. The emotions locked in the prayer do not work by poetic resonance. They emerge and take colour from our knowledge of Jesus, and from our own shifting fortunes at the place where we are. But its core remains, through all shifts between joys and disasters, a fixed point for our will; a set of words to 'say', leaving major work for God Himself to do (*Romans* 8: 26–7). The Lord's prayer can 'only' be said, on some days, by an act of discipline. But the right to say it depends on actions to meet its demands, in every practical way.

When using this prayer with my mother's body, the material now included in Chapter 6 was floating in my mind. It was touched off by my mother's apparent fear of church buildings, and by my own fated alienation from the church. The prayer does not answer such problems, but it does assist them. No final enmity between 'Heaven' and 'Earth' can ever hold. The prayer's genius is to peel away personal irritants, however troublesome, allowing the Kingdom to remain, a city set on a hill that cannot be hid. It forces us to invoke the Holy Spirit tersely, paring everything down to God's Will, and to ours.

(6) 'Give us this day our daily bread'

The word 'daily' enters, attached to 'bread' very simply, but challenging the entire scope of our commitment to the prayer.

To live, we need food for body, mind, spirit, a huge arena. The focus comes in the bodily need which Jesus noted, when hordes of his suppliants were stranded, hungry, on mountains, without any food. Jesus told his disciples to feed them all, on the few loaves and scraps of fish that were available; the disciples had to arrange the multitudes in rows, and wait for bread from Heaven to be given. We have to accept that this situation occurred at least twice in his ministry; and that it took on key importance for the Gospel writers, who would have had the spiritual bread of the Eucharist in mind. There is a great emphasis generally on bread, water, fruit, wine, the Earth's 'natural' resources; and on the proper use that humans must make of these. The earth's harvest must be worked for, reverenced and spread out equally; which means, that practical things must be foremost, in religious lives.

Dostoievsky's Grand Inquisition was wrong to accuse Christ of offering 'only' 'love' and 'freedom', and of neglecting the simpler things that humanity needs. Let us be clear, on this, beyond all doubt, in the West especially; where Governments claim Christ's name, but hate to hear the social truths that he preached. The petition for 'daily bread' is not just one part of this prayer, but its natural pivot. It is the petition which unites, yet severs, the two, contrasting halves. The prayer's first half is rooted in celebration of God and in thanksgiving; the challenge comes from Heaven, to the things of Earth. This present petition is interposed at the centre; and then, the prayer moves to darker, more potentially menacing ground. We turn to our duty to forgive all who harm us, without reservation; and to the link between this, and the healing from God that we need for ourselves. We move on to 'temptation', and pray for the strength to withstand it. We seek 'Deliverance from Evil': the prayer's dark, and strangely threatening end.

Political prophets like Marx and Engels became possible, and necessary, only because Christ's church failed in its most basic, and apparently simple, task. It sold out to princes and to worldly shows and eventually to Inquisition and torture, and took little action (one must except some catholic 'religious', and some protestants) on 'daily bread'. The natural politics of Jesus is 'welfare socialism'; a label that makes sense to all who fought for the reforms which the Labour Party brought to fruition, in Britain, after 1945. Jesus's politics have to rub off on us to some degree, whatever 'our' labels, if we are to use his name and his prayer daily in the presence of God. As long as any classes, nations, races, or individuals under our feet on the pavements starve, while others flaunt plenty, a great evil disfigures the world; and God is mocked.

In a rich country, this should be easy to grasp. During the Second World War our 'rations' were not simply enough for our needs, but were so well balanced, that in health terms this was an excellent time to be young.[2] We must also consider how the 'monetarist economics' of our more recent past, and our present, measure up to hunger in the 'Third World' and to hunger on our doorstep in Europe, as the second millennium after Christ draws to a close.

The starving peoples of the Earth will find no theoretical puzzles in this petition – merely an expression of their growing desperation, as the bread they need fails to appear.

Without bread and water and the other basic needs of the body, human beings grow ill, and waste, and die, in childhood or youth.

There are still millions of men and women in all parts of the world, and around me in London, who are starving today – despite everyone who may be saying this Lord's prayer.

The Lord's prayer cuts deep, in its wider, symbolic reaches; but it is meant first for the starving, who literally, and terribly, have no bread. We cannot say it without shame, unless we are giving some money (within our means, obviously) to cope with the starving. 'No salvation without the Church' is a dogma favoured by 'Christian' sects who claim a corner in 'salvation'. 'No salvation while anyone starves' has the merit of being Christian, at least.

In an age like ours, political systems are hard for religious people to live with. They take our money in taxes – which is fine, in the fields of education, health, clean air and water, basic public 'infrastructure' – but less good when mixed with wasteful bureaucracy, with the promotion of killing through arms dealings, and with economic usury as a new social 'ideal'. It was the same to a degree in the first century AD and luckily, Jesus addressed the crux head-on. Pay your taxes to Caesar he told us, don't stir up subversion; but remember, the 'things of God' are specially trusted to us.

Personal giving of money is desperately needed in the 1990s, even though it is no proper substitute for justice, and for a more orderly world. At present, we can best give money through the big, organised charities, most of which are supported by, but not run by, church sects.

Ideally, we should join charities that call to us, and should be prepared to give more than money to their work. We have to make sure they are properly administered, and that we are not being fleeced by rogues. But feeding and housing the poor is such a priority for Jesus – as this prayer witnesses – that churches using his name must be somehow shamed into doing more than they currently do. Until church congregations are open to the homeless on their doorsteps, and reaching out to the overseas starving, no other dogmas or exhortations can get off the ground. Church halls should be adapted to local needs, if they are empty (and rate-free); so should unused rooms in vicarages now far too large for their priest. The congregations are the obvious people to run them, pooling their talents and time as an obvious extension of worship and prayer.

This petition is for ourselves and the world, and it is not merely literal; but it is not less than literal: and, until the literal aspect is attended to, 'food' for the mind, and soul, cannot be fully addressed. In fact, all three are clearly interconnected; and the 'higher' levels, as we think them, will stay floating in air unless the foundation exists. The whole petition touches that basic test for 'the kingdom' which Christ gave (in *Matthew* 25: 31–46, and other places), when he was asked whom he will, and will not receive 'as his own', when this life is done.

Neither the prayer, nor religion, can be narrowly 'political'; yet, in the broad sense, a fair arrangement of society must prevail. It must be wrong to have 'food mountains', and earth and water polluted with poisons, and farm animals reduced to money-making machinery, while famine and starvation prevail elsewhere. For economic greed to call itself 'the developed world' is bad enough; for it to call itself 'Christian values' is simply sick. We have transport and communications enough in the world to solve material problems. It is an active will to solve them that we lack.

Politicians do not help. Many impede the giving of help 'on principle'; others, through fears of 'strings attached', or 'loss of face'. But recently, the dogmas of the 1980s and 1990s have introduced a new and spreading harshness in the world. Britain, the USA, Europe have all been infected; the end of the Cold War has spread these doctrines into the East. We are now in a world where 'Christian values' are trumpeted by societies where Mammon is, *de facto*, the reigning god. Money is plundered from the poor to give to the rich. It is a reverse Robin Hood politics, marked by open derision for social welfare and its liberal ideals. The word 'socialism' and the word 'liberal' have been attacked as 'subversive' by new vandals of language, now claiming to serve God's Word.

Capitalism was the system known to Christ in its early form; and for centuries, it remained much the system as he had known it. His parables often used images drawn from money, including terms like 'redemption'. Though the poor were 'his' people, he did not denounce class structures and empires *per se.*

If we look at George Herbert's poems in the seventeenth century, we find that capitalist imagery is still used, very naturally, to devotional ends. This is the period when the debasement of capital first gathered impetus; but Herbert found scriptural uses untained, for devotional ends. The poem which he called 'Redemption' is a fine example. Imagery familiar to Jesus and Paul, and to modern Anglican liturgy, illustrates the universal treasure of 'The Kingdom' inside God's love and grace.

> Having been tenant long to a rich Lord,
> Not thriving, I resolved to be bold,
> And made a suit unto Him, to afford
> A new small-rented lease, and cancell th'old.
>
> In heaven at His manor I Him sought:
> They told me there, that He had lately gone
> About some land, which he had dearly bought
> Long since on Earth, to take possession.
>
> I straight return'd, and knowing His great birth,
> Sought Him accordingly in great resorts –
> In cities, theatres, gardens, parks, and courts:
> At length I heard a ragged noise of mirth
> Of thieves and murderers; there I Him espied,
> Who straight, 'Your suit is granted' said, and died.
>
> (George Herbert, 'Redemption')

This is one of the finest poems I know, about 'the atonement'; and lucid, in complex thinking, as only Herbert can be. The poet uses

Pauline theology, but without commitment to blood-sacrifice. The price Jesus paid, and also offered to his followers as their price of discipleship, encapsulates 'The Kingdom' in the language of Earth.

My concern here is with the nature of 'capitalism' as Christ knew it; and as it was, in substance, until recent times. Towards the end of the seventeenth centry, Locke offered his famous economic version of the 'social contract', which assumed that earthly wealth should equate with our individual needs, ideally; and land ownership be attuned to areas we can personally tend for our needs.

The rise of modern capitalism seemed at first benign to the eighteenth-century 'establishment', though men like Goldsmith and Blake perceived new, radical ills. The enclosures of land ruined many long-established rural communities; the 'industrial revolution' turned cities towards sweated-labour, slum dwellings, polluted air.

According to Dickens, the rise of the Stock Exchange, in the 1860s, turned the minds of wordly people increasingly towards 'Shares'. R.H. Tawney, E.P. Thompson and others have traced the rise, and fall, of socialist movements – inspired by anger, by protest, by revolution brought about by society's greed. As we know, our British Labour Movement was influenced at least as much by Wesley as by Marx and Engels, and Christian doctrines were influential in the rise of the 'welfare state'. A great many individuals gave their lifelong energy to create this – opposed by many powerful 'political' interests and with minimal help from the Church of England (the official church of the state). We have to look to the non-conformist traditions for most of the pioneers of welfare (accompanied, belatedly enough as it was, by attacks on the age-old custom of slavery – whose days should have been numbered, after the powerful Letters of Paul).

A body like the Salvation Army seems purely honourable; but mainstream Christians remained entangled in class divisions and established power.

Is the Lord's prayer a proper place for polemics? It is a proper place for 'Give us this day our daily bread' to be faced, frankly and simply, in the spirit of the language Jesus used. He did not argue, and he did not embroider. It would be hard to find a simpler phrase more often repeated and more studiously ignored. The petition is a plea for ourselves, and a plea for others. It seems clear that Christians must confront it urgently, if they are to speak for The Kingdom with conviction, and rescue themselves from 'the world'. These can be no Christianity, and no Salvation, while anyone starves, unaided, in the streets.

The Eucharist uses bread and wine, as its central action; thereby uniting daily politics to the most sublime religious act. I have to accuse myself of too little regarding this. The 'lust' for worldly goods, even as a safety-net against hardship, is as relevant to the Shakespeare sonnet (129) I quoted earlier, as are the more publicised lusts 'of the flesh'. For Jesus, 'world, flesh and devil' were equal and implacable enemies, of 'The Kingdom' he came from, and preached. I shall return to this later. But we cannot easily use the prayer Jesus gave, on any day or occasion, or in whatever circumstances, so long as we persist knowingly in greed.

I recall that my mother, though a lifelong conservative, hated poverty, and was made deeply uneasy by greed. Throughout her life, she was 'poor', as the world judges. But she knew that she was rich, compared with most people; and her later addiction to television confirmed her in this view. She had few luxuries, but she 'never wanted': a phrase more natural, to many hidden, good people, than is often supposed. She said that 'her money was blessed', and she meant this, as a serious judgement. The phrase was used also by my grandmother before her; and both connected blessing with that sense of 'being watched over' which I have come to understand more deeply, now, than I did when young. Both were alienated from the church, if for different reasons; but their 'guardian angels' belonged with instincts 'not of this world', in the true sense.

I trust today that my mother is back in The Kingdom. May she find that her doubts meant to her less than her faith did, all along.

(7) 'Forgive us our Trespasses, as we forgive them that Trespass against us'

Well: here is the rub. Hard on the heels of a petition looking simple, Jesus asks this different, and surely impossible, thing?

I have suggested that any 'simplicity' in the previous petition is deceptive; when we attend, its challenge cuts very deep. There is no real change of direction in this prayer; we remain throughout with 'The Kingdom'. It is, rather, that 'daily bread' sounds normal; this petition does not.

Jesus makes us ask for a thing the church often preaches but seldom heeds much, in normal times. A few remarkable individuals achieve it – some, among the official 'saints' and exemplars; perhaps far more of them hidden among obscure laymen – or among people who are not consciously 'in' the churches at all.

There are times when most of us attempt 'forgiveness' – with very varied success, if I judge by myself. Christ's doctrine goes entirely against the grain of human nature – including 'natural survival', and other basic instincts born of the world. It is the point where 'the world' and 'The Kingdom' come most into conflict; when the laws of Jesus's 'Father' challenge head-on the laws of space/time. If one puts it this way, it is the starkest reminder that we are truly in exile; and that the place of our testing 'in Earth' is very deeply at odds with 'the eternal' in us.

Can we really think of an enemy, even a trivial one, and honestly say that all our rancour is now gone? Can we confront a deed, or an odd remark that wounded us, and let it be as if it had, somehow, never been?

Can we think of major enemies and even want to forgive them? Murder, rape, kidnap, bullying, fraud, betrayal . . . merely to list such things is horrendous. To ponder them, is more likely to harden the heart, than to make it relent.

And then, there were the atrocities of Hitler's Germany, and Stalin's Russia; and sins (less dramatic?) of the former British Empire, which its once subject peoples still find hard to forgive. At the present, we are seriously faced with a growth of political terrorism; and the attitudes of victims bring forgiveness home, in a vivid light. Some say, they can 'never' forgive – though most realise that their own more normal instincts are peaceful; and know that brooding on wrongs will chiefly do harm to themselves. There are others, like Gordon Wilson, who forgave the IRA for wounding himself and killing his daughter, in full Christian charity; yet who was dismayed when, facing the IRA later, he found no answering love in them.

Our 'global village' forces us, as I write this, to look at Bosnia; and at other parts of the world where atrocities daily occur. The end of the 'Cold War' did not bring a 'peace dividend'. It appears instead to have released old enmities and conflicts, as if the years of 'peace by oppression' had not intervened.

Then, there are relationships that were broken through just one thing said or done wrongly. Few of us have not been agents, and victims, of these. We can ask forgiveness for things done or spoken in anger; but we cannot unsay them, or go back to alter the past. If they were hurtful, the harm is done, and how can use overcome it? If they were true, the rupture must go deep. Even years later, forgiveness is hard, though we may attempt it. But we wonder perhaps, 'What good, does it really do?'

Churches which call themselves 'Christian' have the same problem. This part of the Lord's prayer is a poser indeed. It is not just a matter of the *'filioque'* clause, which first split the church in the early centuries, and remains Christianity's major split still, after most of the Church's history on Earth has passed. There were major further divisions when the secondary church (under the Pope) lost parts to Anglicanism, and then to protestants; and suffered further subsequent splits, that have grown in number, not dwindled, with time. The 'ecumenical movement' started up, in this century, to attempt a healing; but it has run out of steam, as it was surely fated to do. Recent papal pronouncements, and the Anglican crux of women ordinands, reveal how much easier splits are to start, than to cure.

There are further issues that alienate individual Christians; and here, I join (and speak for) a large, diverse band. Bishops fulminate against sex, and mistrust strong love and friendship (which might lead to sex); but they bless armies and battleships, since wars can be 'just'. How can these episcopal heresies be forgiven, if they affect the lives of us and of some whom we love? If our love has been wrecked, and our lives made lonely or outcast by the church's 'dogmas' on sex, how can we forgive – let alone attempt to belong to the church? If our loved ones have been killed in wars caused by power politics, how can we judge the church's 'blessing' of wars as other than cant?

There are some sexual rapes and assaults that are naturally wicked; but these are properly a matter for the criminal law. There are some wars that may truly be 'just', like the war against Hitler; but these are exceptions, in history's roll-call of war.

In most daily living, sex should surely be seen, under God, as a 'personal' matter; but violence should be judged as a crime always, whether it is performed by individuals or by states. It seems to me that even if one can 'forgive' the church its perverse meddlings, one cannot join it while it continues in these paths. Why should one forgive, if there is no amendment? Hypocrisy is not a virtue, in anyone's book.

Jesus's prayer to forgive those who trespass against us goes against the grain of nature; and it is not currently helped, by most of the churches which claim to be 'his'. This must be a central problem, for many exiled from 'religion'. No easy solution to it is in sight. With the passing of time, division becomes habitual. Could we go back now, to repair even the church's first split? If we are asked,

'Does the Holy Ghost proceed from the Father; or does he proceed from the Father and the Son?' this is not among our most pressing concerns. Most of us probably fail to make sense of the Trinity, and think (as I do) that a human Jesus born to Joseph and Mary rings far truer, as prophet of The Kingdom, than does a figure whose mother was half-human ('immaculately conceived, without sin' is the formula), and whose father is not human at all. It is unlikely, however, that Rome and the Orthodox will go back, to solve this crux. The uncurbed extravagance of Rome's papal claims exacerbate it further, even at this time that I write.

But let us also face the heart of the problem, which is deeper than we like to admit. At first sight, do we suspect that the great pre-Christian religions seem more in tune with everyday realities, when it comes to forgiveness, than does Jesus, in his great prayer itself? The Jewish 'eye for an eye, tooth for a tooth' (*Exodus* 21: 24) is still widely followed, even though Jesus explicitly reversed it, in unambiguous deeds and words:

> Ye have heard that it has been said, An eye for an eye, and a tooth for a tooth:
>
> But I say unto you, That ye resist not evil: but whoever shall smite thee on thy right cheek, turn to him the other also.
>
> And if any man shall sue thee at law and take away thy coat, let him have thy cloke also . . .
>
> Ye have heard that it has been said, Thou shalt love thy neighbour, and hate thine enemy.
>
> But I say unto you, Love your enemies, bless them that curse you, do good to them that hate you, and pray for them that despitefully use you, and persecute you;
>
> That ye may be the children of your Father which is in heaven . . . (*Matthew* 5: 38–40; 43–5)

The Jewish precept is still far more typical of churchgoers, in their actual attitudes both to crime and punishment, and to sin and ostracism, than is that of the religious leader whose name they use. The Jews call for vengeance certainly, but also for justice: which is measured to fit the crime; and thereby seen to be fair. With luck, justice concludes an ill episode with the honours even, so that no further vengeful sequels are required. The Greeks discovered 'Justice' also, as we have seen in Aeschylus, removing vengeance from personal action, to an impartial court of law. Yet in transcending vengeance, they contained it also; and from them, the judicial systems of Rome, and Europe, still chiefly descend.

Why do we not all cry 'impossible moonshine', 'infantile dreaming' to Jesus – as some, of course, do? Why, more importantly, do we not only pay mere, mechanical lip-service to Jesus, but *feel and know, against all reason, that he is right?*

This is the heart of the matter, and the huge hope vested in it. This is Kingdom against 'world' as it is fought out in *us*. All that belongs in clock-time is firmly against it: and yes, we are creatures of clock-time; and yes, clock-time was also constructed by God. Yet all that belongs with the 'still point', the lasting moment of 'consciousness', leaps out to meet Jesus's words, with assent and delight. These words indeed are 'remembered' truth, in Plato's sense, *par excellence*. They appeal to everything in us which says, with the Jewish writer of *Hebrews*, that 'here we have no abiding city; but we seek one that is to come'. At the same time, these words have been placed by Jesus, in this daily prayer for us, as a natural sequel to the opening petitions: 'Thy Kingdom come; Thy will be done in Earth, as it is in Heaven'.

Obviously, 'forgiveness of enemies' does not fit with Hobbes' shrewd reading of human nature as a natural mix of self-interest and fear. It does not fit with Gibbon's scholarly and pessimistic assessment of the actual, recorded history of man. It does not fit with Darwin's perception of 'the survival of the fittest', and with the evolution of our species, as we currently perceive it to be. It does not fit with the Hawking Cosmos 'from Big Bang to Black Holes' with violent explosions and timescales utterly alien to human survival and human love. It does not fit with the (currently defunct?) oppressions of Soviet Communism (though these can be traced more to irreducible flaws such as bureaucracy and tyranny that invaded communism, than to any great gulf between the ideals of communism itself and the Kingdom of God). It does not fit with the 'market force' ideology currently masquerading as 'Christian', which is virtually a plunder of the poor by the rich.

Jesus's doctrine does fit, however, with almost all perceived human goodness: whether we look to great acts of heroism and sacrifice from all sectors of history; or to those 'little, nameless, unremembered acts/Of kindness and of love' which Wordsworth defined as 'that best portion of a good man's life'.

So: how can we get our bearings? Jesus's seventh petition must have sounded as totally unnatural to fellow-Jews and gentiles in the First Century, as it does now, in our gut-reaction, to us. And here, I suppose, is the inner genius of this great prayer, still said by countless millions day by day. The prayer can seem to be, and is, very simple. Yet, within its compass, wisdom and innovation strangely merge.

How do 'I' respond? Forgiveness is not easy, in the manner asked for, even though I am quickly able to put 'small' things behind me, as are many people prone to anger from their birth. 'Let not the sun go down on your wrath' made great sense to me, as a child. My family erupted often into anger (except for my mother). I could pitch into white-hot anger myself. By and large, I forget and forgive fairly quickly: but here is the problem: 'forgetting' is easy, if your memory is as poor as mine is and if you are temperamentally disinclined to live in the past. When I don't forget, then those things tend to rankle. I steer clear of the people involved, and phase them out of my life if I possibly can. From time to time, I try to forgive, with the aid of the Lord's prayer. But the healing of memory seems very partial; I don't get it right.

Yet I know that this petition is the heart of The Kingdom; that forgiveness and healing are totally and irrevocably linked, in some ultimate way. The petition reaches the profound, the abyss in us, and is placed there – like a broken-down fence, by the cliff's edge, just warning of death waiting, a few inches beyond.

On the occasion of my farewell to my mother, I think of her goodness: which was wildly off-beam, by normal human standards: by no means fault-free, yet hard, clear and integral; free of artifice or of any tincture of deceit. I recall her regular refrain, about evil: 'she could not understand it', she would say. Why do people do evil, why do they think it? Why do they put horrors like crucifixes in churches, and apparently worship them? Why can't they be kind and gentle; above all, why can't they leave each other alone? Well: this may seem disingenuous; or lacking in elementary self-knowledge. Perhaps it was. Did my mother know her own dark side, until (at eighty-seven) it erupted? And if so, did she regard it as an aberration to be conquered? Or was it repressed in the Freudian sense, as I suspected, so that, though I always knew it was there, and that it was a major aspect of her withdrawal from relationships, it was really hidden from her? If so, her desire for a religion which did not face or include evil could have been a form of escapism; it could have been an instinct at all costs to try to stay safe.

So I leave this open; except to express a conviction that my mother did long for a world in which enemies are forgiven or, better, do not happen at all. She had a great deal to forgive, herself, from those close to her; and she did forgive, though I can only guess at the cost. I fancy that Jesus's call for forgiveness struck her as obvious; and that she belonged to the Kingdom without knowing it, in this very deep way.

My mother did believe in criminal law, and punishment; and here, I imagine that Jesus agreed. He did not confuse forgiveness with the absence of judgement, and realised that, without healing, evil must fester, and destroy. If he were living now, he would not be awarding honours and Oscars to films about multiple murders, but recommending everyone involved in them to search their souls. The forgiveness Jesus spoke of was in the *nature* of his 'Father'; and will be in our nature, to the extent that we can be reunited with God. 'Forgiveness' is not the absence of judgment; it is a principle offered by Jesus, at the heart of 'The Kingdom', finally overriding judgement with a still higher law. And it is a principle with amazing powers of healing locked in it; both for those wielding it, and for those in receipt. It goes without saying, that it cannot be vicarious. We cannot ask forgiveness of a priest, or a psychiatrist, for wrongs we have done to others. We can only seek forgiveness from those we have wronged; and from God.

It grows upon me that I have to learn to believe that God *can* forgive everyone; that no one is excluded, if they can (will?) repent. This is wholly mysterious: but I must prepare to learn total forgiveness. There must be no one whose final forgiveness is in any way blocked by me. It is an area where we must rely chiefly on instinct: no doubt, this is why 'the discernment of Spirits' looms so large, for St Paul. I can readily grasp that I have done things myself which I do not want the world to know about – now or ever; I suspect that this is even true of some who make their business 'exposing sin'. I cannot be talking of a cover-up (at least, I hope not: God knows Himself, and we have to deal with Him). I hope, at least, that there will be no spectacular 'Last Judgement': no final, inclusive *News of the World* scenario. Forgiveness will have to be worked out (surely) in harmony; in some way that heals, and then is left behind.

I have a growing conviction that unless this petition becomes central with me, and I really make headway, there will be no fullness of life for me here, or anywhere else. I am certain that forgiveness and healing are interdependent, in The Kingdom – in a manner that Christ's miracles hinted at, but always darkly; since they were performed here, on Earth. As I grow older, the real effect of this petition is, I think, a really *huge* source of hope. It is unnatural, foolish, impossible, for so many reasons; yet its authority goes straight to the heart. The Kingdom is not in space/time, not 'in the mind', not in the normal 'scheme of generation'. Yet if I can be cleansed and remade, and begin to bear fruit, I belong there: how much, and how, can these things be?

> I have no faith
> that to put a name to
> a thing is to bring it
> before one. I am a seeker
> in time for that which is
> beyond time, that is everywhere
> and nowhere; no more before
> than after, yet always
> about to be; whose duration is
> of the mind, but free as
> Bergson would say of the mind's
> degradation of the eternal.
>
> (R.S. Thomas, 'Abercuawg')

What is the nature of goodness? We return to this key dilemma. Is it synonymous with God, and if so, how does it reconcile with the restraints of the Laws of Thermodynamics in this cosmos, and with invasive Evil which seems, strangely and terribly, to originate elsewhere? In effect, the remainder of the Lord's Prayer bleakly confronts us with this paradox; but first, let us return to this petition, and to the mysteries here.

Goodness does exist, just as Beauty does. The more you look for it, the more you find:

> And I say unto you, Ask, and it shall be given you; seek, and ye shall find; knock, and it shall be opened unto you . . .
>
> If a son shall ask bread of any of you that is a father, will he give him a stone? or if he ask a fish, will ye for a fish give him a serpent?
>
> If ye then, being evil, know how to give good gifts to your children: how much more shall your heavenly Father give the Holy Spirit to them that ask him? (*Luke* 11: 9, 11, 13)

But there is a price, as Plato knew, and Christ verifies. We must first purify our inner lives, and cleanse the doors of perception. Goodness is passing our door, lurking like a flower hidden in undergrowth. It is for eyes to see on Earth, that we ask in this prayer. We are told to pray *as if we had achieved victory, and are indeed in the Kingdom already as we pray.* For by grace, we are indeed in the Kingdom, though lost in the dark; light comes from the Spirit finding a place, as often as we let Him, here in ourselves:

> To be conscious is not to be in time
> But only in time can the moment in the rose-garden,
> The moment in the arbour where the rain beat,
> The moment in the draughty church at smokefall
> Be remembered; involved with past and future.
> Only through time time is conquered.
>
> (T.S. Eliot, 'Burnt Norton')

Christ's church started with a particular acknowledgment: 'Thou art the Christ, the Son of the living God' (*Matthew* 16: 13–20). When Peter arrives at the insight, and says it, he becomes 'Peter' – the rock; the foundation stone. Christ accepts the truth, and says that the keys to Heaven and Hell belong with it. He then binds the disciples to silence, on this truth, that he is 'the Christ'. So Christ's 'body on earth' is founded, and the keys of truth go with it. But the discovery is to some degree secret, and meant to stay so. It depends upon recognition, made when the Spirit offers.

This is the work of the Father, in his dealings with all men; and it dates back to the rules of creation itself. The two things Christ asked of those who recognised him, and whom he recognised, were that they should forgive sins, healing the sick and needy; and that they should be witnesses to his truths in the world. 'Witnesses' are not to be confused with bawling evangelists; rather the opposite, since 'silence' always prevails, beyond noise. Witness is by fruits; by a way of life; by the work of the Spirit. It include 'words spoken in due season' but such words must be sparing, at best.

The terms of 'witness' are set out in a life, not in a document. It is the parables, the signs, the discourses, that we must scan. Christ expected his followers to be poor not rich, in the world's terms; but to bear the singular blessing that went with their calling: 'Where your treasure is, there will your heart be also'.

Clearly, Christ's followers are intended to be healers. And clearly, forgiveness and healing are totally linked. This seventh petition, which is the most obscure in the world's terms, is the very heart of religion seen from within. Christ himself performed healings ('miracles', as we often call them; 'signs' is the word preferred by John). Some call him a 'Shaman', seeking an older prototype. But in truth, the power to heal is a gift that some people appear to be born with, as Jesus was. St Paul describes it as a gift of the Spirit, which individuals may or may not have – along with the Spirit's other gifts. The New Testament records are almost routinely ambiguous on healing and forgiveness, much as Apollo's Oracles were. Christ's own attitude is, no doubt deliberately, obscured. Sometimes, he links healings with penitence, but not always: sometimes, he links healings with 'Faith', but there are exceptions, again. Once, he said that a general lack of faith in the community robbed him of his own powers of healing. His healings were sparing, and they seemed to leave him physically drained. Often, he wanted them to be kept strictly secret though, once or twice, he specifically asked for news of them to be spread.

In John's Gospel, where the signs are not stressed greatly, the oddest of all of them is recounted (it appears nowhere else). This is the raising from the dead of Lazarus, who was a friend of Jesus, and news of whose death moved Jesus to tears.

No sequel is recorded by John, to justify the miracle; and presumably, Lazarus had to endure the death process again. There are two other occasions on which the raising of the dead is attributed to Jesus. One is the raising of Jairus' daughter, which is recounted in all three Synoptic Gospels; but here, Jesus uses the phrase 'she was not dead, but sleepeth', which can be variously read. The other concerns that 'raising' of the widow's son, which is called out from Jesus by compassion. This is told only once (*Luke* 7: 11), and again, the death – if it is such – is recent; the young man is being carried to his burial, when healing occurs.

In *John* (11: 1–44), however, it is made clear that Lazarus had been dead for four days. He is already buried, and his sister Martha uses the striking phrase of the body, 'he stinketh'.

In *Acts*, one 'raising of the dead' is attributed to Peter; otherwise, this radical reversal of nature has played no part in the church.[3]

The Lazarus account stands out in my mind, as it does for many; it is one of the two occasions when Jesus wept. John's gospel seems transfigured throughout, and takes us 'closer' to Jesus than anyone but a friend, and a mystic, could get. The English translation in the

Authorised Version is so deeply resonant, that it is always a shock to hear scholars speak of the original Greek as 'odd', or flawed. I tend to assume that Jesus acted, on this extraordinary occasion, on human impulse; and that Lazarus has to stand, as a wonder apart. Yet the great proclamation of general resurrection is made, at this time (*John* 11: 25–6).

Spiritual healings of bodily ills are exceptional, at all periods. Some are well-attested, by reliable witness, though all leave margins where sceptics can move if they want. From time to time, groups from the mainstream churches have taken healing very seriously; at present, the 'charismatics' come to mind. There are centres of healing which have grown up over the centuries in places associated often, though not always, with a particular saint's appearance. One house of healing which greatly impresses me is the Anglican community formed by Dorothy Kerin at Burrswood, in Kent. I visited it several times in the 1970s, when Edward Aubert was Warden, and Dorothy Arnold (official biographer of Dorothy Kerin) was still alive. I have never felt more immediately aware of the presence of Christ, and the power for healing alive in him still.

A few protestant congregations have become absorbed in healing, some of them taking isolated texts to dangerous lengths. There are sects in the American South where venemous serpents are handled, as part of the worship. This is based on episodes such as Paul's escape from a viper (*Acts* 28: 3–6); and especially on *Mark* 16: 17–18 (the account of the resurrection of Jesus, and its sequel, which appears to most scholars to be a later addition to the text), and on one or two other New Testament texts. There is at least one sect, the Christian Scientists founded in the nineteenth century by Mary Baker Eddy, which calls Christian healing 'scientific'. It builds itself on a denial of any 'reality' to the material world, and ascribes all the ills of the flesh to 'mortal error' arising within our minds.

Jesus regarded forgiveness as life-giving to the spirit, certainly; he associated it with general health, including soul, body and mind. In the early Church, forgiveness was associated chiefly with Baptism; but then, the crux of sins committed after baptism began to loom large. Could these later sins be forgiven also; or was no route to healing now left? Many early Christians deferred baptism to their death-bed for this very reason.

They were willing to gamble on the complete exoneration assured by a last-gasp sacrament; and this, even though a sudden or accidental death might claim them instead, with all their sins unhealed.

At some stage, the Catholic church discovered 'the sacrament of penance' which got round the problem; and 'penance' has been central ever since. Its obvious risk lies in making forgiveness mechanical and, from a religious viewpoint, in giving a dangerous boost to priestly power. Later, most protestants rejected 'sacramental penance' as an aberration, but substituted daily soul-searching in private prayer, with 'General Confession' at worship an added rite. There were sometimes public confessions, at evangelical spectaculars, with emotions blazing and no holds barred. Fortunately, these often merged in a general babble; and 'born again' conversion made up for any embarrassment – provided that no one was storing up notes.

Neither catholics nor protestants have regarded healing as a 'normal' sacrament, or made it a part of the basic church year. The laying-on of hands for sickness has been given when asked for; 'extreme unction' has included prayers for an easy death. When healings do occur, they are usually hidden; and this follows the normal instincts of Jesus himself. When I edited *Christian* (vol. 2, no. 2; All Saints 1974), I felt it was the most remarkable thing I had ever done. The range of witness suggests that healing continues to be part of Christian life in the late twentieth century, in ways identical in variety and paradox to the New Testament accounts. There were certain other accounts – one or two from wholly dependable sources, and still more remarkable – which I decided would be better not used. I doubt whether people should, or could, come to religious belief through 'miracles'.

It seems right that, like paranormal experience generally, all religion should be elusive to rational 'proof'. No doubt, healings are meant for particlar people and, like visions and numinous moments, take their place with the material I shall discuss in Chapter 9.

The assurance of God's forgiveness is important to Christians; and it has a sound base, in our union of body, mind, soul. Sometimes, a definite decision or turning-point (*metanoia*) helps individuals to return to devotion; or helps others to cling on through dark patches when devotion might otherwise lapse. It touches eternal life and is at the heart of our cleansing. Some degree of spiritual healing is always involved, in religious life.

Purely physical healings, with no spiritual content, seem more dubious. They do not easily sit with the laws of space/time. Ageing and death are inevitable, as the normal pattern we follow. When an accident happens, it cannot be later reversed. *Luke* records an occasion when Jesus healed ten lepers, who appealed to him with the words 'Jesus, Master, have mercy on us'. Jesus sent them to the priests, to 'show' themselves; and *Luke* records that they were 'cleansed'. But only one returned to thank Jesus, who seemed somewhat hurt by their casualness: 'Were there not ten cleansed? But where are the nine?' This is followed by the important moment, which is reserved for the one who did come back to give thanks to God. 'And he said unto him, 'Arise, go thy way, thy faith had made thee whole'. We are specifically told that this fully healed leper was a Samaritan.

This story (*Luke* 17: 12–19) is extremely powerful, especially in that final use of the word 'whole'. I feel certain that spiritual healing is central to religion, in all times and places. Physical healing may be an offshoot, but it is by nature exceptional; and intended if and when it happens as a very personal transaction by God.

The medical profession is concerned chiefly with physical healing, and has become based largely on our 'scientific' ethos, and on our perception of 'proofs'. This phase is bound to recede, in the next century; and already, many doctors recognise that mental and physical health are closely linked. Psychic explorers like Yeats and Jung have been pioneers, in our own century, of important aspects of the religious resurgence that is now under way.

We must assume (I think) that medical advance *per se* is 'of God', but that its excesses include dangers of a serious kind. In the sixteenth century, Bacon hoped that science would eventually 'cure death', and so prolong life on earth hugely: (not 'for ever', since accidents happen, and always will do; perhaps Bacon assumed that we should live to become more like the Olympian gods than we currently are). Such extravagant hopes encouraged the worst excesses of science and the downgrading of God from 'Father' to mere abstraction ('First Cause': then, not even that). At the same time, Bacon had not discovered the Second Law of Thermodynamics, and did not foresee this doom to his hopes, implicit in 'science' itself. Most 'Utopian' hopes based on 'science', have forsaken Wisdom, and paid the usual price. In recent centuries, Utopias have turned to nightmares, wherever one looks. Today, we have new dangers – the threat of 'genetic engineering'; and the use of transplant surgery to prolong earthly life as if this, alone, were the greatest possible good. The next century will have battles to fight on both these fronts, and very bloody they are likely to be. The seventh petition of the Lord's prayer, and Christ's healings generally, lose none of their power.

What matters, in religion, is the instinct to heal and the nature of healing disciplines – whether spiritual or physical means are chiefly employed. We need to beware of charlatans, on both sides of this equation. We need to keep our eternal destiny at the front of our prayer.

Petitions for loved ones are as natural to prayer as breathing is to the body. If we pray through compassion, then we know that we pray in the spirit of Christ.

And, if the future is indeed rolling towards us – still fluid in shape and not wholly predestined – then to surround loved people with blessing is not only natural; it is the very nature of love; and certainly pleasing to God.

On the Cross, Jesus prayed 'Father, forgive them; they know not what they do'. Forgiveness – so unnatural to 'the world' and so hard for each of us – is God's simple, painful price, for forgiving us. Very simply, it is God's one demand, for making us whole. We may or may not share Christ's exceptional powers, as a physical healer. What we do receive, in forgiveness, is the 'water of life' which death cannot touch.

This seventh petition becomes especially important, when we note what follows, before the prayer ends. When we use the prayer in the presence of a loved person, just before burial, remembrace of blessing and forgiving gathers, and come to a point.

(8) 'And lead us not into Temptation'

In modern translations, this usually becomes 'And let us not be led into Temptation'. I am not sure of the linguistic ins and outs, but the reasons given are often theological. Modern Christians have told me that they find the idea of God leading them into temptation wrong, or even blasphemous. We lead ourselves into temptation (they say), by uncontrolled passions, by failure of willpower, with Satan stage-managing, up to his tricks. God's part is to rescue us when we fall but, above all, to change us. This petition is our plea to be 'let off' temptations that would be too much for us – a not unreasonable request, to the God who 'knows'.

I see the point of this version, but it has its dangers; are we not put on Earth precisely to be 'tested', in an alien world? Our hope must be for such growth in holiness, over a lifetime, that things inimical to God will gradually lose their sway. In the meantime, temptations will come, and we will fall to them. The continued prayer for forgiveness accepts, and deals with, this. God's grace will co-operate with our will, if we truly let it. But we cannot escape the temptations to which we are prone.

In fact though, I feel that Jesus's prayer probes deeper, and deals with mysteries darker than the 'new version' suggests. I want to return to this, but there is a personal note to insert here – always present; and made so especially, by a death.

Despite the baptism which my mother cherished, I was not brought up as a churchgoer, or made much aware in my childhood and early youth of the person of Christ. I was merely submitted to the routine hymns and fragments comprising 'School Assembly' and to the mainly puritan morals current at the time. I recollect challenging the Trinity once, on the ground of mathematics, and being told not to be impertinent; but also, not to get carried away during maths. The master didn't believe, and knew he didn't; and he knew I knew he knew . . . usual enough. Why should I have tried to disrupt this cosy pattern? I suppose I did take religion seriously, up to a point.

At around the age of seventeen, I drifted into St Mark's, Hamilton Terrace, in St John's Wood one summer evening, and was so dumbfounded by the psalms, that I converted at once. I cannot remember which psalms they were, that evening; but probably any, in the glorious Coverdale version, would have done. For a few years, I explored different types of churchmanship, flirted with Rome (who didn't, then?) – but with St Mark's as anchor I felt happy; even, full of delight. I even had six months (or was it five? – or five weeks maybe?) virtually free (as I thought, 'delivered') from the violent, multivalent goadings of sex. This Anglican commitment lasted through much of my Cambridge days, though evangelicals and Romans between them were very soon snuffing it out. In the end, I was accepted for ordination at an ice-cold conference led by an ice-cold Evangelical, and lost my faith as the letter accepting me arrived (what an escape! . . . and for the Church too, I suppose). Later, I returned to the Church in 1966 and remained until 1978, and was extremely happy again – at least, in the first few years. But again, my mind, body and soul were divided, and I felt that nagging false-in-the-truth tug, towards truth to myself. I wanted (among other things) to pray for my friends, and above all, for my life-partner – who meant, and still means to me, far more than life. But they were the wrong sex for the church, which thrives on hypocrisy – from school assembly to the grave, it came to seem. The church, thinking only of sex, cannot see love clearly, for all its preaching. It has among its members, many sincere, committed Christians, but in its present state of obsession with sex, and confusion about love, it should not claim to be the 'body of Christ'.

This time, I left with a decided bang, a public show-down; and I have reverted to my real religion now (whatever its name is), but without the cherished solace of 'Christian' prayer. At sixty-five, with the deaths of all whom I love most in the world now accomplished, I wonder whether the Church of England and I might yet cohabit (hence, really, this book). But Anglican pronouncements and omissions these days mark a further 'No Entry'. The present pope, if taken seriously, is a nuclear 'No'.

I have missed the chance of praying alone, as I did, in church buildings. It must be presumptious to use sanctuaries which others paid to erect and repair, unless one is exploring a return. I should like to be buried with Anglican rites, if this seems acceptable; I am not an atheist, and cherish a religious end. I cannot make out which way is the real temptation. To join, or not to join? And does the Church care?

Maybe the Church is clear, one way or another . . . so this petition, touching myself, revolves a little on that. But, with Jung as guide, I return to this eighth petition, and resume (but with readers now aware of 'my' picture; and with Jung's *Answer To Job* as cue, coming on time).

'Lead us not into Temptation'. As Jung points out, God does in fact lead into temptation. Three of the most high-profile moments in scripture turn on this fact. Virtue, far from protecting humans (and should we feel personal relief, here?), appears to be the thing that most goads God on. I have in mind Adam and Eve, as first example. They were given instructions by God, which seem specific. But Satan was not stopped, in the slippery and brilliant onslaught he then made. He was able to appear in Paradise, disguised as a serpent; and to use a method of lying for which nothing inside their experience had prepared the hapless first pair.

Then, there is Job. Job was handed over by God to Satan, to be tempted; and all for a wager. Job was a good man, outstanding in every particular, and therefore, he was ideal fodder for Satan's wheeze.

And finally, there is Christ himself: who, at the start of his ministry, was handed over to Satan in exactly the same way as Job. The first verse of Matthew's fourth chapter could hardly be blunter: 'Then was Jesus led up of the Spirit into the wilderness to be tempted of the devil'.

In *Answer to Job*, Jung homes in on the second example; and expands from it to considerations of near infinite scope. *Answer to Job* profoundly impresses me, and is a modern classic, which anyone reading my own reflections will want to turn to (if they have not come across it before). I should make clear that I am not endorsing Jung; and I am not suggesting that he is anything but extremely eccentric (as he well enough knew). These thoughts that follow, did strike me forcibly, when with my mother's body; and I see no way round them, if the prayer is to be prayed in the terms proposed.

Satan bet God that he could take and break Job, if this enterprise were allowed, and given fair wind. God, instead of sending Satan packing, accepted the wager; indeed, Satan seems to be in God's good books; or how does he come up with wagers like this? *The Book Of Job*, in all its grandeur and ambivalence and awefulness, records the result that follows from this very strange pact. Jung, seizing on the book for his own purposes, wrote (in his later years) his own amazing *tour de force, Answer to Job*. Jung approached *Job* mainly, of course, as a practising psychotherapist, but also as a lifelong explorer for religious truth. He uses a method which is not theological, not philosophical, not even psychological or literary, in any ordinary way. It is an approach more in the spirit of a literal fundamentalist, to the extent that he receives the text as 'given', and proceeds from there. It is as though God had wandered on to Jung's couch, as one of his patients, and the *Book of Job* (along with *Apocalypse*, and other assorted scriptures) became a stream-of-consciousness session, with Jung raptly engaged.

Jung concludes that *The Book of Job* records a vital stage in God's self-realisation, and that it was the actual cause of God's need to atone, to man, for divine sins. (To call this a remarkable reversal of the normal notion, that Christ came to earth to atone to God for man's sins, is merely to skate on the surface of Jung's truly brilliant, and subversive, small book.) Jung comes near to discovering that God, so scrutinised, is dangerously schizoid; and that this trait explains the rest of scripture, from beginning to end. In effect, God does 'lead Job into temptation' (Jung says); and then, fails to protect him – indeed, behaves in an extraordinary way. God likewise fails to deal with Job fairly, or at all to restore him (unless the ending, whether it is original or was tacked on later, satisfies anyone at all). We can agree that Satan is the effectual agent of temptation; but it is God who gives the needful permission for this. Satan's destruction of Job's entire life, and the lives of all the people he cherishes, goes well beyond anything one might hope God would allow. Job's friends add to his torment, with a gusto that marks them as true theologians – and with a minimal understanding of Job's exceptional fate. Finally, Job's weakness (for Job is a man, not a god, or an angel) overwhelms him, and he curses the day of his nativity – a truly marvellous passage, like so much of this mysterious, and unfailingly universal, work.

We do not know whether anyone who died in the trenches, or in concentration camps, or in acts of torture or terrorism in our century had anything like Job's 'virtue' at the start. Their ordeal is part of the real world – part of *our* history; and 'Where is God? What is He doing?' are questions that tormented my grandmother, and my mother . . . and how many more?

The text tells us that God has handed Job over to Satan in the first place; and for reasons not wholly clear (or so Jung suggests) to Himself. It is a huge jump to Jung's further notion that God's later incarnation as a man is the result of his own guilty introspection (and Jung has to indict God for continually failing to consult both his 'omniscience' and his close daughter Sophia [Wisdom] – as if God had become abnormally absent-minded in the time, even, of Job).

Still: Jung makes this jump; and perhaps it explains why the same fate overtakes Jesus at the start of his ministry, as that which caused all the trouble for Job? Jesus is handed over to be tempted by Satan for forty days and forty nights in the wilderness. And, though Jesus fared better than Job on that occasion, he was later not spared betrayal, trial, scourging, open ridicule, shameful and painful death on the Cross. He did ask to be rescued 'if it were possible' ('Father, if it be possible, let this cup pass from me'). But it was not possible: and this was foreseen by Jesus, who had been well aware of the death that his preaching would bring about.

Jesus's attitude to his death is depicted in the Gospels as an event he predicted, and even regarded as his real destiny. Very likely, a measure of hindsight surrounds this. Old Testament texts have to be selected, and stretched rather far; by Matthew especially, since he is determined to make Jesus fit the Jewish scheme. But Jesus's teaching of 'The Kingdom' naturally courted danger, since most of his hearers inevitably interpreted it as a threat to Rome (an issue I shall return to). Jesus's own testing was, however, to near destruction; in the precise manner known by Adam and Eve, and by Job. 'My God, My God, why hast Thou forsaken me?' is a terrible cry, echoing another previously tormented human (David – *Psalm* 22).

During Jesus's lifetime, the Jewish expectation was of a 'Messiah' to save Israel from the Romans, not of a 'suffering servant', so the texts most used by Matthew would seldom have been in most minds. Even John the Baptist had doubts in his prison cell, as Jesus developed his ministry. The disciples were half-dazed, and shell-shocked, most of the time.

So: Jesus was well aware, when he gave this prayer, that God *can* lead us into temptation; and that the results can be harrowing indeed. It seems that the greater the virtue to be tested, the more dangerous the testing.

Those with a special sense of mission have to be watchful (yet morbid fears have led numerous Christians in terrible paths).[4] This part of the Lord's prayer is undeniably sombre, with too many resonances (for me) from my mother's troubled quest. Yet is is also, I think, a totally central petition, if we are to feel that Jesus's religion passes the human test, and is universal in truth; as it has to be. None of us can evade human suffering. Many of us confront evil (at times in ourselves). The twentieth century has been grim, on any reading. The old Chinese curse, 'May you live in exciting times' has fallen on us: trenches, gas-chambers, 'cold war', terrorism, ethnic cleasing; a reality of world pollution now upon us; science running out of human control. Yet the great mass of humanity always has been born to slavery or poverty. Roll-calls of terror and torture deface every age. The eighteenth century was as grim, for the great human majority, as less 'rational periods' have more confessedly been. Jane Austen's dream of 'bourgeois order' appeals to us, in certain moments; but it appeals as artefact, not as 'social realism'. It belongs in the realm of art, not of 'life'.

A religion that rings true must confront Evil. It must show Evil conquered, at is uttermost reach. It must have the Cross, and all that led to it. It must have a prayer with a petition like this one, squarely faced.

According to Jung, God sent Jesus into the world to atone for the wrong He had Himself done to Job. Jung sees Jesus as succeeding; but as himself doubting the Father sometimes; since experienced betrayal was to be the heart of his fate.

Then, by a further *tour de force*, Jung turns to *Apocalypse*, where he finds the whole of God's self-understanding and integration, as achieved in Jesus, unravelling again. John, the Apostle of Love (and also Jung thinks, as I do myself, the author of *Apocalypse*) is overtaken by an outpouring of his own dark side – repressed or sublimated before, but now erupting, in old age, in these terrifying visions of destruction and hate. Jung suggests that this 'dark side' remains ineradicable in all of us, and that it is present in the Creator Himself. Jung even implies that God, try though He will, cannot overcome His own ambivalence. Jehovah's chequered relations with the Chosen People, through the entire Old Testament, are only intermittently encouraging about God's 'love' for the human race.

I greatly hope that Jung is wrong about the Creator; even though he is right to push the Mystery of Iniquity into realms that we cannot probe. It is impossible to explain the actual laws of space/time by some creature's slip-up – whether the first humans on earth (very recent), or an erring angel living inside this cosmos at any period following Big Bang, should be chosen for this role. Even more, it is impossible to explain the further dimension of Evil – willed Iniquity – which affects our eternal, as well as our temporal, dimension of life.

Answer to Job is very mythic (and 'Jungian'), as its author intended. We should not forget that, though Jung knew the human heart and its psychic depths as few moderns do, he was not exempt from a love of blarney (if such a hallmark of Ireland can be suspected, in a Swiss). He conjures with riddles that haunt Christian religion – and that keep some people from ever being able to believe in God's Being, or his Love.

Today, I cannot forget my mother's life-long search for God, and her unanswered questions. I cannot forget the fearful eruption, at the age of eighty-seven, of her own 'dark side', or imagine that Jung might not be right about St John (one hopes, not about God). This is the last time I shall pray for her, in her body's presence; and the eighth petition hovers, as I say 'farewell'.

I am sure that my mother was 'delivered from evil' (as Jesus was) – and that the Cross, which she feared, is our earthly 'sign' of whatever this process means. The cost is great, the danger real and lifelong; this daily prayer is less austere and detached than it sometimes feels. I also sense that if I can hope I am still, in some honest way, a 'Christian', this has to do with Jesus *de profundis*, and with God's ultimate integrity beyond the fray.

I return to my basic thesis, that the 'problem' is not 'the problem of evil' as often presented; and especially not, if the 'problem' is attributed to some sin which came about in space/time. The real problem remains the problem of Good: where does it come from? How does it get into the world of Big Bang, expanding galaxies, huge alien spaces where men cannot live; the world whose history is dark, and whose hopes are too easily quenched?

This is a world where the greatest depictions of God are ambiguous, and unable to evade a fear that Love does not always win. Jung, at the end of his long life, claimed to be 'a Christian'. He wrote also that the wisdom we must cling to includes both the light and the dark. In a late 'Face to Face' interview, when asked if he 'believed' in God, he paused – and then said, 'I know'. He also wrote, as he neared his own ending: 'God may be loved; but He must be feared'.

Yet Jesus taught the Kingdom on Earth; and he lived it. He offered a vision to affront our 'common sense' and most of our instincts; yet we find this vision pierces our hearts and does, after all, ring true. No need to rehearse this again, since it is my thesis; but the eighth petition brings it terribly close. Also, I face it now in my own dilemma. Is it a temptation to try to rejoin the Church (if I come to this); or is it a temptation to try not to? Either way, would the church want me? The present signs are not good. I could not bow to the Church without renouncing my greatest experience of love; and so betraying not myself only, but other people far nearer God than I am – an entire, mixed bag, with which I belong. I think that I have to try to be in Christ's 'other flock', and leave him to make sense of me, and judge whether I am fundamentally honest or not.

Most days, if we use the Lord's prayer, God will not lead us into temptation. It may be that only the exceptionally good have to worry: but Christ did insert this petition, into the general prayer. On most days, however, we shall face temptations of some kind; so God's help is something we cannot do without. There are temptations that turn compulsive and destroy, unless conquered; there are temptations with destruction, even murder, at the end of their road. This prayer is seldom made from a drama as stark as Job's; but on some day it could, just possibly, be. The prayer's regularity, in dry seasons especially, is to be welcomed, and not felt as a bore.

Temptations can be to inaction, as well as to action. We may be tempted to avoid the one battle that is or should be central to our lives. The nature and the details of this battle will be known to us, secretly, and may be intended to stay a private affair. On the other hand, 'our' battle may be a cause, such as Martin Luther King's, James Baldwin's, Nelson Mandela's, the Dalai Lama's, which has to be public, by the choice of 'the world'. If our particular battle is general (to help animals, children, prisoners – to save the world from pollution – to fight homelessness), much will depend on the nature of our role. Very few people need to be 'high profile', and the world of the media makes publicity more a temptation in itself, than a help, as things stand. If our own battle involves being denounced as unconventional, or as being God's enemies, only a purified heart and dogged will can help.

The New Testament warns that the Devil can come disguised as an Angel of Light; we truly are in for a bumpy ride. No wonder St Paul urges us to pray 'for the discernment of spirits'. No wonder the last two petitions of the Lord's prayer are specially grim.

We must cling to the truth that our normal vocation is that of healing, and of passing on wisdom; and that our normal work-place is the obvious arena for this. We must salute Beauty and Goodness, when we see them, and recognise that we need pure vision, not 'revelations' or 'visions' out of the normal run. Jesus's teaching and life is a light, blazing around him. This whole prayer is a seamless robe; a city set on a hill.

The words themselves? They are not like Wordsworth or Eliot, in their resonance; they do not sear and amaze, as Shakespeare and Blake may do. But this is their strength: they are a mantra, for daily recital. For a day, a week, a month they feel empty. Then, one day . . . It is ours – the Lord's prayer – as life moves on.

(9) 'But deliver us from Evil'

This final petition is the prayer's culmination. We usually tack on the lovely reminder ('For Thine is the Kingdom, the Power, and the Glory: for ever and ever; Amen') – but Christ ended abruptly (except in Matthew's account, which adds the famous conclusion – but with only one 'ever').

We have rehearsed the essential, near-miraculous insights, of forgiveness and healing. We have recalled the evils attending us here, some difficult, some puzzling to bring into perspective. We have asked for 'daily bread', the immediate need for ourselves and all men; a literal request, with many applications of a spiritual kind. We have prayed not to be led into temptation. And, though God is not likely to have engaged with Satan in a wager on our account, 'the enemy' does go about, as a roaring lion; so we need God's help. Fortunately, we started with a reminder that God is Father; we praised Him; we asked for His Kingdom to come; for His will to rule in Earth as it does in Heaven. This is a marvellous opening, but so it needs to be, given all that follows; and given that the obvious channels for God's will are those of us who are saying the prayer.

May the day bring God's good things to those whom we love, those we forgive; to ourselves.

My mother's coffin was a fruitful place, for this prayer. The words offer themselves; what others are there, to use? The listening, teasing, absent God must be here this day, unless my mother's life, and mine, are to be mocked.

Much though I find to admire in pagans and to dislike among Christians, this prayer is the only one that will do, day by day. I am glad that my mother has reached the place she is seeking. I trust that her final absence from her body, in death's coldness, means that she is present, and youthful again, where we can both, out of time, be together at ease. I hope that God will be found, simple and united; untouched by Evil (*pace* Jung), beyond the earthquake and fire.

Of all catholic dogmas, perhaps the one needed most is purgatory? This earth corresponds to it – poised between Earth and Heaven – yet we do not have the assurance, associated with purgatory, that we will finally be saved. So presumably, there is a further phase of purgatory, far kinder and richer; on the last stages of the homeward treck, after death.

I take comfort from Mahler's Second Symphony, with its blazing affirmations of joy. The trumpets sound for reawakening, but there is no *Dies Irae*: 'no judgment', says the music: 'I come from God and I return to God'. Amen.

IV

'I am come that they might have life, and that they might have it more abundantly' (*John* 10: 10). This saying acts as a golden thread, through the Synoptic Gospels, and then through the luminous maze of St John. Jesus's parables, his signs, his discourses, his daily human encounters, is the Kingdom Incarnate, in one man centred wholly in God.

I have kept to one rehearsal of the Lord's prayer, offered on a special occasion, in an attempt to 'Earth' the prayer. In truth, it includes all life. The prayer is amazingly timeless, adapting to all lives, and all periods. It links our own 'scrap of history' with all mankind, backwards and forwards, as far as the race lasts. It links mankind with the entire cosmic creation; and then, with the Kingdom of God, with its rules for eternity, and therefore, with our own consciousness, in its 'now'.

Jesus could be deceptively simple, like God, but he baffled his hearers. His chosen twelve were lost, for much of the time. His parents were alienated when he left them, to roam with a ragbag of followers, every bit as odd as some hippy communes today. He even rebuked his parents for claiming first call on him, in words that must have pierced them to the heart:

> There came then his brethren and his mother and, standing without, sent unto him, calling him.
>
> And the multitude sat about him, and they said unto him, Behold, thy mother and brethren without seek thee.
>
> And he answered them, saying, Who is my mother, or my brethren?
>
> And he looked round about on them which sat about him, and said 'Behold, my mother and my brethren! For whosoever shall do the will of God, the same is my brother, and my sister, and mother'. (*Mark* 3: 31–5)

Jesus addressed synagogues, astonishing their leaders with his wisdom. Yet soon, they were alienated by an authority in him apart from, and seemingly higher than, theirs. The famous clash on 'The Sabbath' acted as a focus for tension. The dispute ramified and developed, and did not end until he was handed over to the Romans to be put to death.

In using a 'good Samaritan' in a parable, Jesus deliberately affronted ancient custom. Though he had 'come for the Jews', as he more than once mentioned, he clearly had wider horizons in mind. His offer of 'eternal water, springing up to eternal life' was made to a Samaritan woman, whom he met casually, and knew to be a sinner. The women he more normally consorted with included at least one who had been a prostitute, and he was taunted as a 'friend of publicans and sinners' and as a 'wine-bibber'. He had increasingly sharp exchanges with notable Pharisees and other Jewish leaders, culminating in the action of whipping money-lenders out of the Temple. (*John* mentions this incident early, but the Synoptics all place it late.)

On the Cross, one of his most breathtaking promises of forgiveness was made to an unknown thief dying next to him. And when he made the point that we are none of us well-placed to rush to judgment, he chose a woman taken in adultery for his example – even though he took a serious view of adultery, among the very few references he ever made to sexual sins.

In these and other ways, Jesus's teaching not only outstripped the tradition he belonged to, but gave rise to misunderstandings that brought him disrepute. Most serious of all, perhaps, were his progressive revelations that his 'other sheep not of this fold' went even beyond Samaria, and included the whole surrounding Earth. Increasingly, it became clear that he was not taking on the role of expected 'Messiah'. Perhaps John the Baptist's doubts, in prison, arose from this; perhaps it was at the root of whatever caused Judas Iscariot, one of the twelve, to drift away from Jesus, and eventually, to betray him.

In *Acts*, even Peter found it hard to understand that Christianity really was 'for the gentiles', until the strange and moving encounter with Cornelius cleared his mind. Cornelius is described as a virtuous centurion; and it is interesting to read that God sent an angel to Cornelius, as part of the plan. The angel gave a personal assurance that Cornelius's virtue, and prayer, had found favour with God; and that he had been picked for this crucial moment in the direction of the church. Peter, who was still wrestling with the vision sent to him by God, in preparation, was amazed by Cornelius's visit, at first. But then, Peter turned up trumps at the critical moment, allowing the once unthinkable truth to seize his mind. Jesus had perceived this potential, in Peter's original flash of insight: his recognition of 'the Christ' which earned him the title of 'rock'. On this occasion, when Peter faced his first great test as decision maker, the response he made bore out what Jesus had seen. 'Then Peter opened his mouth and said, Of a truth I perceive that God is no respecter of persons; But in every nation he that feareth him, and worketh righteousness, is accepted with him' (*Acts* 10: 34–5).[5]

As we know, it was Paul, 'a Hebrew of the Hebrews', and a zealous persecutor of Jesus and of Jesus's first disciples, who became 'apostle to the Gentiles' in a uniquely important way. Paul considered himself to be as 'true' an apostle as the others, and 'not the least of them' – as he told Peter to his face. Yet Paul was chosen directly by Christ, in the Damascus Road encounter, and followed his ministry before seeking even to meet 'the twelve'.

In Paul's own account (*Galatians* 1: 11–24) it was three years before he met 'them which were apostles before me'. So it seems that he was an apostle by the direct route, not involving what is now called 'the Apostolic Succession'; and it is open to conjecture (from *Acts*) whether he received even a retrospective 'laying on of hands' from an original apostle, or one of their line.

Everything we know of Paul suggests that this was unlikely; and the original twelve were no doubt wary of him – at first, naturally; but even after his whirlwind ministry in pagan lands.

Though Paul's insights are fuelled with incandescent fervour, they all derived from his first, great contact with Christ. And though he did more than any other man to give the church its foothold in history, he became an archetypal example of an individual left to survive on his own, with no help but God's. Whether imprisoned, or shipwrecked, or in other tight corners, he survived with one or two friends (Luke, and Timothy) or, sometimes, alone. He did nothing to harden Jesus's teaching towards formulae not 'felt on the pulses', and he wrote his letters to cope with specific crises as they arose. He would have been amazed if he had known that they would later be included in 'scripture' – and horrified, had he encountered the dogmas foisted off on him, in much later times. His mental gymnastics (like Donne's?) sprang from white-hot experience, seeking any shock-tactic or paradox to bring truths home with the most vivid power.

Paul grasped Jesus's offer of life, 'from glory to glory', and from the gospel material drew out Jesus's central themes. 'Grace' is the thread that guides him, in his own personal version of a Minotaur's maze. Above all, he exulted in 'eternal life' as Jesus depicted it, his agile mind applying the doctrine to all the daily crises of life. Eternal life is not 'immortality' as the Greeks and their gods had known it. It is not 'life after death', devoid of image and charm. It is not (most certainly) a notion of divinity 'infusing' us, which becomes reabsorbed into 'the One' when we separately die. It is life 'in Christ', as we come to know it, when the eternal 'now' of our consciousness links back, with our own 'real' self, in the power of God's love.

'Eternal life' affirms, indeed, the indissoluble union of soul, mind and body that each of us is. We are to be 'raised' at death as particular individuals; released from exile, and restored to the glory seen 'as in a glass, darkly' here on earth. The 'raising from death' starts here and now, as a fact to be realised; as a seed to be nurtured, by the grace of the Spirit of God. Not only is death's sting removed, but death is welcome. Paul would have chosen it gladly, had he not had work still to be finished, here on Earth. In *I Corinthians*

15, he asserts the full resurrection, linking the burial of the dead with spiritual growth 'in Christ' (to use Paul's own, favourite phrase).

Looking back, we see that Christ's claim for divinity, which in his lifetime caused much rending of garments, is a discovery, in himself, of truth that belongs to us all. The alien flawed woman of Samaria is as much a recipient of it as is the mother who bore him; and indeed, as he is himself. One of Jesus's favourite names for himself was 'Son of Man': a phrase not opposed, but united to, 'Son of God'.

'Son of Man' is rich and varied in suggestion, but in essence, it asserts the brotherhood of man *per se*. We are not made 'for this world' but for elsewhere; yet we truly belong, Janus-faced, in Earth, and in Heaven. 'Before the beginning and after the end' – many mansions; 'if it had not been so, I would have told you' (Jesus's words).

This is the place where 'the dance' is: the backward time-flow described by Augustine, and called the 'still point of the turning world' by Eliot. Here, in the given moment, we make decisions which, worked out in 'clock-time', determine our inward progress back towards 'heaven', in God's Spirit; or our move away, into the dark.

We are bound to a particular body, 'given' in history, with its genetic and environmental *data* and all that these mean. In the space/time continuum, love exists – but it is not truly 'at home'. The main rules of 'this world' are cut-throat competition – money, status, power, basic survival – then, sickness or accident, with death at the end. In a time such as ours, genocide, terrorism and pollution are added to war, poverty, prejudice – the unholy trinity that always prevail in 'the world'. The next century will face battles special to itself, only some of which are, as I write this, predictable. But there is also the Kingdom: rooted in our hearts and souls, always flourishing everywhere. It was Christ who named it, and set upon it the stamp of himself.

No evils would have surprised Jesus, who was a realist. He understood the laws of space/time, which hurt us, and which we sometimes find 'Evil'. He understood the mystery of Iniquity, which often works through space/time, but poses a dark threat, beyond our normal reasoning, here on Earth. He wept over Jerusalem, foreseeing its destruction. His images of 'the last days' (*Luke* 20: 8–28) are ample seed for the bible's last book, *Apocalypse* – and sound as familiar to our ears in the 1990s, as they can ever have done in any past time.

Christ's century saw Herod, Nero, Caligula, and political turmoil; it had the poor 'always with us', waiting to experience the Kingdom on Earth. It had slavery, a system then taken for granted, as it usually has been.[6]

It had those standards of judgement by which Jesus's death became inevitable, and his Cross the central symbol for any religion addressing mankind with a believable gospel of hope.

As I write this, Gordon Wilson has had a meeting with the IRA to plead for peace with them, after forgiving an attack in which he nearly died, and his daughter did. His high Christian message of hope was rebuffed, and he was visibly shaken.

Yet this man, who took seriously the most difficult petition of the daily prayer, and its central place in all teaching of God's Kingdom, no doubt accepts that those who follow Jesus's way, share his Cross.

Terry Waite went to plead for hostages, speaking as one man of religion to others. But his mission became enmeshed in power-politics, and he became a hostage himself.

These two men received publicity, by the nature of our age; and they are professing Christians. There are countless others who have risen to forgiveness, grown in inner holiness, amid great atrocities; and they are 'of the Kingdom', whether following Christ, or following some other faith, or shunned by 'The Church'. Christ's teaching is often considered impossibly hard, even by those with no doubt at all of its truth. It is a special grace that the teaching has been followed, in all periods and nations by a great host of 'simple' people, open to God.

The Cross stands as a persistent truth about the world, and its standards. It stands as a persistent truth also about the servants of God.

'Eternal life' was not Christ's invention; it was his discovery of profound countertruths to 'change and decay' (the Second Law of Thermodynamics), operative in those most aware that they have no abiding city, but seek 'one to come'.

Christ announced that 'the Kingdom' is 'home' in all of us, despite space/time conditions. It is to be brought 'home' to the world, by living witness; and will be known by its 'fruit' – where forgiveness and healing become, without mystery, one.

'Resurgam!' is not only a hope, but a truth – more profound than the Cross, even. It is the discovery that the alien values of God's Kingdom do in truth transcend, and transform, the world. They even override 'the world', releasing its prisoners, when we see the Cross as a 'simple' victory for good.

Looked at cynically, the life of Jesus is insane wishful-thinking – a man 'born to be king' (as he thought), but rejected by all men, including his own chosen twelve. Reputation: a sabbath-breaker and blasphemer; friend of publicans and sinners; political rebel and (yes) hedonist – recipient, finally, of a most shameful death.

In Jesus, we find also the most perfect human ever born and the greatest prophet; the 'incarnation' of Beauty, Goodness and Truth beyond even Plato's scope.

To marry Christ's social reputation with his religious status, is the sharp challenge of that phrase so often recurring: 'in, but not of, the world'.

V

The conflict between the Lord's prayer and the 'world' of normal perception is fittingly dramatised in the word 'Kingdom' itself. Jesus, as a first-century Jew, steeped in Jewish writings and open to prophecy, must have been keenly aware of ambivalence in himself. In the event, his teaching of 'the Kingdom' centred almost wholly on the spiritual beliefs which concern us here, but he did not regard 'the Kingdom' as a metaphor for these. The kingdom is real: it is in God's world, where eternal life is. It is real on earth to the degree that the prayer 'Thy Kingdom come; Thy Will be done in Earth, as it is in Heaven' can make it so; especially, through those who daily use the prayer. If I am right, this is the place where our eternal 'now' locates most firmly – as 'future' flows through it into 'past' too quickly to measure, while we choose and act; and cumulatively 'are'. The fight to move this 'Now' of our consciousness from evil choices to choices incarnate in Jesus, is the fight to return healed from exile, when the time for departing comes.

It is perhaps natural that the word 'Kingdom' became part of the problem – for Jesus himself, as well as for those trying to follow in his 'Way'. In this world, 'Kingdom' is a word of power, and usually political. Its relation to good and evil is not intrinsic, but varies with our assessment of 'the state of the world'. Almost certainly, the early disciples were looking for the long-promised Messiah; a King of the Jews, who would exalt Israel above all other nations on earth. The genetic descent of Jesus is important to the gospel-writers, notably to Matthew and Luke. Joseph was traced back to David, and through David to Abraham; the descent 'in David's royal line' was an important aspect of several Old Testament prophecies fulfilled, for the first Jewish Christians, in Christ. This forces upon us the anomaly presented in Joseph who, as father-who-was-not-father, became increasingly difficult for post-Trinitarian theologians to fit in. Not a great many churches are dedicated to Joseph, and his feast-day is 'major' more in theory than in practice. I suspect that he appears even less than Mary, in the New Testament narratives; and the main episode is a visit from 'the angel of the Lord' to reassure him that his wife should not be 'put away privily' for adultery, since her child had indeed been conceived by the Holy Ghost (*Matthew* 1: 18–25). This account appears in *Matthew* only, and seems especially odd, since it follows the long genealogy from which *Matthew* begins. However: a further Old Testament prophecy is invoked, the famous 'A virgin shall conceive'... passage (*Isaiah* 1: 18–25). This striking, if obscure, prophecy presumably regularises the notion that Jesus will be descended from David by way of Joseph; while at the same time, it links Jesus with an expected, political saviour to come, to help the Jews. It is Matthew who records a further angelic visitation to Joseph, warning him to flee with his family into Egypt, to escape Herod's purge. This again is peculiar to *Matthew*, and causes grave problems to historians attempting to locate it in the period where it seems to be set.

In *Luke*, the corresponding genealogy begins by speaking of Joseph as the 'son of Heli', rather than as the 'son of Jacob' (compare *Matthew*), and at the same time, refers to Joseph as the 'supposed' father of Jesus. On the strength of this, some theologians have conjectured that the meaning must be that Joseph was Heli's son-in-law, not his son. And, since Heli is then traced back through David to Abraham (and indeed, to Adam), it is assumed that Mary, also, was 'of David's royal line' and so, a sufficient link of Christ's lineage in herself. Upon these details, I am incompetent to judge; but the matter had importance for the early Christians, and so, for us. My present concern is with the supposed role of Messiah, associated with the great and successful King David; and with the expectations placed upon Christ of a 'Kingdom' wholly different from the one he really proclaimed.

For Jesus, as we know, God was his 'Father'. Jesus even risked the huge scandal of applying to himself one of God's most sacred names, I AM (*John* 8: 58). This is the name revealed to Moses, on the occasion of God's original calling (*Exodus* 3: 14) and used only once more in scripture, in the apocalyptic vision of Christ in Glory in the first chapter of *Apocalypse* (1: 17–18).

In St John's Gospel, it is clear that Jesus intended to provoke the enemies who were engaged in goading him; and that these episodes were decisive, in Jesus's sense of his destiny. Yet it is equally clear that Jesus, for whom God was Father, did not use that word to denote his genealogy; rather, that he used 'Father' to link humanity with himself, not to sever himself from other men. The opening of the famous prayer is the invocation 'Our Father'; and only familiarity can rob this of the shock it must have carried at the time.

It is natural that the first disciples expected Jesus to be the Messiah. John the Baptist, from prison, sent anxiously to enquire. The Baptist had proclaimed the great One who was to follow him, in terms that entailed a difference in kind from himself, and from all other men. This is stressed in Luke especially, in the birth narratives. Mary meets Elizabeth (John the Baptist's mother) after the Annunciation; and the baby 'leaps' in Elizabeth's womb, to greet its Lord. Later, the Baptist came to wonder, in his terrible days in Herod's prison, and the question he sent – 'Art thou he that should come? or look we for another?' – carries a burden of anxiety that bring Jesus ambiguous 'Kingdom' into sharp focus again. Jesus's reply was to send an account of his healing miracles, including the 'raising of the dead'. These events are to be found in *Luke* 7 and 8 – absorbing chapters, in which two accounts of Christ 'raising the dead' are also recounted. My present concern is not with the miracles, but with the context. Jesus sends the Baptist a reply that might, or might not, set his doubts to rest. The deeds of healing were manifestly out of the ordinary; but they had nothing to do with the expectation of a Messiah, or a Saviour King. To us, it is clear that Jesus interpreted his Kingdom in terms of his healing ministry, while the Baptist held other views, that were widely shared. We cannot fail to see that the Baptist regarded Jesus as wholly set apart from humanity; while Jesus regarded himself as humanity realising itself in a fullest possible awareness of the divine.

Why was Jesus betrayed? To the religious leaders of the Jews, his claims became offensive; so much so, that as time went by, they stopped their ears. But they were also baffled; as indeed were the disciples. What *was* Jesus claiming? What was his authority, his identity? How could he challenge old and established customs and laws so radically and even violently, when he seemed less and less like the Messiah, the expected King?

Perhaps Judas, who betrayed Christ, also expected the Messiah, and felt deeply betrayed himself, as this notion proved wrong. The story of Judas is strange, and full of riddles; but the certain thing is that treachery rose from among the disciples, as well as from outside. Ambiguities concerning 'The Kingdom' must take a share of the blame.

For the Romans, Israel was a Province, and far from an easy one to govern. The Jews had their exclusive religion, which was bewildering and awkward, in the militancy that its One God bred. A total refusal to allow their own God to co-exist with pagan deities, was compounded by the unpredictable nature of Jehovah's commands. One has the impression that Pilate did his best to ignore Jesus, but found this impossible, in view of the determined Jewish effort to drag Rome in. From the Roman viewpoint, the Jewish God was harmless, if mysterious; a Jewish King was a different matter indeed. The Emperor could brook no trouble from any part of his empire. A claim to kingship, taken seriously, could not be ignored.

As we know, the Jewish leaders forced Pilate to arrest and try Jesus, by warning him that Jesus called himself 'King of the Jews'. We can admit that Jesus did nothing to improve matters, by his growing animosity to the Temple, and by predictions of his coming death (as these were interpreted later, and perhaps at the time). Pilate had to act, since his own career was at stake; and if he failed, very possibly his life as well. There is every sign that he found Jesus impressive and troubling, but did not regard him as a real threat to Roman power.

In most accounts of the trial, Jesus is depicted as silent; or brief and oracular at best. But John offers a more dramatic version, which is either historic (as I incline to think it), or the fruit of an eyewitness's long meditation, maturing in his own old age:

> Then Pilate entered into the judgement hall again, and called Jesus, and said unto him, Art thou the King of the Jews?
>
> Jesus answered him, Sayest thou this thing of thyself, or did others tell it thee of me?
>
> Pilate answered, Am I a Jew? Thine own nation and the chief priests have delivered thee unto me: what hast thou done?
>
> Jesus answered, My kingdom is not of this world; if my kingdom were of this world, then would my servants fight, that I should not be delivered to the Jews: but now is my kingdom not from hence.
>
> Pilate therefore said unto him, Art thou a king then? Jesus answered, Thou sayest that I am king. To this end was I born,

and for this cause came I into the world, that I should bear witness unto the truth. Every one that is of the truth heareth my voice.

Pilate said unto him, What is truth? And when he had said this, he went out again unto the Jews, and saith unto them, I find in him no fault at all.

But ye have a custom, that I should release unto you one at the passover: will ye therefore that I release unto you the King of the Jews?

Then cried they all again, saying, Not this man, but Barabbas. Now Barabbas was a robber. (*John* 18: 33–40)

The offer of release is in all the accounts, and clearly authentic; the preceding exchange is mainly in John alone. Pilate's concern is clear, as is his verdict on Jesus. 'I find no fault' is unequivocal, and stern. Pilate's question 'What is truth?' is eminently sensible and, given his predicament, to read it as irony would be deeply perverse. Pilate's question, though brief, is highly pertinent. It is hard to miss the genuine desire he has, to hear rather more. Jesus's mode of answer 'Thou sayest' had been habitual with him; as a trick of rhetoric, it is as disturbing as any that Socrates used. But Jesus does outline very simply and directly to Pilate the nature of his 'kingdom', and its entire distinction from the charge upon which he is being tried. In the circumstances, it would have been unthinkable for Pilate to release Jesus unilaterally, and so risk from Jewish leaders the insurrection he was there to avert. He did, however, attempt to turn the crowd's custom of clemency to Jesus's advantage; at the risk of giving offense, as he no doubt did, even in this.

Did Pilate have some sense of what Jesus meant by his Kingdom? The Governor of Judea was 'not a Jew', as he pointed out. He had not followed the ministry of Jesus, except perhaps through official reports. Yet clearly something in Jesus deeply impressed him. This was a most reluctant judicial act, as John makes clear. All four gospels record the notice written above the Cross, in three languages. But the Synoptics give the impression that it was mockery, from Jesus's enemies. John's account is fuller, and wholly different:

And Pilate wrote a title, and put it on the cross. And the writing was,

JESUS OF NAZARETH, KING OF THE JEWS.

This title then read many of the Jews: for the place where Jesus was crucified was nigh to the city: and it was written in Hebrew, and Greek, and Latin.

Then said the chief priests of the Jews to Pilate, write not, The King of the Jews; but that he said, I am King of the Jews.

Pilate answered, What I have written I have written. (*John* 19: 19–22)

If we follow John, the notice was contributed by Pilate, and written in the three languages at his command. Any irony is certainly intended for Jesus's accusers, not for Jesus personally; as the chief priests were well aware. At the least, Pilate was saying, 'This man is the pick of you'. It is likely that the person of Jesus, if not his exact use of language, had conveyed something positive to the universal question as Pilate pondered it, 'What is truth?'

Pilate's last word is brief, and magnificent. It makes him, however oddly, the first gentile witness who ever took a risk for the Kingdom's sake.

That history has treated Pilate as badly as the judicial process treated Jesus, would have surprised neither.[7] They were fully aware of the values of the world. At the Cross, a Roman centurion recognised Christ publicly, according to the three Synoptic Gospels: 'Truly this man was the son of God' (*Matthew* 27: 54). This is very close in wording to the moment when Simon became 'Peter'; and is a remarkable gentile 'first fruit' of Jesus's death.

According to Luke, one of the two criminals crucified alongside Jesus turned to revile him, but the other rebuked this – asking a boon of Jesus (was this in hope, or from pity? – it hardly matters): 'Lord, remember me when thou comest into thy kingdom'.

The 'repentant thief' received words that are now justly famous: 'And Jesus said unto him, Verily I say unto thee, Today thou shalt be with me in paradise'. It is possible, if one follows John, that Pilate was actually the first, however, to bear witness, through the notice he attached to the Cross, and refused to remove. Pilate may be the first gentile who arrived in the Kingdom by way of Jesus himself, on the actual day of the death.

We cannot be sure, one way or the other. But for many reasons, John's account rings true, to me. It is one of the few places where the ambiguity in the word 'Kingdom' is explored openly; and where there is some sign that the claim Jesus really made for his Kingdom went home even to Pilate, in a manner transcending religion and race.

It is a further irony that, after Constantine, the catholic church itself mistook 'the kingdom' for kingship, and turned the church into a haunt of prince bishops and hierarchies. The alliance with political power has continued in subsequent history, wherever politicians have let it. Only Christians in sects at various times persecuted – or under regimes which have renounced the church for a different ideology – have had a chance to follow Christ without the distractions and temptations of worldly power. Some have managed to keep spiritual worship alive, through periods of repression. The emergence on to the balcony of the Moscow White House of Orthodox clergy and worshippers alongside Boris Yeltsin, on the day when the Soviet Empire more or less ended, was an amazing moment. After an interlude of nearly three-quarters of a century, this branch of Christendom appeared to resume, after a rude interruption, as if little had happened.

For Christ, his followers had been 'kings' in their very poverty; his Kingdom, 'not of this world', was all paradox and metaphor, in that the words and symbols of status and power were reversed, to make the new order real. In an ultimate sense, Heaven may be full of treasure, without 'place' or distinction. On earth, where our treasure is where our heart is, the kingdom of God is exiled, in all of 'the world's' own normal terms.

Mary was born poor (however distinguished her lineage). She gave birth in an outhouse, since the inn was full. She lost Jesus to his other 'mother and brothers and sisters' when his ministry started. This is little sign that she understood her son; or his vision; or his mature way of life. At the Cross, she was handed into John's care (in that disciple's own version), but in John's Gospel, little mention of her is made. Luke offers 'The Magnificat', and the account of 'The Annunciation'; but could he have met Mary, in his wanderings with Paul; or did he rely on oral reports? The scriptural material is thin, but has been much embroidered. The Mary who stands as 'Queen of Heaven', on a thousand promontaries and above a hundred thousand altars, is a symbol of Christ's Kingdom. Yet the world, in creating icons and images, and then mistaking art for reality, has all too often converted her to 'its own' – dressing her richly; adoring her as if she were a crowned Queen in truth. The prime truth is lost. Mary is great in Heaven, indeed a queen there, only because she was poor, suffered greatly, endured her role, on Earth.

When we return to scripture, and to Jesus as mediated by its writers, and by his early followers, we find an amazing teacher and man; the greatest in history, I have come to believe. The early church conducted an experiment in communism which proved abortive; but which is interesting equally for the ideals it followed, and for the human traits which caused it to fail. For several hundred years, Christ's followers were poor and uninfluential; some were unpopular militants; others merged with the slave-class, to which they belonged.

We are assured by Christ, and by the New Testament, that we are sons and daughters of God, and matter individually to Him. We are invited by Jesus to take our place in 'the Kingdom', which was the core of his teaching, and the core of the prayer that he left. The Kingdom contrasts starkly and continually with 'the world' – both socially; and in the actual laws governing it, which are not the laws natural to space/time. We are 'in the world' however, to fulfil our destinies; since, like Jesus himself, we came for a reason, with some lessons to learn, and some particular work to do. We are subject to the world's laws, including its power and mortality – though the latter is and must be in tension with the laws of The Kingdom itself. The first five petitions of the Lord's prayer address this directly, placing us firmly as earthly ambassadors of the 'Will', and the 'Heaven' of God. In counterpoint with the sway of the world, and with our own mortality, we claim and pursue 'eternal life', through spiritual refinement and prayer. 'From glory to glory', says Paul, charting the promise: mortal here, till our death; raised immortal, when the end is achieved.

During his own arduous ministry, Paul was faithful, choosing no short-cuts or quick martyrdom on the way. When he met the Athenians and others, he neither looked like a 'king' nor behaved like one; his worldly lot was shipwrecks, beatings, journeyings, in the service of Jesus. He spent much time agonising over his 'young churches', writing letters (sometimes from prison) to answer their questions, or set right their wobblings on the straight, but difficult, Way. Most often he depended on charity, for his resting place. He depended on followers who must often have tired him. I assume that the outbursts against women – their silence in church; their hats during worship – might have come from particular situations. Few vicars or ministers will fail to sympathise; but Paul could not have expected those parts of his letters to become 'scripture' and for some future readers, therefore, infallible law. For the most part, Paul's spirit burned bright in adversity. He could say, 'to me to live in Christ, and to die is gain'.

But the Church? We are forbidden to judge each other (and have no right to); but the church must be judged by the basic, New Testament writ. Christ did not restrict his followers to those who 'knew' him; but to those who did – in his lifetime, and through witness later – special duties incurred in phrases like 'the Body of Christ'. In my view, Jesus did not set up an institution. It was Peter's basic affirmation that he saw as the rock. He might have hoped that Christians would live in charity; or he might, as a realist, have foreseen the storms ahead. In effect, the church split early over matters of dogma; though personality clashes were of course at the core of splits, when 'the world' stepped in. By now, there are so many fragments of the church that discernment is called for. And 'discernment' – God's Spirit in us – is not absolute judgment, and not readily detached from our feelings. It is a gift to be prayed for; with the basic chasm between 'this world' and 'Kingdom' daily kept clear.

In the present century, it has come to seem that there is now a real gulf fixed between most visible churches, and the precepts and way of life embodied in Christ. The gulf exists in creeds and dogmas, some of them coming from early times, framed by half-crazed 'Early Fathers'; most of them, accumulated through the centuries, by numerous sects.

The Orthodox Church, which is the oldest and still in my view far the least tainted, has the Nicene Creed (without '*filioque*'), and Patriarchs and Archimandrites exerting discreet but firm power. It has come through its tests in this century with flying colours; and its grip on imagery gives it a very special power. The icons and prayers converge, on sanctuary and worship; the Russian liturgy, in particular, brings eternity into time in the manner uniquely desired of worship as an act. Week by week, the congregation stand in a place of beauty, seeking the grace to resume their place in the world. At death, the believer's body lies in an open coffin, in the congregation – a lovely symbol of the transition now being made. I am told that the celebrants are capable of dogmatism, and personal failings; but this is well inside the Christian writ. Impressively, the princely robes are kept for the celebration of worship; they are not flaunted outside, or allied with political power. The Orthodox work by witness, not by 'bulls' and edicts. The world seems to affect them little – either in its fashions, its media, or in long periods, like that of Soviet Empire, when it drifts away from them.

The Roman Church, which split off chiefly over '*filioque*', but also on account of the Bishop of Rome's growing pretensions, has become the longest lived, and noisiest, protestant sect. It has accumulated dogmas, bulls, papal claims with each passing century, soaring to 'papal infallibility' during the last hundred years or so. Its 'Princes' have been high profile, and authoritarian, and have imposed their will on the rest of mankind whenever they could. Their own followers are oppressed, with a rigid regime and strong censorship – backed with myths so superstitious that they are told they 'cannot leave the Church, only lapse'. I find it pathetic to hear people calling themselves 'lapsed catholics', a collapse of dignity, unmatched in the other sects. At present, the Roman Faction is headed by a specially authoritarian Pole, Karol Wojtyla, better known by his papal name, John-Paul II.

If Rome was the first protestant church, in the true sense, there have been many more since – and notably, in the last four centuries, including our own. Some of these broke from the pope, going 'back to basics', but choosing 'basics' in varying ways, some extremely bizarre. Others have originated with new revelations or scriptures, centred on a 'discovery'. Often a powerful personality dominates, and esoteric claims to truth, or even to 'salvation', may be made.

The fundamentalist Evangelicals, who claim to regard scripture as 'infallible', run on the tramlines of mainly unpleasing dogmas, based on a ragbag selection of prescriptive and judgemental texts. These sects further divide and subdivide often; and the attempt to make scripture (or even, one translation of scripture) 'infallible' seems a certain recipe for whittling faith down to a few, man-made lies.

A Church like the Anglican has a colourful history; and its present situation in Britain itself, and also worldwide, is a study needing more time than any one lifetime could hope to provide. As churches go, it is comparatively undemanding; and its history has many holy people, great buildings, ancient prayerful parishes, where most temperaments can find some sort of a home. It has the advantage of embracing great diversity; but particular congregations may be narrowly focused on a path of their own. The bishops are part of the secular government (certainly, in Britain), and the church's close political link with the world ('the establishment') has been at war with most reforms, in the nineteenth and twentieth centuries, that Christ would most probably have wanted to see.

For me, it has become impossible to stay in the Church; and this is clearly true, for one reason or another, of others who, ideally, would wish to be there. Faults on both sides (as always): but this is peripheral – since the problem is not of 'authority' (in the Roman sense), but of general tone. The church's obsession with sex never helps things; but its failure to respond to this century is the graver divide. We have homelessness and poverty in the world, and now prevalent in Britain, which are addressed mainly by individuals ('Christian' or otherwise), and not by the Church of the land. Vast numbers of church halls remain shut, when they could give shelter; when they could be used to organise laymen to feed, clothe, counsel, direct those who have fallen out of 'society'. In London, we have admirable initiatives like Centrepoint, and one or two other centres for the destitute based on particular churches; but for the most part, the church is not a natural home for the poor and unhoused. Likewise, the Church of England ignores our major challenges – pollution; dehumanising technology; the economics of Mammon now actually using its name ('Christian values', and the like). One looks to the Synod, and finds it engaged with other topics; such as: are women human enough to be priests; and how satisfy the 'conscience' of members who think they are not?

Churches – like politicians – like to think they are 'failing to communicate'; the truth is precisely the opposite, as they well should know. We live in a time of communication, far too much of it. The church has special privileges in 'time on the media' to present itself more or less as it will. Its major Bishops have seats in our Governing Second Chamber: they can speak there; they can be assured of platforms, if they want to 'speak out'. At present, most initiatives on homelessness, pollution, spirituality come from elsewhere – as do the voluntary bodies whose primary concern is with humans and creatures, and with the preservation – if it is possible still, at this late hour – of God's basic gifts for our home planet here – earth, water, fire, air.

I recognise that a great many individuals follow Christ, in all branches of Christendom; and that holiness is nourished by corporate worship and prayer. I rejoice in places where prayer has been offered, over many centuries; and where silence takes on serenity; the presence of God. I gladly acknowledge those who do Christ's work in and out of season: the Salvation Army, and the Society of Friends, come to mind. I see, too, that cults which spring up, often among young people, come close to Christ's original call 'leave the world; and follow me'.

Unfortunately, modern cults are usually commercialised at the start, or quickly become so. They are frequently led by people more wedded to power than to unworldly truth. Money, drugs, sex seep into religion; so does brainwashing. (The Greeks well knew that Dionysus, if refused his dues at the front door, will arrive at the back.) Worse: most cults seem to make a claim to exclusiveness. I am still amazed when exclusiveness becomes a condition of membership *per se.*

But should I be? Exclusiveness has been a mark of the mainstream churches: 'No salvation outside the Church' is a constant refrain – in the Roman Church, and in many subsequent breakaway sects. The claim to be not just one part of the truth, but all of the truth, is by now a hallmark of more 'Christian' churches than one could reasonably list. It runs to the notion that everyone refusing this particular path to salvation will, quite infallibly, end up damned.

Clearly, many people enjoy exclusiveness. As a sin (close to class-divisions and racism, and all variants of snobbery?), its appeal is demonstrably large. But how did it get into a church preaching Christ's kingdom? And how does it stay there – in the light of the scriptures; and the Lord's daily prayer?

Well: the answers are no doubt many. Discipline is needed, if any body of people is to cohere, and succeed. But surely, 'discipline' as a pragmatic need can be distinguished, from supposed 'disciplines of dogma' that restrict God's grace to a chosen few? Surely, the amazing inclusiveness of the Kingdom can be appraised and again made central to any organised 'church'? 'The Spirit bloweth where he listeth'; 'By their fruits ye shall know them'; 'Those who are not against me are for me' – and the like?

Since our consciousness is tinged with evil, as well as with goodness, we need a city set on a hill, that cannot be hid. To this end, Christ's wisdom is less elusive than many would make it. It is far less rigid than creeds make it seem. I choose a modern poem, on which to draw to a close. R.S. Thomas's 'The Kingdom' comes from *H'm,* in the early 1970s. Like many of his poems, it homes in on deep truths, in simple images, and a mood of deceptive quiet.

VI

The Kingdom

It's a long way off but inside it
There are quite different things going on:

Festivals at which the poor man
Is king and the consumptive is
Healed: mirrors in which the blind look
At themselves and love looks at them
Back; and industry is for mending
The bent bones and the minds fractured
By life. It's a long way off, but to get
There takes no time and admission
Is free, if you will purge yourself
Of desire, and present yourself with
Your need only and the simple offering
Of your faith, green as a leaf.

This poem has something of the economy of Yeat's 'An Irish Airman Foresees His Death'. There are powerful contrasts, which might signify mutual cancellation or a strange fulfilment, since the driving emotion is at once apparent, and hard to pin down. 'It's a long way off': the opening phrase, later repeated, demands teasing clarity of utterance; though whether wistfulness, bitterness, mockery or mystical insight predominate, who is to say? Sufficient that the poem's first half rehearses the essence of the Kingdom as Christ proclaimed it, in some ways enhancing its fairy-tale charm and uncancelled allure.

That this vision resembles neither the Church of Christ in any of its visible branches nor any pragmatic values in the world we know daily, is likewise apparent; with a poignancy related in quality to our ultimate response. Is the poem an indictment of the visible church as an institution (I do not speak of the many good individuals who belong there); or is it an indictment of Christ's original vision as wishful thinking, as some will suppose?

The question is real, for even the faintest would-be believer. Yet, if the kingdom is indeed impossible, how comes its power to haunt unnumbered human lives, including Thomas's own?

In the second part, the price of admission is once again impeccably scriptural, though posed with a simple (or artful) directness that staggers the mind. Sunday by Sunday, such sentiments resound in hymns, ring out in scriptures, are expounded in sermons. Day by day they are prayed, by many of us, in the Lord's prayer. Minute by minute, they are mocked by nine-tenths of us, inside or outside the church.

Note the extraordinary neutrality of the closing lines, actively defying us – since, if we read them aloud, we have somehow to declare ourselves, like it or not. '. . . your faith, green as leaf', 'the simple offering' – simple as curing the blind, mending the world, loving mankind. I recall one of my grandmother's favourite aphorisms, 'not as green as he's cabbage-looking', and wonder whether this (Cockney?) phrase ever reached Wales?

The sting in this poem is surely the appearance of innocence, as its unanswered questions (savage indictment? – betrayed salvation? – pure nonsense?) tug at the mind. I am reminded again of Dostoievsky's Grand Inquisitor, secure in his worldly wisdom and in his office, indicting the Christ who has returned to earth, to see how his church now fares. How dare Christ imagine that his 'terrible' gifts – love, freedom, healing – are still alive, in the church which he founded? How dare Christ imagine that they meet real, human needs? In Dostoievsky's parable, Christ is dumb before his accuser, as he was in his true life. His one reply is to kiss the old man's cheek. The old man burns there; and he releases Christ from a second immolation by Holy Inquisition. But the old man does not change his views.

So perhaps 'The Kingdom' is an ironic vision, close to this Grand Inquisitor? At the moment we think this, precisely, the poem turns inside out, a perfect optical illusion. For a moment, one wonders, how could one doubt the Kingdom at all? The lost paradise, the promised eternity – are these not archetypes, always with us? And is not 'mending/The bent bones and minds fractured/By life' a daily reality among surgeons, psychotherapists, public charities with world support? Is it not the day-to-day exercise of generosity and friendship? Is it not the final tribute, paid by bereavement, to the healing of Love?

Perhaps the self-styled churches of Christ seem to mock it, in dogmatic exclusions; in those acts of judgement and damnation meted out freely to those who had the wrong sort of baptism, or put a stress wrong in their creeds, or who loved the wrong sort of people?

But are these churches not judged, for their boomerang judgements, by the rules of the Kingdom, as set out here? Christ called his Kingdom a leaven, a salt that gives savour, a hidden mystery. Only in aspiration is it a city set on a hill that cannot be hid. Christ said that not all who cried 'Lord, Lord' belonged to his Kingdom; just as he said that many who have not so much as heard of him have a place there. He pointed to children, to casualties, to outcasts, as clues to his meaning: to precisely the people from whom this poem starts.

The whole poem can feel like a fairground, heard in the distance by a child, longing to get there; wondering how it is to be found, and how he is to pay the entrance price; and filled with longing by the thought of wonders in progress, just out of reach.

From here, a return to the poem is simple; and to the scriptural image that clearly lurks. Christ, confronted by a blind suppliant (*Luke* 18: 41) asks the simple question, 'What would you have me to do?' The reply, 'Lord, that I might receive my sight' is granted. And the first image that the blind man sees is Love, looking back.

Like other optical illusions, the poem can turn back on itself once more, leaving us staring blankly at the 'to get/There' clause. A poem of faith, a poem of doubt, or something more elusive? 'Verily I say unto you, Whosoever shall not receive the kingdom of God as a little child, he shall not enter therein' (*Mark* 10: 15). A poem of truth and wisdom, beyond doubt.

VII

In my terms, the poem brings me back to my thesis (though I would stress that neither the poem, nor its author, can be involved in this). From our place in clock-time, registering pain and mortality, the Kingdom is 'a long way off' – perhaps, even cloud-cuckoo land. From our Fifth Dimension, the perspective is otherwise. It speaks to all we recall, all we see around us, of eternal things. At the still point where the dance is, there too is the Kingdom: the Kingdom of God, as Jesus shows it; or a darker Kingdom, in varying degree absent from God. Perhaps a very dark place indeed, shading through boredom to fear; to the very edge of the abyss.

Our choices in the moment where we are, that make our becoming: these are our *raison d'être* in exile: a 'vale of soul making', in Keats's words.

In my next chapter, I shall touch on other intimations of wisdom; on things in nature, and in man's creations, that speak of God.

9

The Eternal in Time

I start from an observation which I believe to be true, though it produces complex problems for philosophers. We live among intimations of the eternal so profuse, that mortality seems afloat on a sea of grace. Love and friendship head the list, for most of us. Then, there are one or two animals, who may have upstaged the whole human scene. Then plants, and the teeming world often called 'Nature', where our language comes close to defeat. How are the greens and browns of woodland to be named, or numbered? Can we begin to discriminate every subtle and shifting shade?

The world of art must of course be added, as our human contribution to created things. And running through all life, we know spiritual goodness and beauty; the ideal reality, of creation, in the vision of God.

Received through the senses, conveyed by nerves to the brain, then appearing as images, our own impressions use, but transcend, the processes of mind. There is no exact scale by which to measure them. At best, they range from normal pleasure in the world about us, to occasional approaches of the sublime. If we are lucky, we may experience a few numinous moments also, in the course of a lifetime.

And finally, life is shot through with 'the holy', if we have eyes to see. 'Holiness' is not much used as a term, and seldom has been; but it is one of the great human experiences, and words. Since it belongs with its objects (unlike the numinous), it can be actively sought for; as one fruit, of a disciplined life. Our mind and senses must be trained in prayer, where emotions count for little, and the discernment of God's Spirit is the gift we seek.

Too easily, tiredness and custom can block out holiness, when we are near to it; particularly, in an age of media reductiveness, seasoned with hype.

II

Rudolf Otto's *The Idea of the Holy (Das Heilige*, 1917), written in the Great War years of bereavement and chaos, mapped areas of religion that elude even routine faith, if our wonder is lost. Otto himself coined the word 'numinous', from the Latin *numen*, and it passed into the language as though it had always been there. C.S. Lewis and J.R.R. Tolkien gave it striking images, in their fictional writings, and a very wide currency that rests, in part, on these. Amazingly, there is no precise English synonym for its meaning, but the Latin is ancient recognition of the thing itself. The numinous can be described as a lightning transfiguration of the universe, in a moment when all that we are is radically changed. The things we experience are God, and we are God with them.

For once, our external and internal world is fused, and uniquely affirmed.

The numinous is very close to 'the holy', and perhaps even the core of it; yet the two experiences are, in fact, different in kind. The holy 'belongs' to an object, whether the object is God, or God-filled. The numinous blows like the Spirit, here and gone like a bird, or like a wave of the sea.

The holy is the root, growth and flowering of life in God's Kingdom, as it becomes real for each one of us by gradual steps. Its character includes several features, which Otto distinguishes: the first, a sense of 'awefulness' suffusing a place, or a time. A classic early example is Jacob's vision, recorded in *Genesis*, where 'the holy' is a direct encounter and commissioning, brought about by God:

> And Jacob went out from Beer-sheba, and went towards Haran.
>
> And he lighted upon a certain place, and tarried there all night, because the sun was set; and he took the stones of that place, and put them for his pillows, and lay down in that place to sleep.
>
> And he dreamed, and behold a ladder, set up on earth, and the top of it reached to heaven; and behold the angels of God ascending and descending on it.
>
> And, behold, the Lord stood above it; and said, I am the Lord of Abraham your father, and the God of Isaac: the land whereon thou liest, to thee will I give it, and to thy seed.
>
> And thy seed shall be as the dust of the earth, and thou shalt spread abroad to the west, and to the east, and to the north, and to the south: and in thee and thy seed shall all the families of the earth be blessed.
>
> And behold, I am with thee, and will keep thee in all places whither thou goest, and will bring thee again unto this land; for I will not leave thee, until I have done that which I have spoken to thee of.

> And Jacob wakened out of sleep, and he said, Surely the Lord is in this place; and I knew it not.
>
> And he was afraid, and said, How dreadful is this place: this is none other but the house of God, and this is the gate of Heaven. (*Genesis* 28: 10–17)

Otto detected in 'the holy' an element of 'Overpoweringness' ('*majestatis*'); and with this, 'Energy; Urgency' (the words he chose himself). Beyond these, there is a perception always present at times of commissioning of extreme solemnity: 'It is a terrible thing, to fall into the hands of the living God'.

Otto further asserts that the holy is beyond description, and beyond analysis. The experience is 'given', and can be received by us through the 'feel' of sacred places. It is experienced most often (I imagine) in ancient churches, and in places where ancient religions have left their structures; and in wild country, of the kind which Wordsworth loved. It also exists as a radiance, in certain people; though if we are to find it, our own vision must be attuned to the things of God. We need prophets and artists to evoke, and arouse, the holy: yet holiness is 'given', and wordless, when the experience comes.

And this is because holiness, though an emotion, is also an object (or 'in' an object, perhaps we can better say). In T.S. Eliot's phrase, it is an 'objective correlative': which is to say, it is a complex human experience most precisely corresponding, in the degree that humanity can receive this, to the Supreme Being Himself, manifest in time and space.

The English translator of Otto's *Der Heilige*, John W. Harvey, put this very well in his Translator's Preface (Oxford University Press, 1949):

> When, therefore, Otto uses so frequently expressions like 'the numinous *feeling*' (*das numinose Gefuhl*) he must not be taken to be merely repeating the claims of 'affect', subjective emotion, to a place in any genuine religious experience. But it would certainly have been better if he had always preferred the alternative phrase 'the feeling *of* the numinous'. The word 'numinous' has been widely received as a happy contribution to the theological vocabulary, as standing for that aspect of the deity which transcends or eludes comprehension in rational or ethical terms. But it is Otto's purpose to emphasise that this is an objective reality, not merely

> a subjective feeling in the mind; and he uses the word *feeling* in this connection not as an equivalent to emotion but as a form of awareness that is neither that of ordinary preceiving nor of ordinary conceiving. Certainly he is very much concerned to describe as precisely and identify as unmistakeably as possible, by hint, illustration and analogy, the nature of the subjective feeling which characterises this awareness; but this is because it is only through them that we can come to an apprehension of their object.

I am in entire agreement with this, as a description of the classic experience of holiness. We find it in Jacob's vision, and in similar passages scattered through scriptures; and in other sacred writings; and in moments known, privately, to ourselves. Earlier, I distinguished between 'the holy' and 'the numinous', as I always wish to, since the former strikes me as a direct visitation of God for His own purpose; or as a special presence impregnating holy places where prayer has been made. 'The numinous' also comes to us from God, and also fleetingly. But it comes for no particular purpose we know of; and with no sequel, except its indelible power within ourselves. It cannot be recaptured, because no place embodies it. It appears to be a moment, in time, when God gives us a rare vision of His own inner life. In this sense, the famous numinous moments evoked in T.S. Eliot's *Four Quartets* (written after Otto's book, and independently of it) are the references I most usually point to, when attempting to convey the quality in its purest form. A phrase like:

> For the roses had the look of flowers that are looked at . . .
>
> ('Burnt Norton')

is a *locus classicus*. It conveys the surprise, and the intensity, totally fused. It readily awakens in our minds, in their role as echo-chambers, any similar moments we have known ourselves. My own experiences of the numinous occurred chiefly in earlier years, as Wordsworth's did. I experienced one or two in the dereliction of the burnt-out Isle of Dogs, in the war years; since it was there that the amazing transfiguration first seized me. On an afternoon in Devon, in a summer of the late 1960s, three numinous moments of extraordinary intensity came, in a period between 3.00 and 5.00 p.m. No moments of comparable power have been granted me since then; and I do not 'expect' any (but who knows?) this side of my death.

The Holy, which is not dissimilar, and for those who seek it may be granted more often, does 'belong' to particular places, where prayer has been made. Like the numinous, it relates neither to reason, nor to man-made ethics. It is always of God's making, not of ours. There is no doubting that when we meet the holy, whether in people or in places, it carries the stamp of God's presence direct to our souls. The holy, encountered in people, we may call 'sanctity'; or 'transfigured goodness' (though this, I have only rarely seen). The holy, found in places, can best be described as 'consecrated serenity' – if this phrase does not underplay its dynamic, and aweful aspects, when we are truly aroused.

Such experiences are dealings between God and our souls very directly; so epistemology must be irrelevant, while they last:

Moments of great calm.
Kneeling before an altar
Of wood in a stone church
In summer, waiting for the God
To speak; the air a staircase
For silence; the sun's light
Ringing me, as though I acted
A great role. And the audiences
Still: all that close throng
Of spirits waiting, as I,
For the message.

Prompt me, God:
But not yet. When I speak
Though it be you who speak
Through me, something is lost.
The meaning is in the waiting.

(R.S. Thomas, 'Kneeling')

It will be noted that R.S. Thomas uses pared-down imagery, often elemental; akin to Jacob's vision in *Genesis*. Thomas finds God almost always mingled with multivalence – in Wales's hillside farms, and their half-brutalised guardians; in experiences of God's absence that drive him, sometimes, to near despair. In poems like 'Kneeling', 'The Flower', 'Sea-watching' he is, in contrast, a poet of vision; conveying holiness more directly than almost any other writer I know.

I begin at the summit of this chaper; which, for the most part, has now to return to the foothills, and lower ground. The problems of epistemology, and of changing human fashion, cannot be bypassed; wrong sign-posts, false turnings, impede our ascent. Yet before leaving the heights, we can reflect upon the riches of holiness that abound daily. Christ's incomparable life is ours, in the Gospel records; and in the immediate fruit he brought, in men like Luke, John and Paul. There is the prayer Jesus left, in its potent austerity. It is a prayer spreading blessings widely, to loved people and animals; to the place where our heart's 'treasure' can be assured of a home. Its release of healing through forgiveness is without stint or measure; yet it is made for sombre days, for patches of grief and terror, as well. We see it best as a prayer for all seasons; rarely a summit itself; more often, a path leading on, through our own mire and fog. It can light certain memories, buried in all of us, when 'We had the experience but missed the meaning' (T.S. Eliot's words).

Perhaps we are all watched over from birth, by presences; as some people intuit. Very certainly, we are closer to God, than we usually know.

III

I start at the summit, and hope to return there. But most of what follows concerns things of an earthier kind. Some naturally religious people are discouraged at certain periods, by the failure of the churches to use the holiness vested in them as of right. Others, drawn to God by strong inner tugs, or deep convictions, still hold back from Him; fearing that personal wishes are overriding their minds.

One basic rule for religion is simple, and well worth restating, before we take the plunge to disputed ground. If you want to know the state of your religion, here is the test. People who pray, believe in God; people who do not pray, do not. By this, I mean regular prayer from the heart, which is not always 'formal'; and which may not be 'church prayer' (where the test of daily life is needed, to be certain of its weight).

In their hearts, people know whether they pray, or not. And I refer not to sudden surges of joy in good times (which are far better than nothing); nor to desperate prayers of last resort, when evils come. I have in mind a witness belonging to our lives, in all aspects, including family, and career; a witness to whatever truly calls out our love and faith. Then, alongside this, and in the end more important, there is regular formal prayer, to build up the will. The Lord's prayer is still the best form of words to use, at the heart of life. It ranges from formal repetition on some days, with the special needs of that day held beside it; to every totally unexpected need, and insight, that life's strange drama can bring.

The habit of prayer, in good times and bad, without emotional promptings, is the mark of a religious quest in progress, and still on track. But the habit has to be formed (or resumed), and aligned to reality. We cannot use the words without meaning. We cannot 'mean' if our actions betray us, or our minds remain blank.

One excellent touchstone is Claudius's attempted prayer in *Hamlet*. He is driven to his knees in private, by the weight of his evil. He has killed his brother, seized the crown, and married his brother's wife, Queen Gertrude. He is plotting now against Hamlet, whom he rightly sees as a threat. As he tries to pray, he senses a total blockage. To pray, he would have to give up his ill-gotten gains: a huge sacrifice, which he will not make ('cannot make', he thinks – but is this correct?)

> My words fly up; my thoughts remain below.
> Words without thoughts never to Heaven go.

While Claudius is kneeling, Hamlet observes him; and ponders killing him, while the chance is there. Then Hamlet draws back. The King is praying, and in God's presence. If Hamlet kills him now, Claudius will go to Heaven, and revenge be lost.

Very rightly, Dr. Johnson found this moment horrible. In willing his enemy damnation, Hamlet is deeply evil himself. At this moment, there is no tincture of God's Kingdom in *him*. Was Hamlet right, in his reasoning? When Claudius rises, he assumes that his prayer has been abortive. It was not 'true prayer' at all, even though he kneeled.

Yet Claudius did fall to his knees, for some driving reason. It is clear that he has dealings with God still, and is not out of reach. The state of Hamlet is darker, and far more dangerous. When Hamlet embarks on murders, including those of his unfortunate school friends, we seem to be watching the destruction of a soul.

The main characters in *Hamlet* are deeply involved in murder. Shakespeare's spiritual insight pervades the play. Claudius's prayer might still help him; yet Claudius persists in evil; and so, it has no good effect that we see. Hamlet might yet be saved by the prayers of those who love him for what he was, or seemed to be (Ophelia; his mother Gertrude; Horatio his closest friend). But as we see him, in Shakespeare's play, he is far removed from any contact with God.

I choose this extreme image for its mystery. Shakespeare looks at prayer in, or near, the abyss. He tells the truth, with his own astounding resonance; and is discreetly absent, as ever; leaving us to judge. It would be foolish to think that far more humdrum lives than Hamlet's are free of drama; or that we can find an easy way off Shakespeare's hook. Our own quest is deadly earnest, whatever our circumstances. The test of praying, or failing to pray, is always 'now'.

If we have lapsed from formal prayer but still know we are 'religious', I suggest a simple, daily resumption of the Lord's prayer. Emotion should neither be forced, nor evaded. The act of will is the factor that counts. God exists, and is about His own business. He can deal with us more readily, if we open a door. We can usefully bear in mind two opposed images, both of which have a place in life's scheme. One is the image of God always waiting, always seeking entrance. He stands at the door, knocking; and will come in if asked. The other, is the image of God Who calls us 'Today', clearly and urgently; saying 'harden not your hearts, as men did of old'. Forty long years they wandered, after failing to heed Him. God was with them, in the wilderness, but not once in that time did He give any further hopeful sign.

So, to the 'problems'. In my fourth, fifth and sixth chapters, I hived off some of these; not scrupling, in the sixth, to challenge the Church. Here, I am striking into pragmatic, normal questions. They are not as arid as they seem, or perhaps I should say, they need not prove arid, if we persist. But certain repetitions, and hard slogs, are hard to avoid.

IV

We know that the 'natural world' comes to us through our senses, nerves, brain cells; without which, we should not get off the ground. I shall have more to say of Locke's 'empiricism' a little later; but it pervaded the Enlightenment Period, and is still lingering among us – despite dents from Berkeley and Hume.

The 'Romantic reaction' against Locke was often defined as 'a rejection of reason'; but this is far too simple a view. The great traditions of Platonism, of Christ's Kingdom, of worldwide mystical and religious commitments, were little touched by European philosophers of the past four hundred years. In the West, scientific triumphalism has cast long shadows over religion; and it is these that most readers will fear, as a threat to faith. But Locke and Newton were Anglicans by profession; Alexander Pope was a Catholic. Einstein was a Christian of sorts (if unusual in this, among those who bandy his name). If we look to our prophets and artists, religion has stayed alive and well, through all cultural changes; just as it does, in mutating forms, today.

By a great paradox, the eighteenth century became not only 'The Age of Reason' for historical labelling, but also, a time of special significance for the counterculture (really 'counter'?) where Wisdom lives on. Bach, and other great composers, produced major religious masterpieces, even if their contemporaries failed to see them as we do, now. The eighteenth century is also the greatest of all periods of Christian hymn-writing. It is the soil where our greatest English prophet, Blake, was born and flourished; and where Wordsworth, Coleridge and Keats had their roots. It would be naïve to think of this century as wholly ruled by the Royal Society; even though the normal run of its prose, and verse, did indeed submit to that Society's impoverishing 'rules'.

Towards the end of the eighteenth century, three 'Revolutions' of incalculable import coincided: 'The Industrial', 'The French' and the 'Romantic'. The first of these marked the moment when science made its long-delayed practical impact, and the age of machines, and technology, really dawned. In effect, humanity as it had been before was superceded; though naturally, this is a judgement of hindsight, and not a view taken at the time. Another age began, as if *ab origine*, whose laws and direction could scarcely be guessed. The nature of humankind did not change, nor did perennial Wisdom. But the world that men and other creatures had evolved in, from their first appearance on Earth, began to fade, as science came of age.

The French Revolution was naturally independent of the other 'Revolutions', though a link, in modern capitalism, can now be observed. In France itself, the Revolution erupted in 1789, shocking all Europe. Elsewhere, its effect was to give impetus to the gradual rise of democracy – which technological science would also encourage, as we now clearly see.

The countries of Europe moved to differing rhythms and patterns, but the underlying logic of their development was the same. In Britain, significant change was contained, in a slower process, marked by gradual but inexorable parliamentary reform. Reform was led by various new groups, and by outstanding individual philantropists; and by an unusual number of creative artists in every sphere of the arts. But they were opposed by the church (as an institution) and by many massed vested interests in long, and increasingly bitter, fights. I have traced the tangled relationship between democracy and education in other places: but the social history of nineteenth-century Britain and Europe has emergent Democracy as a major theme, wherever we look.

For the moment, I shall focus still on the Romantics, and on their 'Revolution' since, though chiefly 'literary', this has profoundly influenced culture, and indeed religious life. Arguably, it was the most important of all three movements, in the sphere of Wisdom. It was the forerunner of what must become a major agenda for the twenty-first century, if our own race, and our planet, are to endure. In tackling the intellectual reductionism of 'The Enlightenment' head-on, and helping to check it, the Romantics opened the way to religious revival of the kind that is brewing now. It will be rooted in rejection of economic competitiveness, and machinery, and greed parading as 'Christian', in favour of economic and social interdependence, and recovered reverence for Earth, Air, Water, Fire.

More flesh will be put on this later; but one splendid paradox calls for mention here. The Enlightenment writers had called themselves 'neo-classical', but their 'classical' credentials more or less started, and ended, with style. 'Imitation' of Homer, Ovid, Horace, Virgil *et al.* abounded, and the metrics of Greek and Roman literature (the latter especially) were imported far more fully into our own. But in content, the 'neo-classicists' are far better thought of as 'pseudo-classicists', in that their emphases were akin to no age previous to their own. Science itself was new, in the form centred on Newton. And Locke's definition of 'Reason' as an exercise in deductive logic to the exclusion of our emotions and instincts, would have shocked almost any 'ancient' writer, or intelligent citizen, to the core.

It is pleasing to note that the Romantics who rescued us, from this 'pseudo-classicism', were men and women who returned to the authentic artistic and religious traditions of Greece. Blake is an amazing prophet, largely *sui-generis;* but his basic principles in 'Songs of Innocence' and 'Songs of Experience' are very closely akin to Aeschylus, Sophocles and Euripides in their major works. The Olympian instinct for balance and integration of opposites is self-evident; with Heraclitus somewhere in the background, as he often is. Blake looks directly forward to Yeats and Jung, in this century, and is a seminal influence on the best in modern literature and thought.

Wordsworth and Coleridge wrote largely from their personal experience, but the traditions of Plato, Plotinus and Christ were the mould in which their wisdom took shape. Keats and Shelley returned to pagan myths and archetypes: and found release, through classical gods, for their own, deep truths. Keats's Odes are among the greatest of all 'classical' poems; and the first of them, 'Ode To Psyche', is a *tour de force*. Keats recognised in Psyche a late, and therefore neglected, Olympian presence. In choosing to become her personal prophet, long after the glory of Olympus had faded, he anticipated a major romantic potential, now realised (again), in Yeats, Jung and other key moderns of weight.

For Shelley, this earth was 'a vale of misery'. For Keats, a 'vale of soul making' seemed the more natural phrase. Both saw clearly that Earth is not our 'true home' despite its beauty, and in this, they link with the traditions of Wisdom we have looked at before. Both of them reverenced Earth, despite its transience. Earth offers to humans eternal intimations, but Earth is not the place where these can, or do, belong.

It will be recalled that I am not writing here as a literary critic; so I reluctantly leave analysis to others, and to my own work elsewhere. I want to turn to an allied series of 'problems', before returning to 'romantic and modern' as my favoured, personal, path for the way ahead.

V

There are some who claim that love of 'nature', in the sense of the external world around us, is a modern invention, unknown to the early world. Aldous Huxley's 'Wordsworth In The Tropics' was a squib that had currency when I was young. Huxley argues that if Wordsworth had been born in a tropical hell of mosquitoes and alligators instead of in the Lake District, he would have experienced fewer 'spots of time', and refreshments to build him up. This cynicism is very typical of Huxley's early novels, and predates the experiments with mescalin that led to *The Perennial Philosophy*, where mysticism takes over, and soars extravagantly to other extremes.

In fact, Wordsworth knew perfectly that by no means all the Earth was a match for his birthplace. He knew of swamps, deserts and climates hostile to humans, since the planet's exploration was far advanced. He lived long enough to become acquainted with the early theories of evolution; and I doubt whether 'the survival of the fittest' would have given him sleepless nights.

We know that Tennyson was disturbed by 'Nature red in tooth and claw', in the early 1830s; and that for him, this insight did also disturb Christian faith, when he needed it most. But Tennyson was still influenced by the notion of God's 'design' in the universe somehow 'proving' His Being, and by the Enlightenment science, which he endorsed. He tended to look for God's love inside space/time, and inside the laws of cosmos, rather than pursuing intimations of the eternal to their origins wholly elsewhere. He still thought that science and human progress were linked together – hence, his role as a notable precursor of Victorian 'honest doubt'. Wordsworth, in contrast, was a true mystic, and his vision never rested on Locke; despite the Enlightenment ideas which he imbibed, very naturally, in his formative years.

The experience of God which is Wordsworth's cornerstone differs in kind from theories rooted in scientific ideas. Wordsworth dealt in 'memorable things', which his verse had captured – both for his own 'future restoration' in old age, when vision faded; and for all future readers, ourselves included, in time to be. For fifty years, he laboured to make *The Prelude* one of those very rare works, which men will not 'willingly let die'.

Our modern theories of the universe would not have changed him or caused him a single impulse of doubt. Wordsworth was Newtonian enough to note the apparent design in creation, but his vision had a different, more powerful, source. He did not expect that men would visit the planets, or other solar systems, in space vehicles. And he did not imagine that they would find God there, if they did:

> For I have learned
> To look on nature, not as in the hour
> Of thoughtless youth, but hearing oftentimes

The still, sad music of humanity,
Nor harsh nor grating, though of ample power
To chasten and subdue. And I have felt
A presence that disturbs me with the joy
Of elevated thoughts; a sense sublime
Of something far more deeply interfused,
Whose dwelling is the light of setting suns,
And the round ocean, and the living air
And the blue sky, and in the mind of man,
A motion and a spirit, that impels
All thinking things, all objects of all thought,
And rolls through all things. Therefore am I still
A lover of the meadows and the woods,
And mountains; and of all that we behold
From this green earth; of all the mighty world
Of eye and ear, both what they half-create
And what perceive: well pleased to recognise
In nature and the language of the sense,
The anchor of my purest thoughts, the nurse,
The Guide, the guardian of my heart, and soul
Of all my moral being.

(Wordsworth, *Lines written a few miles above Tintern Abbey on revisiting the banks of the Wye during a tour, July 13th., 1798*)

VI

But are we not dealing then, some ask, with man-made fashions, of mind and taste? No one can deny that all humans belong to their 'period'. Is this not as evidently true of the Greeks, and of Christ, as it is of ourselves?

My concern in this chapter is with things that originate in their own culture, as all things must do, but are 'for all time' also, to use Jonson's famous praise of Shakespeare.

We are dealing with insights that come to prophets and artists chiefly from 'the eternal': and to this degree, use, yet transcend, the culture and the structures to hand. They were received as 'timeless', whatever their temporal circumstances; and they retain the stamp of the eternal, for us.

Picking up this aspect of 'the temporal' leads to a common challenge, which we cannot bypass. It has no force, for those who love Wisdom; but it has been known to stop genuine seekers for Wisdom in their tracks. We need the help of a Devil's Advocate for this part of the terrain, to clear our minds; and perhaps to smooth a path for some who are still in doubt. I propose to spend some time with the sceptics; recalling the onslaught they made on me, in my early years.

Was 'Wild nature' (nature uncultivated by man) not feared and neglected (some ask us), right up to its invention as 'the sublime' in the eighteenth century? And was this not the work of a mix of eccentric 'Gothick' novelists, long-winded Miltonic imitators; and then, of assorted Romantics and Neo-Platonists, on the margins of life? Perhaps such innovators did have the 'pastoral' tradition, and Longinus, to refer to; but in turn, these were surely very marginal sources at best?

Again: was 'cultivated nature' (the business of farming) not man's economic bedrock; and therefore, not remotely associated, by ordinary mortals, with religion or God?

And were 'formal' gardens not, in fact, a triumph of 'art' and 'nature' in harmony, as is often asserted, but the casual luxury of aristocratic or otherwise rich landowners, 'improving' their 'property' to the whims of fashion, for their own self-esteem?

Here are three types of 'argument' often encountered; so let us look at them next. There are books and theses in all of these areas; and I willingly bow to the scholars who chart their own, special ground. As a literary critic, I have been personally concerned with major and minor changes in literature, roughly from the sixteenth century up the present time. The ability to 'place' unseen passages of prose or verse in their period, is required for teaching literature and, indeed, for reading any literature at all with proper care. One ought to be able to pick up clues relevant to dating texts to within a decade: and often, to spotting the writer; and the actual part of his or her life to which they belong.

The existence of fashion and taste is, then, self-evident; and can be taken to be a general truth. Let us turn directly to fear of the 'wild', of the untamed and unknown in nature; which was understandably widespread among early races and tribes. It still is our chief response to 'nature', if we are shipwrecked; or lost in mountains or deserts; or in any situation of personal danger, today.

Nearly all human beings before the early nineteenth century

lived, worked and died in the place where they were born. For most, this would have been a small town or village, and a small area of surrounding country – the proverbial 'native heath'. How far individual men and women have loved their own terrain, and been enriched by it, is a secret locked with most of them in death. Few could have written of it, for most were illiterate: the fate of the greater part of our human kin. Yet their lives held love, richness, wisdom as their human birthright; and we should be shallow indeed to overlook such a truth. Gray's *Elegy* is widely loved, as 'universal', because it gives a voice to the many with no memorials of their own.

Wordsworth knew, and recorded, a special wonder in childhood; agreeing in this with Christ, and with many before. He knew that when childhood passes, wonder fades quickly; passing into boredom and lethargy, if we let these monsters swallow us whole. There must be a conscious pursuit of beauty, if we are to hold on to vision; along with human empathy, as suffering is perceived to join all mortals in one, common lot.

Throughout history, the horse and the small boat prescribed the normal limits of travel. Beyond the near horizon, *terra incognita* began. Those who did travel, the merchants, sailors, adventurers, soldiers, ambassadors, missionaries, outlaws, went at peril of the elements, which they knew to be indifferent to wealth and fame. Mountains were unmapped and hazardous, and hard to trek through: in good weather, difficult; impassable, when winter came on. Brigands and footpads roamed, living by plunder. Inns were few and far between; and had to be taken on trust.

For many centuries, the churches and religious houses provided lodgings for travellers, offering some measure of safety; as they did for the poor, adrift at their doors. But if you vanished on your journey, you left no traces. For the most part, enquiries would never be made. Search parties could hardly be mounted, by loved ones left waiting. The best you could hope for, was to be turned into a myth.

The sea was feared by the Greeks, for very good reasons. Ulysses was blown around the Mediterranean from Sirens to Cyclops to Circe, the ten-year sport of Poseidon, his resolute foe. Agamemnon's fair-wind to Troy was won by a daughter's sacrifice; and his homecoming was rougher than Ulysses', though the sea was more kind.

For St Paul, the Mediterranean was not the least of his problems. Shipwrecks, lack of companionship, enemies who whipped and imprisoned him, made the protection of his God, Whom he trusted, no less hazardous than the lives of the pagans had been.

Desert folk charted the desert to survive, becoming skilled astronomers. Their inspiration was, in the first place, survival; but they did not miss the attendant sublime. Sailors mastered the waves, gathering knowledge and instinct. The spell of the sea called, and fulfilled them often; not all were swallowed down, to await that day when the sea will 'yield up its dead'.

All nations feared the ills on their doorsteps – hurricanes, earthquakes, floods, droughts, volcanos – Nature's great bag of tricks. But many were clearly aware of beauty in the seasons; and loved their native heath, despite its sullen and threatening moods. We should remember, too, that the dangers of 'gravitation' were understood, as the human first law of survival, long before Newton gave gravitation a name (and was turned, for his pains, into the Enlightenment's notion of a saint).

Education has always been, at root, one part of survival; the basic technique for getting through, in one piece, from cradle to grave. For the rural poor, a bare sufficiency has had to be coaxed from the soil, century by century; lean and fat years alternating, as if to some law.

If we consider those born to slavery – a huge, age-old majority – the stakes of suffering are still more starkly etched. Add to slaves (and servants) all the victims of war, tyranny, injustice, and endless varieties of prejudice, and Gibbon's famous pessimism seems a simple truth: 'History, which is little more than a register of the crimes, follies, and misfortunes of mankind'. Gibbon, surveying his own life, in his *Autobiography*, judged himself exceptionally fortunate in the lottery of life. Born to a ruling class, in a country at peace, and humanely educated, he had lighted on a rare oasis of Reason, in the world's great dark. Greek and Roman learning, in Renaissance, had led on to the New Science, which outshone, he believed, all ages before. British commercial and imperial ambitions gave high hopes for world progress, in a spiral still rising from Descartes, Bacon, Newton, Locke, Hume. Such things were his, 'Gibbon's' heritage, in the few decades that any one life endures. He sensed that the rational oasis would prove, in the end, a mirage; as barbarism returned, to the self-same laws that had governed the fall of Rome.

Looking back, we must surely doubt how far 'reason' did rule, in the eighteenth century; and not least, for those to whom Gray's *Elegy* gave a belated voice. Gibbon's culture never was the resurgence of wisdom, that he thought it. It was an arrogant elitism, bearing the seeds of its certain decay. A society made for its rulers only, at the expense of its workers, invites that scepticism about great buildings and gardens, which is now so often expressed – as if the moral flaws in their 'owners' brought their actual beauty, also, into doubt.

The spiritual bearings are clear, and perhaps always have been to those following religious insights with solid foundation from Greece, Israel and Rome. We increasingly discover parallel traditions in the East (in the long evolution of Hindu culture most notably), which begin to converge on a fresh understanding of pagan and Christian wisdom alike. Gibbon's ethos was built on Intellect to the exclusion of 'wholeness'. It was a luxury for a few; and its superior tone became, for the fortunate, nine-tenths of its charm.[1]

Chaos beyond Gibbon's imagining has indeed happened; and the recovery of Wisdom, if the coming millennium indeed achieves it, will be from sources wholly other than Newton and Locke. The rediscovery of Greek and New Testament values, by way of Romantics, Symbolists and Moderns, has already had a long, uphill battle to fight. Its enemies have been rooted in Gibbon's own culture; greatly assisted by the post-Constantine churches, adding allegedly 'Christian' sanctions to most ruthless political power.

'Except ye become as a little child, ye cannot enter the Kingdom of God.' Jesus of Nazareth's perception is, and always will be, a first rule of Wisdom. For Gibbon's society, children were merely 'little ladies' or 'little gentlemen' waiting to become real ladies and gentlemen when, and if, they survived. Wordsworth, by contrast, understood that childhood is a holy state, with the glory of Heaven still lingering in its hidden recesses. He saw that for most of us, childhood is gone before it is truly noticed; and rarely or doubtingly remembered, when it is gone.

Yet many individuals retain the spell of childhood, as a cherished memory. They seek to recover its essence, in the confused and exiled world of adult quest. They find solace in aspects of their own earliest memories; and in those delicate parts of any small child's consciousness which are most hidden from casual, adult eyes.

In the human heart, very occasional flashes of light only may be perceived, from the people around us; and this is true all the days of our lives. The richest human consciousness will often be veiled to others. Perhaps only rare men, like Jesus of Nazareth, see fully and perfectly and always, direct to the heart.

VII

A word now on what is to follow; the part of this book least hopeful, in any obvious sense.

The speed and completeness of change, in the twentieth century, will most probably make our age infamous in the future, if humans survive. The combined effect of internal combustion engine, nuclear power, the global village of television, have accentuated much that disperses, and reduces, coherence in life. We now hear of 'information technology', about to produce the 'information super-highway'; a development towards an unprecedented isolation, accentuated by 'virtual reality', that could sap the minds and souls of humankind. Molecular biology, genetic engineering, ethnic cleansing, already threaten nature in new, dreadful ways. These things: and the pollution of Earth, Air, Water, the sacred elements, are merging now, along with 'market forces' (or 'The Market') as a *de facto* god.

Such a conjunction of change should be a cheap horror story, a nightmare; a madness festering in some sick, schizoid mind. Instead, it is a synopsis of (some) main directions, taken by this century where I, and my first readers, live. A warped picture, perhaps? It leaves out the good things; it is indeed partial. But read that last paragraph again; and consider: in what aspects is it factually wrong? Does it sound any better, on the second reading?

Bacon's dream that science would reshape nature to man's ideal agenda never did take off, perhaps, as a total shared hope by all men of sense. But it has lingered on, and even now is with us, *in a background acceptance that scientists have the right to do whatever they please*. The notion that all inventions will lead to good, became fixed in our culture. It lingered in writers such as Wells and Shaw, while I was myself at school. The fact that the centuries which produced this vision claimed the title 'Reason', is an irony that the next millennium must ponder, as it tries to mop up the damage we have caused.

Bacon was a man so lacking in any true Wisdom that one is amazed by the vogue his *New Atlantis* achieved. If he had read Shakespeare intelligently (let alone 'been' Shakespeare), his ripest nonsense would never have got off the ground.[2]

As I have already acknowledged, a tradition of Wisdom lived on, in the eighteenth century, though much of it ran somewhat underground. The Cambridge Platonists (John Smith, Ralph Cudworth, Benjamin Whichcote, Henry More) were persuasive voices, from the late seventeenth century. The Third Earl of Shaftesbury is a glowing presence among the Augustans, even though his life was dogged by ill health, and sadly short. All of these (and others) gravitated by natural affinity to Plato's tradition, yet remained 'acceptable', as men of scholarship and birth, to their age.

Coleridge was, of course, philosopher as well as poet, coinciding, in important aspects, with Kant. John Stuart Mill found in Wordsworth's poetry and in Coleridge's thinking a life-saving counterbalance to his own father's deadly empiricism, and spiritually threadbare life. Mill placed Coleridge alongside Bentham, as one of the two seminal minds at work in his time.

Wordsworth and Coleridge both reasserted humanity's natural limits; while extending, once more, our spiritual scope. Their mix of mystical vision and pragmatic stoicism came, at a time when such truths had almost been lost. In placing 'intellect' within the larger sphere of 'Reason', they brought back Plato; and along with Plato, and allied Greek wisdom, the fitting context of Christ's still deeper truths.

They recalled us to the 'immortal intimations' that tease us; and to the deep sense of a home that is, and is not, on Earth. This luck continued with Keats and Shelley; perhaps Keats's famous passage, from a letter, will bear repeating again:

> I am certain of nothing but the holiness of the Heart's affections and the truths of Imagination. What the imagination seizes as Beauty must be truth – whether it existed before or not – for I have the same Idea of all our Passions as of Love: they are all, in their sublime, creative of essential Beauty. In a word, you may know my favourite speculation . . . The Imagination may be compared to Adam's dream – he awoke and found it truth. I am the more zealous in this because I have never yet been able to perceive how anything can be known for truth by consecutive reasoning – and yet it must be. Can it be that even the greatest Philosopher ever arrived at his goal without putting aside numerous objections? It is 'a Vision in the form of Youth', for it has come as auxilliary to another favourite speculation of mine – that we shall enjoy hereafter by having what we called Happiness on Earth repeated in a finer tone and so repeated . . . (John Keats, Letter to Benjamin Bailey, 22 November 1817)

The Romantics returned to their truer and deeper religion just as the *détente* between 'rational religion' and science, based on Newton, started to crack. In the early nineteenth century (some find earlier roots for this), evolutionary theories started to appear. The notion that far from being 'King of the Brutes' humans might be simply one of them brought men and women back to earth, with a pleasing bump. Darwin's *Origin Of The Species* (1859) was a later bombshell, but the shockwaves that spread from it had been detected by sensitive minds some decades before. The debates and frenzies which marked the last thirty years or so of the nineteenth century were signs of popular awakening to a long-creeping intellectual furore.

The 'great Victorians' had been living with 'evolution' and uneasily trying to survive it, for at least twenty, and nearer thirty years, before 1859. In the late century, writers like Ruskin, Morris, Matthew Arnold, George Eliot, T.H. Huxley explored man's 'this-worldly' predicament, and found that religious hopes based on 'reason' were unable to help. They assumed that the failure of the Enlightenment could be equated with the failure of Christianity; and this was unfortunate. But the churches had no one but themselves to blame. Not only had the churches entered into the *détente* with science, staking their power on it, but they had erred and strayed from their Founder from the first century on.

Meanwhile, though Darwin's observations appeared to throw doubt on religion, they encouraged certain types of social optimism as well. If man had evolved 'upwards' from the brutes to his present status, surely great things might still appear, on this upward curve? Though older gods had come into question (the Christian God, in his neo-classical reduction, among them), perhaps 'gods' would emerge, in future, from mankind itself? The notion of an 'Emergent God' flowed from this (though the further thought – that man's machines might, in time, supercede man – was not there at the start). Tennyson toyed with this notion in *In Memoriam*, finding in Arthur Hallam (among other roles) a prototype for the 'more perfect humanity' that the future might bring. Intelligence would also grow, bringing peace and prosperity (a *non sequitur* defying all observation of history: but it scraped through for a while – between *Locksley Hall*, and *Locksley Hall Sixty Years After*, we can usefully say).

Social optimism had its last fling in Shaw and the early Wells. The débâcle, in full swing as I write in the 1990s, offers a bitter, yet exciting, challenge to the century to come.

From now on, I shall be returning further back, for my next discussion, and filling out these hints in a context whose roots are very far back. Let me sum up by celebrating the fine creative minds that held out against Enlightenment dangers; keeping Wisdom alive and well, if in seeming retreat. I shall be returning to 'nature' as a source of eternal intimations; and suggest that most of the problems so far looked at can be left now, safely, to one side.

Let us take as read Life's mortality, and human suffering. Let us leave the history of taste to one side as important, but limited to one aspect only of our engagement with art.

Let us agree that love of wild nature was not invented by Wordsworth (or by Gray or Young or Thomson reaching back before him), and no more came as news, to humans, than Newton's 'Law of Gravitation' did. Men have always known that stepping off a mountain into space is asking for trouble. They have always found mountains to be objects of awe and grandeur, when seen with clear eyes.

Let us agree that 'the pastoral' did flourish in classical literature as an escape, often; from the pressures of the court, or the city, or money-making, or maybe all three. Refreshment for the soul is needed, whatever one calls it; and the pastoral archetype touched always on 'The Golden Age' (or 'Paradise', under another name?) Let us agree that the Renaissance leaders rediscovered the Pastoral as a theme for literature and as a model for landscape gardening – most of them, from direct contact with classical authors and a few, like Shakespeare ('little Latin and less Greek'), by mysterious methods best known to himself.

Let us agree that the aristocrats, who owned most of the land and dictated most of the changes, turned to succeeding generations of 'experts' for a periodic reshaping of their 'grounds', to shifting whims. (Mr Milestone, in Peacock's *Headlong Hall,* is a delightfully comic version of them all.) 'Landscape gardening' has a place, to one side of this story; along with swerving fashions in architecture, wallpaper, clothes, music, books, and all aspects of life.

Let us agree to such things, in the shape of the relative. So now, back to the rest.

VIII

The earliest tribes known to us had holy places, with priests to attend them. Figures such as Shamans, Healers, Rainmakers played vital roles, and were revered by their peers as of right. A few men and women were feared, for involvement with magic. Others were accepted as wise, for their counsel and lore. There were sacred Kings who might be destined to die as Saviours. There were gods requiring worship, and gods (or 'a God') too sacred to name. The Oracles of Apollo were built by the Greeks in wild and sometimes remote places, as if to witness that form and structure require balance from their opposites, if arts as complex as Divination are to work.

A measure of fear surrounds all such customs; but men were not easily to be prized apart from their gods. The spiritual structure was at one with politics and, likewise, with everyday pragmatism. 'Religion' was not a department set slightly apart from life. In difficult times, propitiation of the gods was in order; or sacrifice, if troubles persisted, as a result of our human sins. More usually, feasts and offerings were recurring rituals, adding much of the charm and colour to life.

Systems more allegedly 'civilised' came later, but myths and archetypes are the life-blood of all religion, as they are of art. Men looked to the night sky in wonder, searching its vastness; pondering its beauty as a grace sent to them, by the Maker of all. They learned the ways of deserts, forests, seas (their own native heaths, chiefly); a learning seasoned with awe, as well as with proper fear. There were poisons to avoid or traps to be mapped and studied. There were food and drink needful to life, and herbs helpful in healing. There was sacred knowledge, hard to gain and not readily codified, to be guarded and transmitted by the naturally wise. Such patterns were part of all early cultures, and immediately enriching to 'ordinary' folk. If most men and women have not written or attempted to write poetry in the mode of Wordsworth, their sensibility was surely often kindred to his.

Jehovah's great hymn of delight in His own creation (*Job* 38) is not untypical of Judaism, notably in the great Wisdom Books. In context, Job must have found it puzzling; but God's truth does transcend 'our' problems, however sombre they are. The Psalms are full of praise, set alongside great human suffering: 'It is He that hath made us and not we ourselves; we are His people, and the work of His hands' (Psalm 100).

I suspect that at no period of human history before our own century have men and women ignored God and His works, as we tend to do. Cities, Temples, gardens, pictures, artefacts have all been made 'to the greater glory of God'. Beauty has been the first obvious principle, always, of structure and praise. Doctrines of

Incarnation all bear witness to the Good, and the Beautiful. God's indwelling in all whom we love is Good, touched and tasted – which we also sense to be 'holy ground'.

In this great theme, many aspects seem too obvious to labour; but further time in the foothills of wisdom needs to be spent. It will not be lost on any modern nine-to-five commuter reading this, that time spent weaving through traffic-jams, information technology, videos, 'virtual reality' (*et al.*), is less attractive than most lifestyles known to most previous men.

I have now to turn again to our five senses and their primal function; and then, to our 'spiritual senses' which come to us chiefly in union with the senses themselves.[3]

IX

We need to learn to use our senses, *truly* to use them. We should never fall into taking them for granted or into letting them function slackly, as life speeds by. It is a question of sharpening and training our senses, to the highest pitch.

We all see, hear, touch, taste, smell, if our senses are functioning. We experience sensations as vibrations, conveyed by the nervous system to the brain. There, vibrations appears as a unified, complete picture opening, as if through a window, directly upon the world outside.

This process is involuntary, requiring no willpower. It is a passive process, according to Locke. Coleridge, in contrast, assumed that a major act of creation is at the heart of perception, approximating to the original Divine Fiat itself. This he called 'Primary Imagination', the primal act of perception. But, like Locke, he agreed that when our senses are in good working order, perception is 'involuntary'; or at least, that it appears to be so and therefore, to all intent and purpose, is.

Unless we block off our senses, or are blatantly inattentive, we receive a general sense of 'waking reality' outside, and surrounding, ourselves.

As before, I do not intend to linger with epistemology though, with these major differences between Locke and Coleridge on 'perception' itself, it portentously looms. My own concern is with the accepted fact that sense-data, given properly ordered senses, nerves and brain, come to us naturally; however complex the actual mechanism is. We need no training, even from the moment of birth as a baby, to experience the general reality of the world outside.

But it is all too easy to assume that what is 'natural' is also perfunctory. We drop into the habit of taking the world for granted, since it comes at no cost. We may say we are 'bored' by the same old places; that we would far rather be in Venice, or on the Moon.

Worse: it is fatally easy to assume that sense-data become our picture of the world 'purely' passively; as if no co-operative effort were needed from ourselves, and no stringent training. The phrase 'a rose is a rose is a rose' is now somewhat tiresome. Could we try 'this rose is this rose is this rose' for a change? At least, it draws attention to uniqueness united with the particular; to the strange fact that this rose is no other rose, and that it exists. All too often as life runs by, believing that perception is easy, we receive ideas and images in one clouded blur of habit and haste. We may be missing all but the tiniest fraction of the data presented; along with most or all of the supersenuous glory emanating (as the religious suppose) from the indwelling God.

The 'supersensuous' is the home of the greater realities. But there is wonder enough, in the senses themselves. Unless we attend to our senses closely, we shall neither progress in insight, nor be equipped for the slightest awareness of sacrament in everyday life.

Consider colour, as a property of objects (or, as a quality in objects, as our senses perceive it). Colour is mediated by sight, chiefly; though in normal perception, the other senses contribute things we can scarcely discern. If we say 'green' or 'brown', a general image is called up. It may be of green lino, brown paint, from some foul-smelling basement disfigured by woodworm. I have heard people say that green is 'peaceful', brown 'rather drab'. If one looks closely at human furnishings, there are varieties of colour, but some are dire; very few glow with much life.

The colours of an English wood, or an Italian lakeside, are different. Even on dull days, their varieties are always in play. The greens, browns, blues merge, defying our language to discriminate finely; or even at all. But when the light is at its best between dawn and sundown, how to begin to describe the lambent, the iridescent display? No painter, sculptor, architect or composer can do more than evoke certain aspects of the ever-changing interplay, in whatever medium he or she uses and hopes to extend.

We realise that there are hundreds of greens and browns out there in nature; no, thousands: a hundred at least, in any one, given view. Even in great art, our approximations are limited. The greens and browns we use for painting our houses, or in normal decoration, are strangely subdued and deadened, if we compare them with the least grand tree or shrub that grows nearby.

It was Ruskin who pointed out that many of us see remarkably little of what is there to be seen. He meant the sensuous itself, not any supersensuous qualities lying beyond. He was not even talking of 'perfect' against 'defective' eyesight; though shortsightedness and astigmatism cannot help:

> The greatest thing a human soul ever does in this world is to see something, and tell what it saw in a plain way. Hundreds of people can talk for one who can think, but thousands can think for one who can see. To see clearly is poetry, prophesy and religion all in one.

Ruskin clearly exaggerates, as we sometimes have to, when attempting to state the obvious with arresting force. The converse of this, is that for many adults the visual sense has become so overlaid with associations and reflections and preconceptions, or so debased by laziness, that it scarcely functions in its own right at all. In a similar spirit, Pater wrote a celebrated passage in *Renaissance,* from which I quote a section that is more often analysed for its style, than seriously considered for what is says:

> Every moment some form grows perfect in hand or face; some tone on the hills or the sea is choicer than the rest; some mood of passion or insight or intellectual excitement is irresistibly real and attractive to us – for that moment only. Not the fruit of experience, but experience itself, is the end. How may we see in them all that is to be seen in them by the finest senses? How shall we pass most swiftly from point to point, and be present always at the focus where the greatest number of vital forces unite in their purest energy? To burn always with this hard gemlike flame is success in life.

These late nineteenth-century, aesthetic insights, are a call to attention. They urge us to use and train the senses that keep wonder and beauty open; long after childhood's novelty has faded, and habit grown strong. To dismiss this as 'escapism' is a lazy evasion of

Pater's strong call back to reverence. He calls us back to the world we live in; but by implication also, to religion and art, as normal aspects of life.

The aesthetes did indeed seek 'escape' from man-made ugliness; but this was a noble, even a vital, ideal. Their aim was to inspire *recognition* of ugliness, and then its *rejection*. This ideal alone, perhaps, in a democracy, can save God-given reality from the squalor of tiny minds. Much fine Victorian Gothic and Neo-Classical art and architecture was inspired by the Aesthetes; so were later fashions like *art nouveau*, of which *art deco* can be regarded as a last, fading fling. Morris's *News From Nowhere* may seem naïve today, for its progressive optimism; but just ponder the London of the 1960s that he foresaw as possible, if his hopes had prevailed. Compare it with the actual London of the 1960s; now collapsing, or being demolished (not a moment too soon). Look at the sheer reductiveness and vileness of nearly everything actually built between 1950 and 1978 or so; and ponder how 'escapist' and 'precious' Morris's vision really was.

Luckily, we have escaped now from 'brutalism', into the comparative charm of 'post modernism'. This appears at first sight a resumption from *art deco*, but returns in fact to a lightness and beauty of detail, that we had, in architecture, wholly mislaid. (This makes me anxious to add that the word 'modern', which is in general a good word, and certainly is so in literature, was uniquely debased by its association with architecture in its glass/concrete/'brutalist' phase.)

Any education worth the name will be based on aesthetic instincts; which is to say on the quest for precision, and art, and beauty, in everyday life. Science and art are united in their common passion for seeing things, as nearly as we can, as they really are; which is another way of saying, a passion for loving beauty, and pursuing it as a goal. I have heard Theoretical Physicists exclaim at the beauty of their elaborate equations; and the special beauty of a final reduction, from sheets of complex symbols, to (say) $E = Mc^2$. I have gathered that one overarching ideal of physics is the search for 'simplicity': notably, for a simple (and therefore beautiful) theory of the cosmos that will link Big Bang and Black Holes, Quarks and Atomic structure, in one coherent whole that will 'explain' the manifold parts. I have less often heard literary dons use the language of beauty (though mercifully, we have still had critics like C.S. Lewis, and Northrop Frye on the scene). But Beauty is still a natural and current word with artists, as it always must be; and with every critic and teacher worthy of the name.

As I have said, the 'numinous' is a supersenuous experience, that cannot be courted. It comes, at no foreseen times or places, to rules of its own. The 'holy' is also elusive, but somewhat less wayward, to the degree that it half-belongs with its objects: ancient places of prayer; or certain humans half-transfigured by the indwelling God.

Ruskin and Pater knew that Beauty and Goodness are accessible in, or through, sensations. It follows that training to see, hear, feel, taste, smell with the highest precision and delicacy is a vehicle for vision; as well as a prerequisite for excellence in every field of our life. Such training is not 'vision' itself, and may not lead to it; but without the training, vision will lack its most normal routes. We are recalled once more to ponder the interpenetrations of the sensuous and the supersensuous; but now, with the importance of the former chiefly in view.

Ruskin was not primarily a 'religious' writer. Pater became a Christian agnostic, with an unquenched longing for 'faith'. All religions agree that, beyond clean discipline of the senses, we need to cultivate a settled pursuit of purity. We shall miss purity often, and perhaps for long periods depart from it; but repentance and return are part of all wholeness of life. The habit of spiritual cleansing, and daily prayer, are perhaps the only genuine 'ecumenical ground' across religious divides. For Plato, the 'eyes of the understanding' needed cleansing. Moral purity, fortified by mathematics, was his favoured route. Since he believed that our body is expendable, he downgraded it. And, despite his love of life, he saw denial of the body as a step towards freeing the soul. He rejected sex as a distraction at best, and a potential disaster more or less always. (Perhaps he believed that procreation is its sole, proper use.) It is this negative aspect that attracted the ascetic 'Early Fathers' and 'Desert Fathers'; and started Plato towards his co-option (mostly unacknowledged) as a patron of puritanism, and iconoclasm, in the Christian church. (One should add that Plato retained urbane good humour when pondering sex in the youthful; and in this, he differed strongly from most of the Jews before him, and the Christians to come.)

Sexual excess is indeed a snare, and courts disaster. But this is not synonymous, when acknowledged, with extreme rejection of sex. The danger of excess – and still more, of emotional compulsions and enslavements – was well known to the Greeks, by way of the Olympian gods. It is unfortunate that Plato, in scorning the popular religion, lost sight of great parts of its wisdom. For all his insight and learning, Plato deserted the high ideal of balance; and veered towards abstinence, for his guide. Today, we readily find in Aeschylus, Sophocles and Euripides the really deep pagan genius. Their special affinity with our modern traditions of art and philosophy at their most constructive, offers a major signpost towards a new ethical sanity for the century ahead.

Jesus of Nazareth was Jewish, not Greek, and was steeped in the Pentateuch; yet he was amazingly well balanced in his dealings with sex. He took sexual sins seriously, and held traditional Jewish ethics; but his understanding and compassion outsoared and rebuked 'judgemental' minds. If he differed from his fellow Jews and from the Greeks equally, it was in his daily experience of God as 'Father'; and of God as Indwelling Spirit, source of all healing and grace. For Jesus, 'Eternal Life' is no mere idea, and no mild aspiration. It is the 'sacrament of the present moment': immediate and continuing awareness of God in the 'now' where we live. It is God's Kingdom come fully to Earth, and His Will done here. In this light, Jesus believed that all individuals are unique, and uniquely important. He taught that soul, mind and body are all of a piece and all equally eternal; all divine, or erring, according to their closeness to God.

'Let him that hath ears to hear, hear; let him that hath eyes to see, see.' This was Jesus's normal teaching, as he lived out The Kingdom. And, though Jesus was not a nineteenth-century aesthete, or anything like one, he would have understood both Ruskin and Pater, in the passages quoted above. He differed from them in part by being less educated; less concerned with precise details, of a 'painterly' kind. He differed in being more 'down to earth' in the literal sense (more 'true to Heaven' puts this better, of course).

Purification from excesses is part of Christ's clear teaching. Sexual ethics are touched on, but not obsessively. He had more to say on the misuse of money and power, and on the sin of pride especially, than he had on mishaps related to sex. The individual is cherished if things go wrong, whatever his or her failings. God's pursuit of lost coins, lost sheep or lost sons remains unfailing, whatever the method, and the timescale, He adopts. The indwelling Spirit can and will restore us, however we have strayed from Him, if we open the door where God Himself stands and knocks.

The Father is not far off, but near. He is in each one of us. His

Spirit will move us from glory to glory if we say, and mean, 'yes'. The doors of perception indeed need cleansing, but neither Plato's maths, nor Plato's elitist learning, are part of the Way. Christ is the Way himself. He *knows* his divinity. He is Truth incarnate in mortal flesh, to be seen and handled; Son of Man, Son of God also, in here-and-now life. The Way is open to all of us – at a price.

The price is extremely high; it is 'not less than everything'. It is also amazingly low; none is too poor to pay up in full. The paths of Beauty and the paths of Goodness; how to distinguish between them? How to link both with the ever-elusive, ever-clear path of Truth? Plato had his solution, but it was exclusive. Jesus is both simpler and grander: 'I am The Way, the Truth and the Life'.

So: we are back on the path of reverence, after some detours; spiritually home; despite problems strewn in our path.

Now for another detour, which seems unavoidable; and which will criss-cross with places just touched on, as we continue to climb. The summit before us is holiness in God and man, the world transfigured; the path is still low down, amid mire and mist. A section is needed on the contrasting paths of pagans, and of Christians, during the long centuries which each had first to develop and flourish; and then, for too brief a time, to co-exist.

X

As Robin Lane Fox has pointed out, it was the early Christians who began to lay waste groves, take axes to trees; opening the long haul to political exploitation of nature, as we know it today. The gods of pasture and groves and households were turned into demons. Their centuries of worship were destroyed by fanatics, who hated all gods but their own.

Our art has been a major loser to protestant and puritan iconoclasts; but it was very much later that hooligans of this particular brand came on the scene. We are fortunate that the Orthodox and Roman, and later the Anglican, Communions all patronised, and encouraged, art. Even though they did prescribe art's subject matter, and censor rigorously, their monuments in architecture, painting, sculpture, music, and to some degree literature, enrich us all.

The worst artistic iconoclasm has, then, been protestant; associated, in Britain, with Oliver Cromwell, and the Civil War. But a deeper iconoclasm, against human nature itself if we probe it closely, runs through the entire institutional church (or churches) of Christian times. I have already accepted that, though the first destruction of nature as described by Robin Lane Fox was a rejection of paganism, a deeper problem was there, from the first. This was the soul/body dualism, reinforced by Plato but somehow rooted in Judaism, which severed humanity both from animals, and from the entire external, 'natural', world. Indeed, it turned mankind from his natural position, as one part of Creation, into a lonely being, essentially apart. Man became a special 'image of God', created by separate *Fiat*; first, as benign Lord of the Garden; then, as exile fighting for life, after 'The Fall'. In *Genesis*, Adam and Eve were gardeners, and stewards of Nature; but the Fall disrupted this pattern at its start. Humanity was exiled from Paradise to other regions, and to a life of drudgery. The 'sweat of the brow' replaced pleasure, as guiding light for survival 'East of Eden', in the dangerous world where humans would henceforth live.

As we know, the Jews were forced to be nomadic, by their varied history. Only through nationhood did they seem truly rooted in their own 'promised land'. In the Pentateuch, animals became the stuff of food, and often of sacrifice. Praise and fear of God somewhat usurp 'Nature', as a central preoccupation of Jewish life. The Wisdom Books contain evidence of delight in God's material creation; but delight irrevocably yoked with man's dependence upon God, and consequent sufferings – related, as these usually were, to violations of Law. The Chosen People could no longer see Creation as 'very good', as it had been when new-minted. Job is not alone, in experiencing the downside of virtue itself.

The real disaster came later, and is hard to chart precisely. When did a full-scale dualism take over in the church? The really black day seems to have come when the church declared, and accepted, that animals have no souls. This was a black day for animals; not a good day for man. The natural world was made, it now seemed, for man's convenience. Or perhaps, it had been reshaped in this manner, as a result of The Fall? Man was not only Lord of Creation, but Creation's one masterpiece. All other creatures lived and died by 'instinct', to quite different laws.

This is the tendency I propose to call 'Christian iconoclasm'. It separates Christians from pagans, to the greater glory of pagans. It is the chief assumption that threatens Earth's future, as I write these words; and the chief reason why a recovery of pagan (Greek) Wisdom is at least as important, for the final years of this millennium, as is the wisdom of Jesus – greater though that finally is, for its eternal truths.

Christian dualism does not derive from Jesus of Nazareth. It does not derive – contrary to a widely held view – from St Paul, who was the greatest single follower of Jesus; nor from the tenor of the New Testament books (canonical, rather than apocryphal) when read as a whole. Somehow, however, Christian dualism proliferates in writings from as early as the later part of the first century AD. It became second-nature to most of 'The Fathers' and, therefore, seems implicit in the church from the earliest times.

In the early centuries, this doctrinal warp fed on (and perhaps led to) excessive asceticism. This in turn culminated in an obsession with, and against, sexuality, that has seldom been checked by close reference to Jesus; or indeed, by a close and total reading of Paul. By 'close reading' I have in mind the central discipline of my own academic concern, English Literature, where trained and sensitive perception of every detail and nuance, and above all of structure, is a *sine qua non*. In place of close reading of the Gospels, Paul, and of the New Testament writings collectively, we have two differing versions of 'tradition' which between them, have affected most church-going Christians from the late first century up to ourselves. The first is based on a supposed continuous development of revelation, conducted by the Holy Spirit through priests and prelates; and is known now as the 'magisterium' of the Roman Catholic Church. Much of this is taken on trust by the Orthodox, and even by the Anglican, Communions; though outside Rome, inflexible dogmatism has never prevailed. The second version of 'tradition' prevails in extreme protestant sects, where we find favoured fragments of scripture torn from context to the dictates of piety, and used for new, structured schemes of dogma, dressed up as 'truth'.

Unfortunately, St Augustine offered his own immensely influential backing to Christian dualism. For all his genius, he failed to reject his early Manichean background to the degree that he supposed he had. Very soon, dualism passed, in fact if not in theory, into the alleged *magisterium* of the sect which broke, from the unified church, under the Roman Bishop. The priesthood, when forced into celibacy, no doubt grasped at this doctrine with eagerness, as yet another mark of its growing superiority to a now subservient 'lay' flock.

The aspect that most concerns me, in our present crisis, is the terms that the seventeenth-century Christian *détente* with science were based on, when the 'Enlightenment' warfare ended in truce. Endemic iconoclasm surely played a part here, with scientific assumptions lending new weight to the puritan warp. The Church decided to co-operate with science and no longer oppose it, at precisely the point of maximum harm. I speak of the mentality which placed man's *mind* as his glory at the expense of his *wholeness*; and which led to 'observation and experiment' as an unchallenged technique for establishing truth. The more or less axiomatic view that scientific discoveries will always be for the 'good of man', and must submit to no fetters from higher wisdom, now excuses virtually all violations of every other creature sharing our evolution, and our Earth. We sacrifice both creatures, and their habitats, and their natural rhythms, and their very survival to our 'science' and 'convenience': and this, despite the evident truth that their habitats and rhythms, and our own, are all of a piece.

This is the crux which makes the Christian warp towards iconoclasm so finally horrendous, that the very fate of the Earth is now involved. Unless the next millennium can tame, or better phase out, harmful technology, it will not win in its battle against our near-terminal mess. We urgently need to reassess our actual place in Nature – to return to Wisdom from idiocy – if we are to re-establish the Fatherhood of God in Jesus's terms. We have been set on Earth as exiles, but still as stewards and guardians; and of a second home which, despite mortality, offers us 'intimations of immortality' from our very earliest years and throughout our lives.

The damage brought about by severing man from Creation has its grim harvest ripening with each tick of the clock. Man, made in God's image but in exile, is a dangerous predator, blind to the very virtues of 'Reason' that he has tried to claim as his own. We say Jesus's prayer daily, and still in large numbers; but what does the clause 'Thy Will be done in Earth, as it is in Heaven' now mean? The 'green movements' gather strength, but are still culturally marginal; they have little or no foothold on political power. The Churches are too preoccupied with sex, and women priests, and more sex, to attend at all; except through those few, Christlike members whom our present politicians most love to hate. If professing Christians continue to ignore Jesus's prayer, whilst still mouthing it, others must surely move in to fill the gap. If this further means confronting the churches as active obstacles to the clear will of Jesus, it will not be the first time in history that this pattern has come about.

So: to the late Middle Ages and the seventeenth century, for a moment or so more. The 'war' fought out between science and religion was a bitter one; but it was, from the start, the wrong war. It was an irrelevent skirmish at best (when seen with hindsight: though, like all such skirmishes, perhaps it could not be evaded at the time). It caused grief and pain, to Galileo and other victims, but was a tilting at windmills; not remotely clear-sighted, as a view of the dangers posed.

This actual 'war' centred on the church's accumulated body of dogmas; and especially, on a model of the universe assembled over the years. When science challenged this, through its new observations, it clashed head-on with 'revealed truth', as the church now declared all its own lumber to be. Though there was little in the Bible at stake, if Christ himself is our focus, huge areas of the church's 'authority' were deeply involved. The church's complex model included a pseudo-cosmology, with Earth at its centre, and the Heavens arranged round Earth in nine, celestial spheres. There was a pseudo-history likewise, based on *Genesis*, which was read not as myth and poetry but as literal, and inalienable, fact. The 'history' was compounded by a system of 'dating' worked out largely from the Synoptic Genealogies, first Matthew's but, since it went back to Adam, more especially Luke's. The date of Creation was placed at 4004 BC, or thereabouts, with the generations noted by Luke, and the Old Testament records, the clinching fact. The date 4004 BC marked the beginning not only of man, but of the whole Creation, in the six-day week worked by God, with the seventh day set apart for a well-earned rest.

This timescale was, for the church, non-negotiable. (Even today, literal fundamentalists deny that the dinosaurs ever existed; they explain archeological evidence as demonic devices, meant to deceive.) We have to remember that the doctrine of the Fall of Man is also involved with the *Genesis* story (along with the entire scheme of 'vicarious salvation', through blood-sacrifice on the cross, contingent on this). Our entire space/time cosmos was considered to be of recent date, therefore; and was thought to revolve wholly around man, here on Earth. In these factors, we find the stuff of the Renaissance war between science and religion as it actually raged; until, with help from Newton, an armistice could at last be signed.

In addition (and here, we move to still more important ground, with continuing validity), the church saw science as a new form of magic (a matter well explored in C.S. Lewis's *English Literature In the Sixteenth Century, without the Drama*, a volume in the OUP's 'History of English Literature' series).

Magic is man's age-old temptation to 'understand' Nature's mechanism and secret workings, with the aim of imposing upon it a particular human's will, rather than God's. White Magic (or 'Theurgy') was largely beneficent, and intended for healing (for example, Prospero's main plans in Shakespeare's *The Tempest*). Black Magic in contrast (or 'Goety') was intended to aggrandise the magician himself or herself (for example, Dr Faustus's ambitions, as depicted in Marlowe's play about him; and some, at least, of the huge number of non-fictional old ladies burned as witches at the stake). From the viewpoint of the church, there was no real distinction between black and white magic. Both equally opposed the providence of God. The church also (rightly) believed that magicians sought dealings with spirits. White magicians worked through 'aerial', for the most part benign, spirits. In Black Magic, dealings were with fallen spirits and fallen angels, or even with Satan himself. We have to recall that magic was believed to produce results (as it still is, by occultists); and that witches were burned in England as recently as the eighteenth century, and not decriminalised until well into our own.

The church perceived that the new science was observing nature with the intention of changing it; and that it differed from magic only in terms of its means. Many of the early scientists were magicians also; and this confirmed the perception of science as a search for godlike and forbidden power.

The war, along with its battles, martyrs, landmarks, general progress is well known. The eventual resolution was no final solution, nor could it have been. It came about when the church grasped that scientists and philosophers sympathetic to them were supporting and complementing belief in God with the 'new knowledge', and also, that there was no taste for battle (the reverse, rather) on science's side. Newton's 'Law of Gravitation' gave rational proof of God (as Great Mind and Designer). This notion could be made to consort with the 'Supreme Reason' of Aquinas's School, as if supporting traditional verities after all, but from a new, and now very influential, source. Locke, the major English exponent of The Enlightenment from the late seventeenth century onwards, was a professing Christian. He opposed the Deists in a proper and vigorous way; which reassured the church's anxious Bishops, however hard the actual distinction between Locke, and Deism, is to discern. Locke offered 'rational proofs' not only of God's existence as Creator, but also, of basic moral doctrines; and of an afterlife consisting in rewards and punishments, related to the life we live here on Earth.

The package could encompass God, Heaven, Hell, and the Church fairly comfortably; and, for a century and a half (or thereabouts) after this, the fighting stopped. Magicians and witches continued to be severely punished; but scientists were allies, now, of most rational, religious men.

It was not until Evolutionary Theory appeared on the scene, in the early nineteenth century, that tension built up again, and exploded, in a second great war. Most of the famous Victorians shared the anguish of this new conflict, as they were torn between desire (in varying degrees) to remain 'Christian', and a desire for 'the truth'. This war ended in a messy truce for some people, and in a final break between science and religion for others (our basic position today). Innumerable attempts to keep 'Christian morality' but to find a new base for it, co-existed with the *de facto* secularisation of much Western thought.[4]

This is the war that was in fact fought out between 'science' and 'religion' at the Enlightenment; and includes the tensions still most often discussed, as historians look back. Unfortunately, many people still equate the Church with 'Christ' (or even, with 'religion'), and assume that they are 'unbelievers' because they feel obliged, by untenable dogmas, to remain unchurched. Deep religious instincts may then be equated with trivial wishes or errors left over from childhood; or with human longing for more reassurance than the universe actually has it in it to give. Most of us want, understandably, not to fool ourselves. Nowadays, religious belief is more easily linked with credulity than with wisdom, in the popular mind.

The war that *per contra* should have flared up earlier, failed to: a classic case of the dog that did not bark in the night. The dog does not bark when it is aware of an *'insider'*; and no doubt, mistrust of the human body and of its natural instincts, shared by churchmen and scientists in equal measure, fooled the dog, in this particular case.

The Church which opposed sixteenth-century science as a new form of magic, failed to spot the far greater threat contained in its own *détente* with Newton and Locke. This, I take to be the assumption that man is not only 'king' of the brutes, but also radically apart from them: a creature different in kind; and no longer a steward – rather, a godlike being himself, with a licence to kill. Man's intellect is now a sharp line, drawn between humankind, and all creation 'below'.

The church noticed 'pride', of course rightly, in Bacon's notorious phrase 'Knowledge is Power'. If it failed to see even worse pride in the further doctrine of man's special and unique status among God's creatures, then this must be because the same iconoclasm had, almost always, lurked in itself.

XI

As I have said already, the new doctrine was terrible news for the animals; though they could not know this, as their lives continued, for some centuries still, in the age-old ways. The animals were now judged expendable by humans who, as the 'true image of God', living by Intellect and uniquely Immortal, were chiefly perturbed by traces of 'the animal' left over in themselves. Undeniably, men and women are imprisoned in bodies akin to those of the other, lesser creatures, and are led a strange dance by instincts which no longer strike them as natural and, most obviously and painfully, by sex. Perhaps this was one of God's jokes, as Sterne and similar eccentrics jested? More likely, it was the central 'problem' set us, for our challenge to live a decent moral life.

The upshot was that animals came to be regarded as largely alien creatures. At best, they were conveniently placed to be exploited; at worst, they were disturbing examples of things best avoided in ourselves. Unfortunately, this meant that mankind was on its way now to a completely new age of animal sacrifice. This time, the sacrifice would not be in blood-rites, offered for God's appeasement or glory. It would relate to whatever models, and experiments, might serve the 'good of man'.

Bad news for the animals; bad news for art. Human emotions, as well as instincts, were perhaps 'animal'? They were more clearly 'mortal', it now seemed, than are the works of our Mind. They became interpreted, increasingly, as temptations to confusion and error. They were no longer the positive gateway to truth that most ages have found them to be.

'Reason' was put in control of the Arts, therefore, as well as of the Sciences. Soon after the Restoration (1660) the Royal Society was instituted, to draw up new rules for civilised life. As we well know, prose was adapted to the prime needs of philosophers and scientists, as its main function. 'Poetic' prose was frowned on; along, very soon, with most poetry itself.

A further paradox is that the senses were, if in one aspect only, upgraded. This is in their functional role as the organs which admit sense data from the world outside. The data, transmitted by nerves to the brain, become ideas and images. Discursive intellect, tutored by science, then deduces all 'truth'.

If the 'senses' attempted to lay any further claims to the brain's kingdom, these were increasingly discounted, along with most of man's aesthetic and sensuous past. Poets might use 'fancies' and 'wit' if they pleased, as embellishment, but 'poetic truths', like all others, came from Reason itself. The word 'senses' became tainted, along with 'sensual', 'sensuous', 'sensational' and other derivatives. Even 'sensible' meant the 'basic sense data' in common usage, and not 'commonsensical rather than nonsensical', as it often does now.

The entire vocabulary of emotion and instinct was pushed outside the new, charmed world of urbane good sense. 'Enthusiasts' were the religious dissenters; and by extension, others whose views owed more to intuition than to logic. Even 'an Original' was now a term of dismissal; signifying, as it did, anyone of a nonconformist turn. Religion was supposed to produce enlightened assent, not devotional turmoil. Social *mores* were based on codes and customs, not on impulses of the uncontrolled heart.

'The Classics' remained on the major curriculum for the educated minority, and were even its centre in Universities and Schools. But they were valued chiefly now for rational pragmatic insights; and above all for 'style'. The Olympian gods were 'myths', and 'myths' were falsehoods. Even the Christian 'God the Father' gave way, in effect, to Newton's God, the Great Creative Mind.

From this time on, and even into this century, early tribes and societies were called 'primitive'. The word retains, for many, its adverse undertones, despite the Romantics, and the reappraisal they brought. It is still risky, (but growing less so?), to rediscover 'wisdom' from the earlier world, for application to our urgent, modern needs. Doors were slammed shut, by the Enlightenment, on all wild regions of 'the ancients'; especially when instincts and emotions were involved. Man's 'spiritual' faculties took up residence in the House of Intellect; where they would stay, for as long as Descartes, Locke and Newton remained in control.

In eighteenth- and nineteenth-century Europe, culture was still elitist. It 'belonged' with the rulers and aristocrats, and later with the new moneyed classes as they bought their way in. Most of the population was technically illiterate. Any 'popular' culture was a threat and, for many, a misuse of words.

Unhappily for us, we can now understand how this extraordinary change came about in 'polite society'; and why it lasted as long as it did. The Medieval Church had concocted a similar intellectual ascendancy, though under different auspices, and a different name. The Scholastic Philosophers had equated our human 'mind' with the immortal Angels 'above us'; and our 'body' with the mortal, and instinctual, brutes 'below'. Aquinas refined this framework, incorporating notions from Aristotle; yet the moral bias clearly shows Plato's underground influence, doing its worst. It is profoundly unfortunate that Plato had drawn his Theory of Ideas towards the fatal 'mind' (immortal) 'body' (mortal) dualism, and so helped reinforce that puritan streak which infected the Early Church. Just as pagan reverence for the Earth, and for the whole human psyche, was one casualty, so were any pre-scientific 'fancies' that Reason now failed to confirm. The fitful 'Ancients v. Moderns' debate, conducted in the late seventeenth and early eighteenth centuries, equated 'The Ancients' at their best with 'The Moderns' (that is, in their pursuit of 'reason'); but invariably awarded the palm to 'The Moderns' (themselves) in serious debate.[5] The Moderns scored precisely in Science, the new, crowning glory. For all their belief in 'reason', the Ancients had never discovered scientific method; and had shown no sign of inventing machinery, to touch nature up.

It is now arguable that our major Enlightenment figures seriously deluded themselves, even in that area of 'reason' which they most prized. As we have seen, Greeks and New Testament Christians alike had a deep understanding of human nature, of the kind which is possible only when dualism is felt to be folly in the bones. Likewise, though the ancient world did not choose to tread the path of the later scientists, it would have understood their main ideas, by other names. Above all, its grip on man's mortality, and his natural, inalienable limits, made for a sanity that The Enlightenment virtually lost. The Greeks, and Jesus and Paul, had never heard of the Second Law of Thermodynamics; but then, neither had Locke and Newton, as we readily see. Quotations already given, from Eddington and Betrand Russell, show what a spanner this Law was, when thrown into modern science's works. The Greeks however, did know of 'Necessity': that final power (surely entropy?) to which all things, even the gods, must bow. Jesus of Nazareth knew that God's Kingdom is 'not of this world' though it has a foothold here; and that our 'eternal life' has nothing to do with attempting to prolong our intended, mortal span.

In our twentieth century, the Earth has been deteriorated by technology until its survival is threatened; and still, the church does not set its mind on a cure for this. Women priests reduce pious Anglicans to defections to Rome, and to the invention of 'flying Bishops'. But the preoccupations of Friends of the Earth, WWF, Greenpeace and other such bodies, have yet to stir the Anglican Synod (or the Vatican?) out of their torpor. They still pray 'Thy Kingdom come' and the rest of it (it is part of the Liturgy); at Matins, on certain set days, they exhort the whole creation to praise God, in the 'Benedicite Omnia Opera' ('Oh ye Whales, and all that move in the Waters, bless ye the Lord: praise Him and magnify Him for ever . . .' and so on) The Psalms roll round, with much praise and glory for Earth's beauty interspersing the Psalmist's misfortunes and personal pleas – 'The Earth is the Lord's, and the fullness thereof' . . . Even St Francis is tucked away somewhere, for occasional use (to amuse the children?). He has yet to assume his rightful place, as the leading Green Saint of the modern church.

Despite its own scriptures, and its own Founder, the church still sticks, by and large, with its weird mix of hysterical Early Fathers, and Lockeian aridities of 'moral' thought. The prejudices against free instinct, unfettered creativity, sex guided by love and joy rather than by rigid formulae, are still in place, and resisting attempts at change.

The 'World Picture' of the Middle Ages is known to most arts and science students, often in highly schematised forms. (Dr. E.M.W. Tillyard, the English Scholar, did some damage here.) We can make the error, as Tillyard did, of *reducing* great medieval and Tudor writers to these doctrines. We can make the similar error of imagining that The Enlightenment merely replaced the former 'world picture' with a radically revised 'scientific' version, which removed, however, all the beauty and wisdom, leaving it dead.

It is more useful, perhaps, to note how the 'new picture' of the Renaissance was first merged with, and then largely superceded by, the later picture ('ours') – *without the process ever being clearly articulated, or indeed understood.*

The medieval 'World Picture', though at first deemed to be threatened by the new science, was indeed selectively grafted into it, when peace broke out. By tacit consent, the angels vanished. Science's new optic tubes failed to locate angels; and angelic visits ceased to be a feature of polite life. If you read Milton and Donne, then pass on through Pope and Dryden, to Thomson, Goldsmith and Cowper, you can notice the dignified exit of the angels: no head-on clash; no fuss: just a fading away. For Milton, the angels were still as real as they had been to Aquinas; but Donne felt free to use them, as he pleased, for 'metaphysical conceits'. The process was not announced, and not charted; but little overt grief is expressed. From the viewpoint of theologian, philosopher and scientist equally, the result of their going was clearly for the good. Man was now linked to God uniquely and directly, through his Intellect, without incongruous 'angelic superiors' lingering on, from earlier times. Likewise, man was now linked directly with the brutes, when he turned his gaze downwards; but no longer as one link, himself, in a whole, divine chain. The brutes were useful, as adjuncts at hand for future experiments; and exemplary, as reflections of man's 'lower' and 'mortal' parts come adrift from God.

Bias against sex is at the heart of this picture, with science assisting inherited prejudice, in this underground way. Christianity always adopted and reinforced the original Platonic dualism; against which, Blake would in due time launch blazing, prophetic attacks. Though the sects calling themselves 'Puritan' were still actively persecuted, this was a matter of schism and church politics; it was not the result of any deep moral gulf. The puritan moral thrust pervaded the entire church, catholic and protestant. 'Puritanism' became offensive only when 'enthusiasm' triumphed over urbanity, and exclusive claims to salvation were made by tiny sects. The church was as solidly hostile to sex in truth as it had always been: merely, a little more tolerant in practice than in theory, when it came to that pragmatic hypocrisy required by men-of-the-world. 'Discretion above all' was the (non-puritan) subtext: 'don't be found out'. (If you are, 'all hell let loose': the usual rules.)

I put these things starkly, for convenience. Students of literature, history, arts and sciences trace such trends in their own specialisms, adding the detail and scholarship which experts need.

The first Industrial Revolution was accepted in Christian Europe as 'progress', but already a few cranks and romantics began to revolt. Blake dined with Isaiah and Ezekiel, and conversed with angels; and became one of the truly great prophets of all time. Wordsworth arrived on the scene shortly afterwards; an outstanding mystic, who had the good fortune to have Coleridge to hand. Blake and Wordsworth stand out from most contemporaries by their towering genius; but a growing number of less talented (even untalented) men and women began to look for some way out from the rational trap.

Keats and Shelley were a shade less radical than Blake and

Wordsworth, at least in practice. But Keats was also that rare thing, a genius among poets; and both he and Shelley had, for a confident new century, the glamour of youth. In Keats's major Odes, the enduring multivalence of human mortality finds an expression that delights and teases us to this day.

In our own century, a poet like Yeats and a prophet like Jung have central importance, if one wants to chart the passage of wisdom through, towards the millennium to come. Yeats and Jung fed on the Romantics, but studied many kinds of ancient wisdom with a new depth and insight that related to their lives and works. They were involved with the human heart, and both learned to know it; and they found material from many past cultures fit for their own creative, and practical, needs. They rank among the rediscoverers of the East, of India, of Africa, of South America and of many other ancient cultures; always at the point where Wisdom offers truths unanchored in time. As our century draws to its close, these insights grow in importance; and Christ is re-emerging also, from the long shadows cast around him by his so-called church.

No doubt, the alliance between Church and New Learning was advantageous to both of them, when it came about three centuries ago. It clarified and met the needs which both then had. The Church had its Trinity, afloat on a sea of obsolete dogmas. Newton's God could elide with the Trinity helpfully, somewhere off-stage. And science? In its early days, it was lavish with promise for the future, but threadbare in content: the engines and tools of improvement were slow to appear. Both parties had something to give to the other, and this insight was mutually grasped. The Christian alliance gave to the Church Newton's name, and authority. In return, science became accepted by religion, until such time as its own promised wonders and marvels might really appear.

In the late eighteenth century, Goldsmith grieved over the damage being caused by new, large-scale enclosures; 'The Deserted Village' is a poem that speaks to us still. The arrival of industry, and of towns blighted by industry, came gradually. Blake's 'dark Satanic mills' took note of the process, in resonant symbols – prophetic in scope, but based in real smoke, and grime. The first major scientific constructs to change immemorial landscapes were canals. A new, extensive system was conceived, and quickly built. The canals began to revolutionise men's prospects for travel, and especially, for the large-scale transportation of commercial wares.

The railways came not long afterwards, in the 1830s, rendering canals partly obsolete, in record time.

Very soon, life as it had been known to humanity since the earliest records, became a receding pattern; changed, and beyond recall.[6]

In towns, the effects were dramatic. *Dombey And Son* (1846–8) depicted devastation in Somers Town caused by railway building, and also subtle shifts in ethics as older merchants, like Dombey, were replaced by new *entrepreneurs. Bleak House* (1852–3) recorded the homelessness, squalor and public devaluation of compassion which Dickens saw in his own cherished London, along with dramatic changes in fortune for rich landowners still stuck in the past. *Hard Times* (1854) images a hellish midland city of the Black Country, as dirt, machinery, usury and fact-grinding kill off the soul. 'Coketown' is meant to be typical of the new bourgeois ethos, with men like Gradgrind and Bounderby injecting the moral cant of utilitarianism into this unholy mix.

By 1865, Dickens was ready to depict London as a city symbolised by the Great Dust Heaps in Holloway, where outcasts scavenged in filth and rubbish for mislaid valuables; and by a fog-bound Thames, where other scavengers plundered dead men (some murdered) drifting in the river's murky tides. This great novel, *Our Mutual Friend* (1864–5), surveys the landscape thrown up by a decade of unprecedented change.

Dickens depicted the 'new rich' who come from nowhere, and return to nowhere, and are elaborate con-men (the Veneerings and their circle); the new breed of bullying puritans (Mr Podsnap); the struggling would-be upwardly mobile working-to-lower-middle-class types, strained to breaking point (Bradley Headstone); as well as genteel lower-middle-class snobs (Mrs Wilfer notably) and the very poor, struggling to survive by their wits against terrible odds (Hexam, Riderhood, Jenny Wren, Silas Wegg, and many more). In both Eugene Wrayburn and Bella Wilfer, Dickens studies two wayward people from different but perceptibly contemporary backgrounds, for whose souls the main moral battle of the tale is fought. In this last complete novel, Dickens depicts an even vaster canvas than usual; including the rise of the Stock Exchange, and the new mentality of greed based on the overriding scramble, 'Have Shares'. I know of no better or more absorbing introduction to the shifting social currents of the 1860s. Arnold's *Culture and Anarchy* and George Eliot's *Middlemarch* also belong to this period, which saw the implications of democracy for the future of all aspects of culture and society debated, with new sharpness and point.

When the Industrial Revolution did come, it moved swiftly. By the time of Hardy, 'rural England' still existed (it did in my own childhood in the 1930s, even); but population and economic changes had broken all moulds. Towns were growing and eating the countryside, in mainly grim uniformity, as the old England decayed around them, root and branch. These changes were rightly regarded by Hardy as irreversible; but more and more individuals became concerned by the plight of the new, and desperate, poor. In complex debates on practical topics (education, sanitation, health, transport, labour relations) many creative minds were drawn in and, still more to the point, so were not a few, feeling hearts. The growth of revolutionary movements was both feared, and variously analysed. Social changes in the power-structure, just sufficiently radical to avert total revolution and to accommodate the new, money-orientated middle classes, came to seem, in Britain, a race against time.

A great many individual Christians worked hard for the poor, alongside allcomers. Some were motivated by their own variety of religion (the Salvation Army notably; non-conformists more prominently than Anglicans). A great many good men and women were alienated from the church by its dogmas, or by its seeming callousness, but were committed in their actions to Christ's Kingdom of God. The Anglican church, concerned with its privileged status as the 'Established Church', more often opposed than helped radical reforms. And the Roman sect? Among toiling social reformers it could detect only dangerous liberals, obstructing its *magisterium* and defying its pope. The drawbridge went up, to ringfence the sect against damage. Dogmatism achieved new peaks which medieval clerics might have marvelled at; but mercifully, the power of the Inquisition, at least, had been quelled.

As the century moved on, devastation, not progress, became the hallmark of much technology; and entrenched reaction the stance of the church. Technology did produce benefits, and numerous Christians laboured bravely; but I speak, here, of the overarching social trend. The important gains (in medicine, for example) came slowly; and have often been circumvented by lack of finance, bureaucratic muddle, and the endless ingenuity of bacteria and viruses under threat. Premature mortality increased, if anything, in the nineteenth century, in the world of the 'labouring poor'. Engels' *Condition of the Working Class in England in 1844* was suppressed, for most of the century, in the country it studied. But its facts were true, and novelists were on hand to dramatise them, in major art. Writers as diverse as Disraeli, Mrs Gaskell, Dickens, George Eliot, Henry James, played a part. These were artists trained to see and hear with precision, and disposed to an humane and complex total response. Their work complements the infant trade unions, the Chartists and many protest groups, whose situation called more for polemical skills than for subtle art. Weighty social commissions were set up, as people awoke with reluctance, under these varied proddings, to react to that naked anger of Society's victims which self-interest and apathy cannot, for ever, repress. Dickens was not untypical in choosing to play on fear as well as on compassion, as he demonstrated that the rich are not immune to incipient revolution, and to diseases incubating among the very poor.

Many individuals drawn from all social classes and from all shades of religion and humanism, worked together. They laid together, with a solid determination rare in history, the foundations of what would turn, much later, into the Welfare State.

Blake, Wordsworth and Keats preceded the major upheavals, but their art lent powerful impetus to the century ahead. Their literary influence I have touched on already; so I shall jump to later Victorians like Ruskin, and William Morris, and the work they inspired. Here at last were artistic pioneers of a new counter-movement, with the talent to translate visionary ideals into practical shape. In the USA, their counterparts included Emerson and Thoreau, whose writings sowed seed in fruitful soil. We can think of them now as the founding fathers of the 'green movement' – which stayed underground up to and including most of our own lifetimes; but has emerged in increasingly important initiatives outside mainstream 'politics' and now sets a major agenda for the century to come. Though such men have been sneered at as 'escapists' by the likes of F.R. Leavis, they are classic examples of visionaries ahead of their time. They were neither escapists nor cranks (the other accusation often hurled at them); rather, the 'sighted' few, in a country of the blind.

The early green pioneers set out to refresh jaded spirits, and to fight for beauty and 'nature', in a climate marked by greed and decay. In the USA, the first National Parks came into being; a movement which took on slowly in Britain, and is only now finding its feet. Here in Britain indeed, the cities were the first to feel certain benefits, with the rediscovery of patterns of civic excellence that the pagans had known, in their many centuries, as common sense. If greed had won, all England might have turned into Coketown. Only the vigilance of national pride and decency stood in the way. Parks, squares, gardens, fine churches and civic buildings were designed, with charm and grandeur; along with High Street banks, hotels, museums, libraries; and amazing ornamental structures, such as bandstands and seaside piers. These colourful landmarks, in cities increasingly disfigured elsewhere by jerry-building, have original and lasting power to delight. They must still be seen as a major blueprint for the future, when the world escapes its current obsession with 'market values', and puts art, beauty and serenity first once more, in urban life. In a true sense, men like Arnold, Ruskin and their followers managed to harness a grandeur born of British Imperial energy, to Romantic vision and idealism coming from great poets, prophets, artists, and men of goodwill.

Major achievements in architecture are the most enduring gifts of the Romantic counter-culture; still with us and, if war and nuclear destruction can be avoided, still in good shape to last for centuries to come. Barry's Palace of Westminster, Waterhouse's City Hall in Manchester, the St George's Hall in Liverpool, the Albert Hall in London, the Roman Oratory in the Brompton Road and the Roman Cathedral in Westminster, the Clubs in Pall Mall, Scott's Foreign Office in Whitehall: all these, and numerous churches throughout Britain, and far too many fine civic buildings to attempt to list here, are the core of British Architecture's second Golden Age.[7]

Victorian banks, museums and railway stations bear some resemblance to churches and even cathedrals; the period's genius is bound up with this. Whatever buildings a new age needs for its institutions, are public landmarks; deserving all the vision and ingenuity that the age can bring. The Victorians combed major past periods for inspiration, and adapted new materials, iron and glass chiefly, to their own designs. The Albert Memorial combines Classical, Gothic and Byzantine features to stunning effect, as Londoners like myself are glad to boast. The Crystal Palace, built in Hyde Park for the Great Exhibition (1851) and later moved to South London, criss-crossed modern materials (iron and glass) with soaringly beautiful structures adapted from the past.

Whether we look to the great arched roofs of London stations (St Pancras, Paddington, Liverpool Street); or to the Conservatories in Kew Gardens; or to Ruskin's Museum in Oxford and the two major South Kensington Museums; or to the wharves in London's docklands; or to the famous piers at Brighton, Blackpool, Southend and elsewhere, we observe flamboyance, grandeur and fine design meeting, in ever new ways. London remains an amazing city to enter by rail, and then to roam through, seeking out its endless, and often hidden, delights. One feature is a certain democratic openness, which balances perhaps the Imperial appeal. Most of its finest buildings are for general enjoyment, certainly as a spectacle; and many are freely open (or were until recently) to be seen within.

If you removed from London everything Victorian, you would still have excellent neo-classical works to show. The City of London provides many of these; and Inigo Jones' buildings, Wren's churches, the Nash Terraces, four or five Hawksmoor churches, are part of a legacy I should be loathe to play down. But these are, by London's design, scattered glories: it is the Victorian vision which gives to them, by and large, the contexts they need. Without the Victorian, almost everything that makes London great would have vanished; including its often forgotten glory – the many great parks, squares, vistas and trees.

The proliferating working-class areas were in contrast shoddy and ugly, an amalgam of cheap labour, cheap materials, cheap greed. Yet even here, men like Ruskin and Morris helped to build or inspire charming enclaves. Tree-lined avenues, houses with gardens, leafy and accessible squares, fine terraces of well-paved streets or quasi-Venetian footpaths, created a city pattern that has never been surpassed. There were public libraries, to serve the newly literate; and occasional centres for drama, music, sport, adult education and cultural events. Even street fixtures were designed by craftsmen, whether we have gas lamps, local railway stations, kiosks or public lavatories in our sights. Modest districts such as my own, in Maida Hill, North Paddington, had handsome street-lamps, which remained through the 1930s, and were left even after electric fixtures replaced them, until the vandals of the 1950s came. The houses had front and back gardens, and wrought-iron railings, that survived until the outbreak of the Second World War. Bay windows were common in the lower stories, with moulded flights of steps to porch and front-door. They also had thick walls, making for solid construction and noise protection; and well-proportioned rooms, generous in size. These houses were built for middle middle-class families in the late 1850s; my own house still had bells in each room to the 'servant's quarter' (one or two servants, at most). The original owners moved further out, within ten or twenty years of construction; then further out again, as the suburbs continued to recede over the next hundred years. These Paddington houses were soon colonised by mixed communities; the houses multi-occupied, with a rich mix of human background and type. Elderly ladies in genteel poverty had 'rooms' there, alongside a variety of lower-middle-class and working-class families in flats. There was a considerable Irish community in my childhood – an outpost of Kilburn happily and easily part of the general mix. The properties were well kept up for the most part in the 1930s, and the atmosphere was friendly and safe. Only the war led to visible deterioration; only the merging of Paddington and Westminster, somewhat later, precipitated the crisis afflicting it now (1994). Immediately after the war, however, West Indians and some Africans moved in to the area; greatly enriching it by their colour, diversity of temperament, and initial good will.

Certain enlightened industrialists created communities for their workers, as the nineteenth century adapted to urban life. A few, like Port Sunlight, have their own museum or other cultural centre, and are still well worth visiting. A little later, the 'Garden City' idea had a brief vogue, in suburban outposts. This attempted to retain some element of village charm in urban settings. There were some fine churches, as in Hampstead Garden Suburb, but too few shops, community centres and pubs. The idea was flawed and short-lived, or perhaps, too elitist; but it showed willing, as 'London' won total ascendancy over Middlesex, and over large sections of Essex, Kent, Surrey and Herts.

The Garden City idea perhaps lived on in the 'New Towns', of our mid-century period; but these were now further flawed and debased. The robotic mentality of planners put cars before people; and the curse of 'modern architecture' had us in thrall. Huge tower-blocks, hideous to live in and shakily assembled, existed in virtual waste-lands, void of any human life at home in the streets.

Perhaps some positive features from the original 'Garden City' will receive a green kiss-of-life, in the century ahead? One major aim must be to nurture and extend forests, meadows, wildlife; and to protect and enhance all natural beauty still saved from the wreck. The 'global village' now being created by the Information Highway, must be brought into harmony with revitalised towns and villages, purged of their dross. If we are willing to learn again from the Victorians, and beyond them the pagans, we shall tame the ubiquitous car, our twentieth-century demon, and learn again to put gods and humans first.

We can be glad, even now, that men like Scott, Pugin, Waterhouse, Barry, Ruskin and a host of others, made our city centres grand, and our suburbs as pleasing as a philistine age would permit. The basic battle is still between God and Mammon: it involves the Wisdom spoken of here, in very practical forms.

It amazes me still, that I was invited to call the great Victorian buildings 'monstrosities' in my schooldays; when an anti-Victorian mania, led by blinkered iconoclasts like Lytton Strachey, was at its peak. How could well-meaning teachers denigrate, as they did, London's true heritage, while the slums and horrors of capitalism lay, in starkest contrast, all round? It was suggested to me that major landmarks in Kensington would be improved by direct hits in the bombing; while nearby streets, disfiguring a score of slum areas, went without comment – let alone, any constructive notions, for their post-war life. How could such teachers praise wishywashy experiments of the moment like the Peter Jones Building, as if one slight curve, to relieve monotony, were the height of art? If intelligent people had truly *looked*, as Ruskin suggested, then the concrete disasters of the 1950s and 1960s could never have come to disgrace our times.

Late Victorian poetry was a somewhat lesser achievement, but it too has suffered from culpable neglect. A great number of minor poets were accomplished and pleasing; and have still to be appraised at their true worth. There are poems by Swinburne, Christina Rossetti and Matthew Arnold that achieve greatness (Hopkins was also writing, but his work was suppressed by his church). There is also a much larger body of work that is well-crafted, sensitive, and still highly pleasing to read. Morris's *Earthly Paradise* is now scarcely remembered, but I spent a week of growing pleasure with it, when I recently had time to relax.

The quest for poetic beauty continued into the present century, producing lyrics of considerable charm from James Elroy Flecker, Rupert Brooke, John Masefield, John Drinkwater, and a dozen or more Georgians now scarcely known. This tradition also had poets of greater stature, including Rudyard Kipling, and the currently neglected A.E. Houseman and Walter de la Mare.[8] It took time even for Edward Thomas and Thomas Hardy to be appraised as the major poets that they certainly are.

To note this, is to recall really large areas of beauty still available, if we resist the attempt to marginalise poetry as an 'elitist' preserve. People can rediscover the pleasure of reading poetry before settling down to sleep, if they are willing to forego a little violent TV and video to make time. There is a very rich period between (say) 1860 and 1930, when many poets pursued beauty as a good-in-itself.

They may be surpassed in power by the outstanding pioneers of 'modernism' (Owen, Yeats, Eliot, Auden, MacNeice, Dylan Thomas, R.S. Thomas, Ted Hughes, Thom Gunn and one or two others); but the great should never be made an enemy of the good.

XII

Cultural changes brought by technology are always with us; and seem to speed up, with each decade. This is why the challenge to return to 'wisdom' is and must be so urgent; if salvation of our planet, and even of our souls, is to keep pride of place.

Few guessed that the Great War, 'a war to end all wars' as the optimists called it, would turn out to be 'a war to end all peace' (Bertrand Russell's assessment, towards the end of his very long life). The Soviet Revolution of 1917, at the height of the Great War's frenzy, totally dominated Europe for seventy-four years. A sense of nightmare has increasingly surrounded technology, as any study of science fiction as a *genre* makes clear. T.S. Eliot's *Waste Land* and Aldous Huxley's *Brave New World* are 1920s landmarks. Orwell's *1984* (written in 1948) proved far-sighted indeed.

Since 1948, useful gadgets have accumulated in most households. Benefits such as central heating, refrigeration, air-conditioning, antibiotics should not be downplayed. Yet the central perception of science has shifted radically. The progressive assumptions of the Enlightenment are mercifully fading; and already seem, to many of us, folly and *hubris* on a Faustian scale.

In my childhood, electric light was a novelty; so was the wireless, when it arrived. Did I notice how strange they were, how 'wonderful'? For a day or so, some glow of pleasure lingered around them. Then, gaslight receded as a memory, without initial nostalgia; and trysts with Toytown, Henry Hall and the rest were a matter of course.

Motor-cars and buses were normal; hadn't they always been? We all have a blind spot for the decade or so immediately before our own birth. My parents complained of London's endless expansion, engulfing their remembered childhood countryside; but if they hankered after horse-drawn transport, they did not say so to me. I suppose that electric trams, and the underground railways, had prepared them for mechanical changes in transport in the direction of speed.

I was born in London, and loved it from childhood. My grandmother took me to the royal buildings and parks and ceremonials, her self-assurance and pride flowing over to me. I was in London throughout the Blitz and all subsequent bombing, when a great heightening of consciousness fed on the closeness of death. Particular memories from 1940–1, and 1944–5 eclipse, even now, most later memories. There are whole nights, and sections of day caught, with extraordinary vividness; each one associated with particular bombings, and particular deaths. The sense of those years as 'enchanted' overtops even Cambridge: the other great *mythos* of my early life (Et in Arcadia Ego: no cliché; just 1949–52; the simple, charmed truth).

Though career demands have taken me away from London, I have seized every occasion and strategem possible to get back. If I except the Italian Lakes and Venice, and the English West Country and the Hereford/Monmouth border, and the lost Cambridge of undergraduate memory, every absence has led to a longing to be in the city I really love. London was a glorious place to be born in and to experience as 'childhood'. The war offered further bonds, till death do us part.

So: my early place of exile in space/time seems closer to Paradise, than most humans are lucky enough to get. Perhaps this accounts for my love of Wordsworth and of Wordsworth's lakes, woods and mountains, even though I am sometimes asked how these, and London, are supposed to link. Is it really so odd that intense love of one place spills over in empathy, to meet the love of other people's places; above all, to link with them in shared awareness of 'the eternal in time' (my immediate subject, after all?). My fellow Londoners include Blake, Keats and Dickens – artists and prophets, who shape the world for us all. London drew Henry James – a connoisseur of the beauty of great European cities, who still found, in London's endless variety, a spiritual home. London drew T.S. Eliot, to find images for horror in early days; but to find a place to live as he grew towards *Four Quartets*.

London offers riches enough for anyone, including visual artists (if Constable was rural, Turner was 'ours'). It is the place where I experienced my first numinous moments, that sealed me as 'religious' beyond subsequent doubt. They came vividly on one misty evening in Chelsea, with a fiery sunset arching the Thames. I recall also two separate winter days, in the dereliction of the wartime Isle of Dogs, amid ruined wharves and still cranes. Those strange moments! – taken out of oneself, and amazingly heightened; caught in the scene and in God, beyond expectation or parallel; affirmed in a way that transforms but completes.

Anyone who imagines that the numinous is reserved for rural places of acknowledged beauty, has failed to understand the Spirit of God. He blows when and where He will, for His own reasons. You find Him, if He wants, where you are, at the time He chooses. There is no quest, no seeking, no sequel; it is all out of time. The numinous is indeed the strangest of intimations, since neither its meaning nor its import are clear. I return to a sense that it is akin to the holy, yet distinct in essence. The holy belongs with people or places; it has been earned in one lifetime of prayer, or perhaps in many. It implies some kind of commitment, or some immediate prompting to choice. For me, the numinous is profoundly religious, but divorced from all context. It seems that God suspends space/time and its laws for a moment, leaving one free.

Much of London is scarred and disgraced by ugliness; but so are all cities and countries, and very large part of our lives. Anyone who cannot find the more normal signs of God in London, will be unlikely to find them anywhere on earth.

We start from our native heath, and belong there. Not all the changes that science has caused can alter this. We each have equal access to Plato's verities, and to Christ's Kingdom, which are as democratic as our encounter with the 'meanest flower that blows'; or with some chance person in desperate need. We experience the holy sometimes, the good and the beautiful daily; or we do, if we train our senses, and purge our souls. The numinous may choose to visit us a few times in a lifetime; and if so, it is at one with Wordsworth's 'spots of time', and Eliot's 'Still point of the turning world'.

We are right to find evils in the native heath and to fight them. How else shall we find, and fight, the worse evils in ourselves? As I write, London's homeless proliferate, London's transport and health systems fight for survival; London's social life is threatened by political misrule. Our battle for the Kingdom is on the doorstep: as Dickens found in the last century; and Blake in the century before:

> I wander through each charter'd street,
> Near where the chartered Thames does flow.
> And mark in every face I meet
> Marks of weakness, marks of woe.

In every cry of every man
In every Infant's cry of fear,
In every voice: in every ban,
The man-forged manacles I hear

How the Chimney-sweeper's cry
Every blackened Church appals.
And the hapless Soldier's sigh,
Runs in blood down palace walls.

But most through midnight streets I hear
How the youthful Harlot's curse
Blasts the new-born Infant's tear
And blights with plagues the Marriage-hearse.

(William Blake, 'London')

XIII

This chapter has had to concern itself with pragmatic problems, since all vision, including our own, is beset with these. I want to turn again to the practical aspects of God's presence on earth, as a challenge to action; and then to conclude by returning to the spiritual call of high ground.

I picked 1945 as a focus for certain evils, chiefly those connected with nuclear power. In other aspects, it was the year which saw the victory of Winston Churchill's Britain and its allies over Hitler's exceptional wickedness; and the realization under the new Attlee Government of the Welfare State. This great achievement had been striven for, by outstanding men and women, for well over a century, and was a rare instance of unambiguous political good. The 1940s had the two great British Prime Ministers of my lifetime, and was the century's Heroic Decade: 'Our finest hour', as Churchill ringingly told us; then, our greatest liberal hour, following the war. So: profit and loss together, the habitual multivalence; raised to a high point, by exceptional events.

In 1945, the Bombs did fall in August on Hiroshima and Nagasaki; bringing in a new age for man. As a boy of sixteen, my own feeling was exultation. At last, the war was at an end; the troops would return; London was safe. I record this as simple fact, not needing much comment. Perhaps some other sixteen-year-olds saw further than I did, in the first day, and week, after the news came through. By the late 1940s, the extent of the change, and the terror, had registered. I stayed on the edges of CND for a time, sharing its worries; unable to see much hope, in its attempted campaign.

All babies have tantrums, when they beat their parents; when, frustrated in the moment, they would destroy the whole world if they could. The Dyson family had a strong streak of anger in its make-up, which I had to learn to control myself, as I said elsewhere. In my schooldays, I discovered that I could not be rid of the trait, which is deeply genetic; and saw that its diversion into constructive social action was the best course for myself. Anger still wells up at times, and has sometimes exploded; with bad effects for everyone, myself not least.

I suspect that most humans are tempted to anger in bleak times; it then becomes the deadliest of all deadly sins, unless contained. In many it is weak, and a sign of weakness (there is always a touch of this). Some few men and women have overcome anger by a generalised battle for justice; or by allowing God to transform it, through growing love of creation, to creative prayer. The forgiveness of trespass is a prelude to healing; but this difficult exercise reveals the nature of anger, as a sin very few of us wholly escape.

Until 1945, extreme anger was an occasional component, in some form, in all humans; but no 'objective correlative' could be found. There was damage enough, in family feuds, in murders, in human warfare. But the full range of anger had no means of being fulfilled.

In 1945, the objective correlative entered history. It is now a fact of history, for all future times. Can human reason stand and pass such a test, or will it falter? Can politicians contain it, as they did in the Cold War, by 'Mutally Assured Destruction'; or will groups of terrorists now find a way of getting into the act? Would Hitler have 'taken the world with him', in the last bunker; or would even he have paused, at such a step? Such questions no longer belong (if they ever did) to debate, and PhD theses. They are the stuff and challenge of everyday life.

Part of my contention is that the 'Reason' which comes from The Enlightenment could not have coped with the nuclear challenge; even though Hobbes (an odd man out?) saw a profound need to contain human unreason by deterrent power. Only Wisdom can do the trick; God's Kingdom: and this must be wooed, in part, by massive social change. There is no guarantee of success, at the 'end of human history'. A book like *Apocalypse* does not inspire temporal hope.

We have now filled the world with supposedly 'safe' nuclear power stations, such as the Windscale (aka Sellafield) complex in Cumbria, which is hoping to open Thorp, as I write. We must accept that though such choices are ours – and humans have lived with this power now for half a century – the actual nuclear knowledge can never be unlearned. This is the truth that Science accepted, with childlike optimism, at the Enlightenment, assuming that man's reason would naturally be at the service of the good of man. No amount of 'Ban the Bomb' rhetoric can undo the mathematical equations; or the fact that the British–American alliance chose to use the Bomb in 1945 not once, but twice. Nuclear destruction is an aspect of God's space/time complex that humans now have access to. Is it one potential contained in the fruit of the Tree of the Knowledge of Good and Evil that, in the *Genesis* myth, God denied to men?

1945 was about the time, also, when farming turned from the ancient art of cultivating fruit and vegetation, and certain animals intended for feeding humans, towards treating animals as machines, and the Earth as a theatre for unlimited human greed. Earth, Water and Air have all, in the past fifty years, been poisoned; and the process continues, at escalating rates. The damage already done is past reversal; as is the harmful radiation released by mankind. The time has come when the rescue of Earth's ecology must break through all the linguistic shifts used to discredit it ('cranks', 'luddites', 'living in the past', 'state enemies' if the going gets tough). Earth, Air, Water, all deeply violated, need a radical cleansing; along with Fire, in its new role as human nuclear power.

I do not offer 1945 as a scapegoat; just as a focus; and as the year when 6 August, just after 8.00 a.m. Japanese time, stands out. The ambitions of technology were given a charter in Bacon's *Advancement of Learning* (1605) and similar writings. The actual coming of machines started slowly, but now speeds up. Cold War; genetic engineering; TV and Cable Information Technology; virtual reality; the destruction of rainforests and many species of animal; holes in the ozone layer – such things and more; big changes since 1945, in my own 'scrap of history' (to borrow Philip Larkin's fine phrase). I did not do it; nor most likely, did you. But it is our world; our share in man's heritage. Here is the record of human stewardship in the twentieth century, which we have now to offer to God, with the Lord's prayer daily, along with our praise. Here, too, is our agenda for the coming century and millennium (for 'our children and grandchildren', if 'family values' is the phrase, or reality, that means most to you).

During our period, the Church has agonised about sex, as usual. It agonises now about women priests. Perhaps all this is as Christ would have wished it; many clearly think so; I belong with readers who cannot see things this way. The Church must of course make errors like everyone else, it is not infallible. If its preoccupation with issues such as women priests, rigid dogmas concerning personal relationships, the right of homosexuals to love and happiness should they find it, is its current chief agenda, so be it. Either way, the other issues I have listed seem more urgent; if we are indeed thinking now of 'the Church Militant here on Earth'. Our life on Earth, where the Church belongs, must be seriously intended by God, as a test. One major petition of the Lord's prayer concerns this directly, and should come high in the church's duties: 'Thy will be done in Earth, as it is in Heaven'.

Many individual Christians in the churches witness, in prayer and life, to God's Kingdom. I bear in mind that it may be easier to live close to Christ in the church than it is outside it; and that it may be wrong to judge the church by standards one falls far short of oneself. Just now, I am outside the church, so perhaps I can say this; in the hope that others, deterred from Christ's Kingdom entirely by the church's seeming irrelevance, or by its personal hostility to them, might rethink their own commitment to Christ; and to the Earth; and perhaps, then, again to the church.

In practise, Christians as individuals seem increasingly prepared to work alongside many traditions, for causes which for them have a higher priority, than they currently enjoy in their church. In putting it this way, I hope to avoid *hubris*; and to leave open the personal quest; which is still the thing causing me to write this book at all.

The ultimate challenge of 'eternal life' is the same for all of us. We remain mortal in any period; we remain partly astray. Just now, Christians and non-Christians join, in Earth's current crisis; and perhaps Greek wisdom, as we find it explored in the great Greek Dramatists, offers the balance of values most needed, in so unstable a culture as ours, for Earth itself. The pagans revered the Earth, and saw it as holy. In this, they have clear wisdom to give. No dualistic vision can hope to equal them. If I am right, the church has been influenced by dualism through most of its history, in a way that its Founder was very certainly not.

I find that specific problems are best tackled just now by charities. Some are concerned with one major issue and channel resources directly, to donors' wishes. Most are constrained, by their status, from campaigning with the cutting political edge they would like. The charities get little money from the church (which indeed competes with them); they get none at all from the taxes we all pay to the state. They do attract growing numbers of determined idealists; and they do, in their sphere, solve problems more complex in detail, now, than in earlier times.

Homelessness is widespread in cities, and has spread to many rural areas. Its causes are many; and giving money when asked by chance strangers is more problematic, today, than it used to be. We face new health dangers, HIV among them, which require urgent attention from organisations united, and sharing resources, in a manner that our political and church leaders still find elusive. We need a pooling of food, money, time, and human energy, directed towards society's needs as they currently are. Perhaps Christians should look again at that twice-repeated miracle of the bread and fishes. But then, this miracle is one symbol at the heart of the Mass/Eucharist/Lord's Supper; which is still of key importance to nearly every professing branch of the Christian church.

Prejudice is always with us, like poverty; and it gets worse, not better, as this century moves to its end. Lady Thatcher wanted to destroy 'socialism' for ever; and she took hefty swipes at 'liberalism' with a small 'L'. For George Bush, Liberalism was 'The L Word' as he fought to be the US President, successfully; and Bush's memory stretched back to the post-war, McCarthy years. Now, the ascendancy of 'Market Forces' continues, under Major and Clinton: even though verbal sops are sparingly fed to ecologists, as their influence among the all-important 'electorate' spreads. 'Market Forces' are applied now to health, to education, to the arts, to all aspects of infrastructure, to the public utilities. The ambition of British and US politicians is to see these criteria spread, also, through the former communist world.

A few Christians make a stand, from all parts and ranks of the churches. They are not, for the most part, paid-up Socialists, or Liberals. They are unlikely to be Communists of the Soviet kind. They are merely Christians who pray for God's Kingdom to come, and see this as a prayer leading to action. Men like Bishop David Jenkins of Durham, Bishop Trevor Huddlestone, Archbishop Desmond Tutu still function, along with numerous priests and laymen in their mould. They survive much scolding, and the inevitable accusations of crankiness (accusations which may yield to 'saintliness' if they become too popular; or are safely dead). But they are too few in number to 'be' the church; and younger successors are less in evidence (though, to be fair, it takes time for the media to note them, and, in our period, to make them, in this way, 'real'). The church as a body stays with 'Family Values', 'Victorian Values', 'Christian Values', – the three seeming to merge now, to mean 'hard work', 'market economics', 'sex chaste or discreet'; 'no crankiness, please'.

The Kingdom of God remains in good working order. Its rules have never changed, and never can. It is under Christ's management as usual, with the same prayers and Gospels that he inspired. It still criss-crosses with many members of professing churches, in an age-old (necessary?) dance, with 'the world'.

Let me return, therefore, to the charities, where the Kingdom can be seen directly at work. Charities for the homeless; for the blind; for the ill; for the imprisoned; for the victims of prejudice, or of torture or slavery; for men, women and children with problems; for animals, trees, and all aspects of the life of the Earth. We have to take care that we deal with large, accountable charities; and that we bear in mind certain campaigning bodies which are not allowed charitable status since they are 'too polemical', even though they work inside the law of the land (Greenpeace springs, most notably, to mind).

It is good to know that these charities attract the young in growing numbers; and channel money and energy directly to causes whose purpose is known. Increasingly, the National Trust, the Woodland Trust, the Countryside Commission, assume responsibilities for conserving the land we live in. They belong inside 'the Establishment' on normal assessment, but are still denied resources that they need and deserve. There is growing recognition that humans, and creatures, belong to one eco-system; and sink or swim together, in the end. If I am right, this is the major truth neglected through Christian history; and actually perverted, at the Enlightenment, to baleful effect. Blake's amazing insight 'Everything that lives is holy' has a human origin; but it reaches to the heart of the kingdom of God. We must pray and work for such wisdom, in the coming millennium. Only so, can the damage done to Earth be alleviated, and God's will be done once more in Earth, as it is in Heaven.

I feel bound to mention that even the Arts depend increasingly on private charities, to supplement the funding they can get from 'the market', and by grant from the state. When an elected government is obsessed, as ours now is, with 'saving money', men's creative achievements can be represented as 'minority tastes', 'fads', 'subversion', in any slick speech. For practical purposes, it is best to rechristen the Arts as 'part of the Tourist Industry', if larger government grants are to be humbly sought. But, when we turn to the church, and to the universities, and even to media 'critics', it would be good to hear terms like 'cultural glory', 'spiritual lifeblood' more freely in use.

What other signs of hope have we? More than a few. There are small seeds sown, from which great harvests come. Spiritual undercurrents gather in power, and break surface: some, 'in' the church (house-church movements; parish initiatives in healing, or homelessness; the problematic 'charismatics'); some, 'outside' the church but 'inside' religion, through the commitment of spiritual folk.

The word Wisdom, which I have used in this book as a *motif,* is no longer as challenging as it seemed, a decade ago. In saying this, I realise that Eastern mystics, the Eastern Orthodox Christian churches, and Western mystics have always used it. What I have in mind is the word's recent history among teachers, dons and journalists; and in the media and the normal discourse of the West. For most, the word might just as well have been obsolete; and this, despite evident fruit of Wisdom in the music and literature of the past hundred years.

Wisdom has been returning also, half underground, from new sources; through which the main current of our culture will be seen to have flowed. As in the eighteenth century, the 'establishment' ethos has been opposed strongly, by a sub-culture still in touch with perennial truths. A wholesome undogmatic spirituality belongs with the 'green' movement, which crosses all political landmarks, in its commitment to Earth. The green movement is a broad church indeed, including all comers; its future must be with the young, and with their will to make it prevail.

We must add that modern psychotherapists have opened new routes to ancient, partly mislaid wisdom; including religious wisdom – whatever apparent claims to novelty some may make. There was Jung himself, at the centre of the century; an author who links timeless insights with insights still coming to birth. Psychotherapists and counsellors have a 'feel' for human wholeness, which makes its impact in numerous ways. Some well-known agony aunts reach a very large public; then, there are self-help groups, for many with special needs. Whether people are plagued with drug problems, family breakdown, the pain of bereavement, they will often turn now to groups akin to themselves. The Samaritans are at hand, for those tempted to suicide. Members of sexual, or racial, or other 'unpopular' minorities, find trained counsellors outside the ranks of the church. Unhappily, the church still moves, too often, in its old tramlines, and is the kiss of death to those whose needs do not readily fit.

Explorers of the paranormal are growing in number, and bring open minds to bear in difficult ground. Hitherto hidden or neglected traditions of remote, 'primitive' peoples, are looked at seriously; alongside phenomena that are, distinctively, new. Recent medical advances have brought to light 'near-death' experiences, from people who have been recalled to life through revised modern perceptions of clinical death. There are also serious experiments in telepathy and extra-sensory perception; and in the coincidences which Jung called 'synchronicity', and tried to define.[9]

Along with these trends, I would mention small, independent initiatives, indicative of an important, cultural shift. I have in mind the late Sir Alister Hardy's 'Research Institute for the Paranormal', which collects data on all kinds of religious and numinous experience for students to use. These data resist scientific methods, like all God's dealings; but they reveal that personal spiritual vision is no eccentric, or marginal, aspect of life. Sir Alister was famed in his lifetime as a marine biologist; and his religious commitment grew from his personal life. His Institute is housed now in Westminster College, Oxford, where a mood of neutral scholarly interest appears to prevail. Then, I am impressed by Kathleen's Raine's *Temenos*, which ran as a journal for thirteen issues, publishing work from spiritual leaders of many religions and creeds. *Temenos* is now an embryonic academy for the study of Wisdom; which Kathleen Raine regards as a body of 'knowledge' at or near the heart of spiritual truth. I would also mention *Resurgence*, a journal linking spiritual wholeness with the war against pollution, which has maintained a high standard of good prose, and good sense. It operates from Salem Cottage, Trelill, Bodmin, Cornwall PL30 3HZ (subscriptions), and from Ford House, Hartland, Bideford, Devon EX39 6EE (the editorial and advertising address). It has growing links with the USA, Japan and other world centres, and now, with the somewhat similar Schumacher College (details from The Old Postern, Dartington, Totnes, Devon TQ9 6AE). This college is housed in Dartington Hall, Devon, and runs courses where religion and ecology are normally fused.

I mention these three movements because they impress me; and because readers of a book such as this may know them already, or wish to know they exist. There are welcome signs of interest from recent series of programmes on both BBC 2 and Channel 4; along with the longstanding BBC commitment to Wildlife, linked with the Royal Society for Nature Conservation and the Wildlife Trusts (Patron, The Prince of Wales; address, The Wildlife Trusts, The Green, Witham Park, Waterside South, Lincoln LN2 5JR). It is my hope that these will co-operate with larger bodies, like the National Trust, and WWF, to produce some joint programme for all primary and secondary schools. Already, conservation is part of education. But, in these days of the national curriculum, and of heavy statutary commitments, a niche for the environment should be found in every school in the land.

The smaller environmental bodies have their own identity, and their own *raison d'être*; and independence is important in their life. But some minimal co-ordination of their data, and methodology, would be a ready-made resource of much wider use.

During our century, there was a gallant but doomed attempt to reunite the older churches, by finding common truth acceptable to them all. The 'Ecumenical Movement' made at first some progress, with 'The World Council of Churches' its most visible fruit. The hope was to reassemble scattered Christian sects and resources and places of worship, and to reach out to other religions later, if this could be done.

Some few successes occurred, in the early days, but a blind alley seems its destined end (the intention was good). If anything, the Roman sect under John Paul II and the numerous protestant sects, have grown further apart, not nearer, in recent years. None of these corresponds to Jesus's first twelve (then seventy) followers, who were asked to 'bear witness', to be in 'fellowship', and to do Jesus's deeds. The small churches set up by St Paul may be the best early example of viable organised bodies – but even these caused grave anxieties, as Paul's Letters show. The Galatians were lured back too close to 'legalism'; while the Corinthians interpreted 'liberty' too freely, in Paul's strong view. Our best hope these days could be the Russian Orthodox Liturgy (for fine public worship); and then individual Christians doing God's will together, in the world at large.

If we attempt to branch out to other world religions, all past records of their interactions bring little hope. The Western religions (Judaism, Christianity and Islam) keep their distance, despite Abraham as a common ancestor, far in the past. The Eastern religions proceed from different sources; and are hard for Western minds to grasp, as even Jung knew. Once again, initiatives of the sort I have mentioned, seeking converging 'Wisdom', offer more hope to the world at large than any grand attempted 'reunions' would appear to do.

One further source of hope is in creative artists – if we except the 'brutalist' architects, as a group; and a few individuals who wage war on Beauty elsewhere, in the name of art. Literature and music have flourished, no doubt through the resurgence of Greek strands in our culture; and through the disturbing, multivalence of modern life. 'Exciting times' are good times for artists; who have largely ignored all pressures from academics to lower their sights.

This chapter has been concerned with 'intimations of the eternal in time'; but has been forced, for the most part, to stay on more mundane ground. Perhaps I can finish this section, and this final diversion, with a self-quotation, that might help us to see the peaks again, from however far off:

> The essential aspect is that all revelation is enigmatic; there is no simple union of the timeless with time. We live in a universe which bombards us with impressions, the most powerful and compelling of which are beauty, goodness and truth. These intimations reach us in a darkened form, in union with transience and suffering, and we move as strangers and pilgrims through their path. Always the spiritual qualities co-exist with mutability and enigma – not only in the world of nature, and of human creation, but in the supreme revelation of The Word. For a Christian, this is the quintessence of Incarnation, that God is really, if mysteriously, revealed in mortal flesh. The world of nature falls in place as lesser revelation; the world of art as the distinctive contribution of man. (A.E. Dyson, *Between Two Worlds: Aspects of Literary Form*, Macmillan, 1972)

XIV

The above quotation from a 1972 book reminds me that I have always been a Christian Platonist of sorts, with additions and subtractions; and that the nature of these changes has varied with time. Christ has been central to my life since I was seventeen, despite far too much straying; but my relations with the church have been fragile at best. I know I have 'grieved the Spirit', I hope not finally; but signals on this vital issue are mixed. In all life's great things, there is multivalence; not least, in our crucial relation to The Kingdom itself.

So I return to the Fifth Dimension; human consciousness; set here on Earth to sink or swim, amid mystery and flux.

Our consciousness is shared between the space/time continuum, where we exist in clock-time; and the 'still point of the turning world', the 'now' where we 'are'. Our eternal life accompanies us through this earthly exile; and the particular 'scrap of history' we are destined to live through matters little, compared with our purpose, and quest.

I have called consciousness the 'Fifth Dimension' in its aspect of clock-time, since it is the place where the other four dimensions of space/time become real.[10]

Without an attending and experiencing consciousness, space/time might have some reality; but, since no one would be aware of it, would 'existence' be the *mot-juste* for this? As we know, Berkeley postulated God's consciousness as the full, perfect home for 'reality'.

We humans register as much as our senses, and our attention to our senses, permits. Hume removed God, and landed himself with a 'flux of perceptions' amid which is a consciousness unsure of its status *vis à vis* externality; and not truly able to call itself 'I'.

To this degree, our 'place' in space/time is as Fifth Dimension; but our consciousness has a still greater, and transcendent home, in 'now'. Here, it faces Janus-wise, Eternal Reality, of which the 'now' we inhabit is the chief (the only?) experience we certainly have. We always live 'now', wherever we have currently got to; in all periods when we are conscious, between birth and death.

In this 'now' that we 'are', we experience; we also make choices. These choices are worked out in clock-time; and it is there that we become, for good or ill, the people we are.

As I have insisted, the law of clock-time is inexorably mortal;

the Second Law of Thermodynamics holds sway. But we may and indeed must move spiritually 'from glory to glory', if we are to align our 'now' with the Kingdom of God. We in fact know our 'now' as an outpost of Heaven; or, in its frequent alienations and wanderings, as a staging post in, or near, Hell. In counterpoint with the movement of mortality, which is irreversible and fated, we need spiritual movement towards the gifts 'not as the world gives', that Jesus left. *A fortiori*, we need the fullness which Christ himself lived as a human, and called The Kingdom. The Kingdom stirs in our hearts, despite all our rebellions. It endures, despite the tug of all our distractions related to time.

The great problem is, that we might spiritually deteriorate – without being aware of it; without understanding where we are bound. We might move towards a consciousness accurately described as 'hellish', despite its great illusion of vigour (the 'Dionysiac spell', to place this with the Greeks).

Here on Earth is the battle between Good and Evil that we were born for; the place where the Lord's prayer, and God's help as He gives it, are a daily need. We cannot doubt that the pagans had their own means of grace, along with all other religions; and that the God Who 'is not mocked' does not, in this most vital of matters, mock humankind. We experience much, in this life, as confusion and paradox. But the 'feel' of our inner life, as we learn to discern it, can be known to be moving towards, or away from, God.

Our life is an endeavour to keep the mortal and the eternal moving in tandem; above all, to link these twin aspects of being with God, and the Kingdom of God. We 'belong' to the Kingdom, as Christ told us, and specifically promised. Our sense of exile, itself, is our clearest spiritual guide. If we trust the guide, we shall be in quest of a city: despite every setback; despite all fallings away. If we trust the guide, we shall be open to truth, to judgement: and so, open to 'salvation', healing: unless we choose to reject what we love.

If we lose sight of the quest, and settle to live with the 'this worldly', our vision fades; our most basic sense of The Kingdom may be lost. 'Lost'? – lost, or lost sight of perhaps, for huge periods. 'Forty years long' the Jews wandered astray in the wilderness; not once in that time did God give them a healing sign. Yet Jesus's news is of God still there; still patient and waiting: still seeking and finding – lost coin; lost sheep; lost son.

The holy, the numinous, the visionary are peaks of experience in our own, personal lives. We do well to love and remember them;

to follow the light that they give. We do well to witness to them, as our greatest experiences; especially, if this may attract derision, as in times like our own. They are our touch with reality, even when we know them only in memory; they are there to refresh us, when we come to less happy days.

In this chapter, I have been attempting to make a great, simple assertion; but the complexities of our double status, as men, have had to be faced. The assertion *is* simple, to the degree that religious intimations are simple: remembrance of the lost home we love and seek.

Much that is good and beautiful occurs in clock-time, and is known there; but the great intimations belong with the Eternal direct. This I assert, as inner Wisdom, which cannot be 'proved' by any laws that reason knows. It is Wisdom which rejects linguistic vandals, solipsists, and all rigid schemes of dogma – not as evidently false on their own premises, but as too small; too mean; too shabby; and yes, too absurd.

It is undeniable that the supersensuous rides on the back of the senses; that all intimations have a foot in the world, which the world can 'explain'. To see beyond sensuous to Eternal, to *distinguish,* is called 'Faith' by some people. The word I am using is Wisdom. I find it less ambiguous; more truly universal. Wisdom is humble and grand beyond measure, as all wise people know.

I have returned, with relief, to grand simplicities: using 'simple' as Aquinas did, when he applied it to God. The best part of this book exists in quotations; and these too are simple, in a similar way. Anyone presuming as I do, to speak of the things he aspires to, needs Blake, Wordsworth, Eliot, the scriptures, the mystics, to rise to the theme. I can and must witness, as you must also. But we need 'a great cloud of witnesses' about us, to atone for ourselves, and for our dreadful failures in life.

'It is appointed unto all men once to die, and after that the judgement'. This comes from *Hebrews*. For the gloss, I choose my final dip into T.S. Eliot's greatest poem – at a point where every word, and not least here the parenthesis, is in spirit Krishna's; or so Eliot tells us, further on:

> Fare forward, you who think you are voyaging;
> You are not those who saw the harbour
> Receding, or those who will disembark.
> Here between the hither and the farther shore

While time is withdrawn, consider the future
And the past with an equal mind.
At the moment which is not of action or inaction
You can receive this: 'on whatever sphere of being
The mind of man may be intent
At the time of death' — that is the one action
(And the time of death is every moment)
Which shall fructify in the lives of others:
And do not think of the fruit of action.
Fare forward.

(T.S. Eliot, 'The Dry Salvages')

In the end; and the end is 'Now and Always'; there is a great, final gulf. 'Well done, thou good and faithful servant': or, 'Depart from me; I never knew you'. The world would confuse this endlessly, with its codes and fashions. As well for us, that the judgement is set not in words; but in one whole, human life.

Jesus preached the Kingdom and he lived it. It was his fate to be regarded by the world as disreputable and politically dangerous. He was called a blasphemer, a friend of publicans and sinners, a traitor to Rome. He was put to an agonising death as a criminal, betrayed and deserted, at the age of (around) thirty-three. In this image of betrayal, early death, apparent total failure, we find his closest possible union with the Father God.

I will conclude with quotations from two contrasting writers, both exploring the complex gulf, and the simple truth. First, Wordsworth again, explaining his experience of God's presence and absence; and the role that his art played, as a form of prayer:

Oh! mystery of Man, from what a depth
Proceed thy honours! I am lost, but see
In simple childhood something of the base
On which thy greatness stands, but this I feel,
That from thyself it is that thou must give,
Else never can receive. The days gone by
Come back upon me from the dawn almost
Of life: the hiding-places of my power
Seem open; I approach, and then they close;
I see by glimpses now; when age comes on
May scarcely see at all, and I would give,

While yet we may, as far as words can give,
A substance and a life to what I feel:
I would enshrine the spirit of the past
For future restoration.

(Wordsworth, *The Prelude,* 1805 version,
XI: 329–43)

And now, a hymn by a man whose rhetoric I mistrust and whose dogma I reject; but whose right to speak, of our quest, cannot be missed. The poetry, though austere, charts his own long exploring; and speaks in its conclusion, of bereavement, with very sweet, simple power:

Lead kindly light, amid the encircling gloom,
  Lead thou me on;
The night is dark, and I am far from home,
  Lead thou me on.
Keep thou my feet; I do not ask to see
The distant scene; one step enough for me.

I was not ever thus, nor prayed that thou
  Shouldst lead me on;
I loved to choose and see my path, but now
  Lead thou me on.
I loved the garish day, and spite of fears,
Pride ruled my will: remember not past years.

So long thy power hath blessed me, sure it still
  Will lead me on
O'er moor and fen, o'er crag and torrent, till
  The night is gone.
And with the morn those Angel-faces smile,
Which we have loved long since, and lost awhile.

(J.H. Newman)

Epilogue

I had intended to summarise an agenda for the next century, but find I should merely be underlining points already made in Chapters 8 and 9. Let me then wish the reader godspeed, in 'prayer without ceasing'; and in recovering the words, and reality, which are the birthright of man.

Earth is not our final home, but it is our lodgings; furnished handsomely with God's own presence, despite change and decay. A rebirth of Wisdom is needed, for spiritual renewal; and for the task of saving our Planet, if this is possible, from the incremental harm of the past two centuries.

It was Mikhail Gorbachev who recently said, the world needs a new economics, neither communist nor capitalist, but in essence, 'green'. An unholy alliance of usury, technology and greed have brought us to the edge of the abyss. The next century (and millennium) must see either a new flowering of Wisdom; or the rapid end of man's brief Lordship of Earth.

Let me finish with two poems I have been saving, since between them, they span nearly all I have wanted to say. The first, with the deceptive simplicity of very rare genius, is a vision of what life on this Earth should be:

My mother bore me in the southern wild,
And I am black, but O! my soul is white;
White as an angel is the English child
But I am black, as if bereav'd of light.

My mother taught me underneath a tree,
And sitting down before the heat of day
She took me on her lap, and kissed me,
And pointing to the east, began to say:

'Look on the rising sun! there God does live,
And gives His light, and gives His heat away;
And flowers and trees and beasts and men receive
Comfort in morning, joy in the noonday.

'And we are put on earth a little space,
That we may learn to bear the beams of love;
And these black bodies and this sun-burnt face
Is but a cloud, and like a shady grove;

'For when our souls have learn'd the heat to bear,
The cloud will vanish: we shall hear His voice,
Saying: 'Come out from the grove, My love and care,
And round My garden tent like lambs rejoice.'

Thus did my mother say, and kissed me.
And thus I say to little English boy:
When I from black and he from white cloud free
And round the tent of God like lambs we joy,

I'll shade him from the heat, till he can bear
To lean in joy upon our Father's knee;
And then I'll stand and stroke his silver hair,
And be like him, and he will then love me.

(William Blake, 'The Little Black Boy')

The other poem is from a poet who has helped to mould me, and who now speaks for me, as never before. I can no more co-opt him to my side than I can the other writers most quoted. As ever, the words must echo in each reader's mind, and do their own work:

Happy those early days! when I
Shin'd in my angel-infancy.
Before I understood this place
Appointed for my second race,
Or taught my soul to fancy aught
But a white, celestial thought,
When yet I had not walked above
A mile, or two, from my first love.
And looking back (at that short space)
Could see a glimpse of his bright-face;
When on some gilded cloud, or flower
My gazing thought would dwell an hour,
And in those weaker glories spy
Some shadow of eternity;
Before I taught my tongue to wound
My conscience with a sinful sound,
Or had the black art to dispense
A several sin to every sense,
But felt through all my fleshly dress
Bright shoots of everlastingness.
O how I long to travel back
And tread again that ancient track!
That I might once more reach that plain,
Where first I left my glorious traine,
And whence th'inlightened spirit sees
That shady City of Palm Trees;
But (ah!) my soul with too long stay
Is drunk, and staggers in the way.
Some men a forward motion love,
But I by backward steps would move,
And when this dust falls to the urn
In that state I came return.

(Henry Vaughan, 'The Retreate')

Notes

1. WHERE AM I? MAN'S PLACE IN THE UNIVERSE

1. As I write this I spot a piece by Tim Radford in the *Guardian* 15 February 1993. 'Big Bang cosmology – the belief, supported by a series of recent findings that the universe was born in a single instance some 15 billion years ago – has placed God back on the scientific agenda', Professor Ian Barbour has said. The professor – a former scientist turned theologian – argues that 'Among the many possible universes consistent with Einstein's equations ours is one of the few in which the arbitrary perameters are right for the existence of anything resembling organic life'. The gist of the argument turns on two postulates. One, is the expansion rate of the universe. If it had been 'smaller by a fraction of a million millionth, the universe would have collapsed. If it had been a millionth greater, it would have expanded too rapidly for stars and planets to form.' And second, the forces holding atomic nuclei together. If these had been weaker the universe would be composed only of hydrogen. If any stronger, 'all the carbon in the universe would have converted to oxygen'. He agrees that amazing coincidence is not impossible, but feels that an hypothesis from 'cosmic design' is more likely 'by far'. He then argues that 'Humans might seem insignificant in the immensity of time and space – but the greatest complexity in the universe . . . lay in the 100 million million synapses of the human brain'. The number of ways of connecting these 'was greater than the number of atoms in the universe'. There is a higher level of organisation and richness in a human being than in a thousand lifeless galaxies. It is human beings, after all, 'that reach out to understand that cosmic immensity'.

   Tim Radford also reports that Professor Joel Primack of the University of California, Santa Cruz, 'detected mystic dimensions to some of the ideas implicit in Big Bang cosmology'. After expanding on this, he concluded 'This is science, but it is the kind of stuff religious mystics dreamed about'.

   I quote this simply because it is today's relevant 'piece', as I write; one is bombarded by books, these days, in this borderline realm. For my part, I am content to leave science to the scientists, and regard it all as irrelevant – irrelevant to my 'real questions', that is. But it is reassuring to know that the realm of science is no longer only dogmatic, and no longer closed. Professor Ian Barbour's view of the human brain also chimes in with what I call 'the fifth dimension' – at least, in asserting its internal complexity, and its place where the space/time continuum becomes real.
2. A.E. Dyson, *Yeats, Eliot and R.S. Thomas: Riding The Echo* (Macmillan, 1981).

3. THE FIFTH DIMENSION

1. R.S. Thomas's 'The Kingdom', which is quoted and commented upon as the conclusion to Chapter 8, below (pp. 272–5).

4. THE LINGUISTIC VANDALS

1. A.E. Dyson, *Between Two Worlds: Aspects of Literary Form* (Macmillan, 1972).

5. INSUBSTANTIAL PAGEANT

1. Graham Hough once expressed doubts to me about the breakdown of the 'argument from design' in our Western culture, and wondered whether its virtual disappearance, these days, is fully justified by Hume's arguments, or by anything else. Hough did not believe (if I understand him) in human 'immortality', but he did feel that design, in the cosmos, at least balances the elements of chaos and chance. I note that modern scientists are once more admitting religion to some highly provisional place in their thinking. A journalist complained, recently, that one can hardly read a 'popular exposition' of science these days – as made by scientists – without 'bumping into God'. Hawking would have to be an exception, to prove the rule?

7. THE WISDOM OF THE GREEKS

1. As I prepare this for publication (November 1995), I recognise the recent opening of a great Hindu Temple in Neasden as one of the few inspiring news items of the year.
2. It may be worth noting that the theme 'an eye for an eye, a tooth for a tooth' is extremely natural to men; and well fits with the modern universe 'from Big Bang to Black Holes'. Christ's amazing teaching of 'forgiveness of enemies', as a law of 'The Kingdom', takes us to responses deep in ourselves which conflict, however, with our instinctive responses as creatures of time. The law of revenge and later, to some degree, of 'justice', accords with clock-time, and with a universe where the Second Law of Thermodynamics will hold to the end. This matter becomes central, when I turn to consider the wisdom of Christ.
3. Through most of the play, the Eumenides openly scorn the Olympians, and refuse to accept the jurisdiction itself. In effect, the goddess of Wisdom is tested, in the city bearing her name. The outcome has resonances important for all subsequent history – not least, in a century as violent as our own. The Eumenides would, I imagine, have admired Hardy's Arabella (*Jude The Obscure*), and found a kindred spirit in Greene's Ida Arnold (*Brighton Rock*).
4. I use 'brutes', since the old view is still familiar, that man's 'intellectual'

self corresponds to the 'angels', his sensible self to the 'beasts' (or 'brutes'). It must be apparent in this book that I do not accept this dichotomy, or any forms of gnosticism or puritanism flowing from it. Moreover, most animals are more temperate, by instinct, in their sexual cycles than are most humans. Sexual promiscuity (as habit) is more properly seen as a sexual pattern peculiar to humans, than as an attribute of the 'brutes'.

I see no reason to believe that the rest of the creation is inferior to man in God's sight, and see no reason why it should be. Christ said that every sparrow comes under God's providence. Blake wrote: 'Everything that lives is holy'.

8. THE KINGDOM

1. Evangelical hymnals change 'my' to 'the' in the last line of this, intent to make Wesley refer to the 'one sacrifice' of the Cross. But Wesley wrote 'my', and this is the point of it. The hymn is better unused, then used in a badly maimed form.
2. I came across this, as a recent brief news item, somewhat apart from a fat section of diets 'to help those who eat too much' in the same newspaper.
3. For most of its history, the Church has identified 'raising the dead' with black magic ('Goety'), and looked upon it with horror. Despite texts such as *Matthew* 11: 5 (also *Luke* 7: 22), *Matthew* 10: 8, and allied material, 'raising the dead' has not (to my knowledge) been practised in any Christian church.
4. Numerous 'saints' have gone to extremes of 'self-discipline'; the rules and scruples, in religious orders, often err in this way. I have in mind also tormented individuals, like William Cowper, and G.M. Hopkins – whose differing religious traditions brought them near to despair.

   It is my own conviction that Jesus intended, for his followers, the gifts of the Spirit – joy, love, peace. These are 'not as the world gives', and will always be tested; but they surely remain within the root meanings of the words?
5. In the early church, 'circumcision' proved a magnet for contention, much as 'The Sabbath' had been for Jesus, in *his* break with the Law. It dramatised the revolution Jesus had brought to religion, and the fact that ancient Jewish customs would no longer always hold sway.

   Perhaps one can add that Jesus might have been surprised to find 'Sabbatarianism' still an issue for some, in the twentieth century – albeit, with 'The Sabbath' shifted to Sunday, to honour his own 'rising from the dead'. He might also have been shocked to find the unpleasant habit of circumcision still practised, and even current in bodies supposed to be 'his'.
6. It was Christians who finally made slavery disreputable, however belatedly. Paul's beautiful letter to a personal friend, Philemon, is a plea for a runaway slave, whom Paul adopted as a friend. 'For perhaps he therefore departed for a season, that you should receive him for ever; Not now as a servant, but above a servant, a brother beloved,

specially to me, but how much more to thee, both in the flesh, and in the Lord? If thou count me as a partner, receive him as myself' (*Philemon*: 15–17). And Paul's definitive text on the new freedom he had found 'in Christ' is an amazing programme for life here on earth, as well as hereafter: 'For as many of you as have been baptised into Christ have put on Christ/There is neither Jew nor Greek, there is neither bond nor free, there is neither male nor female: for ye are all one in Christ Jesus/And if ye be Christ's, then are ye Abraham's seed, and heirs according to the promise' (*Galatians* 3: 27–9).

The final clause is addressed especially to Jews, harking back to *Genesis* 17: 19. I suspect that most churchgoers (and perhaps most of us, myself included) have yet to come to terms with the vision of Paul. It is relevant to the debate about 'women priests' in the Anglican church; it is relevant to the Society for the Abolition of Slavery which still exists, and finds slavery widespread today.

It is an extremely useful reminder of the great love Paul was capable of, in addition to his occasional thunderous, and very human denunciations of things he disliked.

7. I find the account of Pilate's hand-washing, in other gospels, also moving. The impression was given, when I was younger, that this was cowardly, or even mocking. Yet it must have taken some courage. The age was extremely conversant with symbols and their importance (up to and including the Eucharist). Those who treat this as though it were a metaphorical action, and so a piece of hypocrisy, are most likely people who have never taken a serious risk themselves.

9. THE ETERNAL IN TIME

1. For my own thoughts on this, see the chapters on Gibbon and Lytton Strachey, in A.E. Dyson, *The Crazy Fabric* (Macmillan, 1965). A fuller discussion of Aldous Huxley's youthful scepticism, and later mysticism, will also be found here.
2. We can usefully remember that those who ascribed Shakespeare's drama to this shallow philosopher, did so because they thought Shakespeare too humble in his education and class to produce such serious work. History may not teach lessons, or recur in cycles; but certain patterns of folly exist, to be seen by all with the eyes to see.
3. It is tragically true that people who lack one, or more, of the senses, miss much of the 'supersensuous' united with them as well. Likewise, those who lack soundness of mind and soundness of their nervous system – or who lose it, through defects at birth, or through later accident, or illness, or the process of age. One gathers that the lack of 'a' sense (such as sight) can be 'compensated' by other senses; but it cannot be truly replaced. We must assume (I think) that God deals in His own way with the seriously afflicted: also, that there are likely to be realities within the *space/time continuum* which are permanently hidden from all of us, because the senses to apprehend them are not ours.
4. By and large, it was the parts of Christian morality concerned with

love and with standards of decency that passed into 'humanism', in Victorian times. The threat of hell-fire proved easier to shed. In the churches, these emphases had their parallel. Today, hell is less used as a threat than it once was. One must add that hell-fire evangelical fundamentalists remain strong in America, and in the murkier regions of the Church of England; and retain an appeal for their counterparts elsewhere. There are also signs of a growing yearning for *dogma,* and the supposed 'security' this offers, in a more and more complex and shifting cultural scene.

5. Swift's satire, favouring the 'ancients' through irony in *Tale of A Tub* and elsewhere, is exceptional; as are the powerful intuitions (rather than the expressed ideas) of Pope.
6. It is interesting that the canals, which cut across the country and had such a short life, soon became a treasured part of the landscape, and a haven of calm. The railways themselves now blend with landscape, and represent our best, immediate hope of rescue from the truly devastating roads and motorways we now have. Perhaps we shall be rescued next time by the failure of oil supplies; perhaps, first, the information superhighway will render most business journeys unnecessary, and begin to kill the roads off, by underuse. The next century will know, and face, its own problems. But, if saving Earth is the highest priority for sanity, health, and human survival, then it is to be hoped that the new millennium will recover, take to heart, and be healed by, the Wisdom on which a book, such as this, can merely touch.
7. We have to go back (in Britain and Europe) to the Middle Ages to equal it; and then (I speak of Europe) back to the great buildings of pagan antiquity, known now in ruins, and through archeological skill. The neo-classical period deserves a mention, but it left no works of comparable originality, beauty and *verve.* In Rome and other notable European cities, the story is different; but here in Britain, even Wren, Inigo Jones and Nash did not wholly add up to a golden age. Their classical imitation was too influenced by mathematics – not only as structural soundness, where mathematics belongs in building, but as an actual feature of the finished facades. Few things comparable to Michaelangelo, or to continental baroque, exist in England; though in the nineteenth century, we can confront all Europe with justified pride.

   I should add, of course, that I am speaking still of our major cities. The heritage left to us by chiefly neo-classical architects in great country houses and gardens is another matter, and gives to England, in particular, a unique, dispersed glory, not fully equalled elsewhere. The contribution of aristocratic patronage and idiosyncrasy makes a further, long story, for which this is not the place. I can add, however, that 'neo-classical' ran to many different forms in Britain – as if the high Victorian skill in mixing and pioneering styles, which does concern me, had deep roots in the English psyche, from much earlier times.
8. Walter De La Mare and A.E. Houseman both occupy territory unique

to themselves, yet universal in relevance. Possibly my lifelong love of them is partly personal, but I regard both as 'great' poets, who belong to 'all time'.

9. It will be noted that I am steering clear in this book, as I do in practise, of spiritualism, magic, the occult, in nearly all of their forms. I recognise that astrology has a major vogue, along with Tarot readings and divination. These are often charlatan; and when not so, many dangers lurk. I recognise that major moderns, including Yeats and Jung, have been magicians, using as well as exploring alchemy, and allied trends. It seems likely that spiritual realities are involved, alongside the psychic; but these are not paths that most men and women can wisely take. I want this book to be independent of the entire area; just as I want it to stand, if it does, apart from dogmatic faith.

   Very recently we have had scares about 'devil possession', and about supposed infant molestation 'recalled', in later life, in hypnotic trance. These episodes have caused great suffering to innocent people, and seem naturally to attract some trendy, as well as some unbalanced, minds. I notice that evangelical Anglicans may be attracted to this 'movement', no doubt linking it with literal fundamentalism of their own, mindless kind.

   For Jesus, and his age, many ills were 'devil possession'; today, we choose to search for psychic causes, that can be cured. In these matters, our modern approach is helpful; and its 'science' is creative, not merely discursive in the Enlightenment mode. The important thing is that evils exist and must be conquered. For wise men, prayer and the indwelling God are the truth, whatever 'language' they use. Jesus cast out 'devils', by his personal gift for healing; he then called people to invite God's Spirit into their lives. In essence, we may need medical help at times, but usually, good counsel suffices; then, regular prayer, and a return to life's normal quest. The central gospel, as Paul said, is 'sanctification': that slow movement, 'from glory to glory', as God's Spirit takes charge.

10. I know that certain scientists already speak of the search for further dimensions of space/time beyond length, breadth, depth and duration. If any such are found and named (or expressed in formulae), then my 'Fifth' can no doubt be adjusted, to the final point, where 'consciousness' is. I have also acknowledged that there may be aspects of space/time not available to our human senses; and if so, these are unlikely to be 'found' – except by mathematics, perhaps? I need to identify 'consciousness' as a dimension, and a key one; and a dimension which – numbering apart – faces Janus-wise to The Eternal, as well as to Time.

Index

Themes which occur throughout, and are the book's substance, are not listed. Examples include Being and Becoming; Death; Mortality and Transience; Evil; God; Hebrew Wisdom; Mysticism; Nature; Pagan; Pilgrimage and Quest; Questions (of meaning in life); Reverence; Satan; Sin and Guilt; Time; Treasure (spiritual); Wisdom; and Witness.

The themes which are listed are in lower case, and include cross-references where appropriate. Many have bearing on the above, unlisted, themes.

Names, whether real or fictional, are in UPPER CASE. A few minor fictional names have been omitted.

Note that quotations in the text are sometimes unattributed. These can be found here, subsumed under the entry for their authors.